DATE DUE

AP 21 03			
JE 11 03			
DE 18 03			

DEMCO 38-296

THE MARKETING GLOSSARY

Key Terms, Concepts, and Applications in

- Marketing management
- Advertising
- Sales promotion
- Public relations
- Direct marketing
- Market research
- Sales

Mark N. Clemente

amacom
American Management Association

discount when ordered in bulk quantities.
For information, contact Special Sales Department,
AMACOM, a division of American Management Association,
135 West 50th Street, New York, NY 10020.

This publication is designed to provide accurate and authoritative
information in regard to the subject matter covered. It is sold with the
understanding that the publisher is not engaged in rendering legal,
accounting, or other professional service. If legal advice or other expert
assistance is required, the services of a competent professional person
should be sought.

Library of Congress Cataloging-in-Publication Data

Clemente, Mark N.
    The marketing glossary : key terms, concepts, and applications in
marketing management, advertising, sales promotion, public
relations, direct marketing, market research, sales / Mark N.
Clemente.
        p.   cm.
    Includes bibliographical references.
    ISBN 0-8144-5030-X
    1. Marketing—Handbooks, manuals, etc.   I. Title.
HF5415.C5414   1992
658.8'002'02—dc20   91-40284
                                                                      CIP

Printing number

10   9   8   7   6   5   4   3   2   1

Contents

Preface

The Marketing Glossary is a one-of-a-kind volume. No other book on the lexicon of marketing combines the features of dictionary, encyclopedia, and working reference guide. Nor does any other book provide—in one, easy-to-use source—clear, practical definitions of the most frequently used concepts in marketing management, advertising, sales promotion, public relations, direct marketing, market research, and sales.

All told, the Glossary discusses more than 1,400 marketing terms you need to know—in theory *and* in practice. It is not a book of one-sentence definitions. Rather, its value to professionals and all others concerned with the field of marketing is that, unlike any other book of marketing terms, it defines the major marketing concepts in encyclopedic fashion, providing you with instructive answers to questions and with solutions to problems facing you in your day-to-day business activities. Terms such as *marketing research, media planning, sampling,* and *sales promotion* are followed by in-depth explanations complete with real-life examples, formulas, and checklists. In other words, you are told not only what a marketing plan is but how one is structured.

Each entry leads with the definition most widely embraced by marketers. Then, if the term has more than one meaning—which is likely, since there are so many areas to our profession—other interpretations follow. The many cross-references, shown in boldface type within or at the end of an entry, are included to point you toward even more information about the concept, which often includes its opposite; the direct mail selling technique *negative option,* for example, is cross-referenced to *positive option.*

Finally, three appendixes are included. Appendix A lists the major trade associations—excellent sources of information and professional development opportunities. Those interested in periodicals servicing the marketing community will find a list of trade and professional publications in Appendix B. And Appendix C includes more than 50 of the most popular books on marketing management, advertising, sales promotion, public relations, direct marketing, market research, and sales—greatly enhancing the Glossary's how-to-oriented focus.

Perhaps more than in any other field, the language of marketing is continually evolving. Consequently, while many of the terms contained in *The Marketing Glossary* can be found in any major work on the subject, numerous concepts of recent vintage such as *Euro-ad*, *green marketing*, and *alternative media* have only recently become part of the marketer's vernacular. In many cases, the Glossary is the first volume to define them.

In the time it took to produce this book, many new marketing terms have likely been coined. Future editions will try to keep pace with the marketing profession's ever-growing lexicon. Readers' suggestions regarding new terms (as well as those they feel should have been included) are welcome.

—Mark N. Clemente

Acknowledgments

Many people contributed directly and indirectly to this book. The colleagues whose input and suggestions were directly incorporated into the manuscript are cited below. Not mentioned are the scores of marketing and communications professionals with whom I've worked over the past 15 years—veteran practitioners I am privileged to have been associated with and whose knowledge and experience have indirectly contributed to the definitions contained herein.

My thanks go to the members of the Editorial Advisory Board: Tom Pletcher, Matt Losordo, Ann Simpson, Jim Erlick, Jeanette Gatto, Tim Powell, Dave Schmittlein, and Sal Luiso. Each of them reviewed my preliminary compilation of terms to ensure that only marketing concepts of the greatest import were included. Subsequently, they reviewed the entries that fell into their respective areas of specialization and offered insightful comments and criticisms. Their input was extremely valuable. Their cooperation was of the highest order.

Several other colleagues participated by providing additional editorial review of entries, research support, and assistance with graphics and computer technology. I thank Arthur F. Chassen, manager of Multimedia Management Communications for IBM; Gilda C. Caputo, Marie M. Seiber, and Hope L. Picker, all of Coopers & Lybrand; and Joanne Newborn of the American Management Association, who served as a research assistant.

My thanks also go to Adrienne Hickey and all the editors at AMACOM. Their suggestions regarding editorial style and content enhanced the manuscript at each stage of its evolution.

I also thank my literary agent, Bert Holtje of James Peter Associates, for his encouragement, advice, and support in every aspect of this project.

Above all, I extend my heartfelt thanks to my wife, Anita, and to our sons, Matthew and Daniel. Their love and inspiration made this work possible. And it is to them that this book is fondly dedicated.

Editorial Advisory Board

A

AAAA SPOT CONTRACT A standard contract between an advertising agency and a broadcast station used in purchasing TV/radio air time in individual markets. That is, the contract is used when an advertiser buys **spot TV/radio** as opposed to network air time. In addition to costs, the contract specifies the number of commercials to be bought, the times at which they'll air, and over what period of time (i.e., daily, weekly, monthly). The 4 A's (**American Association of Advertising Agencies**) developed the contract.

ABANDONMENT The decision to discontinue marketing a product, which may occur at any time. Abandonment is a strategic option in the decline stage of the **product life cycle.** This stage is characterized by severely diminished market demand for the product and a proliferation of competing brands. There are three strategies for abandoning a product:

1. A *milking* strategy, which refers to reducing marketing and promotional expenditures to maintain profits.
2. A *concentrated* strategy, which involves directing all marketing activities at the strongest segment of the market while phasing out marketing to weaker market segments.
3. A *continuation* strategy, which refers to maintaining the level of marketing activities up to a specific date on which the product is to be eliminated.

Also known as *product deletion* and *withdrawal.*

ABCD COUNTIES The A. C. Nielsen Company designation for U.S. counties based on their population and proximity to major metropolitan areas. "A" counties, the largest, include any county within the 25 largest cities in the United States. "B," "C," and "D" counties represent counties of decreasing population sizes. ABCD county designations are used by advertisers in **media planning**.

ABC ISSUE   The issue of a magazine reviewed by the **Audit Bureau of Circulations** to validate the publication's **paid circulation** and other statistical information. Paid circulation is defined as the number of copies sold to people at a price not less than half of the publication's established basic price. Only those publications with 70% or more of paid circulation are eligible to be ABC members and, thus, to be audited. Publishers must submit two ABC issues to supply information for the required **ABC statement,** which is produced biannually. *Note:* Auditing publications is intended to limit misrepresentations of readership figures by publishers. It is protection for advertisers, which base their print media buys on the circulation figures of select magazines. See also **Business Publications Audit of Circulations.**

ABC STATEMENT   Filing required of magazines audited by the **Audit Bureau of Circulations,** which reports the periodical's paid circulation statistics over a six-month period. ABC statements also provide information on the source of the circulation, whether it was generated by subscription orders from magazine insert cards, direct-mail campaigns, or other means. The periodical's selling price, as compared to its **basic rate,** is also required information. Publishers file ABC statements twice a year. ABC statements lend credibility to magazines' circulation figures. This is done to attract advertisers, many of whom view ABC statements as a basic criterion for doing business with a given publication. See also **ABC issue; BPA statement.**

ACCORDION FOLD   A brochure or pamphlet design format. An accordion fold is a sheet of paper that has two or more vertical folds. The folds enable the piece to be stretched to its full length with one pull, similar to the expansion of an accordion's bellows. The design allows the inclusion of copy and illustrations on any and all of the brochure panels. Accordion folds are popular designs because they eliminate the need for binding and stapling—factors that increase the costs of printing and postage. Accordion folds fit into standard-size envelopes for direct mailings. They can also be bound into magazines and other periodicals.

Accordion Fold

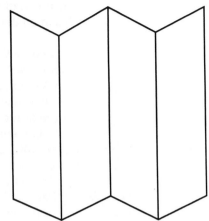

ACCOUNT   **1.** A company that is the client of an advertising, public relations, or other marketing services agency. **2.** A customer of a supplier or vendor company from which the customer obtains particular materials or services.

ACCOUNT EXECUTIVE (AE)   The employee of an advertising, public relations, or marketing services agency who is responsible for servicing one or more clients (accounts). Account executives serve as liaisons between their agency and the client. They're responsible for supervising day-to-day aspects of account work and coordinating all activities involved in program planning and execution. AEs assist in developing strategies, present the agency's strategic initiatives and creative output (copy and artwork) to the client, and monitor program implementation. In sales, an account executive is the person responsible for the overall relationship between a company and its major accounts. See also **account supervisor.**

ACCOUNT PLANNING   The approach to developing advertising in which an agency researcher serves as a key part of the creative team. It is different from the traditional role of the researcher in an ad agency: generating market data for submission to the creative professionals and *not* participating in the planning process. Account planning involves personal interviews with select members of the target market by the agency researcher. The researcher then serves as the consumer's "voice" in the ad creation process. The goal is to develop advertising that closely addresses consumers' concerns and desires. Account planning was pioneered by British advertising agencies. It has since gained popularity among U.S. firms as well as those in other countries.

ACCOUNT SUPERVISOR (AS)   Advertising or public relations agency executive who manages and oversees the work of several account executives. Account supervisors are typically more experienced than AEs. Consequently, they're responsible for higher-level account activities that include supervising the strategic planning done on behalf of clients. Account supervisors handle client relations but not on a daily basis.

ACETATE   A clear plastic sheet used in graphic art production. For example, an acetate can serve as an **overlay**—a protective sheet placed on top of a piece of mechanical art. Acetates are also used in presentations. Thus, a graph that depicts company sales could be drawn on an acetate. Then, acetates showing other graphs can be laid over the original to illustrate changes in sales rates.

ACKNOWLEDGMENT   Written confirmation sent by a manufacturer to a buyer relating to the latter's product order. Acknowledgments inform the buyer that an order has been received and is being processed, or that a customer inquiry or complaint is being handled. Acknowledgments are sent as either postcards or letters.

A. C. NIELSEN COMPANY   A major American market research firm that gathers consumer, trade, and media information to sell to client companies. The company is best known for its television audience measures. However, it also produces bimonthly product data based on an audit of supermarkets, drugstores, and mass merchandisers. The information relates to market share of particular brands; retail prices; the percentage of stores stocking an item; and the levels of promotional activity being undertaken by consumer product marketers. See also **Nielsen indexes; Nielsen ratings.**

ACORN (A CLASSIFICATION OF RESIDENTIAL NEIGHBOR-HOODS)   A way of categorizing households by neighborhood. It is used to segment markets by grouping households into social, economic, and demographic categories based on the household address. Classifications may be by *zip code, block group* (a U.S. Bureau of the

Census term referring to blocks in which 800 to 1,000 people reside), or *census tract* (another census measurement that defines subdivisions of densely populated cities). ACORN was developed by the company CACI of Arlington, Va. See also **PRIZM.**

ACQUISITION A method of expanding a company's sales by acquiring other companies, product rights, or technological processes/materials. That is, acquisition is a corporate growth strategy that attempts to build the company in ways other than internal expansion. See also **merger.**

ACROSS-THE-BOARD Broadcast programming term referring to any television or radio program that airs in the same time period and on the same station five days a week. An example is a TV exercise program that airs Monday through Friday at 11 A.M. Across-the-board programs appeal to advertisers since the shows ostensibly reach the same audience each day. Advertisers often want to send repeated messages to a show's audience (a process known as *strip programming*). Their strategy is that repetition of commercials will elevate product awareness and increase sales. Media representatives often offer advertisers discounts for buying commercial time in all five across-the-board time slots. See also **media planning.**

ACTION CLOSE A **closing** technique used by salespeople, wherein the sales representative proposes to do something that forces the prospect to agree to the sale. For example, the salesperson explains the details of an investment opportunity, then says, "Let me discuss this with your financial planner to finalize the provisions of the agreement." The salesperson must recognize the **buying signals** that indicate the prospect's willingness to agree to a sale. The salesperson must then choose the closing technique appropriate to the given sales situation.

ACTION DEVICE A piece of a direct-mail package that "involves" the reader in receiving the marketing message. For example, an action device might be a scratch-off card indicating that the recipient is a contest winner, or it can involve affixing stamps or puzzle pieces to an entry form to receive a free gift or prize. Action devices were created to increase response rates of direct-mail programs.

ACTION PROGRAM See **marketing plan.**

ACTIVITIES, INTERESTS, OPINIONS (AIO)   A framework for understanding buying behavior based on consumers' *lifestyles*. Consumer buying decisions are influenced by personal characteristics, of which lifestyle is a factor. Activities might include a person's occupation, hobbies, or entertainment preferences. Interests can relate to family, home, or community matters. Opinions may be about social issues, politics, or education. Advertising planning often involves identifying the lifestyle group to which a product is targeted. Ads are then designed to appeal to the AIO characteristics of the target lifestyle group. See also **psychographic segmentation; VALS.**

ACTIVITY QUOTA   Measures of a salesperson's success other than the financial results of his or her sales activities. For example, activity quotas are measurements of the number of letters or phone calls made to prospects; the number of product demonstrations given to prospects; visits to prospects; or the number of formal sales proposals developed. See also **sales compensation.**

ADDRESSOGRAPH   Trademark of a machine that imprints addresses on envelopes. An addressograph uses embossed steel plates that indicate the recipients' names and addresses. The machine presses the plates against an ink ribbon to create the printed information. *Note:* With the advent of computer printing technology, Addressograph machines have become largely obsolete.

ADNORM   Term used in **Starch ratings,** produced by Daniel Starch and Associates, to quantify the number of readers of a given publication who read a particular ad in the periodical. Adnorm is based on several factors: size of the ad; whether or not color was used in it; and the nature of product advertised. The reader's experience with the periodical is also factored into the measurement (e.g., whether the respondent is a regular or first-time reader). Adnorm is stated as a percentage. Thus, an adnorm of 20 means that 20% of the readers of the publication recall having read the ad(s) under review. See also **advertising testing.**

ADOPTER CATEGORIES   Categories illustrating how use of an innovative new product spreads through a population and grouping consumers by *when* they begin purchasing the product. The first group of users are *innovators*. *Early adopters* are the next members of the population who begin to purchase the item. They are followed by the *early majority*, the *late majority*, and *laggards*. See also **diffusion of innovation.**

ADRMP (AUTOMATIC DIALING AND RECORDED MESSAGE PLAYER)   A machine used in **outbound telemarketing.** ADRMPs dial consumers' telephone numbers and activate a prerecorded message when someone picks up the phone. The devices enable a consumer to place an order by letting the person leave a message on the system's answering machine; or they instruct the consumer to punch-in specified digits to be connected with a company sales representative. Also known as *autodialers. Note:* In the United States, legislation has been proposed that would either ban or severely restrict the use of ADRMPs nationwide. See also **random-digit dialing.**

AD SLICK   A **camera-ready** advertisement prepared for distribution to corporate divisions or member companies of an association for placement in local print media. For example, a national car manufacturer will distribute to its dealerships ad slicks that show the company's new models. Dealers use the ad slicks for advertising insertions in newspapers and magazines in their market. Ad slicks often feature a blank space into which the local advertiser can insert its address, phone number, or other information. Slicks of the same ad are developed in different sizes (e.g., full page, half page) to accommodate publications' varying specifications for mechanical art. See also **dealer listing.**

ADVANCE ORDER   A sales order placed far in advance of the requested date of delivery. A buyer usually receives a significant discount when making an advance order because the order is arranged at a time when sales by the supplier are low. For example, a nursery that buys flowers for sale in the spring may place an advance order with its distributor in the preceding winter season. Thus, the nursery would pay much less for the order than if it were placed in the prime buying season for flowers and plants, when the distributor's prices are highest.

ADVERTISEMENT   A paid announcement appearing in a print media outlet that is designed to reach a large audience. The goal of an advertisement is to promote a product, service, organization, or idea. It is designed to persuade, inform, or otherwise influence consumer attitudes. Space for an advertisement is purchased by an advertiser who controls what information will appear. However, an ad's content is often subject to approval by the medium in which it appears. See also **commercial; infomercial.**

ADVERTISING   One of the main elements of the **marketing communications mix** that involves using *paid* media to communicate persuasive information about a product, service, organization, or idea. The key benefits of advertising are providing product information and influencing attitude changes among consumers. Advertising can be targeted to consumers in either narrow or broad geographic areas.

Advertising has three basic objectives: (1) to *inform* consumers about new products, product uses, services available, or other facts that need to be known by consumers; (2) to *persuade* an audience to purchase a product, change brand preferences, or perceive a product differently; and (3) to *remind* consumers about the need for a product or where it may be purchased. Advertising decisions fall into two basic categories:

1. *Message development.* This refers to *what* is to be said. Messages may be intended to create awareness of a brand or to foster a brand image that favorably predisposes consumers to the product. Messages may convey information regarding product benefits or they can be crafted to offset competitors' claims about their products. Messages may also build familiarity of the brand while reinforcing a **unique selling proposition** in the minds of consumers.

2. *Media selection.* This refers to determining *where* advertising communications will appear—the process of **media planning.** Media *categories* include print outlets (newspapers and magazines), broadcast (television, radio, cable TV, and satellite systems), and "out-of-home" (billboards, transit advertising). Decisions on media *vehicles* refer to identifying which individual outlets within media categories will carry the advertising. Vehicles are selected based on comparisons of their ability to reach the target market.

ADVERTISING AGENCY   A company that provides advertising services to marketers. Agencies are considered *full-service* when they offer a comprehensive range of creative, production, market research, strategic planning, and media planning/buying capabilities. *Limited-service* agencies provide only one kind of advertising service (e.g., creative). A typical full-service agency is comprised of four organizational departments. *Creative services* consists of copywriters, art directors, and print and broadcast production specialists. *Account services* is made up of account supervisors and account executives—those professionals handling client relations and overseeing the development and execution of advertising campaigns. *Marketing services* includes media buying and planning professionals, market researchers, and sales promotion specialists. Responsibility for the agency's office management and accounting and finance functions falls under the *administrative services* division. *Note:* See a graphic of an advertising agency's structure under **organization chart.**

ADVERTISING ALLOWANCE   Incentive given by a manufacturer to a retailer for running advertising that features the manufacturer's product. Advertising allowances take the form of either discounts on merchandise (the monetary difference intended to finance the advertising) or cash reimbursements (to cover the advertising expenditures incurred by the retailer). See also **trade promotion.**

ADVERTISING APPROPRIATION   Money allocated for advertising in a specific time period as determined by the advertiser's sales for that period. (Sales are based on either projected figures or those from a previous period.) Advertising appropriations are determined after the company has calculated its manufacturing, administrative, and selling costs, as well as identified the profits it seeks to gain. Advertising appropriations are stated for specific time periods (e.g., 6 months, 12 months, 18 months).

ADVERTISING CAMPAIGN   A program involving the creation and placement of a series of advertisements, conducted in line with established marketing and communications objectives. Advertising campaigns may run for several months or for a few years. Campaigns typically feature different ads that carry a common theme and sales message. Advertising campaign planning is based on the following considerations:

• *Setting advertising objectives.* Objectives may be to *inform* the target audience about new uses for a product or price changes; to *persuade* the market to buy the product over competitors' brands or to enhance the brand's image; or to *remind* the market about the need for the product or where it may be purchased.

• *Establishing the advertising budget.* The budget may be based on a specific percentage of product sales, on the amount competitors are spending on advertising, or on specific objectives (e.g., spending whatever is necessary to accomplish the objective).

• *Creating the message.* This entails developing a creative approach that effectively communicates product attributes and rewards. Advertising professionals will often test the marketing message before, during, and after it appears in the marketplace.

• *Selecting the media.* Decisions on media relate to which consumers are to be reached, through what media categories (print and/or broadcast) and vehicles they will be reached (which newspapers, magazines, or TV and radio programs), and at what times (which publication issues or times of day for broadcast programs).

• *Measuring results.* Evaluating campaign results may include criteria such as communications effectiveness, product sales, or consumer inquiries (e.g., the number of coupons returned by consumers requesting additional product information).

ADVERTISING CHECKING BUREAU (ACB)   A company that furnishes **tear sheets** of advertisements to ad agencies and advertisers. Companies obtain tear sheets from the ACB to ascertain placement of their ads, to assess the ads' impact (e.g., to see in what part of the publication the ads appeared), and to monitor competitors' advertising. The ACB clips ads from daily, Sunday, and weekly newspapers published in the United States. See also **clipping service.**

ADVERTISING COUNCIL   A nonprofit organization that develops and places **public-service advertising.** The Advertising Council was formed during World War II as the War Advertising Council, charged with promoting the sale of war bonds and other governmental policies relating to the war effort. Today the Advertising Council promotes various social, economic, and moral causes. Issues for which it produces advertising include preventing drug and alcohol abuse; crime prevention; fostering better race relations; and generating contributions for organizations such as the Red Cross and the United Way. The Advertising Council is comprised of advertising agencies (that create the advertising at no cost) and newspapers, magazines, and television and radio stations (that donate the time and space for the ads).

ADVERTISING EFFECTIVENESS A measure of consumers' ability to remember advertising messages to which they have been exposed and the persuasiveness of those communications. Advertising effectiveness may be tested prior to the start of an advertising campaign, during the campaign, or upon its completion. See also **advertising testing.**

ADVERTISING MANAGER The corporate executive responsible for executing his or her company's advertising strategy. The advertising manager serves as liaison for the organization's advertising agency. Responsibilities are articulating the advertising objectives, providing necessary information to the agency, and reviewing and approving the agency's media and creative recommendations. Advertising managers supervise the production of materials such as catalogs, brochures, and sales literature, as well as broadcast commercials. They also oversee development and maintenance of program budgets. Advertising managers typically report to the company's vice-president of marketing.

ADVERTISING MODELS Computerized systems that aid in advertising decision making. Advertising models, for example, are used to determine advertising budgets, media selection and scheduling, and projections of **return** (as a result, say, of the size of a direct-mail campaign). In general, advertising models enable the user to ask "what if" questions to generate statistical information about advertising program results. This is done by altering one variable in an equation to determine how other variables will change. For example, a media planner might ask: "What if we increase our advertising 10% on radio station ZZZZ-AM? How many more listeners will we reach?" A computerized advertising model would automatically generate statistics reflecting the increased ad budget and the resultant rise in listenership.

ADVERTISING OBJECTIVES Statements of what an advertisement or advertising campaign is supposed to accomplish over a designated time period. Objectives may be to increase sales, raise product awareness, or change a brand's image. Objectives are based on such marketing decisions as the target market, product **positioning,** or specific elements of the **marketing mix.** Advertising objectives are established and ultimately translated into specific goals.

ADVERTISING RATES   The established prices for space (print media) and time (broadcast) in advertising vehicles. In general, advertising rates are subject to either surcharges or discounts. Rates may carry a surcharge when an advertiser is able to secure a **preferred position** in a magazine or to specify the time at which a broadcast commercial will air. Rates are discounted when an advertiser makes volume purchases (e.g., purchasing ads in all 12 issues of a monthly publication). Advertising *rate cards* are lists of advertising prices. Such cards are included in publications' **media kits.** *Note:* Advertising rates are *basic* costs for space and air time. Nearly all advertising rates are negotiable between the advertiser and the medium.

ADVERTISING RESEARCH   Research that yields insight into a target market or that is conducted to test advertising message concepts. It may be classified as *formative* research, which is designed to acquire background on the beliefs, needs, and buying behavior of target consumers; or it can be *developmental* research, which is used in developing creative concepts before they appear in the marketplace. See also **advertising testing.**

ADVERTISING RESERVE   Advertising dollars set aside for emergency situations in which additional advertising purchases may be required, for example, in a product recall. Advertising dollars may have been budgeted to introduce the product; advertising reserve monies, however, would be used for additional advertising to explain the reason for the recall and to provide instructions to consumers.

ADVERTISING TESTING   Testing that measures the effectiveness of individual advertisements or entire campaigns. Advertising **pretesting** refers to assessing advertising communications before they are disseminated to the target audience. This is done to determine whether the communications effectively get the prospect's attention and relay sales messages persuasively. Pretesting is undertaken by advertisers to identify (and correct) ineffective advertising before it is introduced in a costly, full-scale media program. Advertising **posttesting** is the process of testing advertising communications after they have appeared in the marketplace. Posttesting involves **recall** tests to measure respondents' ability to remember an advertisement's message (e.g., brand attributes, product benefits, campaign slogan). See also **aided recall; PACT; unaided recall.**

ADVERTISING-TO-SALES RATIO   Advertising budgeting technique that bases advertising expenditures on a percentage of a product's sales volume. Advertisers either use sales figures from the past year as a basis for calculating the budget (retrospective), projections of sales for the upcoming year (forecast), or a standard figure based on the competitive climate (e.g., what a competing company or product is spending). Budgeting via advertising-to-sales ratio is determined by using a generalized ratio figure and multiplying it by the sales volume. For example, if sales volume is $500,000 and the ratio is 5%, the advertising budget would be $25,000. In equation form:

$$\$500{,}000 \text{ (sales)} \times 5\% \text{ (ratio)} = \$25{,}000 \text{ (ad budget)}$$

Note: In general, product manufacturers and service organizations spend vastly dissimilar amounts (ratio size) on advertising. Consumer product companies often spend as much as 10% of sales volume on advertising. In contrast, professional services firms usually spend no more than 1% of sales on advertising.

ADVERTORIAL   1. A newspaper or magazine article produced by the medium's advertising department and financed by corporate sponsors. The credibility and implied third-party endorsement of marketing messages in *publicity* ostensibly prompted the creation of advertorials. The sponsoring organization pays to be quoted in the text, which is laid out like editorial material but is labeled *advertising*. A type style different from the host publication's is used to distinguish it as promotional copy. Space ads by the sponsor are often included in the page layouts. Magazine advertorials sometimes may relate to the theme of a given issue, or to one or more articles appearing in it. **2.** An ad that takes the form of a newspaper editorial. That is, it is mostly text, and the topic is usually controversial. See also **advocacy advertising.**

ADVOCACY ADVERTISING   Advertising that espouses a company's, institution's, or person's point of view on a controversial topic. The topic usually relates in some way to the business or special interests of the advertiser. Advocacy advertising addresses topics such as government economic policies, labor-management relations, or ecology. The targets of advocacy advertising may be government agencies, the media, political activists, a particular company, or a company's competitors. An example of advocacy advertising is a private citizen buying newspaper advertising to condemn the high-fat and high-cholesterol content of hamburgers sold by a leading fast-food chain.

AFFILIATE   A television or radio station that contracts with a network to air programming provided by the network. Affiliates may be independently owned, or are a division of the network (an "owned and operated" affiliate). Independent affiliates' contractual relationship with the network is based on exchanging commercial time for news and entertainment programming. Affiliates provide the commercial time, and networks then sell it to national advertisers. Networks contract with affiliates in different regions of the country (with the networks limited by law to a maximum number of affiliations—based on the level of household TV penetration—to be equitable among the three main networks). Having affiliates helps networks attract major advertisers by offering the latter large viewing audiences in multiple markets. Networks arrange the transmission facilities by which affiliates are interconnected for simultaneous broadcasts (co-axial cables or microwave relays).

AFFINITIES   Stores offering the same product lines, with the outlets located in close proximity to each other. For example, on 48th Street in Manhattan there are several musical instrument stores side-by-side. Affinities allow consumers to engage in comparison shopping.

AFTERNOON-DRIVE   The time period from 3 P.M. to 7 P.M., Monday through Friday, which is when a radio station reaches one of its largest listening audiences. Afternoon-drive is a **daypart** occurring during rush hour in large metropolitan areas. (The name of the time period reflects the heavy usage of automobile radios.) The large audience reached during the afternoon-drive is why this time period (and the **morning-drive** time slot) commands the highest advertising rates.

AGE CYCLE   A concept recognizing that consumers' buying patterns and product/brand preferences change as people age. For example, people's recreational activities change from when they were teenagers (e.g., enjoying wind-surfing) to when they are senior citizens (e.g., taking a leisurely ocean cruise). Marketers strive to develop products and services to satisfy changing needs at different points in consumers' age cycles.

AGENCY COMMISSION   Money received by advertising agencies for media purchases they make on behalf of clients in television, radio, newspaper, magazine, and outdoor advertising vehicles. For example, an agency buys a half-page magazine ad for $50,000. The magazine bills the agency $42,500 ($50,000 less 15%). The agency, in turn, bills its client $50,000, then pays the magazine $42,500; the $7,500 commission becomes part of the agency's gross income. Agency commission is granted because agencies save media the expenses of billing and direct selling to advertisers. *Note:* Advertising agency commissions are becoming less commonplace in today's client-agency relationships.

AGENCY NETWORK   A group of independent, noncompeting advertising or public relations agencies that support each other in client service and new-business development. Affiliated agencies may form a national or international network. The network's primary goal is to exchange services and facilities, thus broadening the capabilities the member agencies provide to their respective clients. For example, the client of a Los Angeles-based ad agency may need work done in the United Kingdom, where the agency does not have a local office. The agency would call upon its **affiliate** in the United Kingdom to provide the necessary client-service support. The referring agency may receive a percentage of the fees generated by the work of its affiliate agency.

AGENCY OF RECORD   The firm selected to make all media purchases on behalf of a group of agencies when a large company uses several advertising agencies for its various products and brands. The agency of record coordinates development of all media contracts. It receives payment for placing media advertising on behalf of the other firms—roughly 15% of the 15% **agency commissions** each agency would have received had *it* coordinated the media buying.

AGENT   A person or business whose role is to negotiate the purchase or sale of services or goods to which the agent does not take title. Agents are responsible for identifying customers for their clients' products or services and coordinating the contracts between client and customer. Agents are paid either by fee or on a commission basis. See also **middleman.**

AGGREGATION   Marketing strategy based on the belief that consumers in a given market are all alike. Communications strategy focuses on the common aspects of the market, as opposed to those factors that differentiate consumers. (In this sense, aggregation is the opposite of **target marketing.**) Marketers employing an aggregation strategy use mass advertising and mass product distribution. Marketing communications typically use universal product themes. For example, XYZ Soap is mass marketed as the lowest-price soap available. Here, low price is believed to be a product feature that's universally sought by consumers and, thus, appealing to the broadest possible number of buyers.

AIDED RECALL   A test of advertising effectiveness that measures how much a respondent remembers about a particular ad. Aided recall involves showing a respondent an ad, then querying the respondent about what he or she recalls about its sales message, product offer, slogan, and so on. Aided recall is often used as a **posttesting** exercise. That is, it is a test of advertising effectiveness after the ad has appeared in the marketplace. See also **unaided recall.**

AIRBRUSH   A mechanical drawing instrument used by commercial artists for photo and artwork retouching and for illustrating print advertisements, posters, and signs. An airbrush applies watercolor paint in a very fine spray by means of compressed air.

AISLE ADVERTISING   In-store merchandise displays devised to attract attention and to make the featured product readily accessible to buyers. Aisle advertising displays include *end-aisle* units situated at the end of a row of shelving. *Island displays* are freestanding merchandise units located in an uncrowded area in the store. Aisle advertising designs usually feature the same copy and graphics used in other promotional materials produced by the sponsoring product: print advertising, booklets, coupons, entry forms, and so forth. See also **point-of-purchase advertising.**

ALTERNATIVE MEDIA   Advertising media that do not fall into the standard categories of print (e.g., newspapers, magazines), broadcast (e.g., radio, television), and outdoor (e.g., billboards) media. Examples of alternative media are supermarket video displays that carry ads and sale announcements; ads mounted on shopping carts; ads appearing in trade books. Alternative media were (and continue to be) created to counter heightened competition for consumers' attention in conventional advertising media. See also **clutter.**

ALTERNATIVE PROPOSAL CLOSE A salesperson's **closing** technique that involves asking the prospect to make choices. For example, the salesperson may ask: "Do you think you would like this model in red or blue?" Or, "Would you like me to send this overnight or by regular mail?" The strategy of this technique is to let the prospect make a minor decision, thereby committing the prospect to agree to the sale.

AMERICAN ADVERTISING FEDERATION (AAF) A national trade association whose members are involved in the creation and support of advertising. The AAF consists of advertising agencies and media owners. Other members include vendors and suppliers of materials used in creating advertising (e.g., graphics art suppliers and production houses). The AAF is headquartered in Washington, D.C. See Appendix A for address and phone number.

AMERICAN ASSOCIATION OF ADVERTISING AGENCIES (AAAA) A major trade association comprised of leading advertising agencies in the United States. Headquartered in New York City, the "4 A's" is dedicated to improving the standards of advertising by its member agencies and the industry in general. See Appendix A for address and phone number. See also **AAAA spot contract.**

AMERICAN MARKETING ASSOCIATION (AMA) A leading national organization comprised of marketing professionals and educators. Members include representatives from all marketing disciplines (e.g., marketing research, advertising, and sales promotion). The AMA publishes books, journals, and newsletters. It also maintains a library of books and periodicals relating to all aspects of marketing management and communications. The group is headquartered in Chicago. See Appendix A for address and phone number.

ANALYSIS OF VARIANCE (ANOVA) A statistical method to gauge the degree of similarity or difference between two or more sets of data. For example, to predict the level of return of a direct mailing an analysis of variance calculation would involve mailing to a sample of the untried mailing list and *comparing* the results with the return of a sample from a past mailing list. Ultimately, the calculation would allow for comparison of the two response levels so as to project the return from a full mailing to the untried list.

ANALYTICAL MARKETING SYSTEM   A component of a **marketing information system** consisting of computerized analytical techniques used to extract meaningful information from research data. An analytical marketing system has a *statistical bank* and a *model bank.* The former includes statistical procedures, such as **multivariate analysis,** to draw conclusions from data. The latter is designed to help managers make better marketing decisions by using **models**—sets of interrelated variables designed to represent some system or process.

ANCHOR STORE   A large, well-known retail store that occupies the largest amount of space in a shopping mall. Anchor stores are designed to attract consumers to the center, a fact that benefits the small retail outlets and boutiques that populate the rest of the facility. The term *anchor* connotes a sense of stability for the shopping mall, if only from the standpoint of the center's real estate agent, who has leased the largest segment of the facility's rentable space to the anchor tenant.

ANCILLARY SERVICES   Services offered by a store that do not relate directly to the specific products sold in the outlet. Examples of ancillary services are a gift-wrapping department, layaway plans, and other credit programs. Stores may or may not charge for the ancillary services they provide.

ANDY AWARD   An annual award sponsored by the Advertising Club of New York for the best TV commercial, radio commercial, and best overall commercial produced in the preceding year. Judges are representatives from the New York advertising community, who grade the commercials based on copy, production, and creative selling concepts. See also **Clio Award.**

ANIMATIC   A rough production of a television commercial, developed by an advertising agency to help its client visualize the ad concept. Animatics are produced by filming the sketches on a **storyboard.** An audio track is then added to the footage. Animatics are produced by the creative department under the direction of the account executive. Generally, they are shown to the client for approval prior to the start of film production. Sometimes they serve as a guide for actual production of the spot.

ANIMATION   The process of creating the image of live action by adding motion to inanimate objects. Cartoon animation, for instance, is created by filming individual drawings one at a time. The film is then run at a speed that gives the illusion of movement to the characters or objects in the drawings. Animation is often used in TV commercials. Examples are commercials featuring the Jolly Green Giant (vegetables) and the Keebler elves (cookies). Animation gives advertisers a tremendous degree of creative flexibility since virtually any combination of people, objects, animals, and images may be used to create the desired communication effect. Animation is a very costly process, however. For example, the supercomputers used in animation production may cost up to $5,000 per second for a 30-second TV commercial. See also **claymation.**

ANNOUNCER VOICEOVER   See **voiceover.**

ANTITRUST LAWS   Federal laws regulating trade designed to maintain competition and prevent monopolies. Examples of U.S. antitrust laws are the Sherman Antitrust Act of 1890 that prohibits "monopolies or attempts to monopolize"; the Clayton Antitrust Act of 1914 that outlawed certain types of **price discrimination**; and the Wheeler-Lea Amendment to the Federal Trade Commission Act of 1914 that made **unfair competition** illegal (including deceptive acts or practices). See also **consumer protection legislation.**

AOG (ARRIVAL OF GOODS)   Refers to giving a customer a discount on goods if payment for them is made within a stated period of time. The time period commences when the merchandise arrives at the specific destination. AOG discounts are typically offered to customers who are located long distances from the shipper.

APPEAL   The stated advantage of buying a product, as described in marketing communications for that product: advertising, sales literature, publicity. In general, appeals are directed at satisfying people's basic needs for things such as health, security, prosperity, or accomplishment. For example, the appeal made for a personal computer might be that using the product will help the consumer gain important technical skills. The intended message is: The computer will help the user advance professionally and, ultimately, help him or her reap greater financial rewards.

ARBITRON RATINGS COMPANY   A research company that provides audience measurement data for use by broadcast stations, advertisers, and advertising agencies. Arbitron collects data on 200 local markets (comprising 3,000 counties) in the United States. The information shows how many people in each county view television stations available to them. Counties receiving TV signals from more than one county are assigned to one market or another (an **area of dominant influence**). Arbitron also operates ScanAmerica, a system of 10,000 U.S. households that are equipped with **people meters** to gauge TV viewing patterns, as well as in-home **Universal Product Code** scanning devices that record household members' product purchases. Arbitron is owned by the Control Data Corporation. See also **A. C. Nielsen Company.**

AREA-BY-AREA ALLOCATION (ABA)   A method of allocating money in an advertising budget to specific geographic areas. Using ABA, an advertiser will determine how much to spend on advertising in given geographic locales based on the varying levels of sales in those areas. Sales figures may either be based on established levels of sales or projections thereof.

AREA OF DOMINANT INFLUENCE (ADI)   The Arbitron Ratings Company's designation of television markets. Every county in the United States is exclusively assigned to one ADI. ADI is the market whose broadcast stations reach the greatest share of viewing households in the county, as compared to stations emanating from other markets. For example, the New York ADI includes certain counties in the metropolitan area (from the states of New York, New Jersey, and Connecticut) that view the broadcasts of New York City stations. Audience data are tabulated on areas of dominant influence: viewer demographics, purchasing patterns, media usage. Advertisers often use this information to allocate media budgets geographically. *Note:* The A. C. Nielsen Company's term for ADI is **designated market area (DMA).**

AREA SAMPLING   **Sampling** technique in which geographic areas serve as the primary sampling units. Area sampling involves dividing a geographic locale into smaller areas, then selecting a random sample of those areas. The locale might be divided by **block group, census tract,** or **zip code.** *One-stage* area sampling is when all households in the areas selected are used in the research study. When the households within those areas are subsampled, it is known as *two-stage* area sampling. See also **geographic segmentation.**

ARREARS   Complimentary issues of a periodical sent to readers whose subscriptions have expired. (The activity of distributing them is known as "gracing.") Arrears are sent to readers primarily to allow publishers to meet their **rate base,** which is a guarantee to advertisers of the publication's **average net paid circulation.** Another reason publishers send arrears is to encourage readers to renew their subscriptions, or to use up leftover copies of a magazine issue. The **Audit Bureau of Circulations,** which validates circulation figures, has rules governing arrears. For example, arrears may only be sent for three months after a subscription has expired.

ART DIRECTOR   The senior artist employed at an advertising agency, whose responsibility is the artistic development of all advertising materials. Art directors typically supervise staffs of graphic artists and layout production specialists. In addition, they coordinate retaining freelance artists, photographers, and others involved in designing communications materials. The art director usually reports to the vice-president of creative services.

ARTWORK   Any visual illustration in an advertisement that is not typeset copy. That is, artwork includes photographs, drawings, and charts or graphs (but not copy or headlines). Artwork is produced by an advertising agency's graphic artists under the supervision of the **art director.**

ASSOCIATION OF NATIONAL ADVERTISERS (ANA)   National trade group comprised of companies that advertise nationally. The goal of the ANA is to improve advertising effectiveness. It does so by monitoring industry practices and by sponsoring studies and reports of interest to its members. The ANA is comprised of both manufacturing and service companies. Its headquarters is in New York City. See Appendix A for address and phone number.

ASSORTMENT   Retailing term referring to the range of choices offered to customers. Assortment strategies relate to *depth* and *width* of the merchandise offering. *Depth* refers to the number of choices contained in each category (e.g., a store's assortment of women's bathing suits, including an array of styles, colors, patterns, and prices). *Width* refers to the number of different product categories the retailer features (e.g., beach towels, hats, and sandals offered in addition to bathing suits).

ASSUMPTIVE CLOSE   A **closing** technique in which the salesperson assumes the prospect will make a commitment to purchase. The salesperson proceeds to draw up the paperwork and asks the prospect to sign it, thus committing the prospect to the transaction.

ATMOSPHERICS   The study (and manipulation) of a retail outlet's physical properties, which have a collective effect on consumers' purchasing. Atmospheric variables include a store's architecture, lighting, layout, noise level, and temperature. Retailers attempt to alter store atmospherics to effect higher sales. For example, retailers play music to relax people and to make them predisposed to purchase. Some food store retailers have experimented with creating certain scents and aromas in their stores to make consumers hungry.

ATTENTION, INTEREST, DESIRE, ACTION (AIDA) MODEL   A **response-hierarchy model** illustrating the stages through which a buyer learns of a product and is ultimately moved to purchase it. The model is used in understanding how advertising and selling work. The AIDA model is also used to determine communications objectives. That is, the advertiser's desired response of its marketing communications may be one of four things: to create product awareness (attention), to raise consumers' curiosity (interest), to motivate them to buy (desire), or to move them to purchase (action).

ATTITUDE   A person's positive or negative feelings toward an object or idea. In marketing, attitudes relate to a consumer's tendency to like or dislike a product or to make purchases in a prescribed manner. For example, a consumer maintains the attitude that any purchase, whether large or small, should be based on paying the lowest price. The consumer believes price is the most important purchase criterion and always shops for the best bargain. *Note:* Marketers use *attitudinal research* when developing products and promotional campaigns to gauge the initiative's ability to effect attitude change, or to assess consumers' evaluations of a product or service.

AUCTION   A means of selling products to the highest bidder. Auctions are often employed in selling artwork, used cars, and real estate. Auctions are scheduled for a specific day and time, and are highly promoted in advance to attract participants. The firms that organize them are known as *auction companies* (e.g., Sotheby's).

AUDIENCE DUPLICATION   Consumer exposure to a given advertising message more than once, either in the same medium or in different media. Audience duplication is desirable when an advertiser seeks to reach a target audience repeatedly. It is undesirable when the advertiser wants to reach different people with its separate advertising buys. Audience duplication, therefore, is a factor to be addressed in **media planning.**

AUDIENCE FLOW   Measurement of the program selections of a television or radio audience prior to or following a given program. Household members do one of three things that determine audience flow: (1) They stay with the same station after the show; (2) they change stations to see or hear another show; or (3) they turn off their sets. Tracking audience flow is important for advertisers whose commercials appear between two shows on a given station. That is, advertisers need to know what percentage of the audience will watch the next show and what percentage will switch channels or discontinue watching.

AUDIENCE FRAGMENTATION   Concept relating to the proliferation of broadcast and cable TV stations available to consumers, which has divided audiences into small groups (fragments). It is significant from an advertising standpoint. For example, viewers in New York City can view programs emanating from Boston and Los Angeles. Thus, products being advertised in those far-off markets are not necessarily obtainable in the New York market where the commercials are seen. Audience fragmentation has created problems for advertisers because it complicates analyzing audience size and composition— the information used in **media planning.**

AUDIENCE MEASUREMENT   The practice of gauging the size and composition of a listening or viewing audience. In general, audience size measurements track either the number of *people* or *households* reached by a television or radio broadcast. Five audience measurement methods are commonly employed:

1. *Coincidental telephone method.* Researchers call a sample of homes and ask persons what show they're currently listening to or watching.
2. *Roster-recall method.* Researchers give people a list of stations/ programs in their area and ask them to indicate the ones they recall having seen or heard.

3. *Diary method.* People in the sample households record in a diary information on the stations and programs they watched.
4. *Audimeter method.* Electronic devices (used by the A. C. Nielsen Company) automatically record TV viewing patterns in the sample households.
5. *People-meter method.* Hand-held devices are used by viewers to punch in codes that electronically record TV program viewing.

Note: Broadcast audience measurement is considered *direct* evidence of audience size because the data come from surveys of people who were actually reached by the communication. It is different from print media *circulation,* which measures the number of copies printed of a given publication. Thus, circulation is *indirect* evidence of audience size because it does not include how many and what kinds of people actually read the publication. See also **audience share; households using television; ratings.**

AUDIENCE PROFILE   A composite of audience data that describes the general characteristics of the readers, viewers, or listeners of an advertising **vehicle.** A profile details the audience's traits in terms of demographic variables (e.g., family size, average age, income), psychographic variables (e.g., lifestyles), or geography. Audience profile information is compiled by the media's management for submission to advertisers. Advertisers use these data in determining which **vehicles** to target to reach specific types of consumers.

AUDIENCE SHARE   An audience measurement concept referring to the percentage of households with a television set turned on to a particular program. Audience share is calculated electronically from viewers' homes using **people meters;** or it can be measured through personal or telephone interviews with select household members. In terms of advertising, audience share is a gauge of how many television viewers might receive an advertising message on a given program. See also **audience measurement.**

AUDIMETER   The A. C. Nielsen Company's broadcast audience measurement instrument used to record television viewing patterns among the households being sampled. Audimeters are placed on top of people's TV receivers. The electronic devices provide minute-by-minute records of the shows watched. Specifically, audimeters record the stations watched, viewers' changes from one station to another, and the length of time they spend watching each program.

AUDIT BUREAU OF CIRCULATIONS (ABC)   An independent, nonprofit organization that audits and validates the circulation figures of publications. The organization is comprised of advertisers, ad agencies, newspapers, and magazines. The ABC historically audited only those publications with paid circulations. Recently, however, it began auditing periodicals with **controlled circulations** and those distributed free to the general public. Advertisers use audited circulation figures to make decisions in **media planning**. See also **ABC statement; Business Publications Audit of Circulations.**

AUTHORIZED DEALER   A retail or wholesale outlet that has the exclusive right to sell a manufacturer's product. Sometimes there is only one authorized dealer for a product; in other cases, there may be a select few in a given market. An example of an authorized dealer is an American car dealership that's the only one allowed to sell trucks produced by a given Japanese auto maker.

AUTOMATIC REORDER   What occurs when a company receives merchandise from a supplier based on previously specified terms and/or quantities. For example, a supermarket may arrange to have 10 cases of a household product delivered every two months. In an automatic reorder situation, the buyer gets involved only periodically to review quantities being received (to either increase or decrease the amount) or to change the types of merchandise being delivered.

AVAILABILITY   The television or radio time slots available for purchase by advertisers; also called "avails." Media planners select the programs on which to advertise products. They then work with media representatives to determine the programs' availability and to ultimately secure the media buy. TV and radio station advertising departments furnish lists of available time slots with their respective prices. Prices are based on the shows' estimated **ratings.**

AVERAGE FREQUENCY   Figure referring to the average number of times a person will be exposed to a company's advertisements in different ad media. That is, average frequency describes the number of exposures of an individual or household to an ad in all media carrying the ad. Average frequency is stated as a percentage over a specific period of time (e.g., frequency is calculated for a two-month ad campaign).

AVERAGE NET PAID CIRCULATION   The average number of copies of a periodical sold on a per-issue basis. Average net paid circulation is calculated by dividing the total number of copies sold (subscription and newsstand sales) for a given period of time by the total number of issues printed during that period. For example, assume a monthly publication sold 50,000 copies in a two-month period. The average net paid circulation would be determined by

$$\frac{50,000 \text{ (copies sold)}}{2 \text{ (issues) printed}} = 25,000$$

The average net paid circulation is 25,000. A publication's average net paid circulation is cited in publisher's statements produced by the **Audit Bureau of Circulations.**

AWARENESS   Knowledge in the market of a product's existence, attributes, and availability. Creating awareness is an advertising objective because becoming aware of a new product is the first stage a consumer goes through in accepting it. Advertising effectiveness may be determined by researching how much an advertising communication raised awareness of the product among target consumers. See also **response-hierarchy model.**

AWARENESS-TRIAL-REPEAT (ATR)   A concept explaining the sequence of actions a consumer takes in adopting a new product. Using this paradigm, a consumer moves from being ignorant of a product to becoming a regular purchaser after learning of the product's attributes and availability (awareness), trying the product (trial) and—assuming the trial usage is deemed favorable—buying the product again (repeat).

B

BACK COVER   The back page of a magazine. The back cover is a **preferred position** for an advertisement because it is very likely to be seen and read by a large number of readers. It is often the most expensive advertising space in the publication. For example, in some magazines, the rate for back cover space is calculated as a four-color advertisement, even if the advertiser runs a black-and-white ad. Also known as the *fourth cover*.

BACKDOOR SELLING   Sales technique where a seller bypasses a purchasing agent and attempts to obtain orders directly from other (nonpurchasing) executives in the prospect company. The term connotes a departure from official buying procedures and channels.

BACK OF BOOK   The section of a magazine that appears after the majority of the publication's editorial content. The back-of-book section is believed to have the lowest reader response rate of any section in the magazine. Regardless, rates for insertions appearing in the back-of-book area are usually no different from those for other parts of the publication. *Note:* The back-of-book concept is becoming obsolete as many magazines now include editorial content throughout the publication (e.g., *People* magazine). See also **front of book.**

BACK ORDER   Merchandise that has been ordered but is not available for delivery because the supplier does not have it in inventory. For example, if a pair of hiking boots ordered from a catalog is temporarily out of stock, it is placed on back order. Back order represents an obligation by both buyer and seller to complete the purchase transaction when the product eventually becomes available. However, some suppliers give buyers the option of canceling the order if the merchandise will not be available for a prolonged period of time.

BACK-TO-BACK **1.** The airing of two commercials by the same advertiser in successive order. Back-to-back commercial buys are usually bought by a company selling products that are similar or related in some way (e.g., a shampoo commercial followed by one for hair spray). Back-to-back commercials for the same product are sometimes aired, typically as two 15-second spots. **2.** A programming term describing radio or TV shows that appear one after the other. See also **bookends.**

BACKWARD INTEGRATION A company's efforts to increase sales and profits by expanding operations within its industry. Specifically, it involves building or acquiring businesses that relate to the company's current business. For example, a manufacturing company might acquire one of its suppliers to lessen costs for raw materials and gain greater control over delivery schedules. Backward integration is a strategic planning decision to expand present businesses and develop new ones. See also **integration.**

BAIT AND SWITCH ADVERTISING A deceptive advertising technique in which the seller does not intend to sell a product at its advertised price. The "bait" is used to build store traffic, after which the seller tries to "switch" the buyer to purchase a more expensive item. For example, a retailer advertises a very low price for a computer table, of which it has a very small inventory. The retailer's advertising succeeds in drawing many people to the store, but consumers find the product quickly sold out. The retailer then attempts to get people to buy a more expensive computer table. Retailers found to use bait and switch advertising are subject to disciplinary action by the Federal Trade Commission.

BALANCE SHEET CLOSE A **closing** technique used when dealing with a procrastinating customer. In a balance sheet close, the salesperson writes up a list of pros and cons for either acting immediately or for delaying the purchase. If the salesperson has made a persuasive case, the reasons for immediate action outweigh those for delaying. This approach often makes a compelling case for the prospect to agree to the transaction.

BALLOON COPY   Advertising copy in a print ad where the words spoken by a person in the illustration are enclosed in a circle (balloon), with a line drawn to the mouth of the person to whom they are attributed. This visual technique is borrowed from cartoons and comic strips.

BANNER   **1.** A large strip of fabric featuring an advertising message, product image or slogan, or corporate identification (e.g., company logo). Banners are used in retail outlets to lend visibility to products and special promotions. Often, banners are used at special events to indicate the event theme and the corporate sponsor. **2.** In newspaper layout, a headline that runs across (or nearly across) an entire page.

BAR CODE   A graphic marking comprised of parallel lines of varying widths that is "read" by an optical scanner device. Bar codes are used on envelopes to allow automated postal sorting. They're also used on product packages. Package bar codes are based on **universal product codes,** which identify products, their prices, and their manufacturers. Electronic cash registers scan the code to register the item's price and accumulate data on product sales—information used to track inventory and maintain records of product sales. Bar codes are also used on coupons to generate data on redemption rates. See also **electronic marketing.**

BAR GRAPH   A graphic, comprised of a series of vertical lines representing the object(s) being measured (e.g., market share, sales results), used to illustrate data. The vertical axis is marked by figures indicating quantities; the height of the bars is determined by the quantity of each variable. The bars generally are shown with different markings to distinguish between the objects being measured. Also known as *histogram.* See also **pie chart.**

BARRIERS TO COMPETITION   The economic, political, and technological forces that limit market competition; the factors that make companies' collective ability to enter a market more difficult. Examples are high research and development costs that prohibit companies from developing competing products, insufficient access to distribution channels, and a high degree of product differentiation.

BARRIERS TO ENTRY   The difficulties an individual company faces in entering a market. These may include large capital requirements

Bar Graph

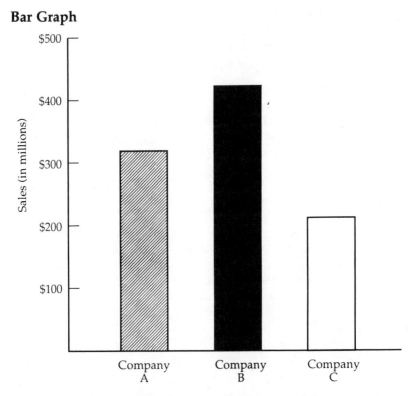

(start-up costs); government policies that can delay entry into a market; proprietary technology; and various economic, political, and legal restrictions. The greater the barriers to entry, the less competition there is for companies already operating in the industry. For example, companies that first produced mainframe computers enjoyed little competition because the technology and expertise required to make them prohibited many companies from developing alternative models.

BARTER   1. The exchange of goods and services without monetary compensation to or by either party in the transaction. For example, a country will provide grain to another country in exchange for crude oil. **2.** In advertising, the practice of selling advertising time or space in exchange for merchandise. The companies that specialize in coordinating this form of exchange are known as *barter brokers*.

BASE RATE   A magazine or newspaper's price for advertising before discounts or surcharges are imposed. The base rate relates to the cost of a one-time advertising purchase. Price discounts are available to advertisers who make volume purchases. Price surcharges may be imposed when advertisers secure **preferred positions** for their insertions.

BASIC RATE The standard published price of a magazine paid by subscribers. Basic rates are determined for single-copy sales, as well as for multiyear subscriptions. The **Audit Bureau of Circulations** requires that a magazine's selling price be at least half the basic rate for its circulation to be considered paid circulation.

BEHAVIORAL SEGMENTATION **Market segmentation** strategy based on how consumers use a product and the buying patterns they exhibit. This segmentation technique defines consumer groups, for example, by when they buy a product (e.g., the product is typically bought for a particular holiday or special occasion); how often they buy it (e.g., first-time users, occasional users, heavy users); or the product features they seek (e.g., quality, service, economy).

BELIEFS The descriptive thoughts consumers have about an item or concept that influence their consumer behavior. Beliefs are acquired through learning and social interaction. Understanding people's collective beliefs is key to developing effective marketing strategies. If, for example, consumers' beliefs about a product are false (e.g., they believe one product is of lesser quality than a competing product), the marketing strategy should attempt to change beliefs. See also **brand image.**

BELIEVABILITY The truth acceptance level of an advertising claim. That is, believability refers to whether or not the advertising message is considered plausible by consumers. In general, advertising is most effective when it is believable and is ineffective when it is not believable. For example, an ad that claims a health product is guaranteed to add 20 years to a person's life would not be believable. Such a claim would create a good deal of product distrust by consumers, and would reflect negatively on the advertiser. Moreover, advertisers are legally obligated to be truthful in their advertising and, from an ethical standpoint, should not make exaggerated claims about their products.

BENEFIT SEGMENTATION **Market segmentation** strategy that groups consumers by the benefits they seek from a product or service. A well-known benefit segmentation study grouped toothpaste consumers by the different benefits they sought: brighter teeth, tooth decay prevention, flavor, and price. Marketers may base marketing mix decisions on the characteristics of a benefit-segmented market.

BETTER BUSINESS BUREAU   An independent organization whose purpose is protecting consumers from deceptive advertising and business practices. Better business bureaus answer consumer complaints and make inquiries into companies against which complaints are filed. The bureaus maintain records of these complaints. In addition to handling consumer calls, better business bureaus produce consumer education programs and materials. There are some 150 local better business bureaus in the United States, each one financed by companies in their respective markets. The national parent organization of the local bureaus is the Council of Better Business Bureaus, Inc.

BIAS   The danger inherent in survey research when questions are phrased to encourage a particular response, and, therefore, generate unreliable feedback. Questions are biased when they create in the respondent a positive or negative predisposition toward the given subject, for example, "Do you feel liberal politicians who favor abortion would condone promiscuity?" The use of the terms *liberal* and *promiscuity* make the question biased. Researchers' bias in survey construction may be inadvertent. Thus, caution must be exercised in developing the wording, sequence, and format of research tools such as questionnaires. Bias must also be recognized and avoided in sampling. See also **interviewer bias.**

BIDDING   An invitation to companies to submit a price quote for the goods or services they provide. Bidding may be *closed* or *open*. Closed bidding is a formal process of soliciting confidential bids (usually from a select list of firms invited to do so.) The contract in a closed bid is generally awarded to the lowest bidder. For example, for a government contract to build a nuclear power facility the supervising government agency announces the call for bids and grants the contract to the construction company offering the best price. Open bidding is less formal. Open bids are generally submitted by a large number of providers (as opposed to a select, pre-established list).

BILLBOARD 1. An outdoor advertising medium. Billboards are large posters (measuring approximately 12′ by 25′) that are displayed in high-traffic locations. They are either erected on platforms anchored in the ground or displayed on exterior building walls or rooftops. The billboard itself is comprised of a series of printed sheets pasted on by hand. **2.** In broadcasting, the brief message, coming before or at the end of a program, that announces the program sponsor or cast members.

BILLINGS The charges made by a marketing services agency to its clients for creative, media, production, and other agency costs. Agencies cite their billings as the amount of gross income generated in a given year. Billings are used to rank firms, and are often viewed as an indicator of an agency's annual growth or decline. See also **agency commission; fee system of compensation.**

BILL INSERT A promotional piece inserted into mailing envelopes, the focus of which is unrelated to the package's informational content. For example, a telephone company may include inserts in its customer billing to promote a community-service activity it is sponsoring. Bill inserts are used to **piggyback** a mailing. That is, they're intended to make the most use of mailing costs being incurred for another purpose.

BILL OF LADING Document used in transporting goods that describes the commodities, quantities, and terms and conditions of the shipment. A bill of lading represents a contract for shipment between a carrier and shipper. It also serves as a receipt from the carrier for the shipment and, ultimately, the certificate of ownership. Historically, bills of lading have been printed forms. Today, however, the information they contain can be transmitted by computer between the participant companies using a technique called *electronic data interchange (EDI).*

BIMODAL DISTRIBUTION Distribution of scores peaking at two points rather than at one when the statistics are charted on a graph. That is, a bimodal distribution occurs when answers to different questions appear with equal frequency. Assume respondents are asked to rank the importance of 10 attributes of a given product. If price and quality are cited by the same number of respondents as being most important, a bimodal distribution occurs. Thus, price and quality appear on a graph as being of equal importance (rather than only one attribute appearing as the most important).

BIND-IN   Promotional pieces, usually printed on heavy paper stock, that are bound into magazines. A response card usually has a perforated edge to facilitate readers' removal of it from the publication. Bind-in cards let readers receive information about a product or service, or they are used to place magazine subscription orders. Consequently, bind-in cards are usually designed to meet U.S. Postal Service size requirements, and frequently feature a postage-paid **indicia** for mailing purposes.

BINGO CARD   Response cards allowing magazine readers to indicate from which advertisers they would like to receive more information. Bingo cards feature a series of numbers that correspond to advertisements in the publication. The advertisements themselves will indicate: "Please circle number 000 on the reader response card to receive more information." Readers mark the numbers and return the card to the publisher, who sends the requests to its advertisers. Advertisers then send product literature, samples, or other materials to the readers. Bingo cards are used in both trade and consumer magazines. In fact, they are used by some publications as an incentive to attract advertising.

BIOGENIC NEEDS   Basic physical needs that people must satisfy: hunger, thirst, a need to breathe. Biogenic needs are different from **psychogenic** (or emotional) **needs,** such as those for love, belonging, security, and self-actualization. The psychologist Abraham Maslow's theory of the *hierarchy of needs* states that people must satisfy their basic biogenic needs before seeking to satisfy their emotional needs. Marketers must understand to what level of a person's needs their products correspond.

BLACK-AND-WHITE   A printed piece that uses no colors. In black-and-white printing, the material features only black ink that has been printed on white paper. Black-and-white printing is considered a one-color process. Thus, it is significantly less expensive than two- and four-color printing. However, it lacks the ability to create vivid images of photographs and illustrations as does color printing.

BLACK BOOK   See **creative black book.**

BLACK BOX CONCEPT A paradigm of the decision-making process that drives consumer behavior. The concept details how marketing stimuli interact with people's personal characteristics and external forces to influence their decisions to buy products. The black box is comprised of three components: *Environmental factors* relate to marketing messages the consumer receives as well as to macroenvironmental forces (such as prevailing economic conditions); *personal characteristics* describe the various interpersonal and intrapersonal forces that make the consumer realize the need for a product and which guide the consumer's search for information and available alternatives; *buyer's responses* relate to how the consumer actually makes decisions regarding product and brand choices, timing of the purchase, and determining the quantity of product needed and an acceptable purchase price. *Note:* In advertising, the black box is used as a model to depict the influence of marketing mix and external variables on consumer decision making. The diagram below illustrates how such elements as advertising and promotion—coupled with the market forces of competition and socioeconomic conditions—collectively impact the action of a consumer who has received an advertising message.

BLACK MARKET Situation existing when merchandise is priced at a high level when the goods are scarce or unavailable in normal market channels. For example, certain American garments not available in foreign countries might be sold in those countries at exorbitant

Black Box

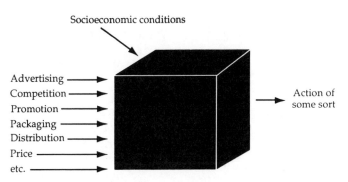

From *Advertising: Theory and Practice*, by C. H. Sandage, Vernon Fryburger and Kim Rotzoll. Copyright © 1989 by Longman Publishing Group. Reprinted by permission of Longman Publishing Group.

rates. Illegal transactions often characterize dealings in black market goods.

BLANKING PAPER   The unprinted border (white edging) of a billboard or other outdoor advertising display that frames the printed image to make it stand out.

BLEED   Artwork in a print advertisement that extends to the edge of the page. Bleed advertisements are designed to capture the reader's attention. The design allows the graphic artist greater flexibility in conveying a visual concept because of the enlarged printing space. Therefore, bleed advertisements are sold at a premium price—an average of 15% above the page's **base rate.**

BLIND EMBOSSING   A graphic art technique in which a raised image is produced on paper without the use of ink. That is, the image is imprinted by physically stamping the paper with a mold. For example, a company's logo might be shown on a brochure or letterhead as blind embossing. Blind embossing is a costly process that can add significantly to the price of the printing job.

BLIND TEST   Product test in which consumers are asked to evaluate products whose identities are not revealed. A common example is

Bleed

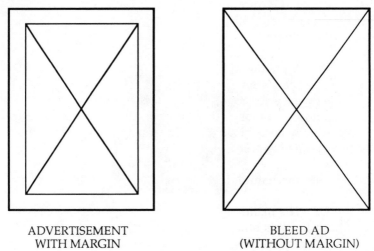

ADVERTISEMENT
WITH MARGIN

BLEED AD
(WITHOUT MARGIN)

the blind taste test conducted for different brands of cola. Commercials show respondents tasting each one and saying which they prefer. The fact that the products in a blind test are not identified enables researchers to elicit unbiased feedback from the respondents.

BLOCK 1. A time period comprised of a successive series of intervals in the daily schedule of a radio or TV station. For example, a block would be the time period from 10 A.M. to noon each weekday. Block also refers to this time period on more than one day during the same week (e.g., 10 A.M. to noon, Monday through Friday). 2. In film production, the process of specifying camera angles/locations or actors' movements for a given production (commercial or dramatic show).

BLOCK GROUP An area of a densely populated city in which 800 to 1,000 people reside, as defined by the U.S. Bureau of the Census. Block groups are subdivisions of **census tracts.** Either may be used as units of study in **area sampling** research.

BLOW-IN The technique of inserting promotional pieces into a magazine using a machine that "blows" the pieces between the pages. These pieces are printed on heavy paper stock and remain in place until the publication is opened. Blow-ins may be subscription order cards or response cards. Blow-in cards capture people's immediate attention, since they can literally fall into the readers' lap. The disadvantage of this promotional device is that blow-in cards are often discarded by an initial reader before an interested person gets a chance to see them.

BLUEPRINT A photographic print of typeset copy produced by a printer for the client's review before printing. Also called "blues," a blueprint shows exactly how a page or series of pages will be laid out with copy and illustrations. The blueprint allows the client to make final changes and corrections to the document before the job goes to press. See also **galley proofs.**

BOARDS See **mechanical art.**

BODY COPY The main section of copy in a print advertisement, as distinct from the ad's other elements: headline, subheads, captions, illustrations. Body copy is designed to sell the product. It explains the product's attributes and benefits to the consumer, and presents a convincing argument to make the consumer want to purchase the item. Also known as *text* or *body text.*

BOILERPLATE COPY   A paragraph or phrase of copy that is standard in all print communications produced by the same advertiser. For example, a company produces brochures for each of its product lines. The brochures all feature different copy, except for a boilerplate paragraph that gives background on the company. The different print and broadcast ads in an advertising campaign might also use some boilerplate copy.

BONUS PACK   A product package containing two items, but the consumer only pays for one. Bonus packs are a sales promotion technique used to introduce new products. For example, a toothpaste manufacturer would use a bonus pack to introduce its new mouthwash, with a sample of the new product included in or alongside the toothpaste box. Bonus packs are also used to highlight a complementary product (not necessarily new on the market) produced by the same company.

BOOKENDS   Two 15-second television commercials for the same product, which are separated by several commercials from other advertisers. Bookends, for example, are used to advertise a popular brand of aspirin. In the first spot, a woman is shown discussing her headache and her plans to take the advertised pain reliever. In the second bookend (three commercials later), the woman appears again to announce that her headache is gone.

BOOKLET   A series of bound printed pages containing an advertising message, product use instructions, or descriptions of a company or service. Booklets generally contain detailed information. Thus, they are used when a sales message is particularly complex. Booklets often accompany product purchases and are used as promotional pieces in direct-mail campaigns. See also **brochure.**

BOSTON BOX   See **growth-share matrix.**

BOTTOM-UP PLANNING   Corporate planning procedure in which an organization's various divisions develop their own goals and plans for review by senior management. In such an organization, divisions create their own marketing plans based on the company's guiding mission and objectives. Bottom-up planning is based on the theory that employees work harder and are more committed to success when they participate in running the organization. Bottom-up planning contrasts **top-down planning,** in which senior management sets the goals and plans for lower management.

BOUNCE-BACK OFFER   A selling device included in a merchandise container that attempts to sell more of the same product. For example, a consumer buys through mail order a gift package containing different blends of tea. Included in the box in which the merchandise was shipped is a catalog promoting these and other tea blends available, as well as related company products (e.g., brewing pots or decorative cups and saucers).

BOUTIQUE AGENCY   An advertising agency that specializes in one aspect of advertising. Boutique agencies offer only creative services (copywriting, art direction) or media planning/buying. Such firms typically maintain small staffs and retain freelance professionals as needed. Also known as *limited-service agency,* both terms contrast the broad range of creative and production capabilities offered by a **full-service advertising agency.**

BOX-TOP OFFER   A sales promotion tactic in which a gift, premium, or free merchandise is offered to the consumer in exchange for a **proof of purchase.** Box-top offers are so named because the company often requires consumers to tear off the package top as proof of the sale. Similar to other sales promotion techniques, box-top offers are designed to get consumers' attention and to make them purchase the product immediately. Box-top offers known as *continuity programs* grant large gifts or prizes in exchange for multiple proofs-of-purchase (e.g., a set of silverware for 25 box tops).

BPA STATEMENT   A filing required of publications audited by the **Business Publications Audit of Circulations.** The statement reports statistical information relating to the publication's paid circulation over a six-month period. Moreover, it includes information on readers' occupations and their industries of employment by **SIC code.** Publishers file BPA statements twice a year. BPA statements are reviewed by advertisers of industrial goods and services to compare the circulations of business publications read by their target audience(s). See also **ABC statement.**

BRAINSTORMING   An idea generation technique used in new product development and in devising strategies for promotional campaigns. Brainstorming is a small-group exercise. The session usually involves 6 to 10 participants who are asked to contribute spontaneous ideas relating to the topic at hand. Participants are told to be free-thinking and to voice whatever ideas come to mind. Spontaneity is essential to effective brainstorming. Also important is a supportive climate free of criticism of the proposed ideas. Rather than evaluating them, ideas should be improved on or combined with other thoughts. It is important to involve people with varying backgrounds in brainstorming meetings. See also **synectics.**

BRAND   The combination of symbols, words, or designs that differentiate one company's product from another company's product. Brand is also used to describe a company's family of products. A brand of coffee, for instance, might include the company's regular ground coffee, as well as its instant and decaffeinated versions. *Trademark* is the legal term for brand. See also **manufacturer's brand.**

BRAND ASSOCIATION   Citing a particular brand in a general product category. For example, a person who says he is going to make a Xerox copy has made a brand association. That is, he has cited a brand name rather than a generic one for photocopying. Brand association is proof of a brand's domination of a consumer's **share of mind** in a particular **brand category.**

BRAND CATEGORY   The generic classification of products and services that all meet the same consumer need. All products in a brand category are similar in that they have comparable attributes and benefits. For example, the various brands of toothpaste (from the same or different manufacturers) fall into the brand category of "toothpastes."

BRAND DEVELOPMENT INDEX (BDI)   A multiple-factor index method used to measure a brand's success in a given geographic area. BDI is determined by comparing brand sales to the area's population and to brand consumption nationally. BDI is calculated for separate metropolitan areas, thus enabling marketers to determine high potential areas for new product introductions and special promotions. It also enables media planners to concentrate advertising in areas where there is a high degree of brand usage, or to direct additional media dollars at areas where brand usage is low.

BRAND EXTENSION   The practice of adding a new product to an existing line of products, with the new product carrying the same brand name. For instance, Nabisco extended its Ritz crackers brand by introducing Ritz Bits, which are bite-size versions. The strategy of brand extension is to make consumers perceive the new product favorably by associating it with the company's established products (capitalizing on the **halo effect** of a successful, existing brand). Brand extensions are usually targeted to a specific segment within the parent brand's general market. Also known as *line extension*.

BRAND IMAGE   How consumers collectively perceive a brand: their thoughts, feelings, and expectations of it. Cadillac cars for many years evoked a brand image of prestige and affluence. Brand image is initially created and subsequently reinforced through advertising.

BRANDING   Creating names and identities for multiple products produced by the same company. Companies adopt one of three branding strategies:

1. *Individual branding*—creating separate brand names for each product without relating them to other company products or the company itself. For example, Procter & Gamble gives individual brand names to products such as Tide laundry detergent and Crest toothpaste. Individual branding is used when products are physically different and/or targeted to different market segments. A benefit of individual branding is that the failure of one product will not endanger the status of another.

2. *Family line branding*—using the brand name on two or more products. For example, tools sold by Sears, Roebuck & Co. all carry the Craftsman brand name. The benefit of family line branding is the ease with which new products are introduced, since new product additions benefit from the established reputation of the family brand name.

3. *Combination of individual and family line branding*—having products carry both family and individual names. For instance, Post Cereals carries the names Post Raisin Bran, and Post 40% Bran Flakes.

This brand name strategy links the benefits of individual and family line branding. That is, it is easy to launch new products while also being able to target separate products to different market segments.

Note: Branding can build a strong seller image, attract loyal and profitable consumers, and help in segmenting markets. Branding, however, has also been criticized for these reasons: It creates trivial product differentiation (e.g., products such as aspirin are virtually identical in their attributes), causes overpricing of products, and creates false social values.

BRAND LOYALTY   A consumer's repeated purchasing of the same brand in a product category. Social and psychological factors determine brand loyalty. Social influences include those exerted by a consumer's family or peer group. Psychological forces relate to the individual's attitudes or beliefs. Companies that engage in **behavioral segmentation** often analyze consumers' brand loyalty status and patterns. That is, consumers may be regular purchasers of a product and never buy another brand (the ultimate in brand loyalty); or their buying patterns may range from occasional brand purchasing to frequent brand switching (the lowest degree of brand loyalty). Marketers, thus, can segment their market based on consumers' varying levels of loyalty.

BRAND MANAGER   Marketing manager responsible for a specific brand in a large consumer products company. Brand managers devise strategy and monitor the market performance of the item. They are typically responsible for making advertising decisions and serving as liaison with retained marketing services agencies. (In large consumer product companies each brand may have its own advertising agency and ad budget.) Brand managers interface with company professionals in research and development, engineering, finance, manufacturing, distribution, packaging, market research, and sales. Also known as *product managers*, they usually report to a group product manager, who oversees several brands.

BRAND MARK   The identifying symbol of a brand. Brand marks include the product logo, package design, distinctive type style, or a combination thereof. Brand mark is different from brand name, which is that element of a brand or trademark that can be spoken.

BRAND NAME　The part of a brand that can be spoken, such as the product name (Maxwell House Coffee) or its slogan (GOOD TO THE LAST DROP). Brand name strategies are conducted by product manufacturers to establish brand identities in the marketplace. See also **branding.**

BRAND PERSONALITY　The image of a product from the manufacturer's standpoint. Brand personality is how the company intends the product to be perceived by the target market and is different from **brand image,** which is how consumers actually see the product and assess its attributes.

BRAND POTENTIAL INDEX (BPI)　A calculation used to predict product sales in a given market and to plan future ad budgets. The BPI is the relationship between the **brand development index** and the **market development index.** The former is the percentage of product sales in a geographic area in relation to the area's population and product sales nationally. The latter describes the relationship between the potential and actual product users in one geographic area, as compared to these figures on a national basis.

BRAND PREFERENCE　The degree to which consumers prefer one brand over another with similar attributes and price. Advertisers attempt to establish and reinforce brand preference through advertising and other marketing communications. Messages often relate to the product's advantages and, in some cases, its long-standing reputation and history of quality.

BREAK-EVEN ANALYSIS　Computation designed to identify the relationship between a product's fixed and variable costs, and revenues-profits based on the number of products sold. Stated simply, break-even analysis is used to calculate how many units must be sold to make a profit. This *break-even point* is determined by the formula:

$$\frac{\text{fixed cost}}{(\text{unit price} - \text{unit variable cost})} = \text{break-even point}$$

Example:

A company invests $500,000 (fixed costs) in developing a new perfume that sells for $20 a bottle (price). Variable costs are calculated to be $10 per unit. Using the above formula:

$$\frac{\$500,000}{\$20 - \$10} = 50,000 \text{ units}$$

The break-even point is 50,000. That is, 50,000 bottles must be sold for the company to cover its initial investment and to realize a profit.

Note: Companies use break-even analysis to forecast profits at different levels of unit sales and at different price points. See also **return-on-investment.**

BREAKING BULK   The practice of breaking up a large inventory of product into progressively smaller quantities as the product moves toward its target consumers. For example, a manufacturer sends a large quantity of product to a warehouse. At that point, the shipment is divided into smaller lots for delivery to the retail outlets served by the warehouse.

BROADCASTER   **1.** A company that owns one or more radio or TV stations. **2.** Also used to describe a person who is a performer (e.g., a news anchor or reporter) on a broadcast medium, or one who delivers or sponsors a commercial announcement on such a medium.

BROADCAST MEDIA   The electronic communications media: television and radio stations, cable TV networks, and satellite facilities. Broadcast media are used in virtually every major advertising campaign because such media reach vast numbers of people either nationally, regionally, or on a market-by-market basis. There are benefits and drawbacks to broadcast media advertising. The main benefit of broadcast media advertising (aside from audience size) is its ability to create vivid product messages that are compelling and very memorable. The drawback is that messages are fleeting and are received by people who do not necessarily want to see the communications. Also, there are numerous commercials, thus hindering the audience's ability to remember everything. See also **clutter.**

BROADSHEET   A newspaper whose pages measure approximately 22" by 15". An example of a broadsheet newspaper is the *Wall Street Journal*. Broadsheets are typically divided into sections, for example, news, business, sports, or entertainment, to increase the ease with which readers find the editorial content they're seeking. They also allow advertisers to place ads in sections of the paper that are likely to be read by their target consumers (e.g., a discount securities brokerage firm advertises in the business section). The large dimension of broadsheet newspapers makes this format cumbersome for commuters on mass transit systems in large metropolitan areas. This fact prompted creation of the **tabloid** style of newspaper makeup.

BROCHURE   An expensively produced booklet that's printed on heavy paper stock and features extensive use of copy and illustrations. Brochures detail products, a company's services, or the company itself. Brochures are used in direct-mail campaigns, as sales promotion pieces, and as **leave-behind** sales literature. See also **collateral materials.**

BROKER   An intermediary authorized to sell, purchase, or rent goods on behalf of an organization or individual. For example, a manufacturer's agent is a broker who sells a line of merchandise by a particular manufacturer. Another example is a **list broker,** who rents mailing lists owned by different publishers. There are two defining characteristics of brokers: First, they never take physical possession (title) of the goods; second, they're viewed as temporary representatives of the organizations for which they work. Brokers' compensation is typically based on commission.

BROWN GOODS   Consumer electronic products such as television sets, radios, and stereos. The name comes from the brown, simulated wood cabinets in which these goods are frequently manufactured.

BUCKSLIP   A slip of paper on which an informational message relating to a product is printed. A buckslip is used to provide new or different product information from that which already accompanies the item. For example, a new use for the product (not described in the product literature) is described on a buckslip. The name comes from the fact that a buckslip is usually the size of a dollar bill.

BUILD STRATEGY   Increasing promotional spending to increase a product's market share. Advertising and marketing expenditures are escalated at the expense, however, of short-term company earnings. A build strategy is one option companies have in determining the future status of a product, product portfolio, or **strategic business unit** (SBU). See also **growth-share matrix.**

BULK CIRCULATION See **circulation.**

BULK MAIL Mail that is sent in large quantities for which the mailer receives discounted postal rates. Bulk mail is sent as either second-, third-, or fourth-class mail. Discounts are determined by the class of mail. Examples of bulk mail materials are catalogs, magazines, and parcels. Bulk mail rates are obtained for direct-mail campaigns, where the sender attempts to limit the cost of large-scale mailings. Companies must pay an application fee and an annual fee to send materials via bulk mail.

BULLDOG EDITION **1.** A daily newspaper's first edition appearing the night before the issue date. For instance, the bulldog edition for Thursday's paper comes out Wednesday night. **2.** Also describes those sections of a Sunday newspaper distributed one or two days before the issue date. For example, subscribers to the Sunday *New York Times* receive the paper's magazine and Arts and Leisure sections on Saturday.

BULLPEN The area of an advertising agency where graphic artists, paste-up specialists, and photo retouchers work. The bullpen houses the materials and computer facilities used in producing artwork and special visual effects in advertising and other communications materials.

BURKE TEST A test of audience **recall** of a television commercial that aired the night before. The day after a commercial has appeared, a sample of respondents is contacted by telephone. The viewers are queried about the spot: specifically, what they recall about the selling points made in the commercial. Burke Tests are one measure of a TV commercial's effectiveness. The research is conducted by Burke Marketing Research, Inc. See also **day-after recall.**

BURST ADVERTISING A media scheduling tactic in which advertising is concentrated to appear during a brief time frame (e.g., over a one-week period), resulting in a "burst" of exposures. Implicit in this media strategy is that there is less advertising, or none at all, at other points in the campaign. Burst advertising is used to accompany new product introductions or is timed to coincide with special promotions. Also known as *saturation.*

BUSINESS ECONOMICS RESEARCH   A form of market research that seeks to generate data regarding short- or long-range sales forecasts; business trends; market pricing; plant, warehouse, or facilities location studies; acquisition surveys; and operations research.

BUSINESS OBJECTIVES   The desired or needed results an organization seeks to accomplish over a specified period of time. Objectives relate to either major problems or issues faced by a company. For example, a company's objective might be to build up its reputation or increase profitability for a product in a specific geographic market. Business objectives typically drive marketing planning. Thus, if the company's objective is to enhance its general reputation, marketing activities might involve public-relations tactics to promote its community service contributions. Setting business objectives gives guidance to a company's activities, as well as provides measures of control and evaluation. See also **strategic planning.**

BUSINESS PLAN   A document used in guiding a company (or a division thereof) toward profitability. Assessing *market potential* is a main element of a business plan. Included in this part of the document is information on the size and characteristics of the potential market(s), the anticipated market share to be gained, and the distribution channels to be employed. Basic marketing activities must also be detailed: promotion tactics, pricing strategies, sales force management, and advertising. Business plans relating to a new product must cite the stage of development at which the product exists (concept, prototype, or ready-to-market) and the item's proprietary aspects vis-à-vis competitors' goods. Start-up companies develop business plans to raise capital from potential investors or lenders. Thus, the plan must demonstrate the viability and potential of the venture, as well as detail management's objectives and the steps that will be taken to achieve them. See also **marketing plan.**

BUSINESS PORTFOLIO   The collection of a diversified company's divisions, product lines, and **strategic business units.** Each element of the business portfolio is related since the divisions' operations are all geared to achieving the parent company's corporate objectives. Organizations periodically measure the performance of units in their portfolio. One way is through use of the **growth-share matrix,** which is a grid used to indicate a unit's performance in terms of market growth rate and its relative market share. See also **portfolio analysis.**

BUSINESS PUBLICATIONS AUDIT OF CIRCULATIONS (BPA)   A nonprofit group that validates the circulation of *trade* publications. The organization is comprised of leading trade and industrial publications, whose circulations are audited semiannually. The purpose of validating circulation numbers is to lend credibility to them. Advertisers base their print media buys, in part, on this circulation information. *Note:* The **Audit Bureau of Circulations** is the BPA's counterpart in that the former audits the circulations of *consumer* publications. See also **ABC statement.**

BUSINESS REPLY MAIL   Postal materials that can be mailed at no cost to the sender. They include business reply cards (BRCs) and business reply envelopes (BREs) used, for example, to order magazine subscriptions or to send payment for a direct-mail offer. Business reply mail is intended to encourage consumers to respond to special promotions. Mailers pay an annual fee for a business reply mail permit, the number for which is printed on all business reply materials. Once a piece of business reply is delivered, the U.S. Postal Service collects the postage due from the permit holder.

BUSINESS-TO-BUSINESS ADVERTISING   Advertising designed to reach business decision makers—that is, purchasing officers, professional users, and others who buy products and services relating to their businesses. (These buyers are different from *consumers*, who purchase goods to satisfy personal needs.) Business-to-business advertising includes

- *Industrial advertising*, which involves promoting goods and services used in producing other goods and services.
- *Trade advertising*, which is targeted at wholesalers, retailers, and others who buy goods for resale or rental.
- *Professional advertising*, which is designed to get professionals either to use a particular product or service or to specify it as the product of choice to others (e.g., advertising to get architects to recommend a particular type of building material to clients).

BUY CLASSES   Categories distinguishing the intricacies of purchasing decisions in the industrial buying process. Companies engage in three types of buy classes: (1) *Straight rebuys* are those involving the routine, repetitive purchase of items (e.g., floppy disks); (2) *modified* *rebuys* are similar to straight rebuys but involve the procurement of new products that cost more or feature new or upgraded specifications (e.g., a new brand of computer monitor); (3) *new buys* are new purchases and therefore involve greater risk and cost to the buyer (e.g., the purchase of a mainframe computer).

BUYER   The person who actually makes the product purchase. Not all buyers make the purchase *decision,* however. For example, a husband may buy a particular brand of dishwashing liquid at the request of his wife, or an office worker might buy supplies that have been requested by a superior. See also **end-user.**

BUYER INTENTION SURVEY   See **buying intent.**

BUYER READINESS STAGES   The levels a consumer moves through in considering the purchase of a product. Success in marketing strategy is based on the ability to *move* a consumer up the various buyer readiness stages. That is, to move the person (1) from simply being aware of a product's existence to (2) being informed and interested in purchasing it to (3) finally being motivated to buy it.

BUYER'S MARKET   An economic situation that favors the buyer rather than the seller. In a buyer's market, product prices are set at levels lower than what the seller would like. For example, when the number of homes on the market exceeds the number of people wanting to buy them, it is said to be a buyer's market. Consequently, buyers would be able to acquire properties at prices much lower than what sellers are asking. A buyer's market relates to industrial purchases as well as consumer purchases. For instance, in a buyer's market retailers can obtain concessions from suppliers (e.g., favorable prices or delivery schedules). See also **seller's market.**

BUYING BEHAVIOR PATTERNS   The variations in buyer decision making that change with the nature, cost, and complexity of the product being purchased. Three types of buying behavior patterns are said to exist. *Complex* buying behavior is characterized by purchases of items that are extremely expensive and there are numerous choices of brands or manufacturers. Examples of purchases in this category are cars, boats, and homes. *Habitual buying behavior* involves the purchase of low-cost, frequently purchased products, such as food staples or personal hygiene products. With *variety-seeking* buying behavior consumers are faced with numerous brand choices of low-cost items, such as brands of soda. Consumers will vary their purchases not because of brand disloyalty but rather for variety. See also **dissonance reduction.**

BUYING CENTER The individuals and groups involved in making corporate purchasing decisions. The complexity of industrial purchasing departments and the purchasing function requires that salespeople study a company's buying center. Buying center members assume several basic roles. *Gatekeepers* control information emanating from or entering the organization. They determine what information reaches other members of the buying center (e.g., secretaries handling incoming calls, or midlevel managers passing on information to purchasers). *Influencers* have the technical expertise to evaluate individual products (e.g., a data processing specialist reviews software products). *Deciders* make the final decision on whether or not to purchase a given product and from which vendor. *Buyers* negotiate the terms and details of the transaction with the vendor. *Users* employ and assess the product (and may have initially recommended its procurement and defined the requisite product specifications). Salespeople analyze a company's buying center by identifying the major decision makers. They also research the different evaluation criteria decision makers establish for different purchasing activities.

BUYING COMMITTEE A specially appointed group of executives responsible for selecting goods and services their company will sell. In retailing, a buying committee is the group that decides on merchandise assortments that will be offered in retail outlets. Buying committees are frequently found in companies that have multiple outlets (e.g., supermarkets and chain stores). In addition to merchandise selection, buying committees also help in planning the timing and logistics of sales promotions and special offers. See also **buying center.**

BUYING CRITERIA Requirements used by companies evaluating suppliers of a product or service. Such criteria may relate to the product itself (e.g., technical specifications of the desired product dictate choosing one supplier over another), the supplier company (e.g., its reputation is the key factor in making the buying decision), or the salesperson with whom the buyer is dealing (e.g., the salesperson's expertise or trustworthiness is important).

BUYING INCENTIVE   Free merchandise, a discount, or a gift given away with a product purchase to motivate the consumer to buy the item. Two common examples of buying incentives are a "buy one get one free" offer and a "baker's dozen" (when you purchase 12 donuts and get one free). Buying incentives are often used by retailers to build store traffic.

BUYING INTENT   The measurement of consumers' intention to purchase a product. Surveys of buyer intent gauge consumer attitudes relating to how they'd act in a particular circumstance—not necessarily their attitudes toward a specific product. A buyer intention survey might use a *purchase probability scale*. For example, respondents would be asked, "Do you intend to buy a car within the next three months?" Surveys of buyer intent are valuable in situations in which advanced planning is involved (e.g., new product introduction or special marketing initiative) or when no past product data exist. Gauging buyer intent is one element of *forecasting*.

BUYING POWER   **1.** The collective amount of income available for discretionary spending by members of a population. **2.** A measure of an individual's financial ability to buy goods and services. **3.** In the context of a corporate hierarchy, the level of influence an individual or job function wields in making purchasing decisions.

BUYING POWER INDEX (BPI)   A multiple-factor index designed to measure *market potential*. BPI is a weighted average based on the population size of a market area, its residents' buying patterns as determined by retail sales, and how much money they have to spend (buying power). BPI is calculated for some 700 U.S. cities and each county in the nation. It is published annually in *Sales & Marketing Management* magazine. Marketers use BPI data to help them decide where and how to concentrate their advertising efforts.

BUYING ROLES   The functions of the people who influence and actually carry out buying decisions. Consumers functioning in social groups assume various buying roles. These include *initiators,* who are the people who suggest purchasing the product; *influencers,* whose assessment of the product or the need for it impacts the buying decision; *deciders,* who ultimately make the final decision whether or not to buy the product and how and where to purchase it; *buyers,* who actually make the purchase; and *users,* who ultimately use the product and may be called upon to assess its functionality. Marketers must ascertain the main players in the buying decision process and the influences they exert in decision making. Thus, the seller of living room furniture might advertise its products in publications reaching both men and women, since research shows that both husbands and wives are usually involved in decisions to buy furniture.

BUYING SIGNALS The verbal and nonverbal cues that indicate a prospect is ready to make a purchase. Verbal buying signals are comments made by the prospect (e.g., "How soon can I receive the merchandise?" or "I'd like to discuss this with my accountant"). Nonverbal buying signals include facial expression and physical actions (body language). For instance, *positive* nonverbal cues might be when the prospect leans forward in his or her chair, nods up and down, or makes open-handed gestures. *Negative* gestures include crossing one's arms across the body, moving away from the salesperson, or clenching the hands. Salespeople are trained to spot buying signals and to use the right technique to finalize the transaction. See also **closing.**

BUY PHASES The procedures in which **buying center** members get involved. Seven buy phases exist:

1. *Problem recognition* occurs when personnel identify a problem that necessitates new product/service specifications or a new supplier (e.g., an assembly-line machine is no longer fast enough to meet production requirements).

2. *General need description* is when personnel develop performance standards to be achieved (for example, personnel specify how fast the new assembly-line machine must operate).

3. *Product specification* involves developing the exact technical specifications for the new machine.

4. *Supplier search* occurs when product specifications are established and suppliers who can meet them are identified.

5. *Proposal solicitation* involves asking suppliers to submit formal bids on the costs to provide the new unit.

6. The *order-route specifications* phase occurs when buying center personnel outline production timetables, costs, and warranties.

7. *Performance review* involves monitoring the supplier's work to ensure contractual compliance.

BY-LINER A newspaper or magazine article ghostwritten by a public relations writer that carries the name (by-line) of the writer's client. A by-liner creates the impression that the client authored the piece—publicity that portrays the client as an expert in the subject area. By-liners are usually developed exclusively for one publication according to its editorial specifications for length and format. However, by-liners are sometimes mass mailed to different publications with no exclusivity implied. By-liners are often accompanied by the client's photograph and a brief biography.

C

CABLE TELEVISION   The broadcast television system in which transmission signals are disseminated to homes via coaxial cables (as opposed to signals sent over the air by networks and independent TV stations). As cable TV becomes available in more and more homes, it is seen as an important advertising medium. Advertising rates for cable TV are often significantly less expensive than network TV rates, yet cable offers companies the ability to advertise products nationally. Advertisers can also enjoy high selectivity in targeting audiences geographically, given the host of cable systems in different regions of the United States. Cable TV is often referred to as "pay TV" because subscribers pay a monthly fee to receive "basic" service. Subscribers may pay additional money to receive "premium" stations, which feature uncut, uncensored movies without commercial interruptions. There are some 8,000 individual cable systems in the United States that reach approximately 55 million households. The number of homes wired to receive cable transmissions is steadily increasing. See also **pay-per-view.**

CALLBACK   The second attempt to interview someone as part of a research study. Callbacks are telephone calls or visits made by a researcher to a respondent who was previously unavailable, or they are interviews that take place after a designated period of time (e.g., after a respondent has tried a product for several weeks and is now qualified to offer an opinion about it).

CALL LETTERS   The Federal Communications Commission's system of designating broadcast stations. Stations east of the Mississippi River have call letters beginning with *W* (e.g., WSBK-TV in Boston). Stations west of the Mississippi have call letters starting with *K* (e.g.,

KMOX-TV in St. Louis). Stations are required by FCC regulations to identify themselves by their call letters throughout the broadcast day and at the start and end of their daily programming schedules.

CALL PLANNING   A telephone sales planning process used by salespeople. Call planning involves defining the objective of the call and devising a selling strategy. Call planning is usually designed to get customer orders. However, the plan may also be intended to get more information about prospects, or to gain permission to make formal sales presentations.

CALL REPORT   A salesperson's status report detailing his or her efforts to generate sales by contacting prospects. Call reports are often required by sales management, who review the frequency with which salespeople make visits to prospects and their success in doing so. Call reports are often used as part of a sales force evaluation program by management. See also **activity quota.**

CALL TO ACTION   The part of an advertising message that tells the consumer what to do—that is, what action the advertiser wants the consumer to take after the latter receives the message. The call to action is typically stated at the end of the communication after the product's attributes and benefits have been discussed. For example, an ad's call to action may be to buy the advertised product, call an 800-telephone number, return a coupon, or write to a congressman.

CAMERA-READY   An artistic layout, comprised of copy and/or illustrations, that is ready to be printed or reproduced through other means. Camera-ready refers to the photographic creation of a printing plate.

CAMPAIGN   A series of promotional messages featuring a common theme and scheduled to run during a designated period of time. Campaigns may be individual advertising, public-relations, sales promotions, or direct-marketing programs; or they may be initiatives that combine more than one of these tactics. See also **advertising campaign.**

CANNIBALIZATION   The adverse effects of introducing a new brand into a product category where the company already has one. The new brand competes with, and, ultimately, takes market share away from the original brand. For example, the Miller Brewing Co.'s introduction of Miller Lite beer proved so successful that it drew significant market share away from the parent brand, Miller High Life. Cannibalization is an inherent danger in **brand extension** activities. Thus, its effects should always be factored into forecasting the profitability of existing brands in the product line to be extended.

CAPTION   A word, phrase, or sentence that describes the visual element of a print advertisement. Captions are used for photographs, illustrations, or diagrams. Captions may appear above or below the visual. Also known as *cutlines,* when captions describe photographs in newspapers or magazines.

CAPTIVE MARKET   A market in which buyers have no alternative product choices other than those offered in the host environment. Examples of captive markets are the clientele in hotels, airports, and railroad stations. People may buy only those products available through vendors in the particular location. Product prices in a captive market environment are usually high due to the absence of competition.

CAR CARD   The advertising posters displayed in transportation vehicles such as buses, trains, and subway cars. Two types of car cards exist. *Overhead* cards are situated above windows in the vehicles; these displays measure approximately 11" by 28". *Bulkhead* cards are larger posters measuring 21" by 33" and are usually located alongside vehicle doors. Car cards are sold as media buys in terms of full-, half-, or quarter-showings. Showings refer to the percentage of vehicles in the transit fleet that will carry the car cards. See also **transit advertising.**

CARD DECK   A direct-mail package comprised of postage-paid reply cards that promote a group of products. Card decks are typically developed by multiple advertisers who sell products targeted at a common market. The products are usually related (e.g., cards promoting an array of computer accessories, books, and supplies). Card decks are produced so as to reduce the advertisers' individual mailing costs. *Note:* Card decks may also be developed by a single advertiser. For example, a business book publisher might develop a card deck promoting its new titles.

CASH AND CARRY WHOLESALER   A type of **limited-service wholesaler** selling products to retailers, who pay for and pick up the product at the wholesaler's location. For example, a retailer drives to a cash and carry wholesaler to buy a set quantity of product, paying cash for the merchandise and taking possession of the goods. Cash and carry wholesalers typically deal in fast-moving (e.g., perishable) products, such as baked goods. See also **truck jobber.**

CASH COW   The product or **strategic business unit** within a company's business portfolio that generates significantly more revenue than the costs involved in maintaining its market share—costs, for example, relating to production and marketing. Cash cows produce enough profits to financially support the company's other portfolio units. Thus, cash cows can be "milked." See also **growth-share matrix.**

CASH DISCOUNT   A discounted price granted to a buyer who makes payment promptly to a seller, or in advance of the delivery of merchandise. In general, sellers offer cash discounts to lessen the time the seller must wait for the buyer's payment. For example, consumers may be offered a 5% discount if they pay their fuel bill before the payment deadline (e.g., the end of the month). The cash discount offered to buyers is usually indicated on the invoice. The designation "5/10, net/30" means that customers receive a 5% discount if they pay within 10 days, or they must pay the full amount within 30 days.

CASH REFUND OFFER   A consumer promotion tool in which a manufacturer offers the buyer a **rebate.** The purchaser returns a proof-of-purchase seal (e.g., a box top or label) to the manufacturer, who sends back the refund amount. Cash refund offers are similar to **coupons.** However, with a cash refund the price reduction occurs *after* the purchase. With a coupon the price reduction occurs at the point of sale. Cash refunds are used for low-cost packaged goods as well as for expensive items such as cars or refrigerators.

CASTING   The process of selecting actors to be used in a radio or television commercial. Advertising is designed to reach specific people and personality types. Thus, casting is critically important in that the target buyers must identify with the actors chosen. The companies that provide actors and actresses for use in commercials and theatrical productions are called *casting agencies.*

CATALOG   A book listing a company's merchandise offering. Catalogs usually include product illustrations, descriptions, and prices. Catalogs are used to sell such items as industrial/office supplies, computer accessories, and gardening supplies. They typically include an order form for customer purchasing. However, most now feature a toll-free number to facilitate ordering. Catalogs are frequently used as direct-mail pieces. These consumer-oriented publications are expensively produced with copy written in a strong promotional tone. They may also be used as sales tools. That is, salespeople carry them on sales visits to show prospects the range of products offered. (Sales catalogs are generally less promotional than their consumer-oriented counterparts.) A catalog's life span is determined by the products it promotes. For example, a catalog produced to highlight a company's Christmas merchandise would have a very short life span of two to three months. Conversely, a catalog describing a company's line of stationery products would have a much longer life span, perhaps as long as two or three years.

CATHODE RAY TUBE (CRT)   A computer terminal with an attached keyboard that enables data input and retrieval. CRT displays are frequently used by companies to input order entries, customer service information, or data used in analyzing consumer purchase patterns. They're also used as market research tools. For example, survey respondents can sit at a CRT that displays the research questions. Respondents type their answers directly into the unit. Researchers may also use CRTs when conducting telephone interviews. The researchers type respondents' answers into the CRT. The benefits of using CRTs for research is that the units eliminate coding and editing, reduce errors, and save time.

CAUSAL RESEARCH   Research designed to identify cause-and-effect relationships between variables. Marketing analysts, for example, would use causal research to illustrate how altering the price of a product affects its market demand. The analysis might show that a price hike will directly lessen demand (a negative influence), but will indirectly raise consumers' perceptions of product quality (a positive influence). The value of causal research is that it illustrates the interrelationship of variables in a given marketing situation.

CAUSE-RELATED MARKETING A promotional campaign devoted to raising awareness of or generating funds for an event or social cause. Companies participate in cause-related marketing to foster goodwill toward their organizations or products/services. That is, corporate sponsorship of such programs generates exposure for the companies in a credible, less-commercial format than selling-oriented marketing communications. Marketing tactics typically employed by the organizations involved in cause-related marketing include new product packaging featuring a campaign logo and graphics, point-of-purchase displays, and advertising and publicity pledging corporate donations based on a percentage of product sales.

One of the first cause-related marketing campaigns involved the Summer Olympic Games in Los Angeles in 1984. Sponsor proceeds financed the U.S. teams' training, uniforms, and other expenditures relating to the athletes' participation. Funds raised through promotions associated with the Statue of Liberty Centennial Celebration (1986) went primarily toward restoring the statue. For example, American Express raised $1.7 million for the statue's refurbishing by donating one cent from every Amex credit card purchase over a specified period of time.

Large cause-related marketing campaigns often involve a central committee formed to solicit corporate sponsors. Its responsibilities also include overseeing promotional activities and coordinating licensing of products that feature the campaign logo. Corporate sponsors' marketing programs usually must be approved by the committee to avoid duplicative marketing efforts by different sponsors and to maintain creative standards.

CEASE-AND-DESIST ORDER A legal directive by an administrative agency or court that enjoins a company from engaging in a deceptive or unfair business practice. For example, a cease-and-desist order might prevent a company from advertising a product in a particular way. Such was the case when a manufacturer promoted its trash bags as being biodegradable and environmentally safe, when the product actually was not. A cease-and-desist order was issued to stop the company from making the false advertising claim. Cease-and-desist orders are issued when an empowered agency feels a company has violated legislative acts governing commerce, competition, and free trade. See also **Federal Trade Commission.**

CELEBRITY ENDORSEMENT The use of a celebrity to recommend a product. That is, the celebrity discusses and then endorses the item. Celebrities are selected based on how well the target buyer will identify with them (e.g., an over-65 film star endorses life insurance for older persons); or they are chosen because their occupation relates to the advertised product (for example, a TV fitness show personality endorses a new exercise machine).

CENSUS DATA   Demographic information about the American population gathered by the *U.S. Bureau of the Census*. Census data are available in several different formats. The *Bureau of the Census Catalog*, for example, is produced quarterly and contains cumulative-to-annual data, with monthly updates. Part I of the catalog lists all publications available from the Census Bureau. Part II lists available data files, special tabulations, and other unpublished materials. Most census data are available at no cost. However, for a fee the bureau can tailor data for a company's specific research initiative, or put data in magnetic tape format.

CENSUS TRACT   The *U.S. Bureau of the Census* term used to subdivide a densely populated city. Census tracts have identifiable boundaries. In general, they designate areas where residents have common social, economic, and other demographic characteristics. Census tracts are one kind of unit used in **area sampling** studies.

CENTERS OF INFLUENCE   People of high social or business standing through whom a salesperson attempts to find qualified buyers. Centers of influence are people who exert power or authority over others, for example, bankers, lawyers, politicians. Identifying centers of influence is a salesperson's **prospecting** technique.

CENTER SPREAD   An advertising layout comprising the two facing pages found in the center of a magazine or newspaper. Advertisers purchase a center spread to run one two-page ad or two separate full-page ads. Advertisers may be required to pay a premium for this **preferred position** in the publication. Also known as *double-page spread*.

CENTRAL BUSINESS DISTRICT (CBD)   The area of a city or town that is populated by the highest concentration of businesses and support services. CBDs typically have high pedestrian and vehicular traffic flows. Consequently, they contain numerous retailers, office buildings, theaters, hotels, and service businesses. Rarely are CBDs defined by measurable boundaries. Nonetheless, they usually are recognized by area residents as encompassing general geographic parameters.

CENTRALIZED SALES ORGANIZATION An organization in which responsibility for the overall sales function is concentrated at the highest levels of management. In a centralized sales organization, the sales force reports to senior management, whereas in a **decentralized sales organization** sales force responsibility and authority are concentrated at the organization's lower levels. Centralized sales organizations are typically found in smaller companies. As a company grows, it will usually move to a decentralized sales hierarchy.

CENTRAL MARKET Location where a large number of the major suppliers or manufacturers of a given product or service may be found. A central market may be a particular facility (a merchandise mart) or it can refer to the location within a city where the large group of product providers are situated (e.g., the garment district in New York).

CENTS-OFF COUPON See **coupon.**

CHAIN RATIO METHOD The research method in which different pieces of secondary research data are combined to estimate **total market potential.** In essence, various research data are linked to form a "chain" of information. For instance, quantifying the market potential for a product might involve combining information on the population in a given geographic locale with per capita expenditures of similar products in that area. Multiplying these two variables results in total annual expenditures for the product in this market. For example, a woman sells a line of cosmetics. Research indicates that there are 100,000 women in her geographic market, and the per capita expenditure for cosmetics among women in this area is $50. That is:

$$100,000 \times \$50 = \$500,000$$

The total market potential of the product is $500,000.

CHAIN STORE A retail outlet that is part of a group of similar stores, all of which are owned and managed by the same company. Chain stores generally carry the same merchandise and often engage in the same special promotions and product offers. The term can refer to one retail outlet within the organization, or to the collective of outlets comprising the organization.

CHANNEL BEHAVIOR   The activities of the people and companies that comprise a manufacturer's channels of distribution. Channel behavior is usually discussed in terms of *cooperation* and *conflict*. Channel cooperation means channel members work together to complement each others' needs and objectives. That is, the members' efforts collectively produce more profits than they could generate individually (which is the ideal scenario for a channel network). Channel conflict refers to when one or more channel members are trying to maximize their own self-interests at the expense of the distribution network's overall efficiency. For example, channel conflict can arise when a franchise (e.g., a fast-food restaurant) maintains poor service that detracts from the franchise's overall reputation.

CHANNELS OF DISTRIBUTION   The interrelated network of people and companies used to deliver merchandise from the manufacturer to consumers. Distribution channels involve a group of agencies or institutions that serve as intermediaries. These agents include *merchant middlemen*, who take title to merchandise and then resell it (e.g., wholesalers and retailers); and *agent middlemen*, who do not take title to goods but who serve as **brokers** (e.g., manufacturer's representatives, sales agents). Channels of distribution vary by level, meaning the *number* of intermediaries involved. For example, a two-level distribution channel would be the sale of produce from a farmer directly to consumers. A four-level distribution channel would consist of a clothing manufacturer selling its product to wholesalers, who sell it to retailers, who then sell it to consumers. Multilevel distribution channels are employed when consumers are numerous and widely diffused.

CHECKING COPY   The copy of a magazine sent by a publisher to an advertiser (or its agency) to allow the latter to review the layout and position of its advertisement in the magazine. The checking copy is normally sent to the advertiser before payment for the insertion is made.

CHESHIRE LABELS   Mailing labels printed on pages of computer printouts that indicate the names and addresses comprising a mailing list. Cheshire labels must be cut by machine and then affixed to envelopes or packages with glue. Thus, they involve more production time than other label formats, which is the reason for their low cost: They are nearly half the cost of **pressure-sensitive labels,** which are precut and provide a gummed adhesive back to facilitate production.

CHI-SQUARE TEST A statistical test used to determine the existence of association between two or more variables, and to see whether or not significant differences exist between them. Chi-square tests are used to determine whether a *test value* is markedly different from a *control value*. For example, a direct-mail package can be tested by modifying the copy and graphics in some pieces in the mailing. A chi-square test would gauge the percentage of return yielded by the standard package (test value), to see if the response rate is significantly higher or lower for the modified package (control value).

CINEMA ADVERTISING Commercials that are screened in movie theaters prior to the featured film(s). Cinema advertising uses commercials that have appeared on television or ones specially created for viewing in theaters (which are typically longer than TV spots). *Note:* As an advertising medium, cinema commercials suffered a setback when some movie studios prohibited on-screen advertising. Advertisers turned to such promotional activities as in-theater product sampling to counter the studios' ban. See also **product placement; video commercial.**

CIRCULAR A form of print advertising used to promote sales or special promotions. Circulars are one-page sheets featuring large illustrations and bold headlines. Circulars are delivered to consumers through the mail or distributed as handouts in retail outlets. They are also employed as shopping bag inserts and as pieces in direct-mail packages. Also known as *flier*.

CIRCULATION Numerical figure referring to how many periodical copies are distributed to readers. Advertising rates for publications are based primarily on circulation figures. There are three main categories of circulation: **Paid circulation** is the percentage of publications actually purchased. Paid circulation is calculated on an issue-by-issue basis or on a six-month average. **Controlled circulation** is the number of readers who receive a publication free of charge (e.g., select members of a given profession or industry). **Pass-along circulation** refers to the number of people who receive a publication by means other than purchase (e.g., publications read in a library or doctor's office, or those given to readers by friends). A publication's total circulation is the combined number of paid and nonpaid subscribers and its pass-along readership. Outdoor advertising, such as billboards and transit advertising, counts circulation figures as the number of people with a reasonable chance of seeing the communication. *Note: Bulk circulation* is a method of circulation in which bundles of a free publication are delivered to specific locations (e.g., a college newspaper distributed in bundles and left at various campus locations).

CLARIFYING   An interviewer's attempt to obtain clearer information from survey respondents' answers to **open-ended questions.** Clarifying involves getting respondents to explain vague or general terms cited in their answers. Researchers will ask clarifying questions such as, "Can you give me an example of what you mean?" or "Can you tell me why you think the product is overpriced?" See also **validation.**

CLASSICAL CONDITIONING   A theory of human learning. Classical conditioning holds that when an external stimulus is repeatedly paired with an unconditioned stimulus, a response is eventually elicited that is similar to the response originally evoked by the unconditioned stimulus. The famous experiment with Pavlov's dogs illustrates classical conditioning. In this study, the researcher linked the sound of a bell with the dogs' expectation of food. Each time the bells rang, the dogs were fed. Thus, through conditioning, whenever the dogs heard the bell (the external stimulus) they automatically began salivating because they expected food (the unconditioned stimulus). In marketing, classical conditioning theory relates to the **stimulus-response theory** of learning, which marketers use to develop routine purchase behavior on the part of consumers. That is, it is used in creating a link between a product and a desired end result.

CLASSIFIED ADVERTISING   Newspaper or magazine advertising that is organized by category (e.g., employment ads, real estate offerings, automotive ads, business opportunities). Classified advertising usually appears in a specific section in the given publication. The advertising layout features copy set in small type with no illustrations. Rates for classified advertising are calculated according to the size of the ad, as determined either by the word count or by the number of lines.

CLAYMATION   An animation technique employing clay figures and objects. Claymation has become a popular technique for television commercials. One well-known ad featuring claymation, created to promote California raisins, showed raisins as pop stars dancing and singing the song "I Heard It Through the Grapevine."

CLAYTON ANTITRUST ACT   Federal legislation enacted in 1914 that prohibits certain types of price discrimination and other practices that "substantially lessen competition or tend to create a monopoly in any line of commerce." The act is a supplement to the Sherman Antitrust Act of 1890. See also **antitrust laws.**

CLIENT   A person or organization who retains the services of an advertising, public relations, or other marketing services agency. A client may be a product manufacturer, service provider, institution, or politician. Also known as *account.*

CLIO AWARD   An international award for creative excellence in broadcast advertising, presented annually at the American Television and Radio Commercials Festival. The gold statuettes are given for outstanding commercials, which are entered in product or campaign categories. The commercials are judged by a panel of advertising creative executives and technical specialists from 10 countries.

CLIPPING SERVICE   A company that monitors the mass media for clients wishing to track the amount and kinds of news coverage they receive. Clipping services are typically retained by public relations firms and corporate PR departments to accumulate editorial clippings. This is done to quantify publicity activities to assess PR program results (usually by a count of the number of clips or column inches), as well as to track public opinion on various issues. Advertising managers also use clipping services to verify the timing and placement of ad insertions, or to survey competitors' advertising. Clients can specify which news outlets the service should monitor based on media (print or broadcast), media category (business, entertainment, sports), frequency (daily, weekly, monthly publications), audience size, and geography. Clients pay a basic monthly fee, but also are charged for the number of news clips in each package (usually $1 per clip). Broadcast news coverage is provided to clients in videocassette or transcript form. Cassettes cost approximately $100 for three minutes of tape. See also **Advertising Checking Bureau.**

CLOSED-CAPTION TELEVISION   Television programs that feature captions for the benefit of hearing-impaired viewers. Such viewers must use a special TV reception box to receive the telecasts. Programs that are closed-captioned are usually indicated as such in the **billboard** announcement appearing at the beginning of the program.

CLOSED-CIRCUIT TELEVISION   A television broadcast, transmitted via cable, that is seen by a specific audience. Closed-circuit broadcasts are shown on monitors in specific locations. For example, a supermarket will feature a closed-circuit TV system to air commercials promoting products on sale in the store. See also **video systems.**

CLOSED-ENDED QUESTION   A survey question that asks the respondent to choose from a list of answers provided by the researcher. There are two benefits to using closed-ended questions in personal interviews and on questionnaires. First, they provide high uniformity of answers (in contrast to **open-ended questions,** which ask respondents to answer in their own words). Second, they are easily processed and analyzed in the tabulation stage of the research.

CLOSING   The final part of a sales presentation in which the salesperson asks the prospect for the order. Closing techniques are used after the salesperson has established rapport with the prospect, explained the product's features and benefits, and successfully handled the prospect's **objections.** The salesperson attempts to identify **buying signals** made by the prospect before using the closing technique appropriate to the specific selling situation.

CLOSING DATE   The date and time when advertising materials must be delivered to a publisher or broadcast station for the advertising to appear in the medium at the desired time. Publishers' closing dates require that all copy, plates or prints, layout instructions, and mechanical art be in hand for the ad to run in the selected issue. Broadcast closing dates require that all broadcast materials be delivered for the spot to air at the scheduled time (allowing station or network management time to review and approve the materials). Publications' closing dates are indicated on the media's *rate cards.*

CLUSTER ANALYSIS A statistical procedure in which people or objects under study are grouped according to common characteristics. The units of study are combined into clusters to allow researchers to identify similarities or differences between them. For example, researchers for a car maker might group makes of competitors' cars into clusters on the basis of their prices or available option packages. Comparisons would then be made for the purpose of developing **marketing mix** strategies to sell the company's own models.

CLUSTER SAMPLE A probability sample in which a population under study is divided into mutually exclusive and exhaustive subgroups (clusters) and a random sample of the groups is drawn. Thus, *groups* of respondents are studied as units. For example, a door-to-door survey project might involve interviewing a cluster of households in a neighborhood of the geographic area being studied. Cluster sampling is undertaken in one or two stages. In one-stage cluster sampling, all of the population elements in the selected subgroup are sampled. Two-stage cluster sampling involves selecting a sample of elements from the subgroups.

CLUTTER 1. The overabundance of advertising and informational messages appearing in a given medium, which compete for readers', listeners', or viewers' attention. 2. A generic reference to the proliferation of marketing messages, which collectively diminish the impact of promotional communications. For example, sales promotion clutter describes the overwhelming amount of special offers and promotions available to consumers and retailers. See also **alternative media.**

COAXIAL CABLE Heavy-duty electrical wire through which cable TV transmissions are sent to subscribers' homes. Coaxial cable is also used to carry telephone transmissions. With the advent of *fiber-optic* cable technology, however, use of coaxial cable is becoming less commonplace (particularly for telecommunications purposes).

COD Abbreviation for "collect on delivery" or "cash on delivery"; the buyer pays for the merchandise when it's delivered. (The buyer may also assume costs for postage and handling.) Sellers offer a COD payment option to give buyers the advantage of a credit order. COD also serves as protection for the seller because the order must be paid for before the merchandise is left with the buyer.

CODE NUMBER   A designation used to identify the source from which sales and marketing materials emanate. For example, code numbers are used on cents-off coupons to identify where consumers obtained them (e.g., magazine, **freestanding insert,** product package). Code numbers are often used in direct-response advertisements with coupons. The advertiser assigns a different code number for each magazine in which the ad will appear and indicates the code on the coupon. The advertiser ultimately groups the coupons received by code number to determine which publications generated the highest responses.

CODING   The process of assigning numbers to survey responses for the purpose of data processing. Data are assigned to numeric classes into which the responses are placed. The purpose of coding is to reduce all the different responses to a question (e.g., an **open-ended question**) to a few types of answers, which may then be easily tabulated and analyzed. See also **data entry.**

COGNITIVE DISSONANCE   The feeling that occurs when a consumer's beliefs and actions are inconsistent with each other. It is a psychological condition, the theory behind which states that humans will alter their beliefs to justify their behavior. Cognitive dissonance is common in consumers after they have purchased an expensive product. For example, a consumer purchases a car and then starts seeing alluring ads for a competing model. Dissonance occurs when the consumer begins to think that he or she made the wrong purchase decision. In striving for cognitive consistency the consumer will typically search for more information about the new car to psychologically justify the purchase decision. See also **dissonance reduction.**

COGNITIVE LEARNING   The theory of learning that refers to a consumer's transformation of environmental stimuli into meanings used to form judgments about objects and behavior. Cognitive learning, in short, refers to the internal workings of the consumer's mind—processing information from the external environment for use in problem solving and decision making. Advertisers study cognitive learning to understand consumer purchasing patterns. The theory suggests the importance of developing marketing communications that influence consumers' perceptions and thoughts. See also **stimulus-response theory.**

COLD CALL An unsolicited or unscheduled visit or telephone call by a salesperson to a potential customer. A cold call may be an attempt to secure a meeting or to gain an opportunity to give a product demonstration. Salespeople engage in cold calling as a means of **prospecting,** which is the process of finding qualified buyers for a product. Cold calling is often done when the salesperson has available time. That is, it is generally a supplemental prospecting activity.

COLLATERAL MATERIALS The various materials and literature used in marketing and promotional activities. Collateral materials include sales kits, brochures, catalogs, newsletters, technical specifications sheets, charts, graphs, and illustrations. Collateral materials are usually developed to support advertising campaigns; or they are used as standard sales or informational materials about a company and its products, or special events and promotions it is sponsoring.

COLOR SEPARATIONS The process of creating color plates for four-color printing. Plates for each of the three primary colors (red, yellow, blue) are produced through a special photographic method. The full-color original to be reproduced, which may either be a photograph or illustration, is separated into the three color plates. A fourth plate is produced for black, to reproduce the illustration's shadows and contrasts.

COLUMN INCH The unit by which print advertising space is sold, its dimension being 1″ by 1″. Newspaper and magazine pages are divided vertically into columns of varying widths. Thus, if a column is 3″ wide and an advertisement is 4″ long, the total column inches to be purchased is 12 (3″ by 4″). Advertising rates are determined by the number of column inches the ad will occupy, so if a publication's rate is $50 per column inch, the 12–column-inch ad would cost $600 (12 × $50). See also **standard advertising unit.**

COMBINATION COMPENSATION PLAN The method of paying a salesperson's salary when the seller's base salary and commission are based on sales volume, profitability, or qualitative factors (such as customer service). The benefit of combination compensation to a salesperson is that it gives him or her the security of a fixed-base income, with the opportunity to gain incentives for outstanding performance. See also **straight commission/salary.**

COMBINATION RATE   A discount on advertising granted by a publisher to an advertiser who purchases space in more than one publication owned by the publisher. For a combination rate to be offered, the advertiser must generally purchase the ads at the same time. Moreover, the insertions must all be for the same-size ad. Combination rate discounts are also granted by broadcasters to advertisers buying air time on radio or TV stations owned by the same broadcaster.

COMMERCIAL   An advertisement for broadcast on a television or radio station. Advertising rates for commercials are calculated in terms of time as opposed to space in print advertising sales. Commercials are either filmed or taped, and duplicate copies are distributed to the stations that will air them.

COMMERCIALIZATION   The final stage of a new product introduction when the item is actually entered into the marketplace. Companies must address several issues when getting ready to commercialize a product: They must decide on *timing* (when the product should be introduced); *geography* (in what markets the product will be available); the *market* (at which target markets or consumer groups will marketing activities be directed); and *marketing strategy* (determining the marketing budget and specific promotional strategies to be employed). *Note:* Some marketing theorists refer to commercialization as the point at which a company first decides to market a product.

COMMERCIAL PROTECTION   Contractual agreement between an advertiser and a broadcaster stating that the latter will not air a commercial for a competitor directly after the advertiser's spot. Commercial protection is a time interval lasting approximately 10 minutes. Thus, the broadcaster is precluded from airing a competitor's product announcement for at least 10 minutes before and after the advertiser's commercial. See also **competitive separation.**

COMMERCIAL TIME   The amount of time on broadcast stations that can be sold to advertisers. Television and radio stations may sell only a set amount of commercial time per hour of programming, as determined by the National Association of Broadcasters. For example, a television network may sell a total of 9½ minutes of commercial time during 1 hour of **prime time** programming: 6 minutes of network commercials, 1 minute and 10 seconds of station commercials, and 2 minutes and 20 seconds of promos or *public service announcements* (PSAs). During non–prime-time hours, networks may sell 16 minutes of commercial time per hour: 12 minutes of network commercials, 2 minutes and 20 seconds of station commercials, and 1 minute and 40 seconds of promos and PSAs. Advertisers purchase commercial time in a variety of unit sizes. For example, 60 seconds of commercial time can be purchased as a 1-minute spot, as two 30-second spots, or as four 15-second spots. See also **dayparts.**

COMMISSION   Compensation paid to a salesperson based on the salesperson's level of performance or activities. Commission is usually based on a fixed formula (e.g., 5% of net sales, 10% of gross profits, $2 for each pound sold). Commission, however, is sometimes based on qualitative factors such as customer service or the accumulation of valuable market intelligence. Salespeople typically must achieve a prescribed level of performance before receiving a commission. For instance, the salesperson might be required to sell at least $5,000 worth of goods before he or she can begin receiving a commission. Salespeople may receive salaries based on *straight commission,* which is compensation determined solely by commission income; or they may benefit from a **combination compensation plan,** which provides a fixed-base salary in addition to a commission or incentives. *Note:* Advertising agencies receive commissions for purchasing media space or time on behalf of clients. See also **agency commission.**

COMMUNICATION CHANNELS   The avenues through which messages are sent. In marketing, these refer to the means by which promotional communications are disseminated to the target market. Communications channels may either be *personal* or *nonpersonal.* Personal channels involve two or more people communicating directly with each other. Examples are face-to-face selling, telemarketing, public speaking, or communicating through personalized mailings. Nonpersonal communications channels involve message dissemination without personal contact or interaction between the message sender and receiver. These channels include media advertising, publicity and other forms of mass communication, and special events (e.g., a store opening). Nonpersonal channels, however, can be used to stimulate personal communications. For instance, nonpersonal communications might be designed to reach **opinion leaders,** on whom advertisers rely to influence other potential buyers through personal communications channels. See also **two-step flow of communication.**

COMMUNITY RELATIONS   The practice of maintaining a favorable relationship between one's company and the community in which it operates. A variety of techniques are used in community relations: distributing newsletters to community leaders and government officials to publicize the company's public service–oriented activities; scheduling speaking appearances by corporate executives at public forums and community events; and sponsoring special programs tied to community development and social-welfare initiatives. Companies may have formal community relations departments, or the organizations' public relations or public affairs group may be responsible for the function.

COMP   1. An abbreviation for "comprehensive layout," which shows how a print advertisement or brochure design will appear in its final form. A comp shows the material with all its copy and illustrations in place. It may appear in the exact dimensions of the final printed piece or may be enlarged. Comps are shown to clients to obtain approval of the materials before the start of final art production. **2.** An abbreviation for complimentary, free of charge. See also **comp list.**

COMPARATIVE ADVERTISING   Advertising designed to build demand for a brand by establishing its superiority over others in the same product category. It involves making direct references to competitors' products (e.g., when Coca-Cola compares itself to Pepsi, or Burger King to McDonald's). There are several keys to effective comparative advertising. First, it is important to compare the brand to others only when the brand has a distinct **competitive advantage.** Next, the competitor's product must be identified but not disparaged. The competitor must not be given too much exposure in the advertising. Communications must be directed and tailored to consumers who currently use or prefer a competitor's brand (as opposed to targeting regular users of the product).

COMPARISON METHOD   A salesperson's technique of responding to a prospect's **objection.** It is an attempt to minimize the objection by comparing the sales offer with something that is acceptable to the prospect. For example, a salesperson may say, "I know this make of window is more expensive than my competitor's. But, the energy savings you'll realize by using our windows will save you money and make our product less expensive in the long run."

COMPARISON SHOPPING   1. A consumer's practice of making a purchase decision based on a review of competing products' attributes, prices, level of quality, or customer-service factors. **2.** An industrial purchasing executive's assessment of competitors' marketing activities such as new items being offered, competitors' pricing strategies, promotional initiatives.

COMPETITION   1. The rivalry among product/service providers attempting to increase their sales, profits, or market share. **2.** All the ways in which a buyer can satisfy *wants* other than by purchasing a particular company's product. In this sense, competition denotes the availability of alternatives to consumers. There are three kinds of competition, as follows: (1) *Brand competition* (also known as *direct competition*) refers to competition by manufacturers offering a similar product; (2) *generic competition* (also known as *indirect competition*) exists when products in totally different categories perform the same function (e.g., an airline competes with other modes of transportation, such as buses and trains); (3) *form competition* relates to products that perform the same function but are designed differently (e.g., a more advanced computer whose functions include those of the less sophisticated computer).

COMPETITIVE ADVANTAGE   ** A defining characteristic or situation that enables a company to differentiate itself from and outperform its competitors. A company's competitive advantage may be its ability to provide superior or unique performance, or to offer prices lower than competitors' prices. For example, Japanese car makers had the competitive advantage of offering high-quality cars at affordable prices. Low labor costs and a high Japanese work ethic made this possible. Another example is a company may offer low prices because it buys its raw materials at a significantly lower cost than its competitors. See also **unique selling proposition.

COMPETITIVE ANALYSIS   ** The process of assessing a company's or a product's performance in relation to its direct competitors. Competitive analyses can be made in terms of product sales, profits, price, quality, delivery, or customer service. Marketing strategy involves analyzing the company's *competitive environment*. This evaluation determines the number of actual competitors, the degree of similarity or difference between their products and the company in question, and various **supply and demand patterns.

COMPETITIVE BID   The process through which government contracts are granted to suppliers that have submitted proposals for providing a product or service. The contract typically goes to the lowest bidder. There are two kinds of competitive bids: *Open bids* are available to any supplier willing to apply; in *closed bids* the government purchasing office invites proposals only from an approved list of suppliers. Bids are prepared according to strict product specifications and terms and conditions of delivery.

COMPETITIVE INTELLIGENCE   Information generated about competitors' businesses and marketing activities for use in developing strategies. Competitive intelligence is accumulated externally through reviewing trade publications or by purchasing data from secondary research sources; or it is gathered internally (e.g., by collecting market information from company executives). Companies collect competitive intelligence for use in making **marketing mix** decisions.

COMPETITIVE-PARITY BUDGETING   The practice of basing the advertising budget on what competitors are spending for advertising. There are two drawbacks to this method. First, it is presumed that competitors' advertising programs are effective and their spending levels are correct. (It is possible to make the same mistakes the other company makes.) Second, competitor ad spending may only be determined after the money has been disbursed. Management, therefore, is basing its budgeting on other advertisers' past decisions.

COMPETITIVE POSITION   The market standing of a company or product in relation to its competitors. There are three basic ways to measure competitive position. The first is by gauging the company's *market position*, which is done by measuring the percent of market share held by competing companies, or by ranking other factors such as quality and service. Another way is by determining the company's *economic* or *technological position*, including such elements as financial resources or patented technologies that the company might hold.

Competitive position based on *capabilities* measures variables such as strengths in management, marketing, or distribution.

COMPETITIVE SEPARATION   The space (in a print medium) or time (on a broadcast station) that separates one advertiser's ad or commercial from a competitor's. Competitive separation is usually made at the request of the advertiser, and it is formally indicated in the contract between the advertiser and the medium. In broadcasting, competitive separation is known as **commercial protection,** which generally stipulates that the broadcaster will not air an advertisement by a company's competitor within 10 minutes of the advertiser's spot.

COMPETITIVE STRATEGY   Marketing strategy in which promotional communications cite competing brands and emphasize a product's superiority over them. Competitive marketing strategy may involve **comparative advertising** or other marketing communications that discredit competing products or may reveal features in one product not found in others.

COMPETITOR ORIENTATION   A corporate planning approach in which a company's moves are dictated by its competitors' activities. A company that adopts a competitor orientation tracks competitors' moves and their levels of market share on a market-by-market basis. Examples of competitor-oriented decisions are a competitor lowers its product price and the company does also; or a competitor improves its distribution in a given market, and the company increases its advertising and promotion there. Maintaining a competitor orientation has two drawbacks. The company may become overly reactive and lose its customer focus by concentrating solely on competitors' actions. Moreover, it makes objective setting difficult because the company does not know in which direction it is heading. That is, its direction is determined by its competitors' moves. See also **customer orientation.**

COMPILED LIST   A mailing list that contains names and addresses that have been culled from publicly available sources: directories, telephone books, rosters of trade or professional groups, public records. A compiled list generally yields a lower response than a **house list** because the latter type consists of people who have already purchased products from a direct-mail seller. Since such people are proven buyers, house lists are significantly more expensive than compiled lists.

COMPLAINT MANAGEMENT The practice of ensuring good customer service by soliciting and acting upon customer complaints. These procedures constitute a *complaint management system.* Companies devise such systems to record, analyze, and respond to written and oral complaints. For example, a company may make every salesperson write a report on each customer who has voiced a complaint. The report would explain the nature of the complaint and the steps taken to restore customer satisfaction. Companies solicit customer complaints to learn how to improve service, as well as to devise innovative approaches to solving customer problems. See also **customer relations.**

COMPLEX SALES FORCE The organizational structure that combines the three basic sales force types: *product-structured, territory-structured,* and *market-structured* sales forces. Large companies that sell a wide variety of products to many different customers in a wide geographic area typically employ a complex sales force structure.

COMP LIST The list of organizations or people who receive free subscriptions to a given magazine or newspaper ("comp" being short for complimentary). People on a comp list are usually influential executives or businesspeople who are important to the continued existence of the publication (e.g., advertisers, sales representatives, key suppliers). See also **controlled circulation.**

COMPOSITION The arrangement on a page of the visual elements of a print advertisement: copy, headline, illustrations. A *composition order* refers to a customer's instructions to a printer for typesetting a print communication. See also **layout.**

COMPUTER GRAPHICS Artwork created by using special computer software and hardware. Computer graphics (i.e., charts, graphs, illustrations) are used in producing print and electronic communications such as videotapes and slide shows. *Note:* The benefit of computer graphics equipment is the ability to make design changes directly on the computer screen and, thus, experiment with different design approaches. See also **desktop publishing.**

COMPUTER-INTEGRATED MANUFACTURING (CIM)   A computer-based management system whose focus is the functional sharing of information between groups in a manufacturing environment. CIM involves automating the flow of information. Data are shared among all departments that directly or indirectly relate to the manufacturing function: engineering, research and development, accounting, shipping and receiving. The goal of CIM is to improve lead times and enhance market responsiveness. Effecting consistent product quality is another aim of CIM technology.

COMPUTER LETTER   A computer-generated correspondence that appears as if it were created specifically for the recipient. Computer letters, in short, are personalized correspondence. They are nearly always included in direct-mail packages. Computer letters are also used in *mail merges,* which are large-scale mailings of business letters whose content is standard except for the recipients' names and addresses.

CONCENTRATED MARKETING   A company's strategic decision to channel its marketing resources at one or just a few market segments. For example, Volkswagen concentrated its marketing at small-car buyers. A company decides to engage in concentrated marketing when it sees ample profit potential in a market segment. Other reasons may be limited resources, or competitors' dominant marketing strength in other segments. The benefit of a concentrated marketing strategy is the ability to achieve a strong market position and build a special reputation. Its drawback is the potential for market segment failure (e.g., people stop buying small cars in favor of larger ones). See also **niche marketing.**

CONCENTRATION RATIO   An indicator of the competitive climate of a given industry. Concentration ratio is based on a number of statistical measurements maintained by the U.S. government (e.g., the percentage of the total industry's sales held by the three or four largest companies operating in that industry). Companies review the concentration ratio to determine the level of competition and the intensity of rivalry in an industry at a given point in time.

CONCENTRIC DIVERSIFICATION   A corporate growth strategy involving the acquisition of businesses that provide new product lines that are similar to the existing product line from a technological and/or marketing standpoint. For example, the manufacturer of kitchen blenders might acquire a company that produces food processors. A result of concentric diversification may be that the new product line appeals to an entirely different set of consumers than the company's current product line. See also **conglomerate diversification; horizontal diversification.**

CONCEPT TESTING   Testing to evaluate a proposed new product or advertisement by soliciting feedback from target consumers prior to full development of the product or ad. Respondents may be asked about an ad: "Are the benefits clear and believable?" "Does the product solve a problem or meet a need?" "Is the price reasonable?" "Would you buy the product?" Responses to these questions are evaluated. The information is then used to enhance the concept's value and effectiveness prior to introducing it in the marketplace. See also **advertising effectiveness.**

CONFIDENCE RANGE   The numerical parameters applied to the results of a research study in making inferences about a total population. Confidence range is the deviation from the test result (usually expressed as plus or minus some percentage) within which the population value falls the majority of the time (usually 90% or 95%). See also **sampling error.**

CONGLOMERATE DIVERSIFICATION   A corporate growth strategy in which a company acquires businesses that have no relationship to its current business. For example, a major retailer acquired companies that offered real estate brokerage and personal financial planning services. The retailer then established space within its stores to house these services. See also **diversification.**

CONJOINT ANALYSIS   A statistical technique in which respondents are asked to evaluate attributes (and combinations thereof) of a given product. Conjoint analysis is often used in developing new products. Through this technique, respondents express opinions and rank their preferences toward the various attributes of the product. Researchers then determine the importance of each attribute as indicated by the respondents' answers. Management then develops the most effective combination of attributes for the product. See also **product design model.**

CONSIGNMENT A selling method in which an intermediary sells goods, the title for which is held by the manufacturer. A consignment selling arrangement may be between a wholesaler and retailer, or between a manufacturer and wholesaler. The selling agreement permits the return of unsold goods. For example, a newsstand retailer may return unsold periodicals to its distributor under a consignment arrangement.

CONSULTANT A professional retained to provide specialized advice on a particular business issue. For example, marketing consultants offer specialized counsel in such areas as public relations and sales promotion. Management consultants are retained to help companies improve efficiency and product quality, design new manufacturing systems, or develop effective organizational communications. Consultants are hired on a project-by-project basis more often than they are on yearly retainers.

CONSULTATIVE SELLING A sales technique in which the seller positions himself or herself as a consultant to the customer. Consultative selling is a low-pressure sales technique commonly employed in **professional services marketing.** Emphasized in the selling situation is the professional's ability to identify client needs. Training for consultative selling involves setting sales objectives and learning interactive skills that help the seller identify client cues—verbal and nonverbal communications that indicate the client's feelings, wants, and needs. Professional services marketers employ consultative selling to market services to existing and potential clients

CONSUMER The person who actually uses a product or service. A consumer is not necessarily the purchaser. For example, a father who buys a bicycle for his son is the product purchaser. The child, however, is the actual consumer. Also known as *end-user.*

CONSUMER BEHAVIOR The study of people's needs, motivations, and thought processes used in choosing one product over another, and their patterns of purchasing different goods and services. Understanding consumer behavior enables marketers to develop products to meet buyers' needs as well as to devise promotional strategies to successfully sell those products. Consumer behavior analysis is based largely on the behavioral sciences. In general, marketers study consumer behavior by assessing the psychological and sociological forces that shape consumers' purchase decision-making patterns.

• *Psychological forces.* These denote a person's cognitive processes; thus, the term implies that psychological forces are unique to each individual. A differentiation is made between *demographic* and *psychographic* variables in studying this aspect of consumer behavior. Demographic factors such as age and occupation affect how people perceive themselves and their external environment. Psychographic factors include the concepts of:

—*Motivation*—relating to the needs that people seek to satisfy and that compel them to buy goods and services. (One of the most popular theories of human motivation is Abraham Maslow's concept of a **hierarchy of needs.** The theory suggests that people have levels of needs, ranging from basic physiological needs to those relating to emotional security and self-actualization. The theory holds that once one level of needs is satisfied, the next level must be satisfied.)

—*Learning*—relating to human behavior that is changed based on experience. Marketers study how individuals learn as a means of analyzing how they form opinions about products and establish procedures for buying them.

—*Attitudes*—referring to an individual's tendencies to perceive or act in a certain way. Consumers maintain attitudes about such things as food, clothes, politics, and religion. Attitudes predispose people to like or dislike a product or to make purchase decisions in a prescribed manner.

—*Personality*—relating to the combination of an individual's traits that leads to consistent responses to environmental stimuli. Personality denotes the characteristics that account for differences between people and that lead to relative predictable responses to certain recurring situations.

—*Lifestyle*—meaning how a person allocates time, money, and effort to pursue desirable objectives. Lifestyle includes a person's **activities, interests, and opinions.** Marketers attempt to identify the relationship between their products and the lifestyles of their target consumers.

—*Perceptions*—referring to the process by which an individual selects, organizes, and interprets external stimuli. Stimuli may emanate from the external environment (e.g., an advertisement) or from internal sources (e.g., a physical need to satisfy hunger or thirst).

• *Sociological forces.* Analyzing consumer behavior also depends on considering the social forces that determine human action because social interaction greatly influences individuals' motivations, learning, personality, attitudes, and perceptions. Sociological forces include:

> —*Culture*—comprised of the system of beliefs, values, and ideas created by a society, the combination of which are passed from generation to generation and reinforced through institutions such as education and religion. Cultural values (e.g., achievement, success, creativity, individualism) are important influencers of consumer behavior because they exert pressures on individuals to desire products that are consistent with the values they hold to be important.
> —*Subculture*—denoting a separate segment of a culture whose members share common traits such as race, nationality, religion, and geography. Members of subcultures usually exhibit similar interests and characteristics, as well as common preferences for things such as art, music, food, and politics.
> —*Social class*—referring to categories based primarily on people's financial income that are characterized by certain behavioral and purchase proclivities of their members. (Social class, however, is not determined solely by income; other factors include level of education and place of residence.) Members of a given social class often exhibit brand preferences for items such as cars, clothing, and recreational activities.
> —*Reference groups*—describing those groups to which an individual belongs, or hopes to belong, that directly or indirectly influence the individual's behavior (e.g., family, clubs, fraternities). Identifying with a reference group exposes people to new ideas and practices, and creates pressures to conform with modes of behavior accepted by the group.

Marketers look beyond the psychological and sociological influences that affect consumer behavior. They attempt to identify who the buyers of particular products are. They also study how buyer decision making is affected by the nature, cost, and complexity of different product purchases. See also **buying behavior patterns.**

CONSUMERISM The organized movement of government, business, and independent groups to protect the rights of consumers.

The consumerism movement gained heightened national exposure with President Kennedy's signing of the Consumer Bill of Rights in 1962. The bill stated that consumers have the right to be safe (from faulty products), to be informed (of a product's negative attributes or inherent dangers), to choose (ensuring market competition and the absence of monopolies), and to be heard (to be able to voice complaints and to have those grievances acted upon). See also **consumer protection legislation.**

CONSUMER MARKET The total number of households and individuals who purchase goods and services for their own consumption. The consumer market is different from the **organizational market,** which is the collective of businesses and institutions that purchase products for resale/rental or to produce other products. Also known as *product market.*

CONSUMER PRICE INDEX (CPI) A statistical measurement maintained by the U.S. Bureau of Labor Statistics that indicates price trends of some 400 different goods and services. CPI is a ratio of the cost of specific goods in a given year compared to their cost in the CPI base year: 1967. This "basket" of goods is grouped into the following classifications: food and beverage, housing, apparel, transportation, medical care, entertainment, and other categories. CPI is used as a measurement of economic conditions in the United States. Also known as the *cost of living index.*

CONSUMER PRODUCTS Products sold to the consumer market. They are grouped into three basic categories. (1) *Convenience goods,* which are bought frequently and where little time and effort are spent by the consumer in making the purchase decision. Convenience goods are usually low-priced and are available in a wide range of outlets (e.g., shampoo, candy, soda). (2) *Shopping products,* for which consumers spend considerable time researching and price shopping at numerous retail outlets (e.g., clothing). (3) *Specialty products,* goods that have unique attributes that consumers hold to be important (e.g., financial investment vehicles, insurance policies, certain kinds of healthcare products).

CONSUMER PROMOTION The variety of sales promotion tools and techniques designed to provide short-term incentives to consumers to stimulate product sales. Examples of consumer promotion devices are product samples, coupons, cash-refund offers and price-packs. Such promotions highlight products or services purchased by consumers. Thus, consumer promotions contrast **trade promotions,** which are geared toward wholesalers, retailers, and distributors.

CONSUMER PROTECTION LEGISLATION The various federal, state, and local laws established to protect the rights of consumers. Such legislation is meant to ensure the quality of consumer goods and honesty in advertising by sellers. Examples of consumer protection legislation are the Federal Trade Commission Act (which prohibited unfair or deceptive business practices) and the Consumer Product Safety Act. The overriding goal of consumer protection legislation is to ensure the safety, quality, and efficacy of consumer products. Maintaining the American free enterprise system and competition are other objectives of these governmental acts. See also **antitrust laws.**

CONSUMER RESEARCH Research designed to yield information about consumers in their roles as purchasers and users of goods and services. Consumer research generates data about people's motivations and their purchase decision making. It identifies the reasons why consumers buy particular products and the factors that influence their brand choices. Consumer research is gathered several different ways: by in-depth interviews, by **focus groups,** and by various tests that gauge advertising effectiveness. Consumer testing may entail inviting people to a laboratory or test kitchen to use and evaluate a product; or the product may be distributed to households for test usage over a period of time, called an *in-home use test.* Consumer panels might also be employed to rate the success of a sales promotion program. Panelists would be asked if they recalled the promotion, what they thought of it, if they took advantage of it, and how it influenced their attitudes or buying behavior subsequently. Consumer research data are particularly important in new product development. Additionally, they are used in advertising planning to aid in developing forceful messages and in determining which media will most effectively reach the target audience. See also **consumer behavior.**

CONSUMPTION People's purchase and usage of goods and services that satisfy their personal **wants** and **needs,** whether those needs are real or imagined.

CONTENT ANALYSIS   A method of collecting data by reviewing communications in books, newspaper and magazine articles, speeches, songs, and so forth. Content analysis has a key defining characteristic: Individual people are not the units of analysis, nor are people directly observed. Content analysis is used to study communications messages or the media carrying them. For example, it may be employed to identify key words or phrases in the news media that positively or negatively describe an organization, product, service, person, or issue. Content analysis is sometimes used to measure publicity results.

CONTESTS   Sales promotion programs in which a prize is given to a consumer who enters the competition by making a product purchase (although this is usually not required of entrants) or who demonstrates a particular skill. For example, a contest might require entrants to create a new slogan for the product sponsoring the contest; or entrants would be asked to take an artistic picture using the sponsoring organization's film or camera equipment. The primary goal of contests is to encourage greater product usage or product trial (e.g., a liquor company's contest to create a new mixed drink requires usage of its brand). Contests offer secondary benefits, however. They generate thousands of names of entrants that can be compiled into mailing lists for use by the sponsoring company or for sale/rental to other direct marketers. See also **sweepstakes.**

CONTINGENCY PLAN   The part of a marketing plan that details the provisions and strategies for dealing with adverse developments that may occur during implementation. Contingency plans outline the steps management will take to deal with negative occurrences like price wars, labor strikes, and product recalls. Contingency strategies are intended to give thought to potential difficulties. Contingency plans are usually detailed in the marketing plan section that deals with *controls,* which describe how the company will monitor the plan's progress and take corrective actions, when necessary.

CONTINGENCY QUESTION   A survey question that is to be completed only by some respondents based on their answer to a previous question. That is, answering one question requires the respondent to answer a subsequent (and related) question. For example:

1. Do you ever make donations to the Democratic Party?
        Yes ☐   No ☐
        a. If yes: When did you last do so?
        ☐ The last presidential election
        ☐ The last gubernatorial election
        ☐ The last mayoral election

The second part of this questionnaire item contains the contingency question.

CONTINUITY   A strategic consideration relating to when advertising will appear. Continuity describes the overall pattern of advertising message transmissions over a specified period of time. There are two basic continuity strategies: Advertisements may be scheduled to appear with the same frequency (e.g., ads running daily during a six-month advertising campaign); or they can be highly concentrated in a particular time frame, followed by periods of inactivity (*burst* advertising). Continuity also describes *how* a particular advertising medium is used. For example, an advertiser may strive for strong continuity by advertising in a single magazine, which would create continuous exposure of the product to the publication's readership. Conversely, the advertiser might sacrifice continuity for the wider audience exposure gained by advertising in several magazines.

CONTINUITY PROGRAM   A sales promotion technique in which consumers are required to collect multiple proofs of purchase over time to receive gifts or prizes. For example, a continuity program might require people to collect 10 box tops to receive a set of dishes or one volume of an encyclopedia collection. The benefit of this sales promotion technique is the ability to effect repeat sales of a product by consumers seeking the premium offer.

CONTINUOUS-LOOP VIDEO   A visual communications medium in which a video display runs a commercial, product demonstration, or informational message over and over again. Continuous-loop videos are common in retail locations or at company booths at trade shows. Messages shown on continuous loop are relatively brief: usually about two to three minutes. See also **video systems.**

CONTROL GROUP   The collection of research respondents that is identical to those in the **test group,** except for the fact that the control group is not exposed to the experimental variable. The goal of using control groups is to measure the impact of the experimental variable to which the test group is exposed. For example, in testing a new medication, the test group receives the medication, while the control group receives a placebo. The effectiveness of the medication is determined by measuring the improvement realized by the test group beyond that which was realized by the control group.

CONTROLLED CIRCULATION   The subscribers of a publication who receive the periodical for free. These subscribers include companies that advertise in the publication, key business executives, and other influential people. Also known as *qualified circulation* or *unpaid circulation*. See also **comp list.**

CONVENIENCE GOODS   Consumer products that are typically low-priced and widely available, and for which consumers spend little time in making purchase decisions. Consumers purchase convenience goods frequently. They often do so on impulse. Examples of convenience goods are soap, razor blades, and candy.

CONVENIENCE SAMPLE   A form of **nonprobability sampling** in which the researcher interviews people who are immediately accessible or easy to reach. Also known as *accidental samples* because respondents are selected on the basis of having accidentally been in the location at which the researcher selects interviewees. The danger of this sampling method is that the researcher may be biased in his or her selection of respondents. For example, the researcher may select only those people who "look like" they will provide good feedback. See also **sampling.**

CONVENIENCE STORE   A retail outlet whose advantage to consumers is its nearby location or store hours. The product assortment in convenience stores is generally limited to key convenience products (milk, bread, shampoo). Consumers typically buy these goods as "fill-in" purchases. That is, they are bought in between the times the consumers do their main shopping for the week or month. Convenience store items are high-priced and the outlets have a high degree of inventory turnover. The stores are generally located in high-population areas and maintain long hours, some staying open 24 hours a day (such as a 7-Eleven store).

COOPERATIVE ADVERTISING   An arrangement in which two or more companies jointly produce or finance advertising. Co-op advertising takes one of two basic forms. *Vertical* co-op advertising involves shared promotional activities between a manufacturer and a local retailer. The advertising is paid for fully or in part by the manufacturer, and the retailer handles placement of the insertions. The manufacturer may reimburse the retailer for the ad costs or may grant an allowance on the cost of the advertised goods. Vertical co-op advertising lets national advertisers promote their brands in specific markets at **local rates,** which are typically lower than national ad rates. In *horizontal* co-op advertising, independent sellers in the same or similar category combine to produce the advertising. A **co-op mailing** is one form of horizontal cooperative advertising.

CO-OP MAILING   A direct-mail technique that is a form of **cooperative advertising.** It involves a joint effort by noncompeting companies (with the same target consumers) to produce and finance a direct-mail package. An example of a co-op mailing is a **card deck,** which is a compilation of business-reply cards promoting products from multiple advertisers. The goal of a co-op mailing is to reduce the advertisers' individual mailing and production costs. This tactic is frequently employed in business-to-business advertising.

COPY   **1.** The words in a print advertisement (before or after printing) or on a TV/radio commercial script. Advertising copy is intended to arouse interest and provide information about the product. In a print ad, copy usually starts out as an amplification of the claim made in the headline. Copy describes the product's benefits and communicates reasons for the reader to want to purchase it. Effective copy must be interesting, specific, simple to understand, concise, believable, relevant to the reader's wants, and persuasive. **2.** In the print news media, the text in a newspaper or magazine article.

COPY-CONTACT   The advertising agency professional who has responsibility for both copywriting and client contact. The copy-contact person gathers input for copy directly from the client and may work with the client to obtain the necessary approvals. Copy-contact professionals generally work under the direction of an account executive.

COPY PLATFORM   A summary outline of the strategy to be employed in developing advertising copy. It defines the basic themes of the advertising and may address such issues as the ad's verbal and visual elements, different messages to be communicated, and the target audience. Copy platforms are developed prior to preparation of the copy and are usually submitted for client approval. A copy platform may also be included in a new business proposal, where it describes the advertising approach the agency will take if it is retained.

COPY RESEARCH   Research relating to analyzing and evaluating advertising copy. It is designed to assess how well the copy meets its stated objectives. Copy research may involve **pretesting,** which is evaluating copy prior to its appearance in the marketplace (to change it, if necessary); or it can involve **posttesting,** which gauges copy effectiveness after the advertising has appeared in the marketplace. Copy research is one form of advertising testing.

COPYRIGHT   The U.S. government's protection of the work of authors, writers, and musicians from being copied, reprinted, or sold without their permission. The Copyright Act of 1976 provides copyright protection for the owner's lifetime plus 50 years. After the copyright expires, the work becomes part of the public domain and may be used by anyone. Copyright protects the expression of an idea but not the idea itself. Advertisements and commercials are sometimes copyrighted.

COPY TESTING   The testing of advertising copy to maximize its effectiveness prior to being introduced in the marketplace. Copy testing differs from copy research in that it tests different approaches to preparing the copy (e.g., trying alternate messages to see which works best). Copy testing is often used in new product introductions to examine the impact of different appeals or descriptions of product benefits. See also **split-run research.**

COPYWRITER   The advertising professional who writes copy for advertisements, TV or radio commercials, direct-mail materials, and other promotional communications. A copywriter works in the creative department of an advertising agency, or may be employed as a freelancer by agencies or corporate communications departments. Copywriters usually work closely with art directors in creating ads.

CORNER CARD   The copy that appears on a direct-mail envelope, the purpose of which is to entice the recipient to open it. The corner card is an important component of the direct-mail piece because the recipient often will open the letter based on the corner card message—the first thing the recipient sees. Examples of corner card copy are "Free Sweepstakes Entry Form Inside!" and "You May Have Won $50,000! Look Inside to Find Out." Also known as *teaser copy.*

CORPORATE ADVERTISING   Advertising that promotes the *image* of a company as opposed to the specific products or services it offers. Corporate advertising is intended to enhance a company's reputation. For example, a major electronics manufacturer provided a multi-million-dollar endowment to a university to establish a center for international management studies. The company ran corporate ads announcing the endowment and explaining its reasons for doing so. The ads provided historical background on the organization and detailed its current management initiatives. Corporate advertising is often undertaken by public companies to increase their investment appeal to existing and potential stockholders. See also **institutional advertising.**

CORPORATE COMMUNICATIONS   The area of communications that is concerned with building favorable attitudes toward a company by its various publics: employees, consumers, stockholders, and the financial community. Most major companies have corporate communications departments that are responsible for external communications, publications development (e.g., annual reports, brochures), and employee communications. Many public relations agencies offer corporate communications services. Such firms are retained by companies that do not have corporate communications departments or that need to supplement their activities in this area.

CORPORATE RESPONSIBILITY RESEARCH   Market research designed to help companies better understand the legal, political, or social environments in which they operate. Examples of corporate responsibility research are ecological impact studies, consumers' "right to know" studies, and social values or policies studies. Corporate responsibility research data are used to help companies become better corporate citizens or to understand the issues that relate to meeting their societal obligations.

CORPORATE STRATEGY   The overall plan a company has for integrating its various elements: divisions, subsidiaries, and so on.

Corporate strategy includes the company's overall mission, which relates to its dominant emphases, values, and general reason for being. Corporate strategy encompasses such areas as financial and human resource strategies, and other issues that affect the organizational structure and its long-term initiatives (e.g., acquisitions, divestments).

CORRELATION ANALYSIS   A statistical technique used to determine the degree to which two variables are related. That is, correlation analysis is employed to identify how a change in one variable relates to a variation in another variable—even though there may not be a direct cause-and-effect relationship between them. For example, correlation analysis may be used to determine how a change in an advertisement's message might affect consumers' ability to recall the communication. Correlation analysis is expressed as a coefficient with a value ranging between 1.0 and −1.0. A value of 1.0 means a strong positive relationship exists between the two variables. A value of −1.0 means a strong negative relationship exists. A value of 0.0 means no relationship exists at all.

COST ANALYSIS   A sales manager's measurement of the cost of sales activities. Cost analysis involves studying expense data, the interpretation of which is used to monitor and assess sales force performance. Data may relate to costs by salesperson, product, geographic territory, or individual customer. Expense data are continually collected and compared to past data, current data, and industry averages. Companies conduct cost analyses to evaluate the varying levels of profitability of individual products or types of customer.

COST OF LIVING   The level of income required to maintain a person's standard of living as symbolized by the acquisition of desired goods and services. Cost of living is an **economic indicator.** *Note:* In periods of rapid price increases in the cost of consumer goods, employers will grant a *cost of living allowance* (COLA) to employees, which is an increase in wages and earnings to enable employees to keep pace with escalations in the cost of living.

COST PER GROSS RATING POINT (CPR)   A measurement method used to compare broadcast advertising vehicles. CPR is a calculation of the cost of the advertising unit (e.g., a 30-second commercial) divided by the rating of the show during which the commercial will air. For example, if the commercial's cost is $5,000 and the rating is 20, the CPR is

$$\$5,000 \text{ (unit cost)} \div 20 \text{ (rating)} = \$250$$

CPR is used to measure the efficiency of media costs when comparing several different broadcast vehicles. Another method of comparing media vehicles is **cost per thousand.**

COST PER ORDER (CPO)   A gauge of the profitability of a mail-order advertising program. CPO is calculated by dividing the sales volume of the orders received by the total cost of advertising for those items. Thus, if the CPO is larger than the average sales per order, the advertising program is deemed unprofitable. Companies use CPO measurements to compare the profitability of the different promotions they undertake.

COST PER THOUSAND (CPM)   A measurement technique used to gauge the cost effectiveness of advertising media purchases. CPM is calculated by taking the cost of the unit of advertising space (print media) or time (broadcast media), multiplying it by 1,000, then dividing the number by the medium's audience size. For example, a magazine with an audience of 100,000 readers charges $5,000 for a full-page ad, so the CPM is

$$\$5,000 \text{ (ad cost)} \times 1,000 = 5,000,000 \div 100,000 \text{ (audience)} = \$50$$

Cost per thousand is a common way to compare advertising buys between media with different-size audiences. The media must reach the same target audience, however, for the comparison to be valid. Marketing managers must realize that CPM is only one criterion. It does not consider other relevant quantitative factors that may determine the advertising effectiveness of the vehicles. For example, a company sells high-priced luggage for vacation travelers. Magazine A (circulation 40,000) and Magazine B (circulation 20,000) are both travel magazines, but A charges less for a full-page ad than B. However, B has a much higher percentage of readers with a household income of $50,000 (which, the company's market research indicates, is the income bracket of most of its consumers). Magazine A has a lower CPM than Magazine B. However, the smarter ad buy would be in B, where more consumers may be reached who have the purchasing power to buy the product. See also **cost per gross rating point.**

COST-PLUS PRICING Pricing method in which a standard markup percentage is added to the direct, indirect, and fixed costs involved in producing a product or service. Price is determined by converting these costs to per-unit costs. Then a predetermined percentage of these expenses is added to achieve the desired profit margin.

COUPON **1.** A certificate entitling a buyer to a discount off a product's established price. The use of coupons is a sales promotion technique used to encourage buyers to try a new product or to increase the quantity or frequency with which current users already buy it. Coupons are distributed via mail, newspaper or magazine inserts, or space advertisements. They may also be inserted in product packages or on the packages themselves. Buyers submit coupons to retailers for money off the product price. Retailers, in turn, submit the coupons to the manufacturer for reimbursement. Also known as *cents-off coupons.* See also **premiums. 2.** A printed form on which a customer indicates his or her name, address, and phone number to order merchandise or request information by mail. See also **direct-response advertising.**

COUPON REDEMPTION See **redemption.**

COVERAGE **1.** In advertising, the percentage of households that can be reached by the various media carrying a particular ad. **2.** In public relations, the appearance of a news story in print or broadcast news media. (Coverage in the PR context is synonymous with publicity.) PR coverage varies by the *amount* of space or time the medium devotes to the story and to its *placement* in the medium (e.g., where it is situated in a publication or when it airs in a broadcast report). PR coverage is measured in qualitative and quantitative terms. Quantitative measures include the number of times a company, product, person, or issue is mentioned in the coverage; the number of column inches devoted to the story; or the length of air time. Qualitative measures refer to the nature of the coverage—that is, whether the coverage portrays the company or product in a positive or negative light. See also **content analysis.**

CREATIVE BLACK BOOK A directory of individuals and companies that supply products and services to advertising and marketing services agencies. Photographers, illustrators, film directors, and producers advertise in the Black Book. In addition to listing their company name, address, and phone number, the suppliers often illustrate their ads with examples of their work. The directory is produced annually as a two-volume set and is distributed in the United States, Europe, and Canada. See also **Green Book.**

CREATIVE DIRECTOR   The advertising agency executive who oversees the creative department. The creative director is responsible for developing advertising from initial concept through production. Reporting to the vice-president of creative services in a typical agency structure, the creative director supervises the work of copywriters, art directors, and layout personnel.

CREDIT CARD ORDER   The process of paying for merchandise by using a credit card. Special promotions are designed to generate credit card orders. For example, direct-response television ads might allow buyers to pay by credit card if they call a toll-free number. Marketers consider credit-card buyers the same as cash buyers. However, they will generally track the two groups separately for record-keeping purposes.

CRISIS MANAGEMENT   Public relations function in which a company attempts to control and minimize damages resulting from an adverse occurrence affecting the company or its products. A product recall illustrates such an instance. For example, Johnson & Johnson exhibited excellent crisis management skills when several bottles of its Tylenol brand pain reliever were found to contain poison. The product tampering resulted in several deaths. Sales plummeted. The company swiftly employed advertising, public relations, and appearances by company executives to assuage the public's fears. Communications explained that the occurrence was an isolated incident. They also highlighted the company's plans to ensure that the incident could never happen again (e.g., through designing new product packaging and format). Through crisis management, the company was able to restore consumers' faith in the product and, thus, save it from extinction. See also **issues management.**

CRITICAL PATH METHOD   Procedure by which large-scale programs involving many phases or elements are managed. This system maps out the varied activities involved in a project, and specifies areas of responsibility and a schedule for completing the required steps. Several of these steps may fall into the critical path. That is, their completion is necessary to move the project forward without incurring significant delays. In planning a conference, determining the location of the event lies in the critical path of this project since logistical details (e.g., issuing invitations) can only be finalized once the site has been selected. See also **PERT.**

CROSS PROMOTION   See **tie-in advertising/promotion.**

CROSS-SELL   A salesperson's attempt to sell a different (e.g., complementary) product to a customer who has already purchased a product. An example of cross-selling is when an accountant attempts to sell clients the firm's management consulting services. Cross-selling may be done in face-to-face meetings, or cross-selling promotional information may be included in the text of written reports or proposals.

CROSS-TABULATION   The statistical technique that seeks to establish an interdependent relationship between two or more variables. The purpose of cross-tabulations (or cross-tabs) is to determine whether or not there are different responses among subgroups in a given sample. For example, subgroups may be determined by demographic characteristics (age, sex, income, size of household), geographic factors (city or region), or usage patterns (awareness or usage of a brand or particular product category). Respondents in these subgroups may be asked whether they feel a particular product is priced fairly. Using cross-tabs, researchers can identify the relationship between people's responses and their subgroup classifications (e.g., respondents in one city may feel the product is fairly priced, whereas respondents in another city believe it is not).

CUES   The minor external stimuli that compel an individual to perform some kind of action. For example, reading an advertisement may be a person's cue to desire and purchase a product. Other examples of cues are reading a newspaper article that favorably discusses a product or hearing a friend recommend it. Cues are generally discussed in the context of **learning,** which relates to changes in individuals' behavior arising from experience.

CULTURAL ENVIRONMENT   See **culture; macroenvironment.**

CULTURE   The system of beliefs, values, customs, and ideas created by a society, the combination of which are passed from generation to generation and reinforced through institutions such as education and religion. Culture is an important aspect of analyzing consumer behavior because cultural values (e.g., achievement, financial success, humanitarianism) create pressures within and on an individual to behave in a certain way. The prevailing cultural values of a given society must be addressed in developing marketing strategy. Identifying the cultural forces that influence human behavior is key to defining and understanding the target market.

CUMULATIVE AUDIENCE Broadcast audience measurement of the number of individuals or households that will be reached by a particular broadcast advertising vehicle at least once during a designated time period. Also known as *cume* and *unduplicated audience.*

CUSTOMER The buyer of goods or services. Customers may be the actual purchasers or the intended purchasers. See also **consumer.**

CUSTOMER DATABASE A computer-based system containing information about customers' purchase histories and buying patterns. Information that is assembled into a customer database is culled from purchase receipts, credit card slips, warranty card returns, rebate applications, or contest entry forms. Customer databases are valuable marketing tools because they contain information on customers who are favorably predisposed to a company or product (since they have already purchased a product or requested information about it). Thus, customer databases are useful in stimulating repeat sales and cross-selling different company products. Marketers also use them to test new products. By targeting the most likely purchasers, companies can estimate a product's success and enjoy the privacy from competitors not afforded by conventional testing methods, such as a **test market.**

CUSTOMER ORIENTATION A company philosophy in which product planning is based on meeting customers' needs as opposed to its own corporate needs. Customer-oriented companies determine customer requirements by researching them through formal market studies and informal discussions with consumers. A customer-oriented company's overriding goal is to meet customer needs better than its competitors do. Customer orientation as a planning philosophy is different from a **competitor orientation,** which is corporate planning based largely on competitors' strategies and actions.

CUSTOMER PROFILE   Buyer descriptions developed by salespeople to depict groups or types of customers based on certain characteristics such as income, occupation, education level, age, gender, and area of residence. Customer profiles provide salespeople with data on buyer traits and behavior patterns. These data are used in selecting the best prospects for a given product or for devising selling strategies. See also **audience profile.**

CUSTOMER RELATIONS   A salesperson's efforts to ensure that clients' needs are never neglected. There are several general policies for maintaining good customer relations. Salespeople must handle complaints promptly and pleasantly, ensuring that the grievances are taken seriously and handled with concern. Next, salespeople must maintain regular contact with customers through periodic visits, telephone calls, or customer newsletters. Salespeople must also continually serve the customer by keeping him or her informed of new developments, by fulfilling reasonable requests, and by providing assistance. Salespeople must show appreciation by giving thanks to the customer for his or her business and by occasionally offering gifts (e.g., at holiday time). See also **customer service.**

CUSTOMER SATISFACTION   A qualitative measure of the degree to which a customer's expectation of a product matches the product's actual performance. Customer expectations, against which product performance is measured, are formed various ways: through information from salespeople; advertising; and input from friends, family, and **opinion leaders.**

CUSTOMER SERVICE   The range of activities a seller offers a buyer after a product has been purchased. Customer service relates to such things as product repairs, support, and the provision of general product information. Customer service also describes the intangible aspects involved in the buyer-seller relationship, for example, courteous and/or prompt service by salespeople in a store or bank. Many companies have customer service departments. Their function is maintaining goodwill between the company and its customers by answering questions, solving problems, and providing advice. Staffers in these departments are called *customer service representatives*. See also **customer relations.**

CUSTOMIZED MARKETING   The practice of designing products to meet each buyer's unique specifications. For example, an airplane manufacturer has only a few buyers. Thus, it designs planes according to each customer's specific product criteria. Customized marketing is generally not economical for most companies. Large companies, however, have the financial and production resources to make minor variations in their products for different market segments. Nonetheless, the principles of customized marketing are being widely adopted by mass market companies. For example, car makers let buyers specify how they want their car manufactured (which color, engine, seat material, options). Even salad bars and self-serve ice-cream parlors are examples of customized marketing in that they let people choose their own combination of fixings.

CUSTOM MARKETING RESEARCH FIRM   A firm retained to conduct research to generate primary data for a client company. A custom marketing research firm generally coordinates the overall design of the research study: producing the questionnaire, conducting interviews, tabulating the data, and analyzing the findings. The resultant information becomes the property of the client.

CUTLINE   A word or phrase that describes an illustration (photograph, artwork) in an advertisement or newspaper or magazine article. See also **caption.**

D

DAGMAR *(Defining Advertising Goals for Measured Advertising Results)* The title of a book by Russell Colley in which the need to set advertising objectives whose results are *specific* and *measurable* is discussed. Colley states that advertising effectiveness should be evaluated according to the advertising's attainment of specific communications goals, not solely on sales results.

DAILIES Newspapers that are published at least five days a week, Monday through Friday. Dailies are a popular ad medium offering several advantages. Ads, for example, may be assigned to specific sections in the newspaper (e.g., a hotel resort ad can appear in the travel section). Dailies also enable readers to clip out a coupon from the ad (or the ad itself) for future reference. The main disadvantage of daily newspapers is that readers quickly discard them. Moreover, reading may be hasty or cursory and there is a high degree of selective reader exposure to different sections (e.g., a person may only read the business section). Other periodicals, such as newsletters, may also be termed dailies if they publish at the aforementioned frequency. The term, however, is usually used to describe newspapers.

DATABASE A computerized system containing an organized collection of data that can be readily accessed for different information needs. Databases enable users to enter, retrieve, sort, edit, or index marketing and general business information. A database management system is often used to categorize data items in different yet related files. See also **customer database.**

DATABASE MARKETING The process of generating computer data on consumers' characteristics and buying patterns for use in subsequent direct-marketing initiatives. For example, profiles of buyers' demographic, geographic, and psychographic attributes are constructed through credit and charge account records, coupon redemptions, sweepstakes entries, and product sample distributions. This information comprises a company's **customer database,** which is used to determine consumers' product preferences to effect repeat sales and to **cross-sell** other products. See also **micromarketing.**

DATA ENTRY   The process of inputting information into a computer for filing and analytical purposes. Data are usually converted to codes before being entered to facilitate storing and retrieving the data. Data may be entered three ways. *Key entry* refers to manually inputting data from a computer keyboard. *Scan entry* employs an optical character recognition device (a **scanner**) that reads data from graphic markings such as **bar codes** on coupons or product packages. *Tape entry* inputs computer-readable data from magnetic tape on which the data are electronically stored. The drawback of using the key entry method is that it requires physical handling of information, leaving open the possibility of human error when inputting data. See also **cathode ray tube.**

DAY-AFTER RECALL (DAR)   A test of advertising effectiveness in which consumers are asked how much they remember about a particular advertisement or commercial the day after seeing it. DAR results are gathered via telephone interviews. Researchers give respondents the name of the advertised product and then ask them to recall the points highlighted in the sponsored message. DAR is designed to assess the extent of brand-name recognition by consumers, and how well the selling points in the advertisement were communicated. See also **aided recall; unaided recall.**

DAYPARTS   Specifically defined segments of radio and television programming schedules that reflect varying degrees of audience size and composition. Media planners review dayparts when making decisions about commercial time purchases. In some cases, media planners buy time by the daypart as opposed to by a particular program. Examples of dayparts are television's **prime time** and **morning-drive** and **afternoon-drive** times on radio.

DEALER   A retailer of merchandise. Dealers purchase and maintain inventories of products to which they have taken title. In this sense, dealers differ from **brokers** and manufacturer's representatives, which do not take title to the goods they sell.

DEALER LISTING   The space in an advertisement by a national company that indicates the local dealers carrying its products. That is, the advertisement is standard except for the dealer listing space, which carries the names and addresses of local or regional dealers offering the advertised item. The dealer listing is usually situated at the bottom of the advertisement. See also **ad slick.**

DEALER LOADER   Any of a variety of incentives given by a manufacturer to a dealer for stocking or promoting the manufacturer's merchandise. A dealer loader might be a gift to the dealer or a discount on goods. Incentives are given to dealers both for carrying specific merchandise and for developing special promotions and product offerings. See also **trade promotion.**

DEALING   Promotional activities that supplement advertising or serve to coordinate advertising with personal selling initiatives.

DECENTRALIZED SALES ORGANIZATION   An organization in which responsibility for sales management tasks is delegated to lower levels of the management hierarchy. It is different from a **centralized sales organization,** in which sales management decisions are made at the highest organizational levels of the company. In a decentralized sales organization, a company has separate divisions, with sales management duties handled by the divisions' sales forces. A decentralized sales structure is appropriate for companies whose divisions sell different products to different markets through separate distribution channels.

DECEPTIVE ADVERTISING   Any advertising intended to mislead consumers. Deceptive advertising is illegal. Advertising is considered deceptive when it makes spurious claims about a product, fails to fully disclose information about it, or otherwise creates false impressions. Advertising agencies, celebrity endorsers, and retailers may all be accused of engaging in deceptive advertising. For example, **bait and switch advertising** by retailers is a deceptive practice. This is where the retailer advertises a low-priced item (that may not be available or is in extremely low supply) to build store traffic and then forces consumers to purchase a more expensive item. The laws prohibiting deceptive advertising are enforced by the **Federal Trade Commission.** See also **consumer protection legislation.**

DECISION MODELS Computer **models** used to evaluate alternatives and assist in problem solving. Decision models are systems that apply scientific methodology to help understand, predict, or control various marketing management problems. For example, decision models are used in making judgments about new product sales forecasting, facilities site selection, media buying, and budgeting. See also **decision-support system.**

DECISION-SUPPORT SYSTEM A computer-based system designed to assist in management decision making. Decision-support systems are comprised of specially developed software and hardware. Management inputs data (quantitative and/or qualitative information) into the system. The system then outputs information describing the implications of specific decisions. (Such systems may also be designed to recommend specific actions.) Decision-support systems enable management to conduct "what if" analyses. For example, management might ask, "If we increase the number of distribution outlets in a given area, what will the impact on sales be in that area?" In marketing, decision-support systems are often used in sales forecasting and in determining media schedules. See also **expert systems.**

DECOY NAME A fictional name and address included in a mailing list to track unauthorized usage of the list. Mailing lists are usually sold or rented to direct marketers on a one-time usage basis. Thus, if a list is used more than once, the list owner will receive materials sent to the decoy name and thereby discover the unsanctioned usage. Inserting decoy (or "dummy") names into a list is a process known as *salting.*

DEFENSIVE WARFARE The **marketing warfare** theory, which holds that the best strategy for a company leading a product market is to defend its competitive position. Three principles of defensive warfare apply. First, the best defensive strategy is "attacking"—that is, introducing new products or services that make the existing ones obsolete. Second, strong competitive moves should always be "blocked," referring to when a market leader introduces a product to copy a competitor's that was first in the market. Third and most important, only market leaders should employ defensive marketing tactics.

DELAYED BROADCAST (DB)   A network television or radio show that is taped for broadcast at a later time in an area that did not receive the initial broadcast (such as in another time zone). For example, a program that airs in New York would be shown on delayed broadcast in California.

DELPHI TECHNIQUE   A judgmental forecasting method in which experts in a given subject area attempt to reach a consensus on predictions of future events. The Delphi technique is a group exercise. Each participant develops his or her own forecast (on such topics as demographic, technological, or economic trends) and anonymously submits it to the group's coordinator. This person reviews all forecasts and develops a summary report. Each participant then prepares another forecast based on this summary, and the process continues until the group members' forecasts converge.

DEMAND   Consumers' collective financial ability and desire to purchase goods and services. Identifying levels of buyer demand is a key part of marketing planning. Determining demand involves using economic measures to quantify the number of potential purchasers in a given product category or geographic locale. Marketers ascertain the extent of demand by comparing the number of consumers desiring a type of product with those who have the financial capacity to purchase it. Demand is influenced by social, cultural, and economic variables that cause it to fluctuate. See also **demand states; derived demand; needs; wants.**

DEMAND-BASED PRICING   A pricing strategy based largely on determining consumers' or distributors' feelings toward the fair cost of goods or services. Prices are determined by market research that illustrates consumer desires and the range of prices acceptable to them.

DEMAND STATES   Varying levels of demand that must be recognized by marketing planners in their efforts to relate **marketing mix** elements to target market needs. Marketing authority Philip Kotler identifies eight demand states: **negative demand,** in which a large part of the market dislikes a product and makes an effort to avoid it;

no demand, in which consumers are indifferent to a product; **latent demand,** in which many customers seek a product benefit not offered by products currently available; **falling demand,** characterized by specific trends or environmental factors that reduce the size of the market; **irregular demand,** in which time factors (season, time of day, etc.) cause fluctuations in product usage; **full demand,** referring to when a company has the full market share it desires; **overfull demand,** in which market demand exceeds the company's ability to deliver sufficient amounts of product; and **unwholesome demand,** where demand for unhealthy products (e.g., cigarettes or alcohol) spawns organized efforts to reduce market consumption.

DEMARKETING   The tactics used to *decrease* market demand for a product. Demarketing involves altering **marketing mix** variables to effect lower demand when it is higher than an organization can or wants to handle. For example, a tourist location attracts more visitors than the facility can accommodate. Demarketing tactics include raising prices, reducing advertising and promotion expenditures, or deleting product benefits. In *selective demarketing* a company tries to reduce demand in a specific market (e.g., one that is less profitable than others). Demarketing may be intended to reduce demand either temporarily or permanently. It is an appropriate strategy when a company is faced with an **overfull demand** state. The concept was developed by Philip Kotler and Sidney J. Levy.

DEMOGRAPHIC ENVIRONMENT   See **macroenvironment.**

DEMOGRAPHICS   The study of a market's composition based on socioeconomic variables such as age, sex, occupation, religion, level of education, race, nationality, income, or family size. Demographic information is useful in analyzing **consumer behavior** because buyer wants, preferences, and product usage patterns often are similar among members of a given demographic category.

DEMOGRAPHIC SEGMENTATION   The **market segmentation** strategy in which the market is divided into groups based on demographic categories such as age, sex, occupation, education, religion, race, or nationality. Demographic segmentation is the most popular segmentation method because much demographic data are readily obtainable from government censuses of the population. Companies that segment markets demographically study changes in population growth trends, the size of consumer age groups, and geographic dispersion of the population. Income trends are also important factors in that marketers must identify how wealth is distributed among households.

DEMONSTRATION   Product sales presentation to provide an inducement to prospective buyers. The seller exhibits the product in use (for example, shows how a new food processor works) or how it will look in its ultimate form (for example, assembles a rowing machine). The seller discusses how the product works and describes its benefits. The classic example is the door-to-door salesperson who gives in-home demonstrations of a vacuum cleaner.

DENSITY   Direct marketing term referring to the proportion of target customers (or potential customers) in a given geographic area in comparison to the total population in that area.

DEPARTMENT STORE   A large retail establishment whose merchandise is departmentalized for the purposes of promotion, service, and accounting. Department stores offer a wide variety of products such as clothing, home furnishings, appliances, and recreational items. They are typically multilevel stores situated either in inner-city locations or suburban shopping malls. Department stores must employ at least 25 people to be categorized as such for census purposes. See also **superstores.**

DEPENDENT VARIABLE   The variable in a research experiment that you are trying to predict or explain. Researchers study the dependent variable by altering **independent variables.** Assume customer attitudes toward service in a restaurant are being studied. Patrons' attitudes, in this case, would be the dependent variable. Independent variables that the researcher might alter would be service by waiters, prices of entrees, and decor. Thus, by changing the independent variables, changes in people's attitudes toward service may be calculated. Researchers are careful to alter only one independent variable at a time in an experiment so they can accurately attribute changes in the dependent variable to the independent variable that was modified.

DEPTH INTERVIEW   A face-to-face, largely unstructured interview in which the researcher attempts to get the respondent to freely express needs, desires, motives, emotions, and so forth. A depth interview usually starts with the researcher asking very general questions. The researcher then moves into more specific questions that probe the respondent's opinions. A depth interview may be so unstructured that it involves no formal questions—that is, the interviewer simply has the respondent talk about the subject at hand.

DEPTH OF EXPOSURE   The level of consumer awareness of an advertising message vis-à-vis the intensity of its exposure in the marketplace. Depth of exposure relates to how much consumers are conscious of the message based on the size (in print media) or duration (in broadcast media) of the advertisements, as well as the frequency of their repetition. In short, it denotes the level of penetration of a message into the **target market.**

DERIVED DEMAND   Demand for a product that results from the consumption of another product. For example, demand for certain industrial products is derived from consumer products that utilize those industrial materials in their production (e.g., the demand for car tires results from consumption of cars, and the production of tires, in turn, influences the demand for rubber and other materials used to make tires).

DESCRIPTIVE LABELING   The method of labeling in which information on the product container describes its contents, size, ingredients, and proper methods of usage. Descriptive labeling is different from **grade labeling** in which the labeling is based primarily on the relative quality of the product (e.g., Grade A meats). See also **unit pricing.**

DESCRIPTIVE MODEL   A type of analytical **model** used to explain or predict factors relating to a marketing problem. Descriptive models employ scientific methodology to understand a mangement situation and to assist in decision making. For example, a descriptive model can be employed to explain the effects of advertising expenditures on sales. The model would be structured to expain how changes in advertising might affect consumer awareness, consumer trial of the product, or usage rates. See also **decision models.**

DESCRIPTIVE RESEARCH   Research that statistically describes a current situation or events that have transpired. Descriptive research seeks to determine the frequency with which something occurs or has occurred. For example, a company is considering introducing a new home-delivery food shopping service. Descriptive research would be employed to estimate how many consumers would be interested in such a service. Descriptive research is often used as a starting point in defining the types of research methodologies that should be used for a given research initiative. See also **evaluative research; predictive research.**

DESIGNATED MARKET AREA   The A. C. Nielsen Company's definition of television markets in which a group of counties constitutes a given viewing area. Counties that comprise a DMA represent the largest viewing audience for the stations in their particular geographic area. All counties in the United States are assigned to one DMA. There is no overlap between them. DMAs are used by media planners in determining broadcast advertising buys. See also **area of dominant influence.**

DESKTOP PUBLISHING   The process of using computer equipment to design and lay out print communications (e.g., brochures, newsletters, collateral materials). Desktop publishing software and hardware are used to create page layouts and cover designs, and to set type. The equipment eliminates the manual preparation of mechanical art. Consequently, it obviates much of the work done by graphic artists and paste-up personnel. Materials designed via desktop publishing are camera-ready. That is, they may be given directly to a printer after being produced by the desktop publishing equipment. See also **computer graphics.**

DIARY METHOD   Audience measurement technique in which people in select households enter information about their media viewing, listening, or reading patterns into diaries. That is, they record information on periodicals read, TV shows watched, or radio programs listened to—information submitted periodically to the research companies conducting the measurement studies. The diary method of television audience measurement is being replaced in some cases by mechanical devices (**people meters**) that automatically record people's TV viewing patterns. *Note:* The diary method is also used to track consumers' product purchasing.

DICHOTOMOUS QUESTION   A type of **closed-ended question** in which the respondent is provided with only two choices. See also **multichotomous question.**

DIE-CUT   Printing production technique in which a special perforation is created on paper or cardboard using a sharp steel die. For example, a die-cut on the cover of a brochure could be a perforation through which the company's **logo** is seen; or a die-cut could be used in a presentation folder to create perforations into which a business card is inserted. Die-cuts are frequently used in producing greeting cards and folded boxes or displays.

DIFFERENTIAL ADVANTAGE   **1.** A situation in which a company can outperform its competitors in one particular dimension of the company's service or product offering. Having a differential advantage enables a company to achieve a sustainable competitive position in a market. However, the differential advantage must indeed be unique and must be communicable to target consumers. **2.** Refers to a specific product's attribute not found in other products in the same category. See also **competitive advantage.**

DIFFERENTIATED MARKETING   A situation in which a company chooses to operate in more than one market segment and develops specific products and promotional strategies for each. For example, a company that produces coffee markets various types such as regular, decaffeinated, and instant. Differentiated marketing typically creates more total sales than **undifferentiated marketing** (in which a company ignores market segment differences and approaches the market with one product offering). However, the costs of engaging in a differentiated marketing approach are high because the company must modify its product (which increases manufacturing expenditures) and incur increased costs for specialized administrative, inventory, and promotional activities.

DIFFUSION MODEL   A type of **model** used in predicting the flow of an innovation through the population. As a decision-support tool, diffusion models help managers estimate the timing with which an innovation (e.g., a new product or advertising message) will spread through the target population. See also **diffusion of innovation.**

DIFFUSION OF INNOVATION   The spreading of an innovative new product through the market over an unspecified period of time.

Innovation is defined as something that is new or perceived to be new. *Diffusion* denotes the spread of the new idea or item from its creator to its ultimate users. Taken together, diffusion of innovation relates to how and when groups come to adopt the innovation. An example of a product innovation is the microwave oven, which had few users when it was initially introduced but became a popular appliance in American homes. See also **adopter categories.**

DIMENSIONAL MARKETING   A direct-mail approach in which the promotional package's contents have dimensions. That is, the package consists of more than printed materials. For example, one dimensional marketing program involved mailing a miniature pool table. Accompanying sales literature had copy that used analogies to playing billiards to promote the advertiser's corporate planning capabilities. Dimensional marketing is a very costly direct-mail technique. Consequently, such packages are sent to small lists of sales prospects (no more than a few hundred at a time) who are generally identified by the advertiser's sales force.

DIRECT ACCOUNTS   A company's customers who are serviced by home-office sales personnel or senior sales executives. The accounts are not assigned to sales force personnel by territory. Direct accounts are usually a company's major clients. They are typically very large buyers who enjoy special arrangements in terms of prices, credit terms, or product design. Also known as *national accounts* or *house accounts.*

DIRECT CLOSE   A salesperson's **closing** technique in which the seller simply asks the prospect for a favorable purchase decision without using persuasive tactics. A direct close approach is used after the seller receives positive **buying signals** from the prospect. The salesperson will typically summarize the major sales points prior to asking for the order.

DIRECT COSTS   Costs relating directly to the production or sale of a product. Direct costs may be those for manufacturing (materials and labor) or for selling (sales force funding). Direct costs can be attributed to one or more of the following segments: a product, sales territory, customer account, or marketing initiative. See also **indirect costs.**

DIRECT DISTRIBUTION CHANNEL   A channel through which the buyer receives a product or service directly from the manufacturer or provider. Direct distribution channels do not involve independent middlemen such as wholesalers, retailers, manufacturer's representatives, and agents. An example of a direct distribution channel is the selling of professional services, where a client receives the service directly from the provider without any involvement by third-party intermediaries. See also **indirect distribution channel.**

DIRECT-MAIL ADVERTISING   Advertising to specific consumer segments using communications delivered by mail as opposed to the mass media. The primary benefit of this direct marketing technique is that it affords great selectivity in reaching target customers.

Direct-mail advertising materials include *letters* (which are often personalized), *self-mailers* (such as folders, brochures, and other materials that do not require a mailing envelope), and catalogs. Target consumers are identified using mailing lists obtained from magazine suscription lists, telephone directories, and other sources of public information, or **house lists** of existing and past customers. Targeting consumers using lists enables the marketer to pinpoint the recipients of the advertising while avoiding the "waste" of promoting goods and services in general-interest media—that is, in media that reach consumers outside the target market.

An important benefit of direct mail is that the advertising message does not compete with other promotional communications. This is different from advertising that appears in publications in which numerous ads compete for the reader's attention, as well as on television and radio stations, which also feature numerous commercial announcements.

Direct-mail packages are generally very detailed and provide ample product descriptions. Thus, direct mail is particularly effective when a sales message is too long or complex to be explained in a print ad or broadcast commercial. As with other forms of advertising, direct mail is intended to generate sales or inquiries that can be followed up by a salesperson or by additional direct mail.

DIRECT-MAIL AGENCY   A magazine subscription agency that uses direct mail to market subscriptions on behalf of publishers. The agency, in turn, receives a commission from the publisher, ranging anywhere from 5% to 100% of the subscription's selling price. Direct-mail agencies utilize promotional approaches such as **sweepstakes**

and *stamp sheets*. The latter is a listing that indicates all the periodicals available and their prices. Publishers retain direct-mail agencies when the former do not have the financial resources or time to generate large-scale subscription orders on their own.

DIRECT MARKETING   The marketing approach in which promotional communications are delivered directly to individual consumers, who are asked to respond by phone, mail, or a personal visit. Direct marketing's central defining characteristic, which distinguishes it from other forms of marketing, is that it is measurable in terms of consumer response. Direct marketing involves techniques such as direct-mail advertising, door-to-door selling, catalog selling, and telemarketing. Direct marketing programs are based on selecting target consumers through use of mailing lists or customer files. The goals of direct marketing are to generate sales or to elicit requests for more information—responses that are followed up by salespeople. Direct marketing has become very popular because of several demographic changes that have occurred in recent years. Two of these are an aging population, which is less inclined to go shopping, and the proliferation of working parents who have less time to shop. Frequent users of direct marketing are magazine and book publishers, credit card companies, catalog houses, and political organizations.

DIRECT MARKETING ASSOCIATION (DMA)   A leading national trade association dedicated to promoting the practice of direct marketing. The DMA is comprised of direct marketing agencies, as well as vendor/supplier companies serving such firms. The group was originally known as the Direct Mail Marketing Association. Its headquarters is in New York City. See Appendix A for address and phone number.

DIRECT MEDIA   The media through which marketing information is disseminated to individual consumers. Direct media include direct mail and the telephone (telemarketing). The term is in contrast to **mass media,** which are those media designed to reach a mass audience (television, radio, newspapers, and magazines) as opposed to specific individuals.

DIRECTORY ADVERTISING   Advertising placed in specialized directories published by government agencies, clubs and fraternities, and trade associations. For example, a building contractors' trade group directory would be a likely outlet for advertising by a law firm specializing in construction claims and litigation. **Yellow pages advertising** is a form of directory advertising, although it is really not a specialized directory for targeting buyers in a given category.

DIRECT PROMOTION   Any activity designed to deliver promotional communications directly to consumers without the use of communications media (e.g., publications, radio, television). Examples are direct mail, telemarketing, and personal selling. See also **indirect promotion.**

DIRECT-RESPONSE ADVERTISING   Advertising designed to evoke an immediate purchase response by the consumer. Its other defining characteristic is that it enables the consumer to respond directly to the advertiser without having to go to a store or a distribution outlet to obtain the product. Examples of direct-response advertising are ads with coupons, **800-numbers,** and interactive electronic systems that allow product ordering from various public locations (e.g., a shopping mall). *Direct-response agencies* are specialists in developing and timing direct-response communications.

DIRECT SELLING   1. A sales approach characterized by personal product explanations and demonstrations, often in the consumer's home or retailer's establishment. **2.** Refers to use of a **direct distribution channel,** where a manufacturer sells directly to users without the intervention of independent middlemen.

DISCOUNT   A product price that has been reduced from its stated list rate. Discounts are offered as an incentive to purchase goods or services. Four basic kinds of discounts are used. *Trade* discounts are those granted to middlemen (e.g., wholesalers, retailers) who carry a manufacturer's goods. *Quantity* discounts are granted to encourage large-volume purchases. *Incentive* discounts encourage the buyer to make payment within a specified period of time (e.g., payment made before its due date). *Seasonal* discounts are offered on merchandise sold at a specific time of year (e.g., the price of Christmas ornaments is lowered at holiday time). Discounts are also often used as a strategy to counter competitors' marketing initiatives.

DISCOUNT STORE   A retail establishment that sells merchandise at prices significantly lower than other merchants. Such stores are able to do so by accepting lower margins and working on higher volumes of goods. Discount stores have several defining characteristics. First, they emphasize national brands in an effort to dispel the perception of inferior quality created by the low price offerings. Second, they operate on a self-serve basis with little customer assistance by store personnel. Third, they carry general merchandise in a wide variety of consumer goods categories. Some discount stores, however, have turned to offering select goods. These *specialty discount stores* offer products in such areas as sporting goods, consumer electronics, and books.

DISCRETIONARY INCOME   The money that consumers have available to spend after having paid for necessities such as food, clothing, and shelter. Marketers of goods that are not necessities, and whose purchase is made with discretionary income, must appeal to consumers' psychological needs (as opposed to their physical needs). This is the case with most luxury goods such as jewelry. Also known as *discretionary buying power.* See also **disposable income.**

DISCRIMINANT ANALYSIS   A statistical technique whose goal is to classify research subjects. In discriminant analysis, the researcher identifies two or more groups to which a person or object could belong. The researcher then determines the discriminating variables that can be used to assign each entity to one of the groups and, thus, predict that group membership. Discriminant analysis is used, for example, to identify what consumer traits are associated with particular brand preferences.

DISPLAY ADVERTISING   Print advertising that appears in the editorial section of a publication and usually features creative use of color and illustrations to maximize communication effectiveness. Display ads vary in size and design. Large display ads attract readers' attention, as does use of color (as opposed to black-and-white ads). Display advertising is different from **classified advertising,** which are print ads categorized under separate headings (e.g., employment, real estate, business opportunities).

DISPLAY LOADER   A premium that is built into a manufacturer's **point-of-purchase** display and that the retailer gets to keep after the display is dismantled. For example, a liquor store display loader may be an oversized bottle of scotch in the shape of a cannon for a special

Fourth of July promotion. After the promotion ends, the retailer disassembles the exhibit and keeps the display loader. See also **trade promotion.**

DISPOSABLE INCOME   The money an individual has to spend after having paid federal, state, and local taxes. Disposable income differs from **discretionary income,** which is the money available for spending after taxes have been taken out and personal necessities have been purchased. Also known as *personal disposable income.*

DISSOCIATIVE GROUP   A **reference group** to which an individual does not seek to belong. The group is one whose values the individual rejects (e.g., a religious cult, an ultra-left-wing political party). Reference groups, which directly or indirectly affect a person's attitudes and behavior, are important to the study of **consumer behavior.**

DISSONANCE-REDUCTION   A type of postpurchase behavior that occurs when a consumer experiences concern over having made the wrong purchase decision. It may occur if the consumer learned new information about the purchased product or heard negative comments about it. The consumer strives to reduce dissonance by seeking more product information (to justify the purchase decision) or by returning the item. Marketers attempt to reduce buyers' postpurchase dissonance. They do so, for example, by sending thank-you or congratulatory letters to purchasers; mailing additional product information (e.g., a booklet on different uses of the item); or highlighting the buyers in company newsletters or promotional materials. See also **buying behavior patterns.**

DISTRIBUTION   1. The series of steps involved in delivering a product from its manufacturer to the ultimate consumer. Distribution decisions involve determining which **channels of distribution** to employ and the number of outlets through which a product will be sold. Companies have three distribution alternatives. **Intensive distribution** is when the company makes the product available in as many outlets as possible. **Exclusive distribution** entails using one particular outlet to carry the product in a given market. **Selective distribution** is when the product is made available in a select few outlets in a market area. Distribution decisions are extremely important in that they affect virtually all other marketing considerations such as pricing, sales force management, and advertising and promotion expenditures. **2.** The extent to which a given product is carried by retailers—that is, the number of retailers that carry a product as compared to the total number of retailers that could potentially carry it.

DISTRIBUTION MODEL An analytical **model** used to support management decision making in the selection and evaluation of distribution channels. Such models are employed to help determine store and warehouse locations, as well as to assist management decisions regarding logistics and inventory management. For example, a distribution model would be used to identify the attractiveness of a potential store site in terms of the target customers' distance from the site.

DISTRIBUTOR The company or individual (usually a wholesaler) that sells or delivers merchandise to retailers. Distributors act as intermediaries between manufacturers and retailers. Distributors typically maintain inventory from different manufacturers. Retailers acquire products through distributors to save themselves the time and expense involved in procuring different products from multiple manufacturers.

DIVERSIFICATION A corporate growth strategy in which a company attempts to build its business through opportunities outside its current business. Companies may adopt one of the following diversification strategies: **Concentric diversification** involves acquiring products with technical similarities to its existing product line (although the products may appeal to new consumer groups); with **horizontal diversification** the acquired products appeal to the company's current customers but are not directly related to the current product line; **conglomerate diversification** entails acquiring products that are totally unrelated to the company's product line and that require reaching new market segments.

DIVEST STRATEGY The act of selling or liquidating a business or product line. Companies adopt a divest strategy when a product's sales decline and its overall market growth rate is decreasing. Divesting a product is done to avoid anticipated losses. The financial resources that had been supporting the product are often channeled to other company products where the resources may be better used. See also **product life cycle.**

DIVISIONAL ORGANIZATION   A form of corporate organization in which the company is comprised of two or more separate units. These divisions operate as individual profit centers, with each headed by an officer who reports to a senior executive in the parent company. Divisions may be responsible for a given business function or product line. For example, a divisional-organized auto manufacturer would have separate divisions for its cars, trucks, minivans, and utility vehicles.

DOGS   See **growth-share matrix.**

DONUT   A prerecorded television commercial with a "hole" in the middle to insert current information. For example, a supermarket that advertises frequently will produce a donut spot to highlight its products on sale each week. The commercial is standard except for the inserted message. Donut commercials save money by eliminating the need to produce a new commercial for each new product offering or sale announcement.

DOOR-OPENER   Any device or practice designed to create opportunities for sales or new business. In direct marketing for a magazine, for instance, a door-opener may be a free give-away that relates in some way to the publication (e.g., a football schedule booklet produced by a football magazine publisher).

DOOR-TO-DOOR SELLING   See **house-to-house selling.**

DOUBLE-BARRELED QUESTION   A poorly constructed **closed-ended question** in that two answers may apply. A double-barreled question causes confusion for the respondent. A well-structured close-ended question must have answers that are mutually exclusive. That is, the respondent should not feel that more than one answer applies.

DOWNSCALE   Term describing consumers at the lower end of the socioeconomic scale. Downscale consumers are people with low incomes and, typically, low levels of education. **Upscale** describes the affluent consumers with sizable buying power and high levels of education and professional standing.

DRAMATIZATION   A thematic approach to advertising in which a product is portrayed in the context of a real-life situation or probem.

For example, a TV commercial for a car battery shows a helpless young woman stalled on a deserted road because her battery failed. The message in a dramatization commercial relates to how product use will solve the problem. See also **slice-of-life advertising.**

DRIVE TIME   The time periods during which a radio station has its highest listenership. *Morning-drive* time is from 6 A.M. to 10 A.M., Monday through Friday. *Afternoon-drive* time is between 3 P.M. and 7 P.M., Monday through Friday. Drive time generally coincides with a metropolitan area's traffic rush hours. The term reflects the large number of automobile radios in use at those times. Drive time is the equivalent of television's **prime time** in that its high audience figures command the most expensive advertising rates. See also **dayparts.**

DROP DATE   A direct-mail term referring to the date on which a promotional mailing enters the postal system. Drop dates often coincide with a particular season or event. For instance, a direct-mail advertising program for summer clothes would have a drop date in early spring. This would enable consumers to receive the promotional information in advance of the buying season for such merchandise.

DROP-IN   A local television commercial that airs during a network broadcast. For example, a network movie will have drop-in commercials by local car dealerships or retailers. Stations are allowed to sell a prescribed amount of time for drop-in commercials per hour of programming. See also **commercial time.**

DROP SHIPMENT   The selling arrangement in which retailers promote goods to which they do not take title. Rather, the promoted goods go directly from the supplier to the customer: The goods are "drop shipped" to the customer. Drop-shipment arrangements usually involve large items (e.g., refrigerators) that are very costly to keep in inventory and to ship. Drop-shipment suppliers generally charge a premium to retailers, who, in turn, pass on the added cost to consumers.

DUB   **1.** The process of reproducing an audiotape or videotape. A dub is created by taking the master print and copying it onto blank cassettes. For example, dubs of a broadcast commercial are produced for distribution to the various stations that will air the spot. Also known as *dupe.* **2.** The process of blending sound into a previously recorded sound track, or combining two or more pieces of video footage into one film. See also **generation.**

DUMMY   A graphic artist's term describing a preliminary layout of a printed promotional piece (e.g., an ad or brochure). The dummy indicates where copy and illustrations will appear and how the pages will be laid out. Dummies are produced to show clients how the printed piece will look upon completion. They are usually prepared for client approval prior to developing the mechanical art.

DUMPING   Selling goods in another country at a price higher than that sold in the seller's own country. For example, steel produced in a foreign country has been dumped when its price is well below the prevailing market price of steel in the country to which it has been exported. Companies that dump products do so to seize market share from competitors.

DURABLE GOODS   Consumer products used over a long period of time. Examples are automobiles, furniture, and large appliances. The sale of durable goods usually requires a high degree of customer service by the seller and lengthy guarantees. Also known as *hard goods*.

DWELLING UNITS   Places of residence where a single person, family, or group of cohesive yet unrelated people live. Dwelling units include single-family homes, townhouses, and apartment buildings (*multiple dwelling units*). Residents of dwelling units generally purchase goods in common. For example, shopping for food and home furnishings is done to satisfy the unit members' collective needs. Mailing lists may be acquired according to dwelling units. A direct-mail campaign for lawn mowers, for instance, would require a dwelling unit list of single-family homes since these properties generally have lawns. (A mailing list of apartments would not be effective in this case.)

E

ECONOMIC ENVIRONMENT See **macroenvironment.**

ECONOMIC INDICATORS Government or commercial indices that reflect economic activity and general business conditions. There are several types: *measures of overall economic performance* (such as the gross national product); *price indices* (like the Consumer Price Index and the Producer Price Index); *labor market conditions* (the unemployment rate); *money and credit market indicators* (such as the Dow Jones Industrial Average, treasury bill rates); *index of leading market indicators* (e.g., money supply, the number of building permits issued); and *measures of major product markets* (such as housing starts or retail sales). Marketers analyze economic indicators when making strategic planning decisions and when projecting demand for goods and services.

ECONOMIES OF SCALE A manufacturer's savings realized by producing a large number of units. For example, it would be extremely costly to produce small amounts of a product whose raw material costs are high. However, as the number of units produced increases, the manufacturer can realize greater production and purchasing efficiencies by acquiring bulk quantities of raw materials at discounted rates. Thus, the larger the production, the lower the per-unit manufacturing costs.

ECONOMIES OF SCOPE The ability of a manufacturer to offer wide product variety while still markedly limiting the costs incurred for manufacturing and distribution.

ECONOMY PACK A sales promotion technique in which two or more items are packaged together to effect savings to the consumer.

An economy pack may feature "two for the price of one," known as a *price pack;* or it can be a *banded pack,* in which two related products are packaged together and priced at a favorable rate (e.g., a package containing toothpaste and a toothbrush).

EDITORIAL CALENDAR   A list of articles to be included in a magazine's upcoming issues. Editorial calendars are distributed to advertisers who use the calendars in planning their magazine media buys and publicity programs. For example, an industrial magazine's editorial calendar might indicate that its November issue is devoted to *computer-integrated manufacturing (CIM).* Thus, manufacturers of computer equipment or firms providing CIM consulting services might want to advertise in this issue. Moreover, public relations professionals serving such companies would attempt to place news items or feature articles in the issue. Editorial calendars are distributed well in advance (generally at the start of the calendar year) to give advertisers time to plan their insertions. Each issue's editorial and advertising **closing dates** are indicated on the calendars. Editorial calendars are included in the **media kits** issued to advertisers.

EDITORIAL COPY   Any reading material in a publication, not including advertising. Editorial copy includes articles, guest columns, departments, op-ed pages, and special sections. Editorial copy is prepared by staffers of the publication or by contributors. It is sometimes referred to simply as *editorial.*

EFFIE AWARD   Award granted by the New York chapter of the American Marketing Association to advertising agencies and their clients whose ad campaigns successfully meet the stated objectives. Entries for these annual awards are judged by a panel of agency executives, advertisers, and other marketing association representatives. Effie Awards are presented each June for campaigns that appeared in the preceding 12-month period from October through September. Gold, silver, and bronze Effie Awards are given to winners.

800-NUMBER   A toll-free telephone number arranged for by a company that enables consumers to order goods and services. These numbers are also used for consumers to obtain product details, voice complaints, or get questions answered by the customer service representatives manning the phone lines. Companies pay to receive 800-

number calls based on high-volume discount rates. Using a toll-free number is more costly than handling customer communications via the mail, but the benefits justify the expense. Toll-free numbers provide customers with fast and personal service. Thus, the speed and facility with which consumers can order products are valuable sales features. For this reason, 800-numbers are nearly always included in brochures and catalogs and are used in various forms of direct-response advertising. See also **900-number.**

ELASTIC DEMAND   Colloquially, the market situation in which market demand for a product increases substantially when there is a decrease in price. Technically, elastic demand refers to when a price decrease causes the percentage increase in the quantity of a product sold to exceed the percentage drop in price. See also **price elasticity of demand.**

ELECTRONIC CATALOG   A communications medium that combines the features of a printed catalog with the benefits of video technology. Electronic catalogs are freestanding units with TV monitors that display merchandise information with product illustrations, descriptions, and prices. Electronic catalogs feature a keyboard that is used by the viewers to select the product(s) for which they want information. Some electronic catalogs permit product ordering directly from the display. These are called *interactive systems.* (*Noninteractive* electronic catalogs require use of a telephone or other communications medium to order products.) Electronic catalogs are placed in retail stores and in high-traffic public locations such as shopping malls. See also **video systems.**

ELECTRONIC MAIL   Messages exchanged between people on a computer network. Correspondence is transmitted via telephone lines by persons using computers equipped with modems. E-mail systems employ *electronic mailboxes,* which refer to the codes that enable users to direct messages to specific recipients. Many companies link themselves to customers via electronic mail systems. Companies use E-mail to receive product orders as well as to communicate company information of interest to customers (sales, special promotions, price changes).

ELECTRONIC MARKETING   The practice of using electronically generated consumer purchase data in marketing and sales promotion programs. Electronic marketing has been used in some supermarkets. Here, the retailer tracks product purchases by consumers, using this information to subsequently target buyers with direct mailings of coupons for the same or complementary products. These supermarkets generate information by having customers use computer-readable cards (employing **bar code** scanner technology) that log data on their product purchases. See also **micromarketing.**

EMBARGO   The publicity practice of issuing a news release with the caveat that it not be used by the news media until after the date or time indicated on the release. See also **release date.**

EMOTIONAL APPEAL   An advertising approach in which the message seeks to evoke a positive or negative reaction in the consumer. The appeal is designed to create tension in the consumer that can be alleviated by purchasing the advertised product. Emotional appeals may play on consumers' fears, guilt, shame, or sexual desires. They tell consumers what they should do (e.g., get a physical, brush their teeth, stay in school,) or what they shouldn't do (e.g., smoke cigarettes, drink alcohol, do drugs). See also **fear appeal.**

EMPLOYEE COMMUNICATIONS   The communications function concerned with disseminating relevant company news and information to employees. Employee communications departments produce newsletters, brochures, and various audiovisual media. Topics include the organization's benefits and compensation program, staff promotions and executive changes, and financial performance information. From a marketing standpoint, employee communications are important to keep staff informed about product or service introductions, customer-service programs, and newly formed alliances with other companies. A company may have a group dedicated solely to coordinating employee communications, or the function may be resident in the organization's public relations department.

END-AISLE DISPLAY   A **point-of-purchase advertising** display used to highlight special promotions and merchandise offerings in supermarkets and discount variety stores. The display, situated at the end of an aisle of shelves, stacks the product so as to be readily accessible to shoppers. Copy and illustrations used on the exhibit are usually the same as other communications in the promotional campaign, such as advertising and coupons. End-aisle displays are designed to catch the consumer's eye and attract attention in order to spark sales of the featured product.

ENDLESS CHAIN   A **prospecting** technique in which sellers solicit referrals from customers, and then solicit other names from the people to whom they were originally referred. Subsequently, each person contacted is asked to provide more names, thus creating a "chain" of referrals. The process can continue indefinitely (hence the term *endless*).

ENDORSEMENT   Advertising that uses a well-known or otherwise respected person who recommends use of the advertised product. For example, a doctor is used to espouse the benefits of a new kind of medication. See also **celebrity endorsement.**

END-USER   See **consumer.**

ENGEL'S LAW   The economic theory stating that as a person's income increases, less money is spent on necessities and more is spent on luxury items. Specifically, as an individual's **disposable income** and **discretionary income** rise, the percentage of income spent on food decreases; the amount spent on housing and clothing remains constant; and the money expended on recreation, education, and luxury goods increases.

ENVIRONMENTAL ANALYSIS   The process of evaluating a company's external environment for marketing planning purposes. Environmental analysis is undertaken to assess the political, cultural, social, and economic forces that may impact the company and its marketing initiatives. The analysis seeks to identify trends that may affect company activities. An environmental analysis is often included in the *situational analysis* section of a marketing plan. See also **macroenvironment.**

ENVIRONMENTAL FORECASTING   The process of anticipating future events to develop strategic plans. Environmental forecasting relates to an organization's attempt to adapt its corporate strategies to a changing environment. Certain market research firms sell forecasting data relating to environmental projections of the economy, population, and technology. Larger organizations have in-house departments that generate forecasting information (e.g., a multinational company's forecasting department studies worldwide forces affecting the company's operations).

ERRATIC DEMAND   Market situation in which demand for a product fluctuates due to seasonal or other environmental variables. For example, the demand for large cars varies according to the price of oil and gasoline at a given point in time. See also **seasonal demand.**

ERROR   In research, the term describing the inherent imperfections in selecting respondents or in recording data. Error is considered to be either *sampling error* or *nonsampling error.*

Sampling error refers to the fact that no probability sample will ever represent the exact characteristics of the total population. Researchers, therefore, must identify the probable difference between survey results and the comparable population figures. The level of sampling error decreases as the sample size increases (although sampling error can never completely disappear). Thus, researchers analyzing survey data apply a **confidence range,** which indicates the range around survey findings for which there's a high statistical probability that the numbers will represent the true population parameter. For example, assume a probability sample of 2,000 households has been drawn to see how many own a VCR. The sample indicates that 40% of the households own one. In this case, the 40% figure would have a confidence range of plus or minus 2% (38–42%) at the 95% confidence level, which means that the chances are 95 out of 100 that the confidence range includes the true percentage of VCR ownership for the entire population.

Nonsampling error describes error that cannot be attributed to the sampling method. Nonsampling error, for instance, can result from respondents not understanding the survey question (and therefore answering it incorrectly), from researchers making mistakes in recording data, or from **keypunching** errors.

ETHNIC MEDIA   Any print or broadcast media designed specifically for a particular nationality group. Most ethnic media are written in the language of the target group. Using such media is effective when selling products widely used by the group's members. Examples of ethnic media are Hispanic television stations and Russian-language newspapers.

EURO-AD   Advertising designed to have mass appeal to consumers in all countries comprising the unified European market. Euro-ads are similar in message, execution, and production standards. They may differ in the language spoken. Euro-ads were created in response to a key dilemma facing companies engaged in Pan-European marketing: overcoming technical and cultural differences in multinational communications without having to produce different advertising for each country.

EUROBRAND   Consumer products that carry the same brand name and are marketed similarly throughout Europe. Marketing of Eurobrands generally involves cross-cultural advertising that appeals to consumers in different countries **(Euro-ads)**. *Note:* Eurobrands also describe the select products that companies kept on the market after reducing their product lines, which many large consumer-product companies did in preparing for the unified European market. One company, for instance, reduced the number of its brands of soap from 10 to 3.

EUROPEAN ECONOMIC COMMUNITY (EEC OR EC)   The economic union of 12 European countries: Belgium, Denmark, France, Germany, Greece, Ireland, Italy, Luxembourg, the Netherlands, Portugal, Spain, and the United Kingdom. The original EC was officially formed in 1958 under the Treaty of Rome. It was established with the goal of effecting economic integration: specifically, abolishing tariffs and quotas and other trade restrictions among the member countries. The EC has cited 1992 as the year when economic unity will become fully realized. (The term *1992* has become synonymous with the integration initiative.) When this occurs, the EC will represent a market of some 320 million consumers. Thus, the European unification is quite significant from a marketing standpoint. Companies from the United States and many other countries are readying themselves to compete in the unified European market. They are doing so by establishing manufacturing and distribution capabilities in countries comprising the EC, or they are forming joint ventures with companies already operating there.

EUROPEAN FREE TRADE ASSOCIATION (EFTA)   A consortium of the countries Austria, Finland, Iceland, Norway, Sweden, and Switzerland. The EFTA was established with the Stockholm Convention of 1959. Its goal was to bring about free trade in industrial goods among the member nations, as well as to expand trade in agricultural products. Similar to the goal of the **European Economic Community,**

the EFTA sought to abolish tariffs and other trade restrictions. *Note:* The United Kingdom was originally a member of the EFTA, but subsequently left to join the EC.

EVALUATIVE RESEARCH   The process of adding value judgments to descriptive data. Researchers compare the data to other data to subjectively contrast or correlate the findings. This is done to identify cause and effect relationships and to develop predictive findings. See also **descriptive research; predictive research.**

EVENTS MARKETING   Marketing tactic in which events are used as a sales promotion and/or public relations activity. Examples are company sponsorships of concerts, film festivals, sporting events, and street fairs. Events give companies the opportunity to create their own medium. That is, events establish an environment that attracts members of a target market where those individuals can be given company information, product samples, and promotional items. Special events often involve appearances by celebrities. For example, one company's events marketing program involved sponsoring a famous rock group's North American tour. The company publicized its sponsorship and advertised the events in newspapers, on television, and on radio. Product samples were distributed at the concerts, as were promotional items such as t-shirts.

EXCHANGE   The objective of all marketing activity; the process by which people give items of comparable value to each other to meet their respective wants and needs (e.g., money in exchange for goods and services). There are several conditions required for an exchange to occur: There must be at least two people, each providing something of value; each must be able to furnish the item or service; and each must be able to accept or refuse the other's offer. To finalize an exchange, there must be mutually agreeable conditions to the sale, a time and place for it to occur, and (in most cases) a contract governing the agreement. Also known as *transaction.*

EXCLUSIVE DISTRIBUTION   The strategic decision by a manufacturer to make its product available in a given market through only one distributor. Exclusive distribution gives the seller territorial rights to offer the product. In such an arrangement, the distributor benefits from the absence of competition by other distributors and the manufacturer enjoys increased commitment on the part of the distributor to market the product. Exclusive distribution is generally used for high-priced, upscale products such as jewelry and expensive cars. Exclusive distribution is the opposite of **intensive distribution,** in which a product is made available in as many outlets as possible. See also **selective distribution.**

EXCLUSIVITY 1. The arrangement between an advertiser and an advertising medium to have no competing products advertised in the same issue or show as the advertiser's products. Securing an exclusivity arrangement usually requires that the advertiser purchase large amounts of space (print) or time (broadcast). See also **competitive separation.** 2. When a public relations professional offers only one news medium a particular story idea. That is, the PR representative agrees not to give another (competing) news medium the story before the first medium prints or airs it. The first medium, thus, has an "exclusive" on the story.

EXPANSIBILITY OF DEMAND The extent to which market demand for a product can be increased by altering the degree of advertising or personal selling. An expansible market is one in which increasing promotional activities can elevate demand (e.g., promoting golf as a recreational activity can lead to more people taking up the game). A market is inexpansible when escalated promotion does little to boost demand (e.g., generically promoting higher education may have little effect on increasing college enrollments).

EXPERIENCE-CURVE PRICING Pricing strategy in which the seller sets a low price to generate a high volume of sales, thereby resulting in a reduction in the average cost per unit. Companies typically engage in experience-curve pricing periodically. That is, they do so at strategic times when it is necessary or desirable to lessen their average unit costs.

EXPERIMENTAL GROUP See **test group.**

EXPERIMENTAL RESEARCH The most scientifically valid research technique. Experimental research involves statistical analyses in which **independent variables** are controlled or manipulated to observe changes in a **dependent variable**—that is, to identify cause-and-effect relationships between those variables. Experimental research usually involves selecting matched sets of respondents (**test**

groups and **control groups**) and exposing them to different treatments. The goal is to determine whether observed differences in responses between those groups are statistically significant. See also **exploratory research; survey research.**

EXPERT SYSTEMS Computer-based systems designed to solve technical or management problems with a level of expertise comparable to that of human experts. Expert systems, a type of *artificial intelligence,* are designed to simulate human reasoning. The systems are based on quantitative and qualitative data (e.g., facts and relationships between facts) that have been developed by human experts. Each system has a knowledge base that can make logical inferences on the knowledge while offering appropriate answers to the problems being addressed. Often, the software provides reasons for the answers it gives. In marketing, expert systems are used in testing advertising messages, as well as executions of those messages in the marketplace. See also **models.**

EXPLORATORY RESEARCH The phase of marketing research that involves gathering preliminary data to reveal the nature of a marketing situation and to gain ideas and insights. Often, hypotheses are developed based on the findings of exploratory research. Exploratory research is useful in breaking down vague problem statements into more precise statements.

EXPOSURE The opportunity for a person to receive an advertising message in a given medium. Both the quantity and quality of exposures are important to advertisers. An advertising medium with a large audience has the potential for many exposures. However, the qualitative aspect of exposures ties to the nature of the medium (e.g., reaching architects with information about a new building product in an architectural magazine yields better exposures than advertising the product in a food publication).

EXPRESSED WARRANTY A written or spoken promise by sellers relating to what they will do if the goods they sell are defective or fail to perform as expected. An expressed warranty applies for a stated period of time. This period begins when the buyer receives a warranty application, not when the product is actually purchased. See also **implied warranty.**

EYE CAMERA   A mechanical device used to observe and measure the eye movements of people reading an advertisement. There are two basic types of eye camera. One takes still pictures of a small spot of light reflected from the eye. The other takes moving pictures of the eye, illustrating changes in the diameter of the respondent's pupil. Eye cameras are used in **copy testing** to see what parts of the text attract the reader's attention. The device identifies where the reader's eyes land first and how long they remain on a given spot. Eye cameras yield information that is used in planning copy layout— that is, in determining the size and placement of type, headlines, and illustrations. See also **advertising testing.**

F

FACING   The exterior surface of a billboard or the position of billboards in relation to each other. For example, with *double facing* two billboards are adjacent and visible from the same direction. *Triple facing* refers to three adjacent billboards visible from the same direction, and so on.

FACTOR ANALYSIS   Analytical technique used to reduce a large volume of research data into a smaller number of categories. Factor analysis is utilized to identify interrelationships among a set of variables to facilitate studying those variables. For example, research data relating to respondents' heights and weights could be categorized into the general category of *size;* or respondents' various hobbies and recreational activities could be combined under the heading *lifestyle.* Here, multiple variables are condensed into general categories to simplify the data analysis.

FACT SHEET   An informational document included in a **press kit** or a package of sales literature. A fact sheet provides data on a company, a product, or special project. Data included on a fact sheet are usually found in other materials in the compilation. However, the data are structured to present the essential descriptive details in a simple, easy-to-read listing. For example, a fact sheet about a new commercial office building would list information in a line-by-line format: height—50 stories; square footage—300,000; exterior—flamed granite.

FAD PATTERN   The demand pattern of a product that quickly achieves great popularity but loses it just as fast. Fad products typically receive a great deal of publicity and enjoy high sales in a short period of time (e.g., the "pet rock" craze). Other fad products become popular every few years (e.g., the hula hoop). Fad products have very short **product life cycles** because such items rarely satisfy important consumer needs. They are usually bought by persons seeking excitement or to distinguish themselves as owning products that are in vogue.

FAIR PACKAGING AND LABELING ACT   Federal legislation enacted in 1966 that requires manufacturers to identify on their packaging the type of product, the contents (ingredients and quantities), and the seller's name and address. The legislation was enacted to ensure that manufacturers don't mislead consumers on product ingredients, or fail to highlight specific safety warnings regarding product contents and usage. The Fair Packaging and Labeling Act is an important consideration for new product manufacturers because they must ensure that they're meeting all government labeling requirements before introducing a new product.

FALLING DEMAND STATE   The market situation in which a product's demand is decreasing due to social or environmental forces. These forces diminish consumers' collective desire to obtain the product or service. For example, college enrollments decline due to shifts in the demographic composition of the market (e.g., fewer college-age people in the market). Marketers faced with products in a falling demand state attempt to restimulate sales either by targeting different consumers, adding new product attributes/benefits, or developing new promotional strategies. See also **demand states.**

FAMILY BRAND   Individual products developed by the same company that carry the same **brand name.** Family brand products use the manufacturer's name and a product descriptor. Examples are Heinz ketchup and Heinz pickles. Employing a family brand approach to product naming is a **branding** strategy. The key benefit of this approach is the ability to easily effect a **brand extension.** That is, the new item can benefit from the established reputation of products already using the brand name.

FAMILY LIFE CYCLE   A sociological concept referring to the changes to a family's composition over time. Family life cycle reflects the variations wrought by births, deaths, marriages, divorces, and so on. Changes in a family's makeup spawn changes in its financial income and buying and behavioral patterns. Marketers can define target markets according to the family's stage in the life cycle. Categories delineating these life cycle stages include:

- *bachelor stage*—young single people who do not live at home
- *newly married couples*—those with no children
- *full nest I*—the youngest child is under age 6
- *full nest II*—the youngest child is over age six
- *full nest III*—older married couples with dependent chidren
- *empty nest I*—older married couples with no children residing in the house and the head of the household is still in the work force
- *empty nest II*—older married couples with no children in the household and the head of the household is no longer working
- *solitary survivors*—older persons living alone, either in the work force or retired

FAMILY PACKAGING   The process of creating variations on a standard package design (or a specific packaging element) to visually and psychologically link related brands. That is, the packages are made similar to show consumers that the products are made by the same manufacturer, for example Oreo cookies. The original brand, as well as the chocolate-covered and double-stuffed versions, all feature the same cellophane packaging, and there are only slight variations of the **brand mark**. See also **family brand.**

FANFOLD   See **accordion fold.**

FANTASY ADVERTISING   A thematic approach to developing advertising (usually for television commercials), which involves using special effects or cartoon characters to create a fantasy situation to sell the product. Popular examples of fantasy advertising are the Jolly Green Giant used to sell frozen vegetables and the Keebler elves, cartoon characters who make baked goods in a tree-house cookie factory.

FASHION CYCLE   Concept similar to the **product life cycle** in that it tracks the market growth and decline stages of fashion products— that is, designs, patterns, and styles. There are three stages of the fashion cycle: *Distinctiveness* is when the fashion is first sought, usually by trendsetters; *emulation* is marked by growing popularity of the fashion as followers begin wearing it; *economic stage* is when the style becomes mass marketed, usually at prices significantly lower than the fashion's original cost.

FEAR APPEALS   An **emotional appeal** made in advertising in which the message is intended to create anxiety in the consumer. The goal is to move the consumer to purchase the advertised product to eliminate this fear. Fear appeals are often used to sell health and beauty aids. For example, fear of social rejection is employed to sell dandruff shampoo via commercials that show unsightly dandruff ruining a person's social life.

FEATURES-BENEFIT SELLING   A salesperson's attempt to convince a prospect to purchase goods or services by discussing a product's attributes and the advantages they will bring to the prospect. For instance, an insurance salesperson will highlight a policy's feature (the ability to accumulate savings) and immediately cite its benefit (offering insurance coverage while also providing an investment vehicle to the buyer).

FEDERAL COMMUNICATIONS COMMISSION (FCC)   The federal governmental agency responsible for regulating the broadcast and telecommunications industries. The FCC designates wavelengths for radio and television stations and issues licenses to them. The FCC, comprised of seven commissioners who are appointed by the president, reports to Congress. See also **call letters.**

FEDERAL TRADE COMMISSION (FTC)   The federal governmental agency responsible for enforcing the Federal Trade Commission Act of 1914, which prohibits unfair methods of competition and business practices. In general, the FTC protects the American free-enterprise system to ensure competition and a strong economy. Consisting of five commissioners, the FTC investigates improprieties in interstate and foreign commerce. The FTC issues **cease-and-desist orders** to prevent unfair methods of competition. See also **consumer protection legislation.**

FEEDBACK   The response from an audience after receiving an advertising message. Marketers cull information from feedback studies to assess how well the message was received and/or to gauge consumer attitudes after having received the message. See also **advertising testing.**

FEE SYSTEM OF COMPENSATION   A method of paying an advertising agency. Under the fee system, an agency will estimate the total cost of its services for the year. The agency projects its hourly costs for creative, media, and account management services. Then the firm generally adds a 25% charge to cover overhead expenses and to realize a profit. Media purchases are billed at their published rates, less the 15% **agency commission.** Materials and expenses incurred from using outside vendors are billed at cost.

FIELD SALES MANAGERS   Sales managers who sell products to customers in the buyers' places of residence or business. Field sales managers may be assigned by region, district, branch, or product categories. In addition to selling, field sales managers are responsible for managing staff salespeople, which includes recruiting, training, and assigning territorial duties to them.

:15   Designation for a 15-second television or radio commercial, as indicated on a script.

FINANCIAL ADVERTISING   Advertising by financial services companies directed at organizations operating in the financial industry or at the investing public (shareholders and potential shareholders). Financial advertisers include investment firms, banks, and insurance companies. Among the products and services they advertise are financial planning, as well as the sale of insurance policies, mutual funds, and other investment vehicles. Some types of financial advertising are regulated by the Securities and Exchange Commission (SEC). For example, advertising of public securities offerings requires that certain information be included in all ad copy. See also **tombstone ad.**

FINDER'S FEE   Payment to an intermediary who brings together people in a business transaction. The finder may be an individual or a company; for example, a dentist receives a finder's fee for sending patients to a periodontist. The fee may be a percentage of the value of the deal or profit resulting from it, or it may be a standard rate (e.g., $500 for each patient the dentist sends to the periodontist).

FINISH   In printing, the texture of a given paper stock. Examples of paper finishes are glossy (coated) stock, dull finish, and textured. Different paper finishes are used for different types of printed materials. For instance, an expensive brochure might feature glossy finish paper for its covers. Letterhead and business cards, however, might employ paper with a textured finish.

FIRST-CLASS MAIL   The most expensive rate for mailing materials since it provides the fastest delivery (aside from special next-day delivery service). The high cost of sending materials via first-class mail is why large-scale promotional mailings are rarely sent that way. An exception would be if the direct mailer wants to avoid conveying the appearance of a promotional mailing and, thus, uses first-class stamps as opposed to metered mail.

FIXED COSTS   Costs that remain constant irrespective of the volume of production and/or sales activity. Examples of fixed costs are insurance, rent, and depreciation. *Total fixed costs* describe the sum of such costs incurred in producing a product. *Average fixed costs* is the quotient resulting from dividing the total fixed costs by the number of units produced. See also **variable costs.**

FIXED LOCATION/POSITION   **1.** The space in a periodical that carries an ad by the same advertiser in two or more consecutive issues. **2.** A broadcast media term referring to a time period on radio or TV for which an advertiser's commercial has been reserved. *Note:* Securing a fixed location or position may require the advertiser to pay a surcharge. That is, the advertiser may be charged a fee above the medium's **base rate** for the specified space or time. See also **preferred position.**

FLACK   Derogatory term for a public relations professional or press agent. Flack is used by journalists to describe PR representatives who are uncooperative with newspeople in the latter's research (such as when they are seeking information on a negative story relating to the publicist's client). The term is also used to describe PR persons who are overly aggressive in pitching story ideas to the news media.

FLAGGING   Graphics or copy on a product package that highlight a particular product feature or offer. Examples of flagging are "50 cents off regular price!" or "special bonus pack!" Flagging may also be used on store shelves to call attention to the special offering. See also **shelf talker.**

FLANKING   The **marketing warfare** strategy for companies trailing the leader in a given product market. The strategy calls for "attacking" a market that does not exist. This entails heeding the three principles of flanking: (1) The flanking move must be made into an uncontested area, creating a new or exclusive aspect to the product; (2) tactical surprise is important to keep competitors from quickly responding to the move; (3) pursuit is just as critical as the attack itself—that is, companies should protect their newly won position by aggressively marketing to boost their market standing.

FLAT RATE   A product cost that is standard for all buyers irrespective of volume purchases or other considerations. For example, some sellers offer a discount on the per-unit price of an item if the buyer purchases the product in quantity. Conversely, selling at a flat rate means the buyer always pays the same price per unit, regardless of volume or other factors. See also **variable pricing.**

FLIER   A one-page promotional piece generally printed on regular 8½" by 11" paper, with copy appearing on both sides. Fliers are distributed to consumers at retail outlets, or they are handed out on street corners or left under car windshield wipers. Fliers are inexpensive to produce. However, many consumers tend to only glance at them or ignore them completely. Also known as a *circular* or *handbill*.

FLIGHT SATURATION   The point at which too much advertising of a product within a brief period of time creates a negative influence on the advertising's effectiveness. Excessive advertising can cause annoyance on the part of consumers, who may stop buying the advertised product for this reason.

FLIPPING   **1.** The use of a remote control device by a television viewer trying to decide which program to watch. The viewer flips through programs, watching a few seconds of each until he or she decides on a particular show. **2.** Sometimes, channel changing during commercials, although this is more commonly referred to as *zapping*.

FLUSH RIGHT/LEFT   See **justification.**

FOCUS GROUP A group interview involving members of a target market, conducted as part of the exploratory stage of marketing research. Focus groups consist of 6 to 10 people and an interviewer who directs the discussion, asking questions to elicit information on the participants' feelings, needs, perceptions, and preferences toward a given issue or product. (To maintain the group members' objectivity, the product is never identified.) Focus groups have an advantage over other personal interview techniques: Small-group dynamics typically lead people to be more open in their responses. However, the danger of the small-group environment is that one or two participants may dominate the discussion. They, therefore, can influence the other participants' opinions. Focus groups yield qualitative feedback. Their key benefit lies in their ability to identify areas that should be probed further through quantitative research. Focus groups are usually conducted in studios where they can be monitored by researchers and videotaped for subsequent analysis.

FOLLOW-UP LETTER A letter sent by salespeople to consumers who have inquired about a product. For example, a consumer who requests more information about a car will be sent a follow-up letter providing additional product information or answering the consumer's questions. Follow-up letters are sent on an individual basis. They are never mass mailed.

FOOD AND DRUG ADMINISTRATION (FDA) The federal governmental agency empowered to set standards for the content of foods, food additives, and cosmetics and the labeling thereof. It also establishes the tolerable levels for unwholesome substances that may be used in food processing (e.g., preservatives). All new drugs must be submitted to the FDA for approval. Applications for them must be accompanied by extensive laboratory test results that attest to the drugs' efficacy and safety.

FOOD, DRUG & COSMETICS ACT Federal legislation enacted in 1938 as a replacement for the Federal Food and Drug Act of 1906. The Food, Drug & Cosmetics Act makes illegal the manufacturing, selling, or transporting of adulterated foods and drugs in interstate commerce. It also prohibits the production and distribution of foods and drugs that are fraudulently labeled. The Food, Drug & Cosmetics Act was amended in the Food Additives Amendment of 1958 and the

Kefauver–Harris Amendment of 1962—the latter relating, in part, to requirements for pretesting drugs for safety and efficacy.

FORECASTING MODEL A **model** used in predicting product sales, market share levels, and other marketing variables. An example of a forecasting model is an *econometric model* that offers diagnostic insights into the effects of variations in **marketing mix** combinations (e.g., the size of advertising budgets, sales force composition, distribution channels).

FORMAT **1.** The general content of a radio station's programming. The format may be all news, country-and-western music, or rock and roll. Different radio formats typically attract audiences of similar demographic characteristics, which has obvious ramifications for **media planning** decisions. For instance, a top-40 radio format attracts a largely teenage audience, which is why products such as acne medicine are often advertised on such stations. **2.** Also describes the nature of a particular television program (e.g., a variety show or situation comedy).

FORWARD INTEGRATION A corporate growth strategy in which a company acquires one or more of its wholesalers or retailers. Companies engage in forward integration to achieve greater control over sales in key markets or control over specific distribution channels. See also **integration.**

FOUR-COLOR The printing process that creates an image that is identical to the original illustration. The process involves developing color plates for each primary color (red, yellow, blue) and one for black (to achieve shadows and contrasts). Four-color printing is used in producing advertisements, brochures, catalogs, and other marketing materials. It is more expensive than **two-color.** However, four-color artwork creates vivid images that provide greater impact than two-color or black-and-white reproductions.

4 P'S OF MARKETING See **marketing mix.**

FOURTH-CLASS MAIL Mail sent with low-delivery priority and at a low postage cost. The U.S. Postal Service does not specify a delivery time limt for this mail. Examples of materials sent via fourth-class mail are parcels and books weighing at least one pound. The fact that

books are often sent by fourth-class mail is why this class is sometimes called *book rate*.

FRAME OF REFERENCE   A social-psychological concept referring
to the way a person views his or her external environment. Frame of
reference describes how the individual perceives external stimuli. It
suggests that people learn and make judgments according to their
view of the world (e.g., a positive, idealistic perspective that colors a
person's general outlook). Studying **consumer behavior** in part involves determining the commonality of consumers' frames of reference as influenced by the groups to which they belong.

FRANCHISING   1. Selling arrangement in which a company (the
franchisor) grants the rights to a person or another company (the
franchisee) to distribute the franchisor's products or services. The
arrangement stipulates that the franchisee will operate its business
according to the practices established by the franchisor, including
using the franchisor's products, promotional materials, and other
company support. The franchisee operates the business using the
trademark and trade name owned by the franchisor. Examples of
franchise businesses are McDonald's, Jiffy Lube, and Midas Mufflers.
2. Also refers to when a government agency grants a license to a
cable TV operator to provide cable service in a particular market.

FREE ASSOCIATION   Consumer research technique in which a
respondent is given a word and asked to verbalize the first word or
phrase that comes to his or her mind. Free association interviewing
is used in advertising research to gauge consumers' knowledge about
and attitudes toward a given product or company. The goal is to
better understand the respondents' buying behavior and purchase
decision making. Also known as *word association*.

FREELANCER   A person who works independently and is hired on
a project-by-project basis. Freelancers in advertising include copywriters, artists, photographers, producers, and directors. Freelancers
are often paid a base fee plus money to cover out-of-pocket expenses
(e.g., materials, transportation); or they may be paid a single fee to
cover their professional time and expenses incurred.

FREE-ON-BOARD (FOB)   Shipping designation indicating at what
location the title to goods transfers from seller to buyer. Consider the

designation FOB/factory, which means that the seller's factory is where the control and title to the goods pass to the buyer.

FREE SAMPLES   Product samples that are distributed at no cost to consumers to allow them to try the product and to encourage future purchases. Free samples are usually packaged in quantities smaller than the actual product package. Such samples are called *trial-size* containers. Free samples are often delivered to consumers via direct mail or are distributed in **events marketing** programs. Issuing free samples is a popular sales promotion technique employed frequently in new product introductions.

FREESTANDING INSERT (FSI)   A printed page or booklet containing promotional information that's inserted into a separate periodical (usually a newspaper). The material is freestanding because it is not printed by the publication or bound into it. Newspaper distributors, which handle the insertion process, charge advertisers a premium to do so. FSIs are used to announce special promotions or to provide consumers with coupons.

FREQUENCY   **1.** The number of times an advertisement or commercial appears during a specified period of time. **2.** Also used as an average to indicate the number of times the communication has been viewed by a person or household during a specified time period. *Average frequency* is determined by dividing the total possible audience by the number of people who have actually been exposed to the communication at least once. Frequency is an important consideration in **media planning. 3.** The Federal Communications Commission designation of wavelength allocations for radio and TV stations, as well as for amateur radio operators and CB radio operators.

FRIEND-OF-FRIEND PROMOTION   A promotional technique in which current customers are given incentives for referring to the seller the names of other people who might be interested in the product or service. An example is an airline that grants flyers free travel tickets if they provide referrals to the airline. This promotional technique is similar in concept to **member-get-member promotions.**

FRONT OF BOOK   The part of a magazine (the "book") that appears before the publication's main section of editorial content. Front of book is a **preferred position** for advertising. Thus, some publishers may charge a premium to companies whose advertising is guaranteed a position in the front of the book. See also **back of book.**

FULFILLMENT   The processes involved in meeting customer requests generated through direct-marketing activities. Such requests may be actual orders or customer inquiries or complaints. A company's *fulfillment system* involves these basic activities: responding correctly to customer requests; mailing out products or information promptly; issuing invoices and recording payments; and generating purchase information for use in subsequent marketing initiatives. See also **customer service.**

FULL DEMAND STATE   The **demand state** in which a company has all the business it needs or desires. That is, the company does not need to increase or decrease demand for its products. Marketing management's task in a full demand state is to maintain this level of demand. Consumer preferences may change and competition may increase. Thus, the company must endeavor to preserve product quality while continually gauging consumer satisfaction.

FULL-SERVICE ADVERTISING AGENCY   An advertising agency that offers clients a complete range of advertising services. Full-service firms offer standard advertising capabilities such as creative services and **media planning** and buying. However, they may also provide project planning (including setting advertising strategies and objectives), as well as activities such as film production, publicity, sales promotion, sales training literature, trade show exhibits, and product name testing. See also **limited-service advertising agency.**

FUNCTIONAL ORGANIZATION   A corporate hierarchy that has departmental managers (e.g., in marketing, finance, research and development, production) who report to the chief executive officer (CEO). It is the CEO who provides overall direction and coordinates corporate activity. A functionally organized marketing department, likewise, has its managers (of market research, sales and product planning) reporting to the senior marketing executive.

FULL-SERVICE WHOLESALER   A company that offers the complete range of wholesaler services. For example, a full-service wholesaler carries stock, offers buyers credit terms and management assistance, makes deliveries, and maintains a sales force. See also **limited-service wholesaler.**

FUND-RAISING   The practice of soliciting financial or other contributions from outside interests. Fund-raising is typically associated with nonprofit organizations such as educational, religious, and charitable groups. Political organizations also engage frequently in fund-raising. Among the most common marketing communications techniques used in fund-raising are telemarketing and direct-mail advertising because they enable the fund-raiser to target people who have contributed before or who have shown an interest in the organization.

G

GALLEY PROOFS   Proofs containing typeset materials before they are separated into pages (e.g., for a print advertisement or brochure). Galley proofs are submitted to a proofreader to make corrections, or they are given to the client for final approval prior to the start of printing production. Errors are correctable most easily at this stage. Galley proofs are often referred to simply as *galleys*. See also **blueprint**.

GALLUP ORGANIZATION, INC.   A Princeton, New Jersey–based marketing research firm. Gallup conducts consumer behavior and attitude studies, local market surveys, telephone omnibus surveys, and advertising tracking studies. The company offers worldwide market research capabilities through its Gallup International Affiliates Network.

GALVANOMETER   A laboratory testing device used to assess advertising effectiveness. Galvanometers mechanically measure sweating in the palm of the respondent. This physiological reaction is equated with interest and involvement as a criterion for gauging the effectiveness of advertising. Many marketers question the validity of this research technique. See also **tachistoscope.**

GATEFOLD   A magazine advertising layout in which an extra page is added to the publication's cover or an inside page. The page extends out, thus presenting an additional page. The resultant ad is particularly noticeable due to its very large size. This costly advertising technique is often used for major new product introductions or to unveil a new advertising campaign.

Gatefold

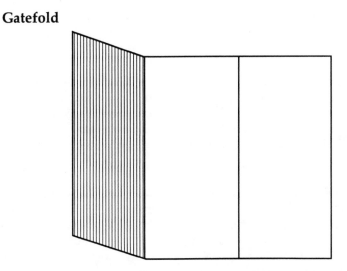

GATT (GENERAL AGREEMENT ON TARIFFS AND TRADE) A multilateral trade agreement enacted in 1948. The goal of the measure was setting rules and principles that liberalize trade between countries—that is, by eliminating tariffs and other barriers to free trade. GATT provides a framework of rules of conduct that govern international trade. Moreover, it provides a mechanism for settling grievances when members maintain that others are in violation of the agreement. See also **European Economic Community.**

GENDER ANALYSIS The process of segregating names on a mailing list into categories of male and female. Marketers do so when selling a product geared specifically to either men (e.g., dress shirts) or women (e.g., cosmetics). Names may be selected based on the designations Mr., Mrs., Miss, or Ms. Lists, however, may not always indicate these titles and the analysis must be done on the basis of first names. Such a gender analysis invariably leads to errors, since some names are used for both sexes (e.g., Robin, Chris, Terry).

GENERAL SALES MANAGER The sales executive responsible for overall coordination of a corporate or divisional sales force. The general sales manager's duties include developing sales policies, strategies, and tactics to support the company's marketing plan. In a large **functional organization** the general sales manager reports to the chief executive officer. Supervision of salespeople in such a hierarchy, however, is the responsibility of the **field sales managers**. In smaller companies the general sales manager supervises all sales-people.

GENERATION   The reproduction of audio and video cassettes from master copies. A copy made from the master is called first-generation tape. A duplication made from that is second-generation tape; a tape made from that is third-generation, and so forth. The clarity and technical quality of the tape diminish with each subsequent generation.

GENERIC PRODUCTS   Products that do not employ a brand name. Rather, they simply cite the product's generic class (e.g., salt, coffee, vitamins) and the manufacturer. Generic products are usually foods and packaged goods. Their packaging is relatively simple, usually including only the generic product name and the required label information. Generic products are significantly less expensive than comparable items. See also **branding.**

GEOGRAPHIC ORGANIZATION   A company whose manufacturing operations are organized geographically. Each unit operates independently but reports to a central corporate headquarters. Geographic organizational units produce the same product but are geographically dispersed to facilitate product distribution. An example is a baked goods company which, due to the need to quickly distribute its perishable products, has production facilities located near its customers. Units in a geographic organization typically handle their own manufacturing and sales. Broader marketing activities are conducted at the corporate level.

GEOGRAPHIC SEGMENTATION   A **market segmentation** technique based on geographic variables. Target markets are defined by neighborhood, city, state, region, or country. Another geographic category is population density (e.g., urban, suburban, rural). A company that geographically segments its markets takes into account the varying consumer preferences in those different areas. For example, a prominent soup company found that consumers in the southwestern United States prefer spicier foods than consumers in the Northeast. The company, consequently, produced a spicy version of one of its soups for sale in the Southwest (while keeping the standard recipe for sales in other regions).

GIFT CLOSE   A salesperson's **closing** technique that seeks to provide a prospect with an added inducement to make the purchase immediately. For example, the salesperson may say, "If you sign this purchase order today, I'll have the product shipped to you tomorrow." The "gift" in a gift close, therefore, is not an actual item. Rather, it is some service performed by the seller to get the prospect to make an on-the-spot purchase decision.

GLOBAL MARKETING   The selling of products in foreign countries using strategies that address the divergent social, cultural, and economic factors in those countries. Global marketing requires different planning from that employed in domestic marketing. A higher level of risk is involved due to fluctuating exchange rates, protectionist barriers, and the high cost of adapting communications. Companies considering global marketing must make decisions relating to the following issues: the foreign country's economic, political, and cultural environment; how to enter the market (either by direct or indirect exporting or through joint ventures with companies in the host country); and the expected **return on investment** vis-à-vis the anticipated level of risk. Also known as *international advertising*. See also **Euro-ad; Eurobrand.**

GOAL FORMULATION   The process of establishing precise points of measurement to pursue corporate objectives. Goals relate to specific levels of magnitude or time. For example, the company's objective may be to increase sales. Its goal, however, would be to increase sales *by 10% over the next six months*. Goals should be as specific and measurable as possible. Companies formulate goals to facilitate management planning, implementation, and controls. See also **marketing plan.**

GOING-RATE PRICING   Strategy in which a company sets its price based on what most competitors are charging for their product or service. A company that adopts this philosophy may set its price slightly higher or lower than the going rate. It will rarely, however, stray too far from the prevailing market price. For example, large oil companies set a price for gasoline. Smaller gasoline retailers who view this as the going rate will charge a few cents more or less than the large companies.

GOOD HOUSEKEEPING SEAL   The Good Housekeeping Institute's seal granted to companies whose products meet consumer protection-oriented specifications set by the institute. Companies granted the seal must advertise the products in *Good Housekeeping* magazine with a minimum page space and frequency determined by the institute. Companies may use the seal on product packages and in ads in other magazines, according to the contractual arrangement with the organization. The Good Housekeeping seal is very well known by the public. It represents an important third-party endorsement of a product. The marketing value of such a seal has spawned the creation of similar designations that attest to healthful products (e.g., low-cholesterol, low-sodium) and those that are environmentally safe.

GOVERNMENT MARKET   The **organizational market** segment comprised of all federal, state, and local government agencies that purchase goods and services. Purchases relate to implementing the main functions of government such as national defense, education, and public welfare. Government buying procedures typically involve open bidding and negotiated contracts. All government buying is overseen by Congress, various budget offices, and private "watchdog" groups. Consequently, government purchasing often involves a myriad of paperwork, lengthy approvals, and slow processing of orders.

GRADE LABELING   A system of classifying products by their respective levels of quality. Grades are either numbers or letters that have been assigned by the government or trade group conducting the evaluation. An example of grade labeling is the designation Grade A (as in poultry) by the U.S. Department of Agriculture. Grade labeling was developed to facilitate comparisons of products by consumers. See also **descriptive labeling.**

GRAPHIC DESIGN   The creation of the visual element of a printed communication such as an advertisement, brochure, sales promotion piece, or product packaging. It involves designing the piece's visual components and preparing the mechanical art from which it will be printed. Included in the process is determining the illustration, typeface, paper stock, colors, and layout. Graphic artists are employed on advertising agency staffs. Some printing and lettershops also offer graphic design services, as do syndicated companies that provide standard designs that are adaptable to different specifications. See also **typography.**

GREEKING   Meaningless words that look like typeset copy that are pasted onto rough layouts of printed materials (e.g., advertisements, brochures). Greeking shows where the copy will be located in the design as well as its type size. Layouts with greeking are usually shown to the art director or account executive for approval. The layouts may also be shown to clients.

GREEN BOOK   An international directory, published annually by the New York chapter of the American Marketing Association, which lists marketing research companies and research service providers. These organizations pay a fee to be listed in the directory. See also **Creative Black Book.**

GREEN MARKETING   The development and promotion of products and/or packaging employing biodegradable components and, in general, protecting the environment. Heightened societal concern over environmental protection prompted green marketing by companies. Examples of specially created "green" products are biodegradable trash bags, disposable diapers, toilet tissue, and food containers, and phosphate-free laundry detergents. The use of biodegradable materials in packaging or product manufacturing has been a creative theme in companies' advertising. Moreover, companies have sponsored special promotions and consumer education campaigns espousing environmental conscientiousness, community recycling, and the use of products made with biodegradable materials.

GROSS AUDIENCE   The total number of viewers, listeners, or readers in a particular audience irrespective of **audience duplication.** That is, the measurement acknowledges that a person may be counted twice in tabulations of two audiences in the same broadcast schedule. Gross audience is different from **cumulative audience,** which indicates the number of people who will be reached at least once with an advertising communication, with an audience member being counted only once. See also **gross rating point.**

GROSS NATIONAL PRODUCT (GNP)   The **economic indicator** that cites the current market value of all goods and services produced in the U.S. economy in a specific time period. GNP consists of personal consumption purchases, private domestic investments, and government spending on goods, services, and investments. GNP statistics are stated in annual terms but are accumulated and released quarterly.

GROSS PROFIT   The numerical difference resulting from subtracting the cost of goods sold from revenues. Gross profit also denotes the difference between the purchase price and the sale price. See also **net profit.**

GROSS RATING POINT (GRP)   A measurement of audience size (viewership or listenership) to quantify a medium's ability to reach a target audience. GRPs are stated in terms of percentage: Each GRP represents 1% of the people or households tuned to a TV program (as compared to the total number of TV sets in the market being studied). GRPs are determined by multiplying the **reach** and **frequency** of the media schedule. Thus, the product of reach and frequency represents the gross duplicated percentage of audience that would be reached by the advertising plan. Comparisons of different media vehicles are often based on their respective **cost per gross rating point.**

GROWTH-SHARE MATRIX   A diagram used in measuring the performance of a company's products, product portfolios, or **strategic business units.** Often referred to as the *Boston box* in recognition of

Growth-Share Matrix

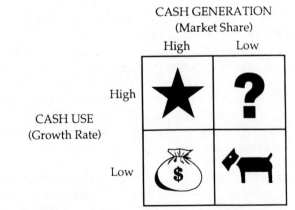

Source: *Perspectives*, No. 135, "The Experience-Curve Reviewed, IV. The Growth-Share Matrix or The Product Portfolio." Reprinted with permission from The Boston Consulting Group, Inc., Boston, Mass. Copyright © 1973.

its creators, the Boston Consulting Group, the matrix contains four quadrants. These indicate the status of units in terms of market growth rate (the grid's vertical axis) and market share (its horizontal axis). Market share is a measurement of the unit's share relative to that of its largest competitor.

Company products and businesses fall into one of the four quadrants according to their positions on the two axes. The units are classified as follows:

• *Question marks*—units that operate in high-growth markets but hold low market share. They require large amounts of financing to cover ongoing costs and to keep pace in the fast-growing market. Question marks are so named because they pose a quandary to management: whether or not to continue supporting them.

• *Stars*—market leaders in high-growth markets. Their high market standing does not mean they necessarily generate positive cash flow for the company because significant financing is required to maintain market share, keep pace with market growth, and fend off competitors.

• *Cash cows*—the most profitable units since they are market leaders in low-growth markets. Cash cows produce enough profits to financially support the company's other products. These units are profitable because the company need not finance capacity expansion (due to slowed market growth) and because they typically benefit from *economies of scale.*

• *Dogs*—units with low market shares in low-growth markets. They require substantial financing and management time. Management must determine the fate of these underperforming units.

Assists in Decision Making

Identifying units' positions in the matrix helps management decide whether or not to continue supporting them. Managers have four basic options:

• *Build*—forgo short-term earnings in an attempt to build long-term market share. This strategy is appropriate for question marks that must grow if they have the potential to become stars.

• *Hold*—maintain existing market share, a strategy necessary for cash cows that must continue to generate positive cash flow.

• *Harvest*—generate short-term cash flow at the expense of long-term profits. It involves reducing expenses to increase profits. This strategy is appropriate for weak cash cows or question marks moving into the dog quadrant.

 • *Divest*—discontinue the product and reinvest resources into other products, which is appropriate for dogs and question marks that the company can no longer afford to finance.

GROWTH STAGE OF THE PRODUCT LIFE CYCLE   See **product life cycle.**

GROWTH STRATEGY   Strategy employed by a company seeking to expand its product's market share at the expense of short-term profits. This is achieved in one of two ways. First, the company may target users of a competitor's product to get them to switch (i.e., attacking its **brand-loyal** customers), or it may target people who have never used the product before. Second, the company can try to expand product use by its current customers (e.g., by promoting new uses of the product).

GUERILLA WARFARE   The **marketing warfare** strategy best employed by small companies battling much larger competitors. Guerilla tactics are based on finding a segment of a market small enough to defend (e.g., based on industry, geographic, or demographic variables). Successful guerilla companies do this by reducing the size of the "battlefield" to achieve superior force. Two other guerilla warfare principles are (1) guerillas must never adopt the marketing or organizational practices of brand leaders, regardless of how successful the former become; and (2) guerilla companies must respond decisively to market changes by exiting the market when circumstances dictate. See also **niche marketing.**

H

HABITUAL BUYING   A consumer's repeated purchase of a product, done so out of habit as opposed to **brand loyalty.** Habitual buying is characterized by low consumer involvement in the purchase decision. That is, little thinking and price-comparison shopping are done. For example, a consumer will regularly buy the same brand of salt because he or she is familiar with it and because there is no significant difference between brands. Marketers plan specific strategies for selling products bought habitually. For example, they will frequently employ price and sales promotions to encourage product trial. Also, they use advertising with visual symbols that are easily remembered and which consumers can associate with the brand.

HALF-TONES   A photoengraving produced from an image shot through a screen. The screen breaks up the artwork into dots of varying diameters, with the density determined by the size of the dots. Ultimately, a print is made. See also **four-color.**

HALO EFFECT   A research respondent's tendency to favorably view a product's individual attributes if he or she has an overall favorable opinion about it. For example, consumers asked to assess a product's features will say they like each feature if they like the product in general. The halo effect also works in the reverse. If a person has a generally negative view of a product, he or she will view its other attributes in an equally negative light. The halo effect is a significant factor in research on consumer attitudes toward advertising and products.

HANDBILL   See **flier.**

HANDLING ALLOWANCE   1. An incentive given to a retailer for handling a promotional program that requires extra work on the retailer's part. An example is a store that handles a manufacturer's coupon redemptions. The extra work involved in doing so is rewarded with an allowance by the manufacturer. Handling allowances take the form of money or merchandise discounts. **2.** An allowance granted to wholesalers as compensation for handling special amounts or types of merchandise. See also **trade promotion.**

HARD GOODS   Products such as TVs, appliances, furniture, and audiovisual equipment. As the name suggests, hard goods are usually comprised of hardware. They are generally *durable goods,* which are items used over an extended period of time.

HARD OFFER   A direct marketer's request for payment to be submitted with a product order. It is different from a **soft offer,** where the company grants the buyer the option of reviewing the product before paying for it. The benefit of a hard offer is that it eliminates the possibility of the company incurring debt expenses. (Some people who accept a soft offer never pay for the product.) Hard offers are not as common as soft offers.

HARD SELL   A salesperson's attempt to pressure a customer into making a purchase. The seller tries to control the sales situation by creating a level of tension. Hard-sell approaches are characterized by insistence on the salesperson's part or by coercive tactics. Needless to say, hard-sell approaches are not well received by customers and should not be employed by salespeople.

HARVESTING STRATEGY   A strategic decision to maximize a product's short-term cash flow. It is made when the company anticipates a deterioration of the market or is contemplating withdrawing its product from the market. Harvesting involves reducing the investment in the product to cut costs and improve cash flow. The cash flow generated is then directed to other areas of the company that need financial support. See also **growth-share matrix.**

HAWTHORNE EFFECT   The tendency of respondents in an experiment to alter their behavior when they know they are being observed by a researcher. The Hawthorne Effect suggests that respondents will change their behavior to meet the observer's expectations. The name comes from an experiment conducted in the 1920s at the Western Electric Hawthorne Works in Chicago. In this study, researchers sought to gauge improvements in worker productivity and satisfaction when work-area lighting was increased. When the lighting was increased, workers were more productive. Yet when the lighting was decreased (but workers thought it had been increased), productivity still improved. The Hawthorne Effect underscores the need for a **control group** in a research study. Comparing the effects realized by the control group with those by the **test group** verifies the true effect of the experimental variable (work area lighting, in the above case).

HEADLINE   The words in a print advertisement that readers notice first. The headline is usually set in very large type to attract the attention of the target buyer and to encourage further reading. Headlines are considered to be the most important part of a print ad because a reader's decision to read the ad is often based on how well the headline arouses interest and communicates the product benefit. Good headlines must make an immediate impact, must promise some kind of reward, must be understandable at a glance, must be specific (not general in the sense that they can apply to other products), and must coordinate well with the copy and illustration.

HEAD OF HOUSEHOLD   Consumer research term referring to the person who is responsible for managing a household and who is the primary source of income. Heads of household are married or unmarried men and women.

HEALTH AND BEAUTY AIDS (HABA OR HBA)   A category of products comprised of hair- and body-care items, cosmetics, nonprescription drugs, toothpaste, mouthwash, and so on. Health and beauty aids are typically grouped in a separate section of a grocery or discount store.

HEALTHCARE MARKETING   Public service–oriented marketing to communicate the physical or mental health benefits of a product or service. Healthcare marketing is conducted by hospitals, clinics, and associations (e.g., the American Heart Association). Healthcare marketing also describes efforts by profit-making companies (e.g., pharmaceutical manufacturers) and facilities (e.g., chiropractic centers) to market their health-related goods and services.

HEAVY-UP   The process of intensifying the level of advertising scheduled to appear during a particular period of time. It is usually a relatively short period (e.g., a week or month). The technique is used when a product is purchased primarily during a specific time or season. For instance, media planners will heavy-up the ad schedule for farm-grown turkeys in the weeks immediately preceding Thanksgiving. See also **continuity.**

HEAVY USERS   Consumers who purchase a given product frequently in comparison to the rest of the market population. A product's heavy users are usually a small percentage of the overall market. However, they constitute a very large portion of the product's total sales. Consequently, many marketers direct much of their promotional efforts at this group.

HIDDEN PERSUADERS, THE   An exposé of the advertising industry, written by Vance Packard. It discusses how some advertisers base their creative strategies on Freudian psychological theories of human motivation. That is, advertisers strive to spark consumer purchasing by preying on people's deep-seated (unconscious) motivations. The book was one of the first to accuse the advertising industry of manipulative exploitation of consumers' psyches. Published by Pocket Books, Inc., New York, 1957. See also **subliminal advertising.**

HIERARCHY OF EFFECTS   A paradigm of consumer purchasing used to describe how advertising works. It illustrates how a consumer passes through stages from being unaware of a product to being in a state ready to purchase it. The hierarchy of effects model theorizes that people move through the phases of awareness, knowledge, liking, preference, conviction and, ultimately, purchase. Marketers attempt to understand this hierarchy in planning to *move* their target audience from being ignorant about a product to wanting to purchase it. See also **attention, interest, desire, accessibility model.**

HIERARCHY OF NEEDS   The psychologist Abraham Maslow's theory of motivation that seeks to explain why people are driven by particular needs at different times. Human needs, the theory states, are arranged in a hierarchy according to their order of importance. Once a person satisfies an important need, he or she attempts to satisfy the next level of need. The hierarchy moves from high- to low-order needs: *physiological* (hunger and thirst), *safety* (security and protection), *social* (love, sense of belonging), *esteem* (self-esteem, recognition, status), and *self-actualization* (self-development). The model is used by marketers to understand how different products meet consumers' different levels of need.

HIGH-DEFINITION TELEVISION (HDTV)   An emerging video technology that gives a television picture the same sharp image and sound as a motion picture. HDTV describes the new technology's application for wall-size video displays and computer screens. High-definition television sets are expected to be quite costly when they are introduced in the mid-1990s: approximately $5,000 each. The cost is expected to drop once sales begin increasing.

HIGHER-INVOLVEMENT MODEL   An advertising medium requiring the consumer to be actively involved in receiving the ad message. Most print media are considered high-involvement models because they are read. That is, the consumer works at receiving and comprehending the media's content. In contrast, with **lower-involvement models,** the consumer passively receives information. Examples are radio, TV, and other broadcast media.

HIGH-INVOLVEMENT CONSUMER BEHAVIOR   Pattern of consumer purchasing in which the buyer spends a significant amount of time researching a product and comparing alternative brands. Items bought with this degree of decision making are typically expensive goods or those that have significant personal consequence to the buyer. Examples are large-scale purchases (homes, cars, or boats), or purchases of a highly emotional nature (a life-insurance policy or a cemetery plot). See also **low-involvement consumer behavior.**

HISPANIC MARKETING   A type of **ethnic marketing** in which American consumers of Hispanic descent comprise the target market. Hispanics represent one of the fastest-growing population groups in the United States. Consequently, there has been a proliferation of Spanish-language media (print and broadcast), as well as marketing services companies that specialize in Hispanic advertising and communications. Some marketers mistakenly treat the Hispanic market as a whole without considering the cultural differences between Hispanic subgroups such as Mexicans, Cubans, Puerto Ricans, Costa Ricans, and Central Americans. Effective Hispanic marketing must take into account the socioeconomic and cultural dissimilarities of these subgroups.

HISTOGRAM   See **bar chart.**

HIT LIST   A salesperson's list of names of potential cutsomers he or she has decided to pursue. The list consists of people who are both weak and strong prospects, usually in priority order (the strong prospects are the ones who receive the most attention). A hit list is used to generate leads that can ultimately be turned into future business. The percentage of prospects who have been made into customers is referred to as the *hit rate*. Salespeople track their hit rates to gauge the success of their lead-generation activities. See also **prospecting.**

HOLD STRATEGY   The strategic decision to preserve a product's existing market share. Implied in this strategy is maintaining the necessary levels of production and promotion required to do so. Hold strategy is usually discussed in the context of the **growth-share matrix.** This is where products, product lines, or **strategic business units** are categorized on a grid that illustrates the units' varying cash flow characteristics and market standing.

HORIZONTAL DIVERSIFICATION   A strategy by which a company seeks to grow by acquiring or developing products that are geared to its current customer base. The new products, however, are technologically different from the existing product line and require different manufacturing processes. For example, a videocassette manufacturer may begin developing videocassette racks to hold the tapes. See also **diversification.**

HORIZONTAL HALF-PAGE   An advertisement that occupies the upper or lower half of a newspaper or magazine page. When two facing pages in the periodical feature horizontal half-page ads by the same advertiser the advertisement is called a *half-page double spread*. The cost for such a layout is generally the same as for a full-page ad.

HORIZONTAL INTEGRATION   A corporate growth strategy in which the company tries to increase sales and profits by expanding within its own industry. For instance, a company would acquire one

Horizontal Half-Page

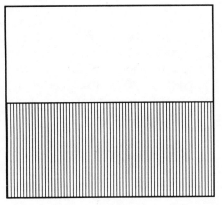

or more competitors that market the same product as the acquiring organization. See also **integration.**

HORIZONTAL MARKETING SYSTEM   A situation in which two nonrelated companies combine resources in pursuit of a marketing opportunity. For example, a soft-drink producer joined forces with a liquor manufacturer to market drink mixers under the liquor company's name. The companies felt that using the liquor company's name (and the soft-drink maker's manufacturing and distribution expertise) would enable them to effectively reach their target market: spirits drinkers. Companies establish horizontal marketing systems when seeking to effect marketing, production, or distribution synergies; or they do so when they lack the individual resources to successfully capitalize on a marketing opportunity. See also **vertical marketing system.**

HORIZONTAL PUBLICATION   A trade magazine whose content is geared to people in a general business area as opposed to a specific industry or profession. Consider, for example, a magazine or newspaper on office management. A publication on this subject would be read by administrative managers in companies in virtually every industry. See also **vertical publication.**

HORIZONTAL SALES ORGANIZATION   A sales force organization that employs both company and outside salespeople who are assigned sales responsibility based on geographic location, type of product, type of customer, or specific selling function.

HOUSE ACCOUNT   See **direct accounts.**

HOUSE AGENCY   A company's own advertising agency staffed by its employees. Large companies may establish house agencies to save on media commissions and to exercise complete control over advertising planning and implementation. The drawback of using a house agency is the loss of an outsider's unbiased point of view on advertising decisions (a benefit of retaining an outside firm). House agencies occasionally take on their own clients.

HOUSEHOLDS USING TELEVISION (HUT)   The A. C. Nielsen Company term used in estimating the number of households in a geographic area that have their TV sets turned on at a specific time. HUT level is stated as a percentage. It is based on the number of sets turned on as compared to the total number of TV sets in the geographic area under study. For example, an area has 10,000 TV sets. When 1,000 of those sets are turned on, the HUT level is 10 (10,000 $\div$ 1,000 = 10). A television program's **audience share** is stated in terms of HUT. Thus, a program with a 10 share indicates that 10% of all households using television were watching that program. HUT level can be determined for the entire United States (network programs) or for individual markets (local programs). See also **audience measurement.**

HOUSE LIST   A mailing list comprised of current customers and people who have made inquiries relating to a product(s). House lists are considered to be the best-performing lists. That is, they will generally yield higher responses than **compiled lists** because the former contain the names of people who have already shown interest in the product. Companies will sometimes sell or rent their house list to other direct marketers.

HOUSE ORGAN   A magazine produced by a company, the editorial content of which relates to the company itself. The audience of an *internal* house organ are employees. *External* house organs are developed for a company's clients, customers, or persons interested in its corporate activities (e.g., shareholders). House organs feature articles and news items portraying the company in a favorable light. Topics usually relate to the company's growth, product development activities, technological advances, and staff promotions. See also **newsletter.**

HOUSE-TO-HOUSE SELLING   **Direct-selling** method in which salespeople make sales calls on individual consumers at the latter's homes. The sales calls are made either with or without an appointment. Examples of wares sold house-to-house are Fuller Brush (personal grooming) and Avon (cosmetics) products. The changing nature of the American work force, however, has lessened the amount of house-to-house selling by companies. That is, with more families having both spouses working, there are fewer people at home during the day to receive the sales calls. Also known as *door-to-door selling*.

I

IDEA GENERATION The process of devising concepts for new products and promotional campaigns. In **new product development** the process begins with top management's definition of the target market and the specific corporate objectives to be achieved. Ideas may come from company employees (e.g., salespeople, manufacturing executives), or from outsiders (e.g., sales representatives, wholesalers or retailers, scientists). There are several commonly used idea-generation techniques. One of the most popular is **brainstorming,** in which members of a group session spontaneously suggest ideas. See also **synectics.**

ILLUSTRATION A print advertisement's primary visual element. Illustrations include photographs, original artwork, cartoons, or diagrams. They often show the product itself or the product in use or ready for use. Illustrations may highlight the product's special features (e.g., how a station wagon's rear door opens). The role of an illustration is to attract attention, to select prospects for the product advertised, and to interest prospects in reading the copy. To maximize total communications effectiveness, the illustration must complement and reinforce the ad's other elements: the **copy** and **headline.**

IMAGE Consumers' perceptions of a product, company, individual, or institution. Image is what people *believe* to be true about something. Companies frequently conduct image analyses to assess the market's perception of their products. Image analysis gauges *familiarity* (where consumer responses range from having never heard of the product to being very familiar with it). It also measures attitudes in terms of *favorability* (responses rank product attributes from being very unfavorable to very favorable). Image analysis gives marketers insight into the specific communications challenge confronting them. For instance, products whose image is low in terms of familiarity must be marketed to raise public awareness. Products low in consumer preference must use communications that create favorable attitudes among buyers.

IMAGE ADVERTISING Advertising whose goal is to sell a product by creating an image for it, as opposed to highlighting its attributes. Image advertising can portray a product as being sophisticated, reliable, or prestigious to own. Image advertising seeks to create an aura around a product that enhances its desirability to consumers.

IMPLEMENTATION The process of carrying out the elements of a marketing plan. The activities being implemented relate to specific *tasks* (e.g., conducting market research, creating advertising), according to set *time parameters* (a schedule for completing activities), and according to specific *resource allocations* (dollar amounts budgeted for the various activities).

IMPLIED WARRANTY An unstated promise (not written or spoken) by sellers relating to what they will do if the goods they sell fail to perform as expected or are defective. Assume a consumer has purchased a mechanical toy in which batteries are included in the purchase price. If the batteries are not enclosed in the package, an implied warranty suggests that the seller will furnish them, even though this particular situation is not cited on the warranty application. See also **expressed warranty.**

IMPRESSIONS The total number of individuals or households receiving a single exposure to a print or broadcast advertisement or publicity mention. See also **gross audience.**

IMPULSE BUY A purchase that involves no planning or forethought on the consumer's part. It is a spontaneous purchase made in response to a sudden urge or external stimulus (e.g., a **point-of-sale** display). Impulse products are a specific category of *convenience goods*. These low-cost items (such as candies, disposable lighters, diet or recipe pamphlets) are often situated near checkout counters in supermarkets and discount stores because many consumers will spontaneously pick them up when paying for their other goods.

IN-BOUND TELEMARKETING   The direct-marketing practice in which sales representatives handle incoming telephone calls from customers who are placing orders, making inquiries, or voicing complaints. For example, customers calling a toll-free **800-number** are using an in-bound telemarketing system. Today many in-bound systems are automated. That is, customer calls are first handled by an answering machine, which instructs callers to punch in select digits to be connected with company representatives in different departments. In-bound telemarketing is different from **out-bound telemarketing,** where salespeople call current and prospective customers as a means of direct selling and qualifying leads.

INCENTIVES   Items given by companies to consumers to motivate purchases or to distributors to reward sales performance. Consumer sales promotions often involve incentives such as coupons, rebates, and discounts. Examples of **trade sales promotion** incentives are merchandise discounts to wholesalers or retailers, or special prizes or vacations to salespeople. *Incentive pay*, for instance, describes a bonus given to a salesperson for a particular achievement.

INCOME GROUPS   Demographic categories based on income brackets. Income groups are collectives of people with different levels of purchasing power. For example, yachts would probably be marketed to the income group earning more than $250,000 a year as opposed to the group earning $25,000 a year. Members of the same income group often exhibit similar product wants, preferences, or usage patterns. See also **socioeconomic classifications.**

INDEPENDENT STATION   A broadcast station independently owned and which is not affiliated with a network. According to Federal Communications Commission regulations, an independent station carries less than 10 hours of prime-time network programming per week. Independent stations are usually small local stations. The exceptions are **superstations,** which are independently owned but are broadcast nationally.

INDEPENDENT VARIABLE   The variable in a research experiment that explains or predicts differences in the **dependent variable.** For example, if the effectiveness of a direct-mail package is being tested, respondents would be asked to assess different *test packages*, which may vary by copy or enclosures. Here, respondent reaction is the dependent variable (that is, what is being predicted). The characteristics of the different packages are the independent variables used to illustrate the varying levels of effectiveness as indicated by the respondents. Also known as *predictor variable*.

INDICIA The graphic on a mailing envelope indicating that postage has already been prepaid by the mailer. The indicia is located in the upper right-hand corner of the envelope. It shows what class of mail is being used (first-class, second-class, bulk rate, etc.) and displays the permit number and permit holder's name. An indicia is obtained by the U.S. Postal Service. It is used by companies on various forms of **business reply mail.**

INDIRECT COSTS Costs that cannot be assigned directly to marketing expenditures. Indirect costs include expenses for a company's rent, overhead, taxes, insurance, and so on. Indirect costs are different from **direct costs,** which are expenses that can be traced to specific marketing entities (e.g., sales commissions, advertising expenditures, sales force salaries, and travel expenses). Indirect and direct costs are factored into *profitability analyses,* which are used to assess such marketing activities as sales force performance.

INDIRECT DISTRIBUTION CHANNEL Distribution in which merchandise is delivered to consumers by way of independent **middlemen.** That is, the distribution channel employs wholesalers, retailers, brokers, or manufacturer's representatives who deliver products to consumers. See also **direct distribution channel.**

INDIRECT PROMOTION The dissemination of promotional information to consumers via nonpersonal channels of communication (e.g., the mass media). The main goals of indirect promotion are to make a product or service known to the market and to present it in the most favorable light. The opposite of indirect promotion is **direct promotion,** which involves activities such as house-to-house selling and telemarketing.

INDUSTRIAL ADVERTISING Advertising designed to promote goods and services used in producing other goods and services. For example, the maker of a materials handling system will use industrial advertising to reach manufacturers in need of such a factory floor installation. See also **business-to-business advertising.**

INDUSTRIAL BUYING BEHAVIOR   The patterns and buying procedures of groups in the **organizational market.** Industrial buying practices differ significantly from those by consumers. They are characterized by highly professional, detail-oriented purchasing activities. Purchases are usually large-scale acquisitions of raw materials or office equipment and supplies. Salespeople dealing with the industrial market study **buy classes,** which are the varying levels of intricacy of purchase decisions based on the nature of the goods and their costs. Marketers also study **buying centers** (the individuals and groups who participate in industrial buying decisions) and **buy phases** (which delineate buying center processes in making purchase decisions).

INDUSTRIAL MARKET   The segment of the **organizational market** comprised of organizations that purchase goods and services to make products that are sold, rented, or furnished to other companies. Examples of industrial market sectors are the construction industry (whose companies buy building products used in real estate development) and agriculture (where companies buy chemicals used in making fertilizer and other farming products).

INDUSTRIAL PRODUCTS   Goods sold to companies making other products. They include equipment and mechanical parts; raw materials; and **maintenance, repair, operating items.** In general, industrial products are used in conducting business or industrial manufacturing activities. In this sense, industrial products are different from **consumer products,** which are goods purchased by members of the general public for personal consumption.

INELASTIC DEMAND   Colloquially, the market situation in which an increase in product price has virtually no effect on its market demand. Technically, inelastic demand refers to when a price increase causes the percentage decrease in the quantity of product sold to be less than the percentage increase in price. Inelastic demand exists when there are few or no product substitutes or competitors. Demand is inelastic also when buyers do not readily notice a price increase or when they feel the increase is justified due to enhanced product quality or inflation. See also **price elasticity of demand.**

IN-FLIGHT PUBLICATION   A magazine distributed for free by airlines to passengers on their flights. The editorial content in in-flight publications includes many business topics (geared to frequent business flyers) as well as travel-related articles. Advertising is by national advertisers and local retail stores and restaurants in the cities to which the airline flies. Most airlines offer in-flight publications, which are produced by companies specializing in this type of periodical.

INFLUENCER   The member of a **buying center** who convinces others of the need for a product or the choice of a particular brand. This person may also define the product specifications and participate in evaluating alternatives. Implied in the term is the person's ability to alter the behavioral and/or psychological states of other buying center members.

INFOMERCIAL   A program-length television commercial designed to look like a regular TV show. Infomercials use such techniques as panel discussions or on-camera interviews to reference the sponsoring product or service. Infomercials might discuss "how to make a million dollars a year in real estate," or "miracle cures for baldness." Infomercials have been criticized by governmental and consumer groups for misleading viewers. That is, it is often difficult to differentiate between them and noncommercial TV news reports or programs. Regulations have been proposed, however, that would require multiple identifications of the infomercial's sponsor at different points in the broadcast.

INFORMATION SEARCH   **1.**   In consumer purchasing, the act of obtaining information about a product (or different brands) before making a purchase decision. Consumers conduct information searches by reading articles and advertisements, and by talking with family, friends, and experts. **2.**   In industrial buying, the act of purchasing executives accumulating information on vendors or suppliers when seeking to fulfill a given product or service need. See also **buy classes.**

IN-HOME MEDIA   Media that are seen, heard, or read in people's homes. In-home media include newspapers, magazines, television, and radio. **Out-of-home media** are seen outside one's dwelling, for example, billboards, outdoor displays, transit advertising, or skywriting. See also **alternative media.**

IN-HOME USE TEST   A form of market testing in which a consumer tries a new product in the home and reports back to the researcher conducting the study. People are selected to use the product for a limited time and, ultimately, are asked for feedback on their likes and dislikes. In-home use tests are designed to help researchers identify problems with a new product and to spot unexpected usage patterns or servicing requirements. The tests are intended to solicit input from consumers regarding their purchase intent and attitudes toward the product.

INNER-DIRECTED   Describes a consumer's purchase that is based on satisfying an inner need, consistent with his or her own values. For example, a person will buy do-it-yourself home-improvement products to fulfill the need to be self-sufficient. In **outer-directed** buying purchase decisions are based on consumers' perceptions of how they think other people view them and their actions. See also **VALS.**

INNOVATION   The introduction of a new product or one that is perceived to be new by the market. Consumer adoption of an innovation occurs in phases in a process known as **diffusion of innovation.** The term *innovators* describes the first people to adopt an innovation, as well as those companies that introduce innovative products. See also **adopter categories.**

IN-PACK ADVERTISING   Advertising materials inserted into product packages. Examples of in-pack advertising materials are coupons (for the product or a complementary one) and free gifts and premiums (e.g., toys enclosed in a cereal box). In-pack advertising premiums offer consumers instant gratification and serve as an incentive to repurchase the product or another of the company's items.

INQUIRY   A consumer's request for information about a product. Inquiries may be unsolicited. That is, a consumer may have simply heard about a product and wants more information. However, much advertising is designed to generate inquiries, such as ads with coupons and an **800-number.** Inquiries represent valuable sales leads because consumers have already shown interest in the product. Salespeople generally follow up on inquiries with letters and phone calls.

INSERT   A separate page of promotional information that is enclosed in a print advertising medium. For example, inserts are included in newspapers (**freestanding inserts**) or are bound into magazines. Bound magazine inserts, for example, might be order forms that accompany an ad in the publication. These inserts are sold as advertising, the design and production of which are handled by the advertiser. Inserts are used in nearly all direct-mail packages. They may be materials that provide additional product information, or they are items offered free to the recipient (e.g., bookmarks, calendars).

INSERTION ORDER   A purchase order for print advertisements. Insertion orders specify the placement of the ad, as well as its size, price, and publication date. A copy of the advertisement is usually included with the insertion order. The term *insertion* is used to describe the ad itself. Media planners prepare *insertion schedules* for advertising campaigns to outline their purchases in various media.

INSIDE COVERS   **Preferred positions** of magazine advertisements, often sold at an extra charge to the advertiser. There are two types of inside covers. The inside front cover (also known as the *second cover*) appears behind the publication's cover page. The inside back cover (also called the *third cover*) appears before the magazine's back cover. The magazine's back cover is another preferred position. In fact, it is often the publication's most expensive advertising space because so many people are apt to see and read it.

INSTALLMENT   A credit technique in which the buyer pays for a product by making a series of payments over time. The payments are usually for the same amount. Installment amounts are calculated by dividing the total amount due by the number of payments. For example, a $500 purchase might require 10 payments of $50. There are benefits and drawbacks to this credit method. The main advantage is that an installment offer will likely generate a high sales response because consumers perceive the product as costing less when not required to make a lump-sum payment. The drawback is that the company's billing costs are increased and its receipt of cash is slowed.

INSTITUTIONAL ADVERTISING   Advertising promoting the name, image, or reputation of an organization as opposed to the products or services it provides. Institutional advertising is designed to create public awareness of the organization and/or improve its reputation in the marketplace. See also **corporate advertising.**

INSTITUTIONAL MARKET   The segment of the **organizational market** comprised of institutions that purchase goods and services for persons in their care. Examples are schools, hospitals, nursing homes, churches, colleges, clubs, and prisons. Marketers must recognize that institutions have special buying needs and requirements. For example, most institutions are nonprofit enterprises. Thus, their budgets are typically low and buying procedures are highly detailed.

INTEGRATED MARKETING   The strategic combination of **marketing communications mix** elements to sell a product—that is, coordinating advertising with publicity, sales promotion, merchandising, and direct-marketing activities to ensure the marketing message is being disseminated consistently in all communications reaching the target audience. Integrated marketing has gained popularity as a strategic approach due, in part, to advertiser discontent with lessening media advertising effectiveness wrought by the proliferation of ads (**clutter**). The upturn in integrated marketing activity also coincides with the increase in direct marketing, database marketing, and other tactics that more accurately define and reach market segments.

INTEGRATION   A company's attempt to generate additional sales and profits by acquiring businesses related to its existing one. There are three forms of integration: *Backward integration* refers to the company acquiring suppliers (or developing a supply capability) to enjoy greater control over materials procurement; *forward integration* involves acquiring retailers or wholesalers; *horizontal integration* refers to the company taking over one or more of its competitors (assuming it is not precluded from doing so by government regulations).

INTENSIVE DISTRIBUTION   The distribution strategy in which a product is made available in a market in as many outlets as possible. The benefit of this strategy is that the product is widely available to consumers. Its drawback is that retailers show little commitment to promoting the product since their competitors also offer it. Intensive distribution is different from **selective distribution,** which is when a product is made available through only a few outlets in a market. See also **exclusive distribution.**

INTERACTIVE TELEVISION The use of video and telecommunications technology to let consumers receive product information and order products directly from manufacturers. Merchandise is shown on a video screen (e.g., television or computer monitor) and consumers place orders by using an attached keyboard or a touch-tone telephone. Interactive television, however, is used for purposes other than shopping. Viewers, for instance, may conduct banking transactions or play video games using such systems. One kind of interactive television system is a *digital broadcasting network*. A group of people on a computer network receive text, images, or statistical information disseminated by the system sponsor (e.g., a bank). The viewers are able to access information or services at their convenience. See also **video systems.**

INTERCEPT INTERVIEW An **interview** arranged by a researcher who stops people and asks to question them for a survey. The researcher usually stands in a high-traffic public location (such as on a city street corner) where he or she is likely to meet a large and diverse group of people. The drawback of intercept interviews is that they must be brief. Second, the selection of respondents is done via **nonprobability sampling,** which leaves open the possibility of interviewer bias in choosing which respondents to query. See also **judgment sample.**

INTERMEDIARY See **middleman.**

INTERNAL REPORTS SYSTEM The part of a **marketing information system** that provides current data on sales, costs, inventory levels, accounts receivable and payable, and so on. Managers use this internal information to identify problem areas and to spot opportunities and trends. Managers also use internally generated information in various marketing activities such as marketing analysis, planning, implementation, and control.

INTERNATIONAL ADVERTISING See **global marketing.**

INTERNATIONAL ASSOCIATION OF BUSINESS COMMUNICATORS (IABC) A worldwide association of communications and public relations professionals. The goal of the IABC is to foster communications excellence and to contribute to its member companies' organizational communications effectiveness. Headquartered in

San Francisco, the IABC has more than 11,000 members in 40 countries. See Appendix A for address and phone number.

INTERNATIONAL STANDARD SERIAL NUMBER (ISSN)   The number assigned by the U.S. Library of Congress to each serial publication such as magazines, newspapers, and newsletters. ISSNs are used to identify publications, as well as to catalog them and track subscription orders. Retailers use ISSN designations to record sales of publications and to place orders for them. According to U.S. Postal Service regulations, a periodical's ISSN must appear within the periodical's first five pages. It is usually indicated on the periodical's **masthead.**

INTERPERSONAL VARIABLES   The socially generated forces that affect people's knowledge, values, beliefs, and ideas, and that ultimately influence their buying behavior. Marketers seeking to understand **consumer behavior** and purchase decision making factor into their analysis interpersonal variables as determined by culture, subculture, reference group, and social class. These sociological phenomena are important determinants of human action. Thus, marketing planning addresses their impact on the members of a given group. The goal is to help define target market characteristics and to devise appropriate **marketing mix** combinations. See also **intrapersonal variables.**

INTERPRETATION   One of the steps in the process of how a consumer gains awareness of advertising or a particular product. Specifically, interpretation relates to how advertising messages are received and understood by consumers. The study of how people interpret external stimuli is important in developing effective advertising. Interpretation is generally discussed in the context of **perception.**

INTERSTATE COMMERCE COMMISSION (ICC)   An independent regulatory agency established in 1887 that is empowered to "foster the preservation and development of a national transportation system adequate to meet the needs of the commerce of the United States, the U.S. Postal Service, and national defense." The regulations established by the ICC can have a major impact on a company's product distribution channels and strategies.

INTERVAL SCALE   See **ratio scale.**

INTERVIEW   The situation in which a researcher asks questions of a respondent to collect survey data. Interviews are conducted several different ways. They may be done in face-to-face encounters, in which the researcher asks questions and records the respondents' answers; they can be conducted over the telephone; or they may be done by mailing questionnaires to a predetermined group of respondents who are asked to return the forms. Interviews may also be conducted in group settings. See also **focus group.**

INTERVIEWER BIAS   The opinions or prejudices a researcher may exhibit (consciously or unconsciously) that influence a respondent's answers. Interviwer bias may result from the researcher's actions, body language, or choice of words. For example, interviewer bias would be created if the researcher asks, "Don't you think the president is doing a very good job?" The way this question is phrased is subjective. An objective phrasing would be, "How would you rate the job the president is doing?" Thus, how an interviewer asks a question is one form of interviewer bias. Interviewers must be totally objective so as to elicit reliable feedback from respondents.

INTRAPERSONAL VARIABLES   The psychological forces that influence an individual's knowledge, values, beliefs, and ideas. The term relates to a person's cognitive processes. Thus, it implies that intrapersonal variables are unique to each individual. Identifying the impact of intrapersonal variables on human action is necessary in analyzing **consumer behavior.** Social scientists distinguish between *demographic* intrapersonal variables (i.e., age, occupation, economic standing) and *psychographic* intrapersonal variables (which relate to the concepts of motivation, learning, perception, attitudes, and personality). **Interpersonal variables** describe human action as influenced by sociological forces. Together, these variables lend insight into target market characteristics and help marketers devise effective **marketing mix** combinations.

INTRAPRENEURSHIP   A new product development approach in which corporate management allows an employee to spend time creating product ideas and the company finances the approved products' research and development. (The employee is typically not a member of the company's new product development team.) A well-known product developed by an intrapreneur was the Post-It pad—adhesive-backed note pages that can be removed from papers without ripping or leaving a mark on the paper. Post-It pads were developed by an executive at the 3-M Company.

INVENTORY   Merchandise or the dollar value of it in storage at a given point in time. Companies engage in *inventory control* to maintain a desired level of available merchandise because a company needs ample inventory to ensure that sales will not be lost or deadlines missed. However, there are dangers of having too much inventory on hand. For example, the costs of storing large amounts of inventory are high. Moreover, the merchandise is subject to loss, theft, or damage. Another danger is that market demand will fall, and the company will be unable to sell the merchandise. *Inventory turnover* is the number of times an average amount of inventory is sold over a designated time period (e.g., annually).

INVESTOR RELATIONS (IR)   The communications function geared to maintaining favorable relations with a company's shareholders. Investor relations professionals typically employ newsletters and other print media to communicate information about the company's financial performance. IR professionals often coordinate production of the company's annual report. They also help organize annual shareholders' meetings. IR professionals frequently get involved in communicating management's position in certain problem situations (e.g., a hostile takeover attempt). A company may have a department dedicated solely to IR, or the function is handled by its public reations department. However, some communications firms specialize in providing IR services.

INVOLVEMENT   The level of importance a consumer places on a given product purchase. Involvement varies according to the degree of relevance a product has to the buyer. A high-involvement product, for example, is one that has a significant magnitude of emotional consequence to the buyer (e.g., a health insurance policy). A low-involvement product is not linked to important personal consequences or goals (e.g., a low-cost convenience product). Marketers attempt to predict the level of involvement consumers will bring toward the purchase of the seller's product. The companies determine their **marketing mix** combinations accordingly.

INVOLVEMENT DEVICE   See **action device.**

IRREGULAR DEMAND STATE Market situation in which demand for a product varies significantly by season or the time of day, week, month, or year. The situation is characterized by high demand at certain times and low or nonexistent demand at others. For example, a museum has very high demand on weekends but is slow during the week. Likewise, commuter trains are quite busy during peak hours but sit idle at off-peak times. Marketers faced with an irregular demand state strive to alter the pattern of demand. They may do so by creating special promotions and incentives to raise demand during sluggish periods. See also **demand states; seasonal demand.**

ISLAND DISPLAY A freestanding **point-of-purchase** merchandise display situated in an open area of a retail outlet. That is, an island display is not located near shelves or checkout counters. Rather, it is placed in an area that allows shoppers to pick up the featured merchandise from any side of the display.

ISLAND POSITION The position of an advertisement or commercial where it is not surrounded by ads from other advertisers. In a publication, an island position means that editorial content appears before and after the advertisement. On a broadcast station, island position refers to where the commercial airs in the middle of a program, with no other paid announcements made during the commercial break. An island position is desirable to advertisers because there is no competition for people's attention from other ads. See also **competitive separation; commercial protection.**

ISSUE The copies of a magazine, newspaper, or newsletter that bear the same date or special content. For example, the final issue of a monthly magazine is called its December issue; or an issue may carry a specific name describing, say, a once-a-year theme (e.g., *Life* magazine's "The Year in Pictures" issue). Issue denotes that all copies of the periodical contain the same editorial and advertising content. The exception is a periodical featuring **regional editions,** in which case the advertising varies according to where in the country the publication is distributed.

ISSUES MANAGEMENT The practice of dealing with potentially adverse circumstances prior to their reaching crisis proportions. For example, a company's issues management program might involve public relations and lobbying to influence legislation which, if enacted, would harm its sales or competitive position. See also **crisis management.**

ITEM NONRESPONSE BIAS   A form of **nonsampling error** that arises when survey respondents are unable to or refuse to answer a question. Questions that have a high degree of item nonresponse bias alter the survey findings. For example, if 40% of the respondents did not answer a particular question, the survey findings would be markedly different than if every respondent answered it. Item nonresponse bias may occur if the question is so poorly phrased that it is misunderstood by respondents; or it can happen if many respondents hold neutral or negative feelings toward the question topic. See also **bias.**

J

JINGLE   A song created especially for a radio or TV commercial or an advertising campaign. Some jingles are instrumentals, but most feature lyrics that address the product and its attributes or benefits. Jingles are designed to be catchy and memorable.

JOBBER   A **middleman** who buys goods from a manufacturer or importer for sale to retailers. Although the terms *jobber* and *wholesaler* are often used interchangeably, jobber generally refers to a small-scale wholesaler. For example, a jobber typically has limited warehouse capacity (or none at all) in comparison to larger wholesalers. *Note:* Jobbers are often the middlemen in **drop shipment** arrangements, which involve retailers promoting goods to which they do not take title. See also **limited-service wholesaler.**

JOB TICKET   A tag or envelope that is attached to a printing job or piece of mechanical art to indicate instructions to production personnel. In addition to instructions, a job ticket generally lists the date, the advertising agency that produced the materials, and the client for which they were prepared. Job tickets are also used as a checklist for in-house production personnel: If more than one department in an ad agency is responsible for different aspects of the job (e.g., typesetting, proofreading, artwork), each group checks off its work on the job ticket when finished. Thus, the job ticket also serves to track various production phases and the personnel who handled them.

JOINT VENTURING   Two companies combining resources to exploit a marketing opportunity. Joint ventures are common when a company attempts to market its goods in a foreign country. That is, the company will arrange to have the goods made available through a company already operating in that country. Joint ventures can be established formally or informally. An informal arrangement, for example, involves the companies merely sharing production or distribution facilities. A formal arrangement is characterized by combined ownership and control as determined by the companies' proportionate financial investments. Companies establish joint ventures when they need to obtain capital, add managerial expertise, or limit their financial or operational liabilities.

JUDGMENT SAMPLE A form of **nonprobability sampling** in which the researcher selects respondents based on the belief that they will provide the needed information. Judgment sampling does not involve random selection of respondents. Thus, such samples are not based on statistical techniques nor do they result in statistical conclusions. Also known as *purposive sample*. See also **bias; sampling.**

JUNIOR PAGE Describes the size of a magazine ad that would be a full page in some publications or a portion of a page in others. A junior page generally measures 4⅜″ by 6½″; thus, it would be a full page in periodicals with pages of this size. However, it would just be a part of a page in larger format magazines (and editorial copy would appear above, below, or beside the ad). When two junior page ads appear on facing pages in a large-format periodical the ads are called a *junior spread* or a *pony spread*.

JUNK MAIL 1. A derogatory term for *direct-mail advertising*. It is usually used by people who object to receiving unsolicited promo-

Junior Page

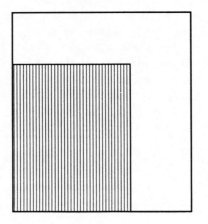

tional mail. **2.** Also used by direct-mail industry professionals to describe mail that is undeliverable because it is addressed incorrectly.

JUSTIFICATION   Typesetting term referring to when lines of copy extend evenly to the end of the right and/or left margins. Copy that is justified is also called *flush*: Flush right is copy extending to the edge of the right margin; flush left is text that stretches to the edge of the left margin. Justified copy is the opposite of **ragged left/right** text, which is copy with uneven margins on the right and/or left sides of the page.

JUST-IN-TIME PRODUCTION (JIT)   An inventory management philosophy which holds that manufacturers need not maintain more inventory than necessary at a given point in time. The theory is that rather than stockpiling parts and components, companies should receive inventory in the specific quantity they need to meet their immediate production schedules. JIT denotes a synchronization between suppliers and manufacturing production timetables. Companies adopt JIT production to reduce their inventories and lead times. The main benefit of JIT is a greater level of adaptability to sudden market changes in demand or materials availability.

JUST NOTICEABLE DIFFERENCE (JND)   The minimal difference in a product that is apparent to consumers when the item's attributes are modified. JND is of concern to manufacturers who are considering increasing or decreasing a product's quality or price. For example, manufacturers are concerned with achieving a JND that is recognized by consumers when increasing quality. Conversely, they are concerned with a JND that is not apparent to buyers when decreasing quality or increasing price. *Note:* Just noticeable difference is generally discussed in the context of **Weber's Law**—the psychological theory that is used in marketing to describe consumers' tendency to assess a product based not on its individual attributes but rather on the perceived difference between the product and other brands.

K

KEY CODE   A graphic designation included in an advertisement or printed communication that is used in tracking responses to that communication. Key codes are generally numeric or alphanumeric codes. Advertisers use key codes to analyze the effectiveness of the promotional materials and, ultimately, to evaluate product sales resulting from them. For example, key codes are used on coupons in direct-response magazine ads. The advertiser can review the coupons returned and quantify the coupons coming from different magazines to determine which drew the greatest response.

KEYLINE   1. In graphic arts, an outline drawing that shows all the visual and typographical elements of a layout. A keyline shows the exact size of the type, artwork, and illustrations, as well as their respective positions in the design. **2.** A marking—such as that on the **overlay** of a piece of mechanical art—that indicates a particular printing or design instruction. For example, a keyline shows a printer exactly how a color border should appear around a chart or graph.

KEY PUNCH   A mechanical method of entering research data for tabulation purposes. It involves punching holes into a special computer card that features 80 vertical columns and a dozen or so horizontal columns. The process involves use of a keypunch machine that punches the holes and "reads" them based on the specific code being employed. The data are input into the machine via an operator using a keyboard similar to that on a typewriter. Each keypunch card provides the data supplied by or about the **unit of analysis.** See also **data entry.**

KIOSK   A freestanding display used to provide merchandise information. Kiosks are usually situated in retail stores or in shopping malls. Some kiosks employ video technology. That is, they house **electronic catalogs** that present merchandise information on a video display. Such kiosks often allow the consumer to order products directly from the unit, usually by hitting keys on an attached keyboard. Many kiosks are not electronic, however. Rather, they provide product information via illustrations and copy on the display itself. Kiosks are sometimes manned by a company sales representative.

L

LABEL **1.** A printed strip on a product package that names the item and describes its contents. Label information also details the product's uses and its manufacturer and often features an illustration of the product. In one sense, a label serves as an advertising medium, especially when **flagging** is used on the package to announce special offers, discounts, or product promotions. **2.** In direct mail, the small piece of paper or sticker on which a mailing address appears. Mailing labels come in a variety of formats that differ in cost and production requirements. Two types are **Cheshire labels** and **pressure-sensitive labels.**

LATENT DEMAND STATE A market situation in which significant demand exists for a product that is not on the market. That is, a large number of people share a strong need for a product that has yet to be developed, for example, a harmless cigarette. Companies have been unable to develop one. Therefore, latent market demand for the product cannot be satisfied. The marketer's task in contending with a latent demand situation is to measure the potential market's size and develop a product that meets demand in the best way possible. For example, companies have experimented (with little success) with "smokeless" cigarettes to meet the latent demand for a safe tobacco product. See also **demand states.**

LAW OF DEMAND Theory describing the relationship between a product's price and the amount of product taken by the market. The theory states that the lower a price is, the higher demand will be. That is, more sales will occur when, all other things being equal, a product is priced at a low level.

LAW OF DIMINISHING RETURNS   The economic concept that once a certain point has been reached, additional resources will first produce increasing returns, then declining, and, finally, negative returns. Consider a company that is attempting to fund its sales force. The law of diminishing returns states that increasing the amount of selling expenditures will at first produce increasing sales revenue. Over time, however, additional financial input will result in less—and finally no—increase in revenue.

LAYAWAY   A service provided by retailers whereby a consumer pays for a product in several installments and takes possession of the item when full payment has been made. Layaway plans are one type of **ancillary service** provided by retailers.

LAYOUT   A rough design of a print advertisement. The layout is a plan for the ad that shows what the final printed piece will look like. Layouts indicate copy, illustrations, graphics, type style, and so forth. They differ in terms of how accurately they depict the finished artwork. For example, a *rough layout* may simply be a sketch of the ad. A *comp*, or comprehensive layout, shows the ad's elements in their exact dimensions. A layout person is the graphic artist responsible for developing a layout and, ultimately, producing the mechanical art. Layouts are developed for client review prior to the start of graphic production.

LEAD GENERATION   A salesperson's practice of identifying the best possible prospects (leads) he or she can approach via sales calls or visits. Salespeople employ several lead-generation techniques: They ask current customers for names of other people who might be interested in their product or service; they join trade or professional associations to make contacts; they scan magazines and other data sources to identify people and opportunities; or they speak before business and professional groups (as well as author articles in publications reaching those groups) to publicize themselves and their product offerings. See also **endless chain.**

LEADING QUESTION   A survey question, biased in its phrasing, that influences the respondent's answer. That is, a leading question either intentionally or unintentionally gives a clue to the respondent on how to answer the query. The resulting response, therefore, is unreliable. An example of a leading question is, "Don't you think the senator's prompt visit to the scene of the disaster was the right thing to do?" The positive terms in the question ("prompt" and "the right thing") suggest to the respondent that he or she should answer positively as well. See also **interviewer bias.**

LEAD IN/OUT **1.** Broadcast media term referring to programs that precede or follow another program. A lead-in program is one that is shown prior to another program; a lead-out is a program that is shown after it. **2.** A brief monologue that introduces a show. See also **audience flow.**

LEARNING The ways an individual's behavior changes based on his or her experiences. Learning is one of the key factors that influences **consumer behavior.** Learning theories highlight the interaction of a person's motivations, external stimuli (cues), and reinforcement. Marketers attempt to build demand for their products by influencing people's learning and by creating positive reinforcement of consumers' purchases. That is, marketers strive to effect positive reinforcement so that the consumer "learns" to appreciate the company's products. For example, if consumers are happy with the computer they purchased, they will be favorably predisposed to other products by the same company (e.g., computer printers, floppy disks, other accessories). See also **stimulus-response theory.**

LEAVE-BEHIND Literature that is left with a customer by a salesperson after the latter's sales call. A leave-behind may be a catalog, brochure, or flier that contains information on the seller's product or service and includes his or her phone number and address. Leave-behinds are designed to keep the seller's products in the customer's mind after the sales call. Also known as *leave piece*.

LETTERHEAD Specially designed stationery that features a company's **logo** and address and phone number. (Some professional services organizations, such as law firms, also list their partners and principals on their letterhead.) Direct marketers often develop special letterhead for given promotional mailings. For example, a direct mailing to generate newsletter subscriptions may feature the newsletter's logo on the letterhead. Such letterhead might also cite a different address than the publisher's address. That is, it would indicate the address to which responses should be sent.

LETTERSHOP   A company that produces large-scale mailings for direct-mail campaigns. Included in its services are printing the package materials, collating and folding them, inserting them into envelopes, labeling and sorting them (according to U.S. Postal Service regulations), and transporting them to the post office. Some lettershops offer clients creative services such as promotional copywriting and graphic design. Some also will handle the acquisition or compilation of mailing lists.

LICENSING   The practice of selling the rights to use a trademark, patent, or proprietary manufacturing process. The company that purchases the licensing rights is called the *licensee*. The seller, the *licensor*, receives a flat fee or royalties. Companies seek to obtain licensing rights on names, symbols, or well-known personalities for use in selling new or existing products. The benefit of using the licensed image is the ability to gain immediate consumer acceptance of the product. For example, a well-known car manufacturer licensed its name to companies that produce skis, sunglasses, and other items. In international marketing, licensing is a way for a company to gain entry into a foreign market. Here, the licensee is a company already operating in the host country. The benefit to the licensor is a low-risk way to enter the market. The benefit to the licensee is the ability to gain production or management expertise, and to sell a well-known product without having to incur start-up costs.

LIFESTYLE   A person's pattern of living—in other words, how an individual functions in his or her physical environment. Lifestyle is an important element of studying **consumer behavior** because persons who maintain similar lifestyles often exhibit similar product preferences and usage patterns. Lifestyle is often defined by a person's activities, interests, and opinions. It is a common criterion for **market segmentation**. See also **psychographic segmentation**.

LIFESTYLE GROUPS   The company S.R.I. International has classified American consumers into nine lifestyle groups. These value lifestyle groups (**VALS**) describe general personality traits and patterns of living of the people in them. The classifications suggest that consumers move through the groups in developmental stages. That is, each stage affects persons' attitudes, behavior, and psychological needs, which change over time. Major corporations subscribe to lifestyle group data from S.R.I. International. Companies use this information in formulating products and marketing strategies to effectively identify and reach market segments defined by lifestyle.

LIFETIME PROCEEDS   Concept referring to the number of mail-order purchases made by a customer over a prolonged period of time. It describes the total profits and losses related to that customer's purchase history as tracked by a given mail-order company.

LIFT LETTER   A brief note in a direct-mail package that provides information intended to induce the recipient to purchase the advertised product. Lift letters typically start by saying, "If you've decided not to buy this product, read this note." The lift letter goes on to describe a special offer or discount to people who agree to the offer. Lift letters are usually signed by the publisher or president of the company issuing the mailing. They are called lift letters because they are designed to "lift" the level of response to the mailing.

LIKERT SCALE   Statements used in survey research to gauge the degree to which the respondent holds a given attitude. Respondents are given a statement and asked to indicate whether they "strongly agree," "agree," are "uncertain," "disagree" or "strongly disagree." Likert scale statements are usually laid out as a matrix of items and answers. The benefit of this format is that it's an efficient use of space on the questionnaire. Respondents also find these questions relatively easy to complete.

LIMITED-SERVICE ADVERTISING AGENCY   An advertising firm that specializes in a particular advertising activity. Such firms typically offer only creative services or **media planning** and buying. For example, a limited-service firm might offer only copywriting or art direction services. Limited-service agencies are normally retained on a project basis, as opposed to yearly retainers. Limited-service agencies are different from **full-service advertising agencies,** which offer the full complement of media, creative, production, and planning capabilities.

LIMITED-SERVICE WHOLESALER   A wholesaler that offers one or just a few of the services typically provided by a **full-service wholesaler.** That is, a limited-service wholesaler provides some, but not all, of these wholesaler services: carrying stock, offering credit, making deliveries, maintaining a sales force. See also **cash and carry wholesaler; rack jobber; truck jobber.**

LIP SYNCHRONIZATION   Film production technique referring to the coordination of spoken dialogue with the visual of a person speaking the words. In short, "lip synching" involves correlating the film's audio track with its video track. An actor may be shown singing a song that is actually being sung by another person. That is, the actor is mouthing the words. This visual is then synchronized with the audio track of the vocalist who sang the song.

LIST BROKER   A company that coordinates the compilation or rental of mailing lists. The company works on behalf of the list owners and is paid on commission—a percentage of the rental fee. List brokers frequently offer consulting services in addition to list procurement. They advise clients on which lists to rent and often evaluate list performance. List brokers offer clients many types of *compiled* and *house* lists that are targeted at particular market segments.

LIST PRICE   The standard retail selling price of a product prior to the application of a discount. A product's list price is indicated on its price tag. Additionally, it is indicated in merchandise catalogs and on purchase orders and invoices.

LOCAL MEDIA   Print and broadcast media that serve an audience in the same geographic area as the media's location. For example, a local newspaper is distributed to readers in the city in which the publication is produced and printed. Advertisers in the media's geographic area benefit from **local rates:** prices for advertising space or time that are discounted for local advertisers. National advertisers pay a higher cost for advertising in local media than local advertisers do.

LOCAL RATES   Discounted advertising rates granted by media to advertisers in the media's area. Local rates are lower than those charged to national advertisers. Many national companies engage in **cooperative advertising** with local retailers to benefit from ad purchases at local rates. Under such an arrangement, the national advertiser has the retailer place the ads to receive the discounted local rate.

LOGISTICS   The procedures involved in controlling and allocating resources in manufacturing, physical distribution, or purchasing operations. (Resources include both materials and manpower.) Logistics involve the overall management of activities involved in delivering finished goods from the point of origin to the point of consumption. Logistical activities may include demand forecasting, inventory control, materials handling, order processing, warehousing and storage, and customer service.

LOGO   **1.** A design, symbol, or series of words that identifies a product or organization. Logos may be a **trademark,** which is a name or designation that distinguishes a product from its competitors. **2.** In journalism, a one-piece line of type that bears the name of a publication. Also known as *logotype.*

LONG-RANGE PLANNING   The process of developing and implementing initiatives to achieve specific objectives over a prolonged period of time. Long-range planning involves assessing the attributes and resources of a company vis-à-vis the changing threats and opportunities of the environment in which it operates. Long-range planning is based on developing action plans and budgets; analyzing internal and external forces that may have an impact on the company's operations; establishing specific goals and objectives; creating strategies to achieve them; and developing performance measurements to monitor the program's success. Long-range planning may relate to general-business planning or to marketing planning.

LOSS LEADER PRICING   A pricing strategy by retailers in which the cost of a popular product is lowered and widely advertised to build store traffic. Retailers acknowledge that they will take a loss on profits. But they do so under the theory that consumers who have purchased one product below cost will be less reluctant to pay full price for others in the store. Also known as *leader pricing.*

LOTTERY   A type of contest used in sales promotion programs. It requires that a consumer make a product purchase that qualifies him or her for a random drawing for a prize. Lotteries differ from **sweepstakes** in that the latter do not require consumers to make a purchase to qualify for the prize. According to U.S. Postal Service regulations, lotteries are illegal for direct-mail promotions because they are deemed to be gambling.

LOWER-INVOLVEMENT MODEL   Advertising media that require little or no active participation by the consumer to receive the advertising message. Examples are radio, TV, and other broadcast media. With lower-involvement models, consumers are not consciously seeking information but rather, are passive recipients. That is, information is unconsciously absorbed as opposed to being actively sought and interpreted. Advertisers must recognize that using lower-involvement models requires repeatedly exposing consumers to the advertising message to ensure its effectiveness. See also **higher-involvement model.**

LOW-INVOLVEMENT CONSUMER BEHAVIOR   A consumer's purchase of a product done with little thought, price comparison, and decision making. The consumer is typically unconcerned with specific brands or choices because there is little personal consequence to the purchase decision, nor does it relate to important goals held by the consumer. An example of low-involvement consumer behavior is the purchase of low-cost convenience goods such as soap or candy. *High-involvement consumer behavior* refers to a great deal of deliberation going into the purchase decision, for example, when the consumer buys a car.

M

MACROENVIRONMENT   The collection of external market forces that influences a company's ability to sell its products and services. Companies must examine the following macroenvironment forces when devising marketing strategies:

• *Economic environment*—comprising the economic variables and developments that affect people's ability and willingness to purchase products (i.e., employment levels, inflation, interest rates, supply and demand patterns).

• *Demographic environment*—relating to the study of the population of target buyers, particularly with regard to their geographic dispersion and income levels and distribution.

• *Social-cultural environment*—referring to the sociological factors that shape consumers' attitudes and behavior and that, ultimately, influence demand patterns (e.g., cultural attitudes such as a society's values relating to marriage, family, education, professional achievement).

• *Political-legal environment*—relating to, for example, monetary and fiscal policies such as taxation, environmental protection laws, and regulations prohibiting certain kinds of advertising (e.g., laws disallowing cigarette advertising on television).

• *Technological environment*—referring to new technologies that impact a market by changing the ways people use products (e.g., introduction of the microwave oven and its spawning of new products, such as microwavable entrees and trays).

• *Competitive environment*—relating to the process of assessing competitors and the attributes of their product offerings.

Marketing planners are generally unable to control macroenvironmental forces. However, they must attempt to understand the nature of these forces and forecast their direction and intensity. Marketers then develop **marketing mix** combinations to capitalize on positive macroenvironmental forces or to counter negative forces. See also **microenvironment.**

MADA (MONEY, AUTHORITY, DESIRE, ACCESS)   Criteria used in sales forecasting and in measuring market potential. Marketers attempt to characterize a population by assigning MADA attributes to it. That is, companies strive to quantify the consumers who have the financial means to purchase a product (money); have the power to make the purchase decision (authority); have the interest in buying the item (desire); and have the ability to physically obtain it (access). Using MADA attributes is a starting point in devising marketing strategy.

MAGAZINE   A periodical whose editorial content is topical and reports a given subject using in-depth detail. There are two basic types of magazines: *Consumer magazines* report information of interest to the general public (e.g., *Time*, the news magazine, and *People*, which covers celebrity news and human-interest features); *trade magazines* cover news of interest to businesspeople in specific industries. Magazines are published either weekly or monthly, although some are produced quarterly. Magazines are printed on paper that is generally of a higher quality than newsprint.

MAGAZINE IMPACT METHOD   A form of **recall** testing that gauges the communications effectiveness of magazine advertisements. Via this technique, respondents are asked to read a magazine, close the publication, and then describe the ads they remember in the issue. The research findings ultimately cite the percentage of readers who remember a particular ad and can describe it accurately. Additionally, the data quantify the respondents' level of recall of an ad's sales message as well as its overall persuasiveness. The magazine impact method is conducted by the Gallup & Robinson company.

MAGNETIC TAPE   Tape used to store computer-readable data. Magnetic tape is employed in several different marketing applications. For example, magnetic tape is used in **data entry,** where research statistics are entered into a computer system. It is also used for direct-mail lists: The client receives a rented or purchased list on magnetic tape from which he or she prints out the list or modifies its entries.

MAGNUSSON-MOSS WARRANTY/FEDERAL TRADE COMMIS-SION IMPROVEMENT ACT   Federal legislation enacted in 1975 that empowers the FTC to establish rules on consumer warranties. Specifically, the act requires consumer product sellers to clearly indicate whether a written warranty is a *full* or *limited* warranty. Moreover, the act gives the FTC greater jurisdictional power in curbing unfair and deceptive acts and business practices.

MAILING LIST   A compilation of the names and addresses of target customers. Mailing lists are created by companies for their own marketing initiatives (e.g., compiling lists of all past and present customers), or they are purchased or rented from **list brokers,** companies that specialize in list compilations.

Mailing lists are compiled several different ways. Perhaps the most popular method is through listings of magazine subscribers. Lists of readers are an excellent means of targeting people in specific industries (e.g., *Institutional Investor, MIS Week*) or with distinct areas of interest (such as *Field & Stream* or *Sports Illustrated*). Lists may also be developed based on zip code, when the marketer seeks to reach consumers in a particular geographic area or income level (as dictated by the zip code). Credit card lists are another means of list compilation, with the names of people who have purchased goods using a credit card.

There are two basic types of lists. *House lists* are assembled by companies with the names of their own current and past customers (or, perhaps, people who at one time responded to a promotional offer). Companies use house lists for their own marketing programs or sell or rent the lists to other companies involved in direct-mail solicitations. *Compiled lists* contain people's names culled from directories and other sources of public information such as trade association rosters and telephone books. House lists are generally more expensive to obtain than compiled lists because the former contain people who have already purchased products via direct mail. Compiled lists are comprised of people who are not proven direct-mail buyers.

Mailing lists must be periodically reviewed to incorporate address changes and to delete the names of people who are no longer customers. See also **merge-purge.**

MAIL ORDER   The practice of promoting and distributing products through the mail. The defining characteristic of this marketing approach is that there is never face-to-face interaction between buyer and seller. *Mail-order advertising* is designed to promote goods available through the mail. It encompasses several different tools and techniques. The most common of these is catalogs. Catalogs are distributed by mail and product ordering is effected the same way. However, mail-order companies often use **800-numbers** to allow consumers to place orders by phone. Direct-mail packages and space ads are the other common forms of mail-order advertising.

MAINTENANCE, REPAIR, OPERATING (MRO) ITEMS   Classification of the various products and supplies used in a manufacturing environment. *Maintenance* items are used in preserving manufacturing equipment and ensuring its functionality (e.g., cleaning supplies, mops). *Repair* items are the products needed to keep equipment in sound working order (e.g., machine lubricants, new control switches). *Operating* items are the products used to actually run the manufacturing equipment (e.g., fuel oil).

MAJOR ACCOUNTS   A company's customers that are so important they require special treatment and attention. Major accounts are handled by senior sales representatives or managers specially assigned to the accounts. Contact with major accounts is frequent to ensure the customers' ongoing satisfaction. Also known as *key accounts*.

MAKEGOOD   A credit of advertising given to advertisers when a medium is unable to run their advertising at the time or in the form originally planned. For example, a magazine will grant a makegood when it is unable to run an ad in the position contracted for, or if the insertion is unreadable due to a printing error. Broadcast stations grant makegoods under four basic circumstances: when they are unable to air a commercial at the desired time; when a spot has to be canceled due to unavoidable circumstances; if video transmission is interrupted or is of poor quality; and if the advertising fails to deliver the audience size or composition as contractually agreed upon. Makegoods are generally reruns of the advertising spots, as opposed to financial reimbursement for the amount of time or space purchased.

MALL INTERCEPT INTERVIEW   Interview arranged when a researcher stops people in a shopping mall to request the interview. There are two drawbacks to this method of surveying respondents. First, mall intercept interviews generally must be brief. Second, because this is a form of **judgment sampling,** there is significant room for **interviewer bias** in choosing which people to interview.

MANUFACTURER'S AGENT   An independent salesperson working in a specific geographic territory who sells products from several noncompeting manufacturers. The products are typically related in nature and are distributed via the same channels to the same range of customers. Manufacturer's agents are remunerated by **commission** and generally have extended contracts with the manufacturers. As a result, they often possess some authority in setting product prices or establishing terms of sale. Also known as *manufacturer's representative.*

MANUFACTURER'S BRAND   1. Merchandise carrying a manufacturing company's name as opposed to a reseller's name (a **private brand**). For example, Whirlpool's line of washing machines, driers, and dishwashers are manufacturer's brands, all of which carry the company's name. 2. Products that have been licensed for sale by other companies outside the manufacturer's product category. For instance, a well-known clothing manufacturer may license its name to companies who use the name on their perfumes and jewelry.

MANUFACTURING-DRIVEN COMPANY   A company that places primary emphasis on manufacturing requirements at the expense of marketing (e.g., customer service) considerations. A manufacturing-driven company strives to ensure smooth production schedules, low manufacturing costs, and high-volume production. (Customers on back order have to wait for goods.) A **marketing-driven company** places primary emphasis on satisfying customers. In a marketing-driven company, production schedules would be altered to accommodate customers' needs (regardless of the cost overruns and overtime work schedules that would be incurred).

MARGIN   1. The numerical difference between the price of a product and the cost to produce it. 2. In printing, the distance between the copy/artwork and the edge of the page. See also **bleed.**

MARKDOWN   A reduction in selling price. Markdowns are made to stimulate demand for a product or are established to capitalize on reduced costs for materials or manufacturing.

MARKET   **1.** The group of potential buyers with the desire and financial means to purchase a product. Marketers distinguish between two basic types of market. The *consumer market* consists of individuals who purchase goods for their own use or benefit. The *organizational market* is comprised of businesses, industries, governments, and institutions that purchase products for resale or for use in making other products. Companies identify *target markets:* the people with access to the product who collectively represent a group with the level of buying power that justifies special marketing initiatives designed to reach them. **2.** The geographic location where buyers reside (e.g., the Japanese market, the Canadian market) or the particular place where the marketing exchange process occurs (e.g., a store).

MARKET ATTRACTIVENESS   Market appeal that is based on several factors. These include the market's size or the annual rate at which it is growing. *Economic/technological* factors include inflationary forces (affecting people's ability to buy the product), **barriers to entry,** and the availability of raw materials (or a lack thereof). *Competitive* forces include the number of rival companies and their respective competitive strengths. *Environmental* factors relate to such things as governmental regulations and the extent to which the product or service is socially acceptable.

MARKET ATTRACTIVENESS–COMPETITIVE POSITION MATRIX
A multifactor model developed by General Electric and the McKinsey consulting firm. It is used to make decisions on entering or remaining in a market. The matrix is based on two factors: **market attractiveness** and the **competitive position** of the company (or its products) vis-à-vis rival companies. It is also known as the *9-block matrix* because the two dimensions are divided into three levels. See also **growth-share matrix.**

MARKET-BY-MARKET BUY   A media buying approach in which broadcast commercial time is bought in different markets one area at a time. It is different from a **network buy** in which the advertiser makes one buy and its commercial airs on all local stations affiliated with the network. Advertisers make market-by-market buys when they want to target their advertising at specific geographic markets. See also **spot TV/radio.**

MARKET COVERAGE   Term relating to distribution decisions as well as to the types of products offered by a company to different market segments. As a distribution concept, market coverage describes the number of outlets in a given market through which the product is available. Market coverage is the percentage of the number of outlets where the product is available in comparison to the total number of potential outlets in which the product could be offered. Market coverage as a product offering concept describes strategies relating to what types of product to offer to which parts of a market. For instance, in *single-market* strategy, the company concentrates on one segment of the market (e.g., a car manufacturer that only develops models for small-car buyers). A *product specialization* strategy relates to the decision to make one product for all segments of the market. A *market specialization* approach refers to the decision to develop all products for a particular market segment. In *selective specialization*, a company develops different products for different market niches. *Full coverage* is the rare situation in which the company makes different products for each individual customer.

MARKET DEMAND   The total amount of product purchased by a group of consumers in a specific market at a particular point in time. Market demand is measured three ways. *Product levels* gauge market demand by product type, form, company sales, industry sales, or national sales. *Space levels* refer to market demand as determined by territory (region, nation, world). *Time levels* gauge market demand over short-, medium- or long-range time periods. Companies prepare estimates of market demand as part of their ongoing planning. See also **total market potential.**

MARKET DEVELOPMENT   A company's attempt to expand the market in which it is operating. Companies may enter new market segments by broadening the geographic parameters of their business or by using new distribution channels. Second, they can attempt to convert nonusers of their product either by lowering the price or by directing special promotions at them. Third, companies can increase product usage by current customers by creating new product uses.

MARKET DEVELOPMENT INDEX   The ratio between a brand's potential and actual customers in a given geographic area in comparison to the total number of potential and actual customers of the brand nationally. Market development index is used as an indicator of the sales potential of a given brand or product category. See also **brand development index.**

MARKETING DRIVEN COMPANY   A company that bases its key operating (e.g., manufacturing) decisions on meeting customer needs. For example, manufacturing complications and cost overruns that may be incurred in meeting those needs are of secondary importance. In a **manufacturing-driven company,** primary emphasis is placed on ensuring smooth production and low costs. In contrast, a marketing-driven company makes every effort to satisfy its customers. Marketing decisions dictate manufacturing schedules, and there is little concern for the overtime costs and other complications that can result from meeting customer needs. See also **customer orientation.**

MARKET GROWTH RATE   The annual increase in a market in which a business operates. Market growth may be stated in terms of population, product sales, or other factors. (A market growth rate in excess of 10% is generally considered high.) Market growth rate is one variable cited in the **growth-share matrix,** which is used to evaluate the performance of products, product portfolios, and **strategic business units.** Increasing a market's growth rate may be a marketing strategy unto itself. For example, a company that manufactures compact-disc players might strive to increase market growth for its product. It would employ generic advertising to persuade people to discard their stereos and audiocassette players in favor of the newer compact-disc technology.

MARKETING   The complex, interrelated series of activities involved in creating products and services, promoting their existence and attributes, and making them physically available to identified target buyers. Marketing is comprised of four distinct processes: (1) developing the product or service; (2) establishing a price for it; (3) communicating information about it through various direct and indirect communications channels; and (4) coordinating its distribution to ensure product accessibility by target buyers. See also **marketing mix.**

MARKETING AUDIT   The process by which an ongoing marketing program is evaluated. The goal of an audit is to spot problem areas and to devise actions to improve performance. A successful marketing audit must be *comprehensive*—that is, it must review all aspects of the marketing program and not just problem areas. It must be *systematic*—that is, it should involve a series of diagnostic steps that address the marketing environment, internal marketing resources, and current marketing initiatives. The audit must be conducted by an independent person who's well-versed in the company's guiding mission and who can make an objective assessment. The audit should be conducted as a matter of course and not only when crisis situations arise. See also **marketing controls.**

MARKETING BUDGET   The financial element of a marketing plan. The budget details how money will be allocated in the pursuit of the plan's goals and objectives. For example, it will state how much is to be spent on market research, sales force funding, advertising, and other forms of promotion. Budgets are developed to guide the actions outlined in the plan. That is, a review of the budget can help identify deviations from the plan (e.g., areas where more money is being spent than was originally budgeted) as a means of devising corrective actions and assessing plan performance.

MARKETING CHANNELS   The interdependent organizations a company employs to make its product available for consumption. Channel organizations include wholesalers, retailers, manufacturer's agents, and other intermediaries involved in product distribution, sales, and promotion. Companies must decide which channel alternatives to pursue. These involve the *number* and *kind* of channel intermediaries to utilize. For example, the company must determine if it is efficient to make products available through retailers (in which case, it must generally employ wholesalers to effect distribution to retailers) and how many retailers should be used. *Channel management* is an ongoing company task. This process begins with selecting the right intermediaries to employ and engendering a sense of teamwork between them and the company. Moreover, channel management involves periodically evaluating the performance of intermediaries. Performance is measured either against the intermediary's own past achievements or its performance in relation to other intermediaries in the channel system. See also **channel behavior.**

MARKETING COMMUNICATIONS MIX   The activities employed to communicate product information to present and potential customers and to other publics. The marketing communications mix consists of four major tools: advertising, sales promotion, publicity, and personal selling. A variety of tactics are employed in each of these areas. In general, marketing communications decisions involve determining what to say, to whom, and how often. These decisions comprise a company's *communications strategy*. Strategy development involves identifying the target audience and its characteristics; establishing communications objectives (e.g., getting consumers to become aware, like, or develop a preference for a product); deciding on **communications channels** (personal and/or nonpersonal channels); setting a communications budget; and determining how to monitor communications effectiveness and consumer feedback. Also known as *promotion mix*.

MARKETING CONCEPT   The business philosophy dictating that successfully achieving organizational goals is based on determining customers' needs and meeting them more effectively than competitors do. This marketing focus is different from a selling focus in which the organization seeks to meet its own needs as opposed to those of its customers.

MARKETING CONTROLS   Measures enacted to help a company monitor and evaluate its marketing activities. Controls help a company determine if its activities are being performed efficiently and effectively. There are four basic kinds of marketing controls: *Annual-plan controls* gauge ongoing performance as measured against activities in the annual plan (the goal is to take corrective actions when necessary); *profitability controls* are undertaken to assess the actual profitability of products, territories, or trade channels; *efficiency controls* are used to determine ways to improve the impact of different marketing tools and expenditures; *strategic controls* are conducted to examine whether the company's basic strategies are consistent with its external market opportunities. See also **marketing audit**.

MARKETING DIRECTOR   The executive in a corporation who oversees all marketing functions. In a typical organization, the marketing director supervises the company's advertising, sales promotion, marketing research, and public-relations activities. Each of these groups is headed by a manager, who reports to the marketing director.

MARKETING INFORMATION SYSTEM   The system of collecting and disseminating relevant market information for use by company decision makers. The system is structured to sort, analyze, and distribute information to help managers make better, faster, and less risky marketing decisions. Designing a marketing information system requires determining what information is needed. For example, an advertising manager needs data to compare the effectiveness of a print ad appearing in several magazines; a product manager requires information on competing products to formulate strategies for the brand under his or her management. A marketing information system should consist of four basic elements:

1. *Internal reports*—statistics on sales, inventory levels, cash flows, and accounts receivable and payable. Information is compiled through invoices, shipping and billing documents, sales reports, and receipts.

2. *Marketing intelligence*—information on developments in the company's external marketing environment such as competitor activity, changing customer needs, and existing or potential distribution problems. Data are compiled by reviewing books, newspapers, and trade publications. Additional input comes from discussions with customers, suppliers, distributors, and company salespeople and managers.

3. *Marketing research*—quantitative and/or qualitative data that address a specific marketing problem or situation facing the company. Market research is compiled from *primary* or *secondary* research sources.

4. *Analytical marketing*—statistical procedures to analyze the data generated by marketing research. Research analysts use descriptive, verbal, graphical, or mathematical **models** to review data in light of the specific marketing problem or situation.

Marketing information systems vary in their levels of complexity. A system may be as simple as manually tabulating responses generated by a coupon in a print ad; or it may employ intricate computer analyses that track sales or customer buying patterns by city or region.

MARKETING MANAGEMENT   The process of establishing marketing goals and devising and implementing tactics to achieve them. Implicit in the marketing management function is setting goals that are based on a company's internal resources and external market opportunities. Marketing management is an ongoing process. That is, it involves periodically altering strategies to respond to marketplace changes that pose new threats and opportunities.

MARKETING MANAGEMENT ORGANIZATION   One method of organizing the marketing function in a corporation. Marketing activities are handled by functional specialists (in the areas of research, advertising, sales, public relations, etc.). These specialists report either to the marketing director or to a group marketing manager or product manager. The marketing management structure is common in large companies that produce numerous products sold to different consumers through different distribution channels. See also **marketing organization.**

MARKETING MANAGER   The corporate executive responsible for overseeing marketing activities relating to a particular market or product. These activities include research, product planning, pricing, distribution, and promotional communications. A marketing manager's basic duties involve developing and implementing marketing plans, and monitoring their execution. Marketing managers become expert in understanding the needs and practices of a given market. Consequently, they provide valuable input regarding customer needs to other corporate departments such as research and development, sales, manufacturing, and technical services.

MARKETING MIX   The four controllable variables a company regulates to effectively sell a product. Also known as the *4 P's of marketing,* which refer to product, price, place, and promotion.

  1. *Product*—an entity possessing objective and subjective characteristics manipulated to maximize its appeal to target consumers. Products may be objects (goods), services, activities, places, people, or organizations. Products that are objects fall into two categories:

  a. *Industrial goods* are used in producing other products and are typically sold to manufacturing organizations. Industrial goods are further categorized into raw materials, equipment, fabricated materials, and supplies.

b. *Consumer goods* are designed for individual use by the general public. Consumer goods are grouped into three categories:
- *Durable goods* are used time and again and their life expectancy is more than three years. Examples include televisions, appliances, and furniture. (Durable goods also are referred to as *hard goods*.)
- *Nondurable goods* have a shorter life expectancy than durable goods. Examples are clothing and other textile goods. (Nondurable goods also are referred to as *soft goods*.)
- *Packaged goods* are created by manufacturers and are sold through retail outlets. Examples include food, toiletries, and household products.

2. *Price*—setting a product's cost to maximize sales and to enhance product image among the target consumers. Price is the most flexible element of the marketing mix, as well as the only one that generates revenues (the other "P's" generate only costs to the company). Nonetheless, price is inextricably linked to these other elements. Since a product's price relates to the tangible and intangible characteristics of the item (i.e., product features, store locations in which it is available), price planning is done in concert with decisions on distribution, promotional tactics, and product management. *Note:* Price is particularly important in its influence on consumers' perceptions of the product, which ultimately have an impact on sales volume and profits.

3. *Place*—the tactics and distribution channels used to make a product physically available to consumers. Manufacturers consider the following three distribution alternatives:

a. *Direct channels* involve selling directly to consumers (such as in the case of perishable goods and certain specialized products requiring demonstration of use).
b. *Indirect channels* rely on the use of retailers, wholesalers, industrial supply houses, manufacturers' representatives, and agents. (Although it is a more costly method, companies can reach many more consumers via indirect channels than through other distribution techniques.)
c. *Multiple channels* involve using a combination of direct and indirect channels. Marketers, however, must be cognizant of potential rivalries between channels (e.g., competing stores that may refuse to carry the same goods).

Place considerations also relate to physical distribution of the product, for example, warehousing, packaging for transportation, type of transportation employed, and the number of distribution points.

4. *Promotion*—the marketing and communications tactics used to alert target consumers to the features, benefits, and availability of a product. Marketers employ four basic promotion techniques to persuade consumers to purchase their product: advertising, personal selling, sales promotion, and publicity.

MARKETING MIX MODEL   A type of **model** used in management decision making regarding the optimal combination of marketing mix variables: product, price, place, and promotion. That is, the model enables management to estimate the market response to different combinations of these variables. The goal of using a marketing mix model is determining the most effective grouping of these variables for different products and marketing situations.

MARKETING MYOPIA   Concept relating to when a company emphasizes in its marketing of a product the item's attributes rather than the item's ability to meet customers' needs. Thus, marketing myopia is when the company does not highlight the benefits or services inherent in a product's design. Rather, it emphasizes only the product's physical characteristics. See also **marketing concept.**

MARKETING ORGANIZATION   The ways the marketing function is organized in a corporation. Marketing organizations may be *functional organizations* in which separate marketing functions are headed by managers (e.g., advertising, sales, research) who report to a vice-president of marketing; *product management organizations* in which individual products are assigned to product managers, who coordinate and oversee the work of functional specialists; *marketing management organizations* in which major accounts are assigned to marketing managers, who supervise the work of functional specialists; and *divisional organizations* in which a diversified company has divisional marketing departments, headed by managers who report to a central corporate marketing department.

MARKETING PLAN   Document detailing the objectives, strategies, and activities to be employed in marketing a product or service. In most large consumer-product companies marketing plans are prepared for individual brands. The collective of plans comprises the company's overall *marketing program*. Implicit in this framework is the need for consistency between marketing plans, as well as between the plans and the company's guiding mission and corporate objectives. A marketing plan consists of several basic sections:

1. *Executive summary*—a synopsis of the plan. It briefly describes the product or service, recommended strategies and tactics, and specific goals and objectives. Also referenced are the financial investment required and the projected results. Results may be defined in terms of increased market share, sales, profits, or **return on investment.**

Note: Managers who read numerous marketing plans (venture capitalists as well as senior management and marketing executives) often read no further than the executive summary. Thus, it is critical that this section clearly outline the plan's major elements and persuasively communicate its potential and likelihood of success.

2. *Situational analysis*—addresses the internal and external variables affecting the company and its product(s). It includes quantitative and qualitative projections for the marketing actions being proposed. Among the situational variables reviewed are industry developments affecting the marketing environment such as new competitors, technological innovations, environmental issues, and socioeconomic and political developments that may impact the marketing strategy. Projections of performance indices (i.e., income, net profit, losses, etc.) are made based on extrapolations of past data and the subjective input of experienced managers. An assessment of strengths and weaknesses of a product, as well as those of competitors' products, is usually included in the situational analysis.

3. *Goals and objectives*—details the desired end results of the marketing actions. Goals and objectives are usually stated in terms of sales volume, profits, or gains in market share. Objectives outline, in general, what achievement is desired (e.g., increased return on investment). Goals are the *specific* aims of the objectives (e.g., to increase return on investment by 20%).

It is important that goals and objectives be articulated clearly. This helps in defining managers' specific areas of responsibility and in helping to assess progress and performance.

4. *Marketing strategy*—describes the activities and tactics that will be employed to reach the goals and objectives. Marketing strategy is devised by addressing three basic areas:

- *Select markets*—defining who the market is, as determined by either a **mass marketing** approach or a **target marketing** approach.
- *Positioning*—identifying and communicating the differentiating characteristics of the product versus those of competitors.
- *Marketing mix*—combining the variables that a company controls (product, place, price, promotion) to establish or reinforce its competitive position.

5. *Marketing controls*—details how marketing plan performance will be assessed using quantitative and/or qualitative criteria. Controls are useful in periodically gauging the success of the plan and in devising corrective actions, where necessary.

6. *Budget*—details the financial resources to be allocated in implementing the marketing plan. Costs include those for product development, distribution, and promotional activities. The budget may also include personnel costs (e.g., salaries of managers responsible for carrying out the initiative).

Also known as *action program.*

MARKETING PLANNING   The process of devising strategies, activities, and specific goals and objectives related to marketing a product or service. Formal planning is deemed essential to successful marketing. Planning encourages systematic thinking by management, forces management to clearly identify goals and objectives, and leads to greater coordination of activities. Planning also enables management to periodically gauge the success of the marketing initiative and, if necessary, to take corrective actions. See also **marketing plan.**

MARKETING RESEARCH   Information that relates to a specific market opportunity or problem, and the process of collecting, analyzing, and reporting this information. Compiling market research requires determining what market data are needed. It also calls for devising a strategy for generating usable information in a cost-effective manner. Accumulating relevant market research data involves four steps:

1. *Define the marketing problem/opportunity.* Usable information can't be generated without knowing the marketing situation. Examples of marketing situations include declining sales in a particular

region or city, or low levels of product awareness among target consumers. Once the problem is defined, researchers then set research objectives. Thus, their objectives might be to determine why sales are declining, or to identify the reasons for low product awareness. Identifying the problem is necessary to determine the type of research required. There are three basic types:

- *Exploratory research* gathers preliminary data to help clarify the nature of the problem. For example, exploratory studies would have been employed to identify that sales are declining in the market under review or that product awareness is low.
- *Descriptive research* gauges the magnitude of the marketing problem. It would be used to determine *how much* sales are declining or how low product awareness actually is among target consumers.
- *Causal research* attempts to identify causes and effects. It would be employed to see if sales increase if the product's cost is lowered, or if consumer awareness is raised by advertising in different media.

2. *Develop the research plan.* This involves determining the most efficient way to gather needed information, and the time required to do so. The research plan will identify

- *Information sources* to be used. Information may be accumulated from *primary* or *secondary* sources. Secondary data are information available from within the company (e.g., from its **marketing information system**) or from published sources such as government periodicals, trade publications and books, or commercial data from *syndicated service research firms.* Primary data are information gathered specifically for the company, which involves scientifically selecting and interviewing people individually or in groups. *Note:* Companies often begin the research process by reviewing secondary data to see if problems can be identified without having to collect primary data, which is significantly more costly and time-consuming. Secondary data can also help in developing research hypotheses that lend direction to the research initiative.
- *Research approaches* to be used. If primary data are needed, they can be generated by one or more of the following approaches: **Observational research** involves studying relevant consumers or the setting in which they purchase products. (Thus, researchers may station themselves in stores to witness consum-

ers' purchasing activities and may interview them about their purchase decisions.) **Focus groups** may be assembled to interview consumers in a small-group setting on their purchase decisions and product perceptions. **Surveys** may be used to gauge consumers' knowledge, beliefs, preferences, or attitudes. **Experimental research** involves using groups of interviewees who are subjected to different research treatments. Researchers control extraneous variables and attempt to identify how the different groups respond. Responses are then reviewed to see if the differences are statistically significant.

- *Research instruments* to be employed. Questionnaires are a common type of research instrument. They are used in face-to-face or telephone interviews by a trained researcher, or questionnaires are self-administered by the respondent. Mechanical instruments may also be used. These include *galvanometers,* which measure a respondent's physical reactions in response to exposure to a particular picture or ad; and *tachistoscopes,* which flash an image to a respondent at different intervals, after which the respondent describes his or her level of **recall.**

- *Methods for selecting respondents.* Researchers must develop a **sampling** plan to determine which respondents will provide the research information. The sampling plan identifies who should be interviewed (e.g., product users or nonusers), how many people should be interviewed (large samples give more reliable results than small samples), and the procedure by which respondents are selected (e.g., probability or nonprobability samples).

- *Methods of contacting respondents.* Information may be accumulated through telephone interviewing, questionnaires mailed to respondents, or personal interviews with respondents.

3. *Collect the information.* Various manual and technological methods can be employed. Manual data collection may simply involve the researcher writing down respondents' answers to interview questions. Technological tools include computers and electronic communications hardware. Examples of the latter are *cathode-ray tubes* and *data-entry terminals.* These allow researchers to input respondents' answers directly into a computer, thus obviating the need for editing and coding (called CATI—computer-assisted telephone interviewing). *Note:* Collecting information is usually the most costly phase of the research process and the one most liable to error because respon-

dents may be unreachable, may refuse to be interviewed, or may give false or biased answers.

4. *Analyze the information.* Pertinent findings must be extracted from the collected data. Information is tabulated. Then, statistical techniques and decision **models** are used to discover additional findings.

MARKETING RESEARCH MANAGER   The company executive responsible for providing research services in a corporation. The research manager generates research data (by reviewing *secondary* research sources) or oversees the work of retained market research firms (in developing *primary* data). In large companies, the marketing research manager has staff support in accumulating data for use in marketing decision making.

MARKETING STRATEGY   The collective of a company's marketing goals and objectives and the measures it will take to achieve them. The marketing strategy is outlined in (and often used synonymously with) the company's marketing plan. The strategy may be either for specific products or for the entire company. Activities to achieve the strategy are established for a specified period of time.

MARKETING WARFARE   Marketing strategies based on military tactics described using terms from various militaristic undertakings. Which marketing warfare tactic to apply depends on the company's position in the market. That is, being the market leader requires tactics different from those employed by a small company seeking entry into the market. The concept of marketing warfare was popularized in the book *Marketing Warfare* by marketing consultants Al Ries and Jack Trout. This book, published by McGraw-Hill, and others on the topic cite marketing case studies that illustrate the tactics employed by companies battling competitors in the same product category. See also **defensive warfare; flanking; guerilla warfare; offensive warfare.**

MARKET NICHE   A narrow market segment that a company targets because the segment is free of competitors yet offers significant sales potential. Serving a market niche is a common tactic of small companies because the niche is unattractive to (and, therefore, unserved by) the company's larger, more powerful competitors. Examples of market niches include a management consulting firm offering its services only to small clients (who are generally overlooked by larger firms); and a manufacturing company setting its prices either at the low end or high end of the market where there are no competitors. See also **niche marketing.**

MARKET ORIENTATION   The approach to developing and selling products in which product planning begins with identifying customer needs. A market-oriented company begins the product development process by basing product design on customer requirements. The marketing department suggests new product ideas to other groups in the company such as purchasing, research and development, and manufacturing. Once a product idea is approved, the various groups begin assembling the needed materials to manufacture and market the item. A market orientation is different from the "traditional" process of developing and selling products. Here, it is the research and development group that conceives product ideas. Once management approves the promising concepts, materials procurement and manufacturing commence, and the marketing department is assigned the task of selling the item. The drawback of the traditional approach is that the customer is viewed at the end of the process. Thus, little customer information (if any) is collected to design the product and improve its functionality.

MARKET PENETRATION   The strategies to increase the market share of the product in markets where the company already operates. Companies try to achieve greater penetration by getting current customers to buy more of the product. Or, they can try to attract competitors' customers or get nonusers to become users. Market penetration strategies generally involve aggressive promotion and new distribution tactics. It is similar in concept to **market development.** See also **penetration strategies.**

MARKET POSITIONING   See **positioning.**

MARKET PROFILE   The descriptive aspects of a market used as a guide to developing marketing strategies. A market profile describes a group in terms of the similar traits of its members. These can relate to demographic characteristics such as age, sex, and income bracket; or to similarities in lifestyle as indicated by people's activities and interests. A market profile can also be based on socioeconomic factors such as supply and demand patterns.

MARKET SEGMENTATION   The practice of dividing a market into groups of buyers for whom special products or **marketing mix** strategies are developed. Companies engage in segmentation when they cannot effectively serve all customers in a large market (e.g., when consumers are too numerous, widely dispersed, or have different buying requirements). There are four basic ways to segment a market.

1. *Demographic segmentation.* Groups are based on age, sex, religion, race, nationality, size of family, and so on. Dividing a market by demographics is the most popular segmentation strategy because demographic data are easy to measure and obtain. Much of the data are available through government censuses of the population. Also, buyer wants and product usage patterns can be very similar among members of the same demographic category.

Note: Sometimes researchers combine two or more demographic variables to segment a market (e.g., combining age and income bracket). This process is known as *multiattribute segmentation.*

2. *Geographic segmentation.* A market's composition is grouped by nation, state, region, county, city, or neighborhood. Other geographic variables are population density and climate. *Note:* A company that segments markets geographically must decide in which area(s) to operate. If it attempts to operate in all markets, it must take into account the different buyer needs and preferences of the areas' population.

3. *Behavioral segmentation.* Groups are defined by how members use the product and/or perceive its benefits. Behavioral categories may include *purchase factors,* relating to when people buy the product (e.g., Christmas, Mother's Day); *benefits,* or the particular aspects of a product the group members hold to be important (e.g., improvement to lifestyle, health, or socioeconomic standing); *usage status and rates,* referring to whether or not members use the product (nonusers, first-time users, regular users) and the frequency with which they do so; *loyalty,* gauging members' predisposition to trying competitors' products; and *attitudes,* referring to members' feelings toward the product (i.e., enthusiastic, positive, indifferent, negative, hostile).

4. *Psychographic segmentation:* The market is divided into groups based on lifestyle, characterized by members sharing common activi-

ties, interests, and opinions; or personality, relating to members' commonality in terms of being, for example, independent, impulsive, self-confident, thrifty, or prestige-conscious.

Many segmentation options are available to marketers. However, segments must meet four criteria. They must be

1. *Measurable.* The size and purchasing power of the segment must be quantifiable. Many segmentation variables are difficult to measure. For example, it is impossible to measure the market size of all people who like the color red. However, it is possible to measure the market size of people who like red cars (by identifying annual car sales broken down by color).

2. *Accessible.* The segment should be easily reachable (through communications) and can be served (via product distribution and delivery). For example, American armed forces personnel stationed in the United States are an accessible market to American companies. Those personnel stationed around the world are a much less accessible market.

3. *Substantial.* The segment must be large enough and have sufficient purchasing power to financially justify the specialized marketing activities.

4. *Actionable.* The company must have the staff and resources to effectively reach the segments identified. Attempting to approach more segments than can actually be serviced jeopardizes the success of the overall initiative.

Once a company has segmented its market, it generally engages in one of three marketing strategies: **differentiated marketing, undifferentiated marketing,** or **concentrated marketing.** See also **market targeting.**

MARKET SHARE   The proportionate quantity of unit or dollar sales of a company in a given market. Thus, market share is the amount of money spent by consumers on the company's brand, as compared to the total amount of money spent by consumers on all competing brands in the same product category. Companies periodically conduct market share analyses to monitor their marketing programs and to ensure that their sales and profit goals will be achieved. Market share analyses are also undertaken as a **marketing controls** exercise to detect problems and to take corrective actions, where necessary. Also known as *brand share* and *share of market.*

MARKET-STRUCTURED SALES FORCE   A sales force structure in which sellers specialize in particular market segments. That is, separate sales forces are established for different industries or for large customers within those industries. For example, a computer company establishes sales forces for customers in the finance/brokerage industry, for automotive companies, and for manufacturing concerns. The benefit of a market-structured sales force is that sellers become expert in the market's (or a customer's) specific needs. The drawback is that travel and selling costs can be high if the various markets or companies within them are widely dispersed. See also **product-structured sales force; territory-structured sales force.**

MARKET TARGETING   A company's decision on which groups of buyers to pursue after it has engaged in **market segmentation.** Targeting is based on an evaluation of the market potential of each segment as determined by such factors as market size, growth, competitor activity, and the company's own resources and corporate objectives. Once a company has defined its targets, it must decide on one of three strategies: **undifferentiated marketing, differentiated marketing,** or **concentrated marketing.** Then the company must devise **positioning** strategies to distinguish itself from competitors serving the same market segment(s). See also **target marketing.**

MARKET TESTING   A key phase of the product development process in which a new item is exposed to a sample of the market to gauge consumer reaction. Market testing simulates the eventual marketing of a product. It is designed to yield information about buyers, market potential, and the effectiveness of promotional communications. A common form of market testing is introducing the product in a **test market.** Here, the product is marketed in a geographic locale that is representative of the total market. The goal is to evaluate product performance on a small scale before embarking on a costly full-market **rollout.**

MARKUP PRICING   Setting a product's retail price based on a percentage increase in the item's wholesale price. For example, a 10% markup on a product whose wholesale cost is $200 is $20. The markup price (retail cost) would be $220 ($200 + $20). Thus, the markup percentage refers to the difference between the wholesale cost and retail price.

MASS APPEAL   A marketing approach designed to reach the broadest audience possible. A mass appeal strategy ignores the different characteristics and needs of consumers within market segments; rather, the appeal is designed to be universally acceptable to all possible product users. Using a mass appeal is usually an ineffective strategy. However, it is sometimes appropriate for primary (generic) advertising. For example, an advertising campaign promoting beef as a popular American food makes a mass appeal to consumers of all demographic and psychographic categories.

MASS MARKETING   A marketing strategy in which a seller develops one product offering for all buyers in a market. The seller mass produces and mass distributes the item in an attempt to maintain low production costs and low prices. The rationale for mass marketing is attempting to serve the largest market possible. A well-known example of mass marketing was Henry Ford's offer to consumers of only one car (the Model-T) in just one color (black). A mass marketing strategy is generally ineffective, which is why companies have embraced **target marketing,** in which different products, prices, distribution channels, and promotions are developed to meet consumers' varying needs and preferences.

MASS MEDIA   Publications and broadcast stations that reach large segments of the general public. Publication groups include newspapers and magazines (and some newsletters). Broadcast media encompass radio and television (including cable TV). Billboards and transit advertising are also considered mass media. Mass media are essential to marketers seeking to reach large numbers of people via advertising, publicity, and sales promotion.

MASTHEAD   **1.** Information in a newspaper or magazine that indicates the publication's ownership and its editorial and advertising staff. This printed section, which usually appears on the table of contents or editorial page, provides the publication's address and circulation information. **2.** The line of type stating a publication's name, also known as *flag* or *banner*.

MATERIALS REQUIREMENT PLANNING (MRP)   An inventory planning approach for manufacturing operations. It is designed to integrate material procurement and manufacturing schedules, as determined by output requirements. The goal of MRP is to minimize costs and lead times and to maximize production efficiency and product quality.

MATRIX QUESTION   A type of **closed-ended question** in which statements are listed vertically, and the responses available to respondents are horizontally laid out (e.g., "yes and no" responses or "agree-disagree" choices). Matrix questions are useful in conserving space on a questionnaire and are considered to be easy to complete for respondents. An example of a matrix question is:

1. Indicate next to each statement below whether you strongly agree (S.A.), Agree (A.), are Undecided (U.), Disagree (D.), or Strongly Disagree (S.D.):

	S.A.	A.	U.	D.	S.D.
a. An MBA degree is essential to a successful career in marketing.	☐	☐	☐	☐	☐
b. Marketing professionals should have extensive training in the behavioral sciences.	☐	☐	☐	☐	☐

MATURITY STAGE OF THE PRODUCT LIFE CYCLE   See **product life cycle.**

MEAN   The arithmetic average calculated by adding the number of values, then dividing their sum by the number of values. For example, the mean of $10 + 5 + 20 + 25$ is determined by adding these figures (which total 60), then dividing by the number of values $60 \div 4 = 15$. *Note:* The weakness in using mean as an average is that it's affected by extreme cases. For instance, if the incomes of five millionaires were averaged with those of two low-paid laborers, the mean would be misleading as an indicator of the group's average income. See also **median; mode.**

MECHANICAL ART   **Camera-ready** art that is photographed for use in printing ads, brochures, and other collateral materials. Mechanical art is produced on a sheet of white cardboard, attached to which are all the design elements: typeset copy, artwork, photographs, and illustrations. Developing the mechanical art is the final phase of the graphic design process. Also known as *mechanicals* or *boards*.

MEDIA   The various channels of communication used to disseminate information. Media provide news, entertainment, and specialized/technical information. In advertising, media are grouped into four basic categories. *Print media* include newspapers, magazines, newsletters, and directories. *Broadcast media*, also called electronic media, include radio and network and cable television. *Out-of-home media* refer to billboards, transit advertising, and posters displayed in public places. *Direct-mail media* are catalogs and other printed materials delivered to consumers via the mail. See also **alternative media; communication channels.**

MEDIA BUY   The purchase of advertising space (in *print* and *outdoor media*) and air time (in *broadcast media*). Media buys are based on several criteria and procedures. In general, they are the advertising vehicles that will best reach the *target audience* (from a demographic and/or geographic standpoint). Media buying is one of the services provided by an advertising agency; however, special *media buying services* also exist. See also **media planning.**

MEDIA BUYER   The ad agency employee who coordinates the purchase of advertising space and time. Media buyers are part of the marketing services department in an ad agency. Larger agencies have media buyers that specialize in certain media: *time* buyers for broadcast buys, *space* buyers for print media purchases, and *outdoor* buyers for billboards and transit advertising.

MEDIA BUYING SERVICE   A **limited-service advertising agency** that offers media buying as its sole capability. Some of these firms provide **media planning** services as well.

MEDIA FLIGHTING   A method of scheduling advertising for a given period of time, followed by a period without advertising, then followed by another round of advertising. Media flighting is different from **continuity,** which is advertising scheduled evenly over a particular interval. A media flighting strategy is used when an advertiser has limited funds or if a product has only seasonal appeal (e.g., an item bought only during the Christmas season).

MEDIA KIT An informational package about an advertising medium that provides data on its audience and its advertising rates. Media kits give details on the size of the medium's readership or viewership/listenership, the audience composition, and (in print media) specifications for camera-ready art for advertisements. The costs for advertising in the medium are detailed on a **rate card** that is included in the kit.

MEDIAMARK RESEARCH, INC. (MRI) A market research firm that compiles data on consumers based on demographic and lifestyle characteristics. Additionally, the company provides data on specific products and brands purchased, and the print and broadcast media consumers watched prior to buying them. MRI data are compiled annually based on clusters of residential neighborhoods. Consumers in samples from 20,000 households in these clusters are queried through personal interviews and questionnaires.

MEDIA MIX The strategic combination of media used in an advertising campaign. The mix may include a blend of print, broadcast, and outdoor advertising. Media mix strategies relate both to the selection of appropriate media and to decisions on the spending levels to be allocated to each. See also **media planning.**

MEDIAN The middle case in a ranked list of numerical observations. In a set of numbers arranged from lowest to highest (or vice versa), median is the middle number—that is, half of the set of observations fall above the median and half fall below it. Consider the numbers 25, 30, 45, 50, and 55. The median here is 45, since it is the middle number in the series. Median might be used in analyzing the average value of consumer response to a direct-mail offer: If the median were $75, half the purchases were less than $75 and half of them were more than $75. *Note:* The advantage of median is that it's not affected by extreme cases, which distort the **mean** of a range of values. See also **mode.**

MEDIA PLACEMENT The process of generating print and broadcast publicity. *Placement specialists* are the public relations professionals who coordinate this function. Entailed in the process is targeting publications where publicity is desired, and contacting the media's editors to arrange for coverage. (The resultant publicity is referred to as a placement.) Large public-relations agencies have media placement departments. Staff in these departments generally report to the agencies' account executives on a client-by-client basis.

MEDIA PLAN   The document detailing the media strategy for an advertising campaign. The media plan states the goals of the effort, a definition of the target audience, and the **media mix** to be used. It also indicates the specific advertising vehicles that will be employed, as well as a rationale for media selection and scheduling decisions. Media plans detail the *options* available for individual advertising insertions, such as the size of a print ad, use of color, and its position in the publication. Options for broadcast buys include the length of the commercial and its time of airing.

MEDIA PLANNER   The advertising agency executive who reviews and selects advertising media on which a client should advertise its products. Media planners determine media buys based on comparisons of quantitative (audience size) and qualitative (audience composition) attributes of the media under review.

MEDIA PLANNING   *Media* refers to the contexts in which the advertising message appears. Media planning strives to maximize the message's effectiveness by placing it in advertising vehicles that reach the defined target audience. Media planning is one of the central aspects of developing advertising strategy.

There are four basic questions to ask in media planning.

1. *Who should be reached?* Media selection is based on choosing advertising vehicles whose audiences best meet the description of the target market. For example, tennis equipment would be advertised in a magazine read by tennis enthusiasts.

2. *Where are they located?* A market is always dispersed, to some degree. Different media must be used to reach people where they live. Thus, advertisements might be in a Los Angeles daily newspaper if the seller is trying to reach consumers in that city, or in community newspapers to teach people in specific neighborhoods therein.

3. *What is the nature of the message?* Different advertising approaches require different media. For example, if a product's use must be demonstrated, television would do so more effectively than print advertising. Similarly, advertising a floral bouquet would be more effective in a four-color magazine ad than in black-and-white.

4. *When should the advertising be scheduled?* Print media issue dates and time units in broadcast media allow advertisers to choose when

their messages will appear. Audience composition and size vary with the time at which advertising appears. For instance, to reach a large number of businesspeople, radio advertising might be bought in the **afternoon-drive** time slot when they are traveling home from work.

Media Categories

Different types of media offer distinct benefits. They also have discrete drawbacks. The basic media categories are:

• *Newspapers*. Advertising in newspapers offers flexibility in terms of where advertising can appear in the publication (e.g., placing financial services ads in the business section). Another benefit is that newspapers allow readers to clip out ads for future reference. The drawbacks of newspaper advertising include their short life span (they are discarded soon after being read) and the fact that many readers just scan the publication without focusing closely on content.

• *Magazines*. Magazines offer audiences that are highly segmented by subject matter (e.g., consumer magazines, trade publications, special-interest magazines). In comparison to newspapers, magazines are kept longer before being discarded. The main drawback of magazines involves their long production lead times. These prohibit advertisers from making last-minute changes to their advertising insertions.

• *Television*. Advertising on TV provides the impact of combining sound and visual images, as well as wide geographic reach. Moreover, messages can be scheduled at specific times in different shows. TV advertising planning is facilitated by the ample audience data available on a program-by-program basis. The main disadvantage of TV advertising is its cost: Producing high-quality commercials is expensive, as is the cost of commercial time (although this is not always the case with cable TV). Television also lacks the ability to target specific market segments, especially from a narrow geographic standpoint.

• *Radio*. Radio offers well-segmented audiences, especially in large metropolitan areas. Production costs are low and it is easy to specify the time of day at which the advertising airs. However, radio messages are usually brief. Consequently, they do not allow advertisers to provide detailed product information. Another drawback is that limited research data are available on radio listenerships (which complicates comparisons between different stations).

Comparing Media Buys

Media planners compare advertising vehicles based on three criteria.

1. *Reach*—the number of people/households that would be exposed to an advertising message at least once during a given period of time.
2. *Frequency*—the number of times a person/household would be exposed to a message over a period of time.
3. *Impact*—the *qualitative* aspects of a medium (e.g., selling athletic equipment would have a greater impact in a sporting magazine than in a gardening magazine).

Advertising comparisons are conducted using two basic measures: **cost per thousand** and **cost per gross rating point**. See also **alternative media**.

MEDIA RELATIONS In general, an organization's active and reactive dealings with the news media. Media relations is often used synonymously with publicity (e.g., a media relations campaign to promote a particular product or issue). However, the term also describes a company's efforts to maintain a beneficial relationship with the media. For example, a media relations gesture might involve making company experts available to provide explanations of technical topics for reporters' edification (even though the interviews will not always result in publicity for the company).

MEDIA REPRESENTATIVE A salesperson retained by a publication or broadcast station to sell advertising. Media representatives ("reps") generally handle several noncompeting media. For example, a rep would sell advertising for only one radio station in a given market. Media representatives sell to agency media buyers. Reps give presentations to buyers on their media's audience size and composition, ad rates, and special issues and discounts. Reps are generally compensated on a commission basis.

MEDIA RESEARCH The various analyses conducted on the size, composition, and behavior patterns of media audiences. Advertising executives, for instance, undertake media research to study how consumers use media (e.g., how long they preview a show before deciding whether or not to watch it, or what people do with a magazine once they're finished reading it). See also **audience measurement.**

MEDIA TOUR   The scheduling of a series of news media interviews (usually in a particular market) to generate publicity on a given topic. For example, Post Cereals and Sanka hired fitness personality Jack LaLanne to lead exercise rallies in 15 U.S. cities. Media tours involving newspaper, magazine, radio, and TV interviews were scheduled for him in each market. The publicity was designed to build attendance at the rallies and to promote a free exercise equipment promotion that was part of the PR campaign. **Media placement** specialists arrange the interviews on a media tour. An account executive typically shepherds the spokesperson to each interview.

MEDIA TRAINING   The exercises involved in preparing a company executive or spokesperson to give news media interviews or presentations. Spokespeople hired for publicity campaigns often undergo media training. The process typically involves arranging mock interviews (with PR people playing the role of journalists). The spokesperson learns verbal and nonverbal techniques to effectively communicate the promotional message to be imparted, as well as tactics for responding to questions from hostile reporters. The spokesperson's performance is then critiqued. Suggestions are made to enhance his or her presentation skills. Often, these mock interviews are videotaped to facilitate the critiquing process.

MEDIA WEIGHT   The overall strength of an advertising program as determined by the number and size/length of advertisements and the frequency with which they appear in the marketplace. Thus, the media weight of an advertising campaign relates to the total size of the audience delivered by the collective of advertising messages disseminated to the market.

MEMBER-GET-MEMBER PROMOTION   A sales promotion technique used to recruit new customers by providing an incentive to current customers who make referrals. Consider a book club. Members who give the club's management the names of friends who might be interested in joining might receive free books or discounts if they successfully recruit new members. Member-get-member promotions are similar to **friend-of-a-friend promotions.** The difference is that the latter involve providing incentives to any person who provides referrals, even if the person is not a customer.

MERCHANDISING   The activities undertaken to ensure a product is available to its target consumers and prominently visible in the stores in which it is sold. In retailing, merchandising relates to product and product line decisions. These involve determining which merchandise should be offered to which consumers, in what outlets, at what times, and in what quantities. Merchandising also describes the tactics used in physically displaying products in stores. That is, it relates to decisions on in-store promotions and **point-of-purchase advertising** displays that present products in a favorable light to the buying public. See also **planogram.**

MERGE-PURGE   The act of consolidating two or more mailing lists, the goal of which is spotting duplications and deleting unwanted names. A merge-purge is done, for example, when combining a rented list with a **house list** of customers. Assume the seller wants to send literature to potential customers instead of current customers. The rented list could be merged with the house list; then, from the combined list, the names of people to whom the seller does not want to send literature could be purged.

MERGER   Situation in which two independent companies combine to form one organization. A merger represents a corporate growth strategy for both companies involved. That is, their union is intended to capitalize on market opportunities that they might otherwise be unable to realize if operating individually. *Note:* A merger differs from an **acquisition** in that the latter occurs when one company gains control of another. In an acquisition, the acquired company essentially ceases to exist because its operations officially become part of the acquiring organization's business.

MESSAGE   The information sent from a communicator (e.g., advertiser) to a receiver (e.g., consumer). In advertising, the message is the information the seller wants consumers to receive upon reading or viewing the ad. For instance, the message in an ad for a savings bank might be, "Your money will earn more interest in our bank than in others." Messages, whether implied or stated explicitly, must be readily understandable to the target audience. **Message development**

is one of the key elements of devising advertising strategy. See also **appeal.**

MESSAGE DEVELOPMENT   The strategy of determining what is to be said in advertising. Success in advertising is based in large part on effective message development. Message development begins with setting communications objectives. That is, once the target market and its characteristics have been identified, the advertiser must decide on the desired audience response, such as creating general awareness of the product, arousing interest, or creating a desire to purchase it.

Designing the Message

There are four decisions involved in designing an effective message. They relate to:

• *Message content*—what the advertising **appeal** should be. That is, what is the reason the audience should act. Content generally involves formulating the benefits of purchasing the product (e.g., quality, economy, value, performance).

• *Message structure*—how the message should be logically stated. Advertisers have the option of structuring the message to draw a conclusion for the consumer, or to allow the consumer to draw his or her own conclusion. (In general, in the most effective advertising the ad raises questions and allows consumers to draw their own conclusions.)

• *Message format*—how to state the message symbolically. In a print ad, for instance, format relates to the options of size of the ad, headline style, use of color, and so on. In radio advertising, format includes decisions on the announcer's voice quality, rate of speech, and inflections. Television commercial formats vary according to the spokesperson's (or actor's) image, clothes, body movements, and so forth.

• *Message source*—who should say the message. In general, sources should be perceived as expert, trustworthy, credible, and likable. The goal is to have the consumer hold a positive attitude toward the source.

METROPOLITAN STATISTICAL AREA (MSA)   The U.S. Bureau of the Census's designation of a metropolitan area. MSA describes a geographic area consisting of several different counties, the core of which is an urban center inhabited by at least 50,000 residents. For example, the New York City MSA encompasses the counties of Westchester, Fairfield (Connecticut) and Bergen, Hudson, and Essex (New Jersey). See also **area of dominant influence.**

MICROENVIRONMENT The largely internal, organizational forces that influence a company's marketing activities. Each of the following microenvironmental forces must be addressed in determining **marketing mix** combinations:

• *Company* forces relate to the firm's guiding mission, objectives, and policies (which involve procedural standards and indicate the need for cooperation and a shared sense of purpose between divisions within the organization).

• *Supplier* forces refer to the companies that provide supplies or raw materials needed to produce the product. (Implicit in the selection of suppliers is the need for standardized procurement procedures, evaluation criteria, and quality controls.)

• *Marketing intermediaries* include financing sources (bankers, venture capitalists, insurers, etc.), **middleman** companies (i.e., wholesalers, retailers), physical distributors (warehousers and transporters of goods and services), and marketing services firms (advertising and public-relations agencies, market researchers).

• *Publics* are groups that have an actual or potential effect on marketing activities. Publics may be categorized into *welcome* publics (those whose support is beneficial to marketing programs—e.g., satisfied customers); *unwelcome* publics (groups that will hinder marketing activities—e.g., consumer advocates and watchdog groups); and *sought* publics (the groups that would support marketing initiatives but whose cooperation needs to be secured—e.g., **opinion leaders**).

See also **macroenvironment.**

MICROMARKETING The direct marketing technique that utilizes consumer purchase and demographic information to target individual buyers for special promotions and marketing programs. An example of micromarketing is the so-called **electronic marketing** programs used by some supermarkets. Here, the retailers track information on a buyer's purchase history and demographic characteristics to target him or her for special promotions (e.g., direct mailings of coupons for products the customer is likely to be interested in). See also **database marketing.**

MIDDLEMAN   A company that serves as an intermediary in the movement of goods from a manufacturer to the ultimate consumer. Two examples of middlemen are wholesalers and retailers. Wholesalers buy goods from a manufacturer and, in turn, sell them to retailers. Retailers are the middlemen who sell those goods to consumers, often through multiple store outlets. See also **channels of distribution.**

MILKING STRATEGY   A company's attempts to generate the maximum amount of profits from a product in the near term, at the expense of the item's long-term profit potential. This is done by increasing promotion or production expenditures to achieve optimal profits. A milking strategy is used when the profits from the product are needed elsewhere in the company (e.g., for another product or for a particular function, such as research and development). The strategy is also employed when a company considers withdrawing the product from the market. See also **abandonment.**

MODE   The most frequently observed attribute in a range of values. For example, if the respondents to a research study were aged 20, 25, 28, 28, 29, and 30, the mode would be 28. Mode, like other statistics such as the **mean** and **median,** is used to reduce raw data into a manageable form for analytical purposes.

MODEL   Computer-based systems that assist in management decision making. They employ mathematical formulas that enable management to ask "what if" questions regarding particular situations or problems. In marketing, models are used to determine **marketing mix** combinations, media budgets, sales forecasts, and site selections. See also **decision-support system.**

MODIFICATION STRATEGY   See **product improvement.**

MODIFIED REBUY   A **buy class** situation in which an industrial buyer seeks to change a needed product's specifications, price, or delivery requirements. In a modified rebuy situation, the buyer has purchased the item before and, thus, has had experience in procuring the product. However, the product's attributes are different from the first time the buyer purchased it (and the buying procedures or suppliers from whom it must be obtained will vary). Buy classes describe the varying levels of complexity in the industrial buying process.

MONOPOLISTIC COMPETITION   A competitive market situation that combines the characteristics of a **monopoly** and **pure competition.** In this environment, many companies sell products that are veritable substitutes for each other. Consumers perceive the products to be different, even though the goods are functionally similar. Companies effect product differentiation by altering **marketing mix** combinations, for example, devising proprietary aspects of the product, creating unique packaging, or trademarking a name or design attribute. As a result, companies create mini-monopolies by establishing product traits that appeal to narrow market segments.

MONOPOLY   A market situation characterized by the absence of competition, for example, products-services are offered by a privately regulated body (e.g., an electric utility), or a company that has exclusive access to a product or the materials used in manufacturing it (e.g., a proprietary computer chip needed to make all models of a consumer electronics product). Since there is only one provider in a monopoly, a company can set prices as high as it likes. The danger of this, however, is causing public discontent and, consequently, people's refusal to buy the product. Another danger of excessively high prices is the possibility of attracting competitors, lured by the prospect of generating substantial revenues from nominal sales. See also **oligopoly.**

MONTHLY   A periodical published on a monthly basis. Many magazines and newsletters are monthlies. These typically have longer production lead times than periodicals published daily or weekly. See also **dailies.**

MOOD ADVERTISING APPROACH   Advertising that contains no explicit claim about the product. Rather the claim is suggested by the mood created around the item. For example, billboards for a chewing gum brand show smiling young adults enjoying recreational activities. The mood is "fun." Thus, the ad makes an association between chewing this brand of gum and engaging in youthful, fun activities.

MORES   The norms of behavior dictated by a particular society. Mores are the accepted patterns of behavior to which people must adhere to conform to a society's social and legal requirements, and to ensure its ongoing existence. For example, mores prohibit child abuse. There are laws and regulations that ensure people's compliance with this. Mores differ from *folkways,* which are also norms of behavior, but noncompliance has little consequence to the continued existence of the society (e.g., dressing in a way that is socially unacceptable). See also **consumer behavior.**

MORNING-DRIVE   The time period on radio from the hours of 6:00 A.M. to 10:00 A.M., Monday through Friday. This time slot, and the **afternoon-drive** time segment, represents a radio station's largest listening audience. Therefore, advertising rates are usually highest for these periods. Morning-drive gets its name from the fact that a large number of automobile radios are in use during this time slot (when people are driving to work). See also **dayparts; prime time.**

MOTIVATION   1. The psychological forces that move a person toward or away from certain actions, activities, or objects. 2. In marketing, motivation refers to a need that a person strives to fulfill. Motivational forces are grouped into two categories: *Primary motives* relate to general product classes (e.g., a motive to purchase a new car to satisfy the need for transportation); *selective buying motives* relate to choices within those product categories (e.g., choosing one car over another because it is large enough to accommodate a family and belongings). People are often unaware of the motives that shape their buying behavior. Thus, the challenge to marketing planners is trying to understand how basic motives arise and the various forms they take.

MOTIVATIONAL RESEARCH   Study of factors influencing consumers' purchasing decisions. It is designed to help marketers understand how people make product choices and how different advertising appeals influence decision making. Motivational research generally involves *in-depth interviews* with consumers to identify their motives in choosing products. The research also may ascertain how consumers perceive product categories. For instance, motivational research showed that consumers resist prunes because they are wrinkled and, thus, remind consumers of old age. Data generated through motivational research are used in **new product development** and in creating advertising and marketing communications.

MULTIATTRIBUTE SEGMENTATION   **Market segmentation** based on two or more **demographic** variables. For example, a company may segment the market based on consumers' age and income brackets, which is useful because consumers who have the same annual income but are of different ages will typically exhibit different buying patterns and personality characteristics.

MULTICHANNEL MARKETING SYSTEM   A marketing system that utilizes multiple intermediaries in moving goods from a manufacturer to the ultimate consumer. That is, several different wholesalers or **retailers** would be used even though they may, in fact, compete with each other. General Electric employs a multichannel marketing system. The company makes its large home appliances available through department stores, discount stores, and catalog houses. It also sells the appliances directly to builders of large housing tracts, which, therefore, compete with the retailers carrying the products.

MULTICHOTOMOUS QUESTION   A type of **closed-ended question** in which the respondent is presented with three or more alternative choices. The respondent is asked to select the one that most closely corresponds to his or her position on the given subject. A **dichotomous question** is one that offers respondents only two choices (e.g., "yes" or "no"). See also **questionnaire.**

MULTIDIMENSIONAL SCALING   A measurement used to compare people's feelings about the similarities of products and their preferences among those products. Respondents' answers are charted as points on a scale. The distances between those points illustrate the respondents' perceptual and preferential differences. For example, the scale on page 226 is based on consumers' feedback about three different types of vacuum cleaners (points 1, 2, and 3), where axis X gauges product value (price) and axis Y measures product quality. In this example, consumers perceived vacuum cleaner models 1 and 2 to be similar in terms of quality and value; model 3 is perceived to be of similar quality but of lower value. Multidimensional scaling is used to determine the importance a target market places on different product features and attributes. See also **positioning.**

Multidimensional Scaling

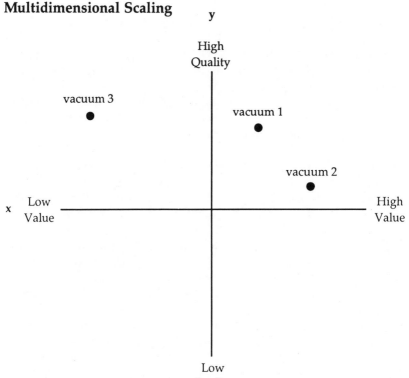

MULTIMEDIA   **1.** An advertising initiative involving the use of different media. For example, newspaper advertising would be used to support the primary media buys made on radio and television. Most advertising campaigns involve the use of multimedia in order to benefit from the different qualities of each medium, as well as to reach the same consumers more than once. **2.** An audiovisual presentation consisting of such diverse elements as videotape, slides, and computer graphics.

MULTINATIONAL CORPORATION   A corporation that operates manufacturing facilities in foreign countries and markets its products internationally. Companies operating multinationally typically seek the low labor costs in foreign countries as well as other economic and operational benefits. See also **global marketing.**

MULTIPLE-CHOICE QUESTION   See **multichotomous question.**

MULTIVARIATE ANALYSIS   In research, the analysis of several variables simultaneously. The goal of multivariate analysis is identifying statistical relationships between variables or within sets of variables. That is, it is used to ascertain the dependence between variables (through such techniques as **multiple regression analysis** or **discriminant analysis**); or it is used to gauge the interdependence of variables (via such techniques as **factor analysis, cluster analysis, conjoint analysis,** and **multidimensional scaling**).

MUSICAL ADVERTISING APPROACH   The approach to broadcast advertising in which music is employed to communicate the product message. Music may be used in the background, or the actors may sing a **jingle** about the product. For instance, a consumer electronics store showed a group of 1950s "doo-wop" singers crooning about the store and its product line.

N

NARROWCASTING The strategy of reaching small yet highly defined market segments with specialized broadcast programming. These market segments are narrow in terms of geography and/or subject matter. For instance, a company can produce a show about current Broadway musicals that airs only on a Manhattan cable TV station. Programs that are narrowcast lend advertisers the opportunity to reach the shows' highly segmented audience. Thus, a Manhattan dance studio can advertise on the aforementioned show to attract local residents who are interested in learning to dance. The proliferation of radio stations and independent and cable TV stations in the United States spawned the ability to narrowcast.

NATIONAL ACCOUNTS Salesperson's term for customer companies whose operations transcend regional territories. That is, a national account may have multiple divisions that require different products, services, or delivery schedules (e.g., a department store chain, with many products and retail locations). Companies establish *national account management divisions* when they have several such customers. These groups are staffed by managers who act as liaisons between their company and the customer. Implicit in this role is serving as a link between the groups within the sales manager's company (e.g., manufacturing, research and development) and the customer company (e.g., their different divisions or departments).

NATIONAL ADVERTISING **1.** Advertising by a company whose products are sold nationally. Advertising may be purchased in national media, or can be placed in regional or local media on a market-by-market basis. **2.** Also refers to ads that appear in national media (e.g., *Time* magazine, a television network).

NATIONAL ADVERTISING REVIEW BOARD (NARB)   The advertising industry's self-regulatory body. The NARB is comprised of advertising agency professionals, executives from national advertisers, and laypeople who hear complaints about deceptive advertising. Such complaints, which question the truthfulness or accuracy of advertising claims, are usually first heard by the National Advertising Division (NAD) of the Council of Better Business Bureaus. An appeal made on a ruling by the NAD is then submitted to the NARB for resolution.

NATIONAL BRAND   A brand that is sold nationally, as opposed to one marketed only in specific regions or cities. National brands are often owned and advertised by their manufacturer (e.g., IBM computers, Zenith television sets).

NEAR-PACK PREMIUM   Gifts or discounted items that are too large to include inside or to attach to the product being promoted. In the store, near-pack premiums are situated close to the product display so as to visually and physically link the product and premium. For example, a men's shaving kit might offer a travel-size can of shaving cream as the near-pack premium. The cans would be situated alongside the display housing the shaving kits. Offering near-pack premiums is a sales promotion technique.

NECK HANGER   A tag hung around a bottle's neck (e.g., soda, wine) that serves as a coupon or an informational device announcing a contest or special product offer. Neck hangers are used as part of sales promotion programs.

NEED-DIRECTED   Term describing a consumer purchase that is based on an individual's need for survival and sustenance. Need-directed purchases are those based on people's physical requirements rather than on their desire to be socially accepted (*outer-directed* purchases) or to be self-sufficient or highly individual (*inner-directed* purchases). See also **VALS.**

NEEDS   The essential things that support human biology and the human condition, for example, food, clothing, shelter, and social belonging. Marketers distinguish between people's **biogenic needs** (those relating to physiological requirements for food and drink) and

psychogenic needs (e.g., the need for emotional security). See also **hierarchy of needs.**

NEGATIVE APPEAL   Advertising that highlights the negative things that can happen to a person as a result of not using the advertised product. Negative appeals create anxiety in the consumer. The advertising suggests that use of the product will alleviate the anxiety. For example, negative appeals are used in selling mouthwash. That is, the advertising suggests that not using the particular brand of mouthwash will cause bad breath and thus ruin one's social life.

NEGATIVE DEMAND STATE   The market situation in which a significantly large number of consumers dislike a product or service and may try to avoid it. Examples of negative demand state products or services are vaccinations, dental work, and elective surgical procedures. Marketers confronted with a negative demand situation must understand the reasons for people's dislike of their product. Marketers must attempt to change people's beliefs and attitudes. They can do so by changing the product or service's design, lowering prices, or developing different promotional approaches. See also **demand states.**

NEGATIVE OPTION   A direct-mail selling method in which a consumer receives a regularly scheduled product shipment unless he or she specifically refuses it. For example, a record club will send members one new record each month. A notice is sent to members announcing the next month's arrival. The consumers have the option of agreeing to receive it or notifying the company that they prefer not to. Companies generally send reply envelopes to members to enable them to respond to the offer. However, the envelopes are usually not *postage paid* (as is the case with other kinds of **business reply mail**) in order to discourage people from returning the notices that serve as a refusal of the next offer. See also **positive option.**

NET PROFIT   The numerical sum that results from deducting a company's expenses incurred from its amount of total revenues. Expenses include items such as a company's overhead, salaries, and research and development and manufacturing costs.

NETWORK   1. A group of radio or television stations that are affiliated to broadcast the same programs and offer advertisers national or regional advertising coverage. Networks are comprised of a parent organization (that produces the programming) and **affiliates** (that are the stations with transmission facilities linked with the network to receive and air the programming). Affiliates are either owned by the network (called *owned and operated* stations) or are independent. Networks take one of four basic forms. *National networks* broadcast in cities across the country. Thus, advertising purchased on these networks is broadcast in all markets where the network has affiliates. *Regional networks* broadcast only in specific regions (e.g., the Southeast). *Cable networks* use satellite transmission facilities to disseminate programming. *Tailor-made networks* are formed on a one-time basis, usually to air a single broadcast. Advertisers benefit from buying network commercial time because by making only one purchase they are able to air ads in multiple markets and thereby reach large numbers of consumers. Stations benefit from being affiliated with networks because they receive programming that would be too expensive to produce themselves. Member stations also enjoy the ability to attract local advertisers wanting to run commercials during popular network programs. **2.** A group of noncompeting advertising or public-relations firms that exchange information, services, and client contacts. Such groups comprise an **agency network.**

NETWORK BUY   A broadcast advertising purchase that enables the advertiser to air its commercials on all stations affiliated with a network. Thus, the spots are broadcast in multiple markets via only one purchase. Ad scheduling in a network buy may be concurrent. That is, a commercial can air at the same time in all markets. Or, commercials can be staggered to air at different times, which might be the case with an advertiser wanting to air commercials to coincide with its product's varying availability in different markets. A network buy contrasts a **market-by-market buy,** which is advertising time purchased in one market at a time.

NEW PRODUCT DEVELOPMENT   The process of conceiving, developing, testing, and introducing new products into the marketplace. The process generally involves these stages:

• *Generating new product ideas.* This begins with management's statement of the new product objective, for example, whether the product is intended to generate high cash flow, or to allow the company to enter a new market. Idea generation involves ascertaining customer needs and wants. New product ideas may come from internal sources (e.g., company managers) or external sources (e.g., retailers, independent sales representatives). One common idea generation technique is **brainstorming.**

• *Screening ideas.* This stage involves generating as many new ideas as possible, then reducing the number to a manageable few. A company's goal in this phase is to assess product ideas, discarding poor ones and pursuing those that show promise. A company, therefore, can make one of two mistakes in the idea screening stage: It can dismiss a good new product idea, or it can permit a poor idea to be developed.

• *Developing and testing concepts.* In this stage, new product ideas are developed into finer concepts. The company will determine the potential users of the product and decide on the benefits (attributes) the product should provide. Additionally, thought is given to competitors' offerings to devise appropriate product features and pricing levels. This phase also involves having a sample group of target consumers react to the product concept.

• *Developing a marketing strategy.* Greater attention is paid to the target market in this phase. The market's size, structure, and the behavior patterns of its members are all studied. Moreover, how the product will be positioned is determined and preliminary forecasts of potential sales, market share, and profits are made.

• *Conducting business analysis.* This phase entails evaluating the financial attractiveness of the product concept and the marketing strategy. Sales, costs, and profit projections are measured against the company's corporate objectives. Estimates of sales and profit projections are developed in greater detail. If the company is satisfied with these projections, the process moves into the next phase.

• *Developing a prototype.* Here, the product goes into research and development for the purpose of creating a prototype. (This phase of the new product development process requires the largest financial investment.) The company tests whether the product is technically and commercially feasible. The product development stage is also where the product is exposed to consumer testing of its actual performance (safety and efficacy).

• *Conducting market testing.* The product is given a name, is packaged, and a preliminary marketing program is developed. The goal of this phase is to elicit market feedback on the product and the chosen **marketing mix** (e.g., promotional) variables. An example of market testing is introducing the product in a **test market,** which involves marketing the product in one or more test cities to forecast future sales and to gauge the effectiveness of marketing strategies. In other words, a test market is a *dress rehearsal* prior to a full national rollout.

• *Commercialization.* This stage involves actually introducing the product into the marketplace. Prior to introducing the product, the company must make decisions on timing (when to introduce it), geography (in which markets), the market (selling the product to which market segments), and marketing strategy (determining the marketing budget and the specific promotional strategies to be employed).

See also **intrapreneurship.**

NEW PRODUCT FORECASTING MODEL   A **model** used in forecasting the market performance of new products and services being introduced into the marketplace. Such a model can generate forecasts regarding product trials by first-time buyers, as well as purchases by repeat buyers. Information used in a new product forecasting model may be based on a similar product already available in the market (e.g., its past sales figures), or on subjective information provided by management. Consumer research data may also be input to generate forecasts.

NEW PRODUCT MANAGER   The corporate executive who coordinates the **new product development** process. The new product manager identifies new product needs of the market. He or she then develops and tests these concepts with consumers prior to actual research and development of the item. New product managers are generally found in large consumer products companies that produce numerous items in many different product categories. See also **intrapreneur.**

NEWS CONFERENCE   A public relations event to generate publicity. In a news conference, a company, institution, or individual releases newsworthy information to a specially assembled group of news media. The events are used to announce new products, services, or corporate activities. (Such events are also held to communicate company responses in *crisis communications* situations.) News conferences typically involve speeches and presentations by senior company officials. These are followed by a session in which the executives respond to reporters' questions. One-on-one interviews are sometimes arranged after the formal proceedings, which often include a breakfast or lunch. Materials summarizing the news being announced are distributed in **press kits.** Organizing and monitoring the results of news conferences are coordinated by corporate PR managers and/or their agencies.

NEWSLETTER   A publication that resembles a small newspaper and whose content is geared to a highly specialized audience. Information contained in newsletters is generally not provided in general news media because the information is so specialized that it is valuable only to people who function in the specific technical or business area. For example, newsletters such as *P.R. News* and the *Media Industry Newsletter* are written for professionals in the fields of public relations, media, and marketing communications. The level of detail contained in their editorial content is generally of interest only to professionals in these industries. Newsletters are generally sold through subscriptions. Rates range from a few dollars to several hundred dollars a year. See also **house organ.**

NEWSPAPER   A periodical whose editorial content describes events that occurred recently and are of interest to the people whom the publication is designed to serve. For example, a newspaper in a major metropolitan area reports on topical events and situations affecting the people living in the city and suburbs comprising the readership area. Newspapers are published either daily or weekly. Some are produced monthly. However, these are more accurately categorized as magazines even though they may be printed on newsprint—the light, inexpensive paper stock on which newspapers are printed.

NEWSPAPER SYNDICATE   A company that sells news and entertainment information for publication in newspapers. Syndicate offerings may be editorial (news stories, columns), illustrations (photographs and artwork), or items for readers' amusement (cartoons, puzzles, horoscopes).

NEWS RELEASE   A promotional communication written in the form of a news story that is used in generating publicity. News releases provide either hard news or background information on a company's products, services, or special activities and initiatives. Releases are subjective news stories written to position the company in the most favorable light. Releases are generally rewritten by editors to delete explicit sales language prior to being run in news reports. See also **video news release.**

NEWSSTAND CIRCULATION The number of copies of a periodical sold on newsstands and retail outlets. A periodical's newsstand circulation is distinct from copies sold through subscriptions. Nonetheless, newsstand circulation is part of a periodical's **total paid circulation.** That is, newsstand circulation is added to the number of subscription copies sold to arrive at the periodical issue's total paid circulation.

NICHE MARKETING The marketing strategy to serve a narrow market segment that's unattractive to and unserved by larger competitors. The market niche may be a particular customer type, a geographic area, a product feature, or a price-quality level. In general, a niche must be of sufficient size to be profitable, while being unattractive to competitors. There is a danger to a niche marketing strategy: The market segment may dry up or become attractive to competitors. For this reason, it is prudent to engage in *multiple niching* (attacking two or more niches) as opposed to *single niching*. Niche marketing is generally undertaken by small companies or by divisions of large corporations. See also **guerilla warfare.**

NIELSEN INDEXES The A. C. Nielsen Company indexes relating to consumer activities such as their product purchasing and TV viewing habits. Index information is available to advertisers on a subscription basis. Three of the indexes provided by the company are:

• *Nielsen Food & Drug Index.* It measures consumers' product purchasing in retail outlets. The index provides data on products in specific categories, reporting on the sales volume and inventory levels of various brands.

• *Nielsen Station Index (NSI).* NSI is an audience measurement service. Analyses of more than 200 markets in the United States generate data on the size of local TV viewing audiences, as well as the demographic characteristics of the audience at different points in stations' programming schedules.

• *Nielsen Television Index (NTI).* NTI generates audience size estimates for all commercially sponsored network programs. Data are collected via the use of the company's **audimeters** as well as through viewer entries into diaries. NTI also provides demographic information about viewers.

Note: Both NSI and NTI information is used by media planners in making media buy decisions.

NIELSEN RATINGS   Statistics measuring the number of people viewing a particular TV program, as tracked by the A. C. Nielsen Company. "Nielsens" are based on the total number of households whose TV sets are tuned to a given program for at least six minutes. This measurement, cited in terms of **gross rating points,** is just one of several produced by the Nielsen organization. See also **Nielsen indexes.**

900-NUMBER   A special telephone number that allows consumers to call a company or advertiser at a flat rate. For example, for 75 cents, consumers can call the 900-number from any location to receive product information or to hear a recorded message providing news or entertainment material. These telephone numbers are similar to **800-numbers** in that they are designed to encourage consumers to call the company at a reduced rate. The difference is that 800-numbers are *toll-free* calls.

NO-DEMAND STATE   The market situation in which consumers are uninterested in a product offering. Assume that the product is a Broadway musical. If reviews of the show were negative, people would not want to see it, thus creating a no-demand situation. The marketer's task in confronting this type of **demand state** is to persuasively link product benefits to people's needs and interests. Thus, advertising for the musical might highlight positive information about the show that was not included in critics' reviews.

NOMINAL SCALE   The classification of objects into groups that have no inherent order or value. In other words, a nominal scale (also known as a *categorical scale*) is a measurement in which numbers are assigned to nonnumerical objects as a means of identifying them (e.g., male/female, user/nonuser). See also **ordinal scale; ratio scale.**

NONDURABLE GOODS   Consumer products that are soft to the touch (in contrast to **durable goods**) and that have shorter life expectancies than durable goods. An example of a nondurable good is linen. Also known as *soft goods*.

NONPRICE COMPETITION   The marketing approach in which products are differentiated in terms of promotion, packaging, delivery, or customer service. With **price competition,** products are marketed as being preferable in terms of their cost (in comparison to competitors' offerings). See also **pricing.**

NONPROBABILITY SAMPLING   Sampling technique in which certain members of the population under study have a greater chance of being selected than others. There are three factors on which a nonprobability sample could be based: *judgment* on the part of the researcher selecting the respondents; *convenience*, in that the respondents are located near the researcher; and *quota*, based on a prescribed number of interviewees in several different categories. Nonprobability sampling is used primarily in the initial stages of the market research process when hypotheses are being developed. The hypotheses are then tested in the latter stages of the process via **probability sampling.** See also **convenience sample; judgment sample; quota sample.**

NONPROFIT MARKETING   Marketing by organizations not seeking a monetary gain from their activities. These not-for-profit groups include religious, charitable, educational, political, and social services organizations. Such groups use **fund-raising** as their primary means of financing their operations as well as to externally promote their services and mission. Typical fund-raising activities include direct mail and telemarketing. Non-profit organizations may also undertake **institutional advertising** to highlight their history, objectives, and philanthropic or social service contributions. See also **social marketing.**

NONRESPONSE BIAS   The degree of error in survey research caused by the fact that not all people who were identified to be interviewed can, in fact, be queried. For example, people move or their addresses are incorrect, thus decreasing the number of responses to a mailed questionnaire. Nonresponse bias is a source of **nonsampling error.** Researchers must consider nonresponse bias when planning and conducting survey research. See also **item nonresponse bias.**

NONSAMPLING ERROR Imperfections in the quality of research data that can result in bias and inaccuracies when analyzing survey results. Nonsampling error can occur when respondents misunderstand a question, refuse to answer it, lie, or have an inaccurate memory. It can also occur due to researcher mistakes, for example, if data are input incorrectly or if the interviewer is biased in terms of verbal or nonverbal cues exhibited in the interview.

NORMS The accepted patterns of behavior as dictated by a given society. Norms are rules of conduct that determine how people act and, thus, can ultimately influence their product needs and preferences and their buying behavior. Norms reflect the values of a society and state what actions are appropriate (e.g., you should be dressed when you go outside) or inappropriate (e.g., you should not go outside naked). A society will grant rewards for adherence to norms. Conversely, punishment is given to those people who don't conform to norms. See also **mores.**

NTH-NAME SELECTION A method of drawing a sample of respondents from a list by selecting names based on a prescribed interval. For example, every fifth person on the list may create the sample. The size of the interval is based on the size of the list and the number of names needed. Thus, if 1,000 names are needed from a list of 10,000 people, a 10th-name selection would be made. Nth-name selection is used to create a *random* sample that represents characteristics of the entire population (the list). See also **probability sampling.**

O

OBJECTION   A prospect's refusal to agree to a salesperson's offer. Prospects raise objections based on either psychological or logical factors. Psychological objections include the prospect's resistance to interference (the sales call itself), or reluctance to give something up or make decisions. Logical factors may relate to the prospect's objections to price, terms of the sale, or the seller or seller's company. Handling objections is an essential selling skill. In general, a salesperson confronted with objections must maintain a positive approach and take steps to overcome the objection.

OBJECTIVES   The business or financial results a company needs or wants to achieve during a specified period of time. A company's objectives, for example, might be to raise its market share or increase profits. Objectives are more general than **goals.** (For example, a goal would be to increase market share by 10% in that time period.) Nonetheless, objectives must be stated in clear terms and must be measurable. Objectives provide guidance to a company's operations, as well as create measures of evaluation and control.

OBSERVATIONAL RESEARCH   Research technique that involves observing people or settings to record data on consumers' behavior and other relevant environmental factors. For example, researchers will station themselves in a store to observe buyers and, perhaps, interview them on their purchase decisions; or researchers might visit competitors' stores to study the outlets' architecture and layouts. Observational research can be used to supplement statistical information or to form hypotheses that might be probed through **quantitative research.**

OBSOLESCENCE   The situation where a product becomes out of date or is no longer used by the market. For example, stereo turntables are reaching obsolescence as the market comes to favor compact-disc and audiocassette players. Thus, turntables (and the albums played on them) are being manufactured in lower and lower numbers. *Planned obsolescence* refers to the practice of intentionally building products so they will need to be repaired or replaced after a certain period of time (thus requiring repurchase). Planned obsolescence carries a negative connotation.

OCCUPATION GROUPS   Categories that relate to **consumer behavior** as determined by a person's area of employment. People's actions and buying patterns are influenced to some degree by the occupation groups to which they belong. For example, a blue-collar laborer will buy bowling equipment for his recreational activities. Conversely, a white-collar executive will buy golf equipment. Marketers attempt to identify the occupation groups that have an interest in their products; or they may develop products specifically for such groups (e.g., a computer software company develops different programs for lawyers, accountants, and engineers).

ODD-EVEN PRICING   Method of pricing designed to make the cost of a product psychologically attractive to consumers without markedly lessening the desired profit margin. For instance, a $5 item would be priced at $4.99 (odd-pricing) to create the impression that the product is less than $5; or a product would be priced to end in a whole number or in tenths (even-pricing) such as $10.00, $100.00, or $.50.

OEM (ORIGINAL EQUIPMENT MANUFACTURER)   A company that buys industrial products that will be incorporated into other manufactured goods. OEM companies use these goods to produce items that will ultimately be sold in the industrial or consumer market. For example, a company that makes telephones functions as an OEM in purchasing the internal circuitry that's used in their production.

OFFENSIVE WARFARE   The **marketing warfare** strategy for companies occupying second or third position in a product market. Offensive warfare entails attacking the market leader, basing activities on three principles: (1) Consider the strength of the leader and focus the attack on lessening the leader's market share; (2) find a weakness in the leader's strength and attack at that point; and (3) launch the attack on as narrow a front as possible—that is, attack only one of the leader's products at a time.

OFFER TEST   A test of a direct-mail package on a small scale prior to conducting a full mailing. Specifically, an offer test refers to altering the prices, terms, or quantities of the product offer to see which draws the highest response. For instance, an offer test for a business newsletter may entail stating different subscription prices: $100 in one package, $150 in another, and $200 in another. Whichever price is deemed most acceptable to consumers (based on the returns achieved) would be used for the full mailing.

OLIGOPOLY   Market situation in which a few large sellers of a product dominate the market. The competitors in an oligopolistic environment monitor each other closely and often react to each others' pricing moves. Smaller product providers may exist in an oligopoly. However, they typically are followers who mimick the marketing activities of the dominant sellers. See also **monopoly.**

ONE-MORE-YES CLOSE   Salesperson's **closing** technique based on the theory that people will make a habit of saying yes. Thus, the seller will ask questions about the prospect's feelings toward the product—queries the seller *knows* will elicit positive responses. The seller's final question (which he or she hopes will also be answered affirmatively) asks the prospect to agree to the sale.

ONE-ON-ONE INTERVIEW   **1.** In research, a personal interview between one respondent and one researcher (as opposed to, say, a **focus group** interview). **2.** In publicity, a reporter queries an executive or spokesperson in private instead of in a group session with other reporters, such as at a news conference.

ON-PACK PREMIUM   A free gift or coupon that is attached to a product package. The premium may either be taped, banded, or otherwise adhered to the package. There are two dangers to using this sales promotion technique. First, if the premium is bulky, it may complicate a retailer's displaying of the product on store shelves (perhaps discouraging him or her from doing so). Second, on-pack premiums invite theft. That is, the premium can easily be ripped from the package by shoplifters.

ON-SPEC   Short for "on speculation," referring to creative work done by an advertising agency for which it has not been officially contracted. Doing work on-spec means the agency will be paid for its efforts only if the client uses the material. Working on-spec is usually done by agencies seeking to build their reputation.

OPEN ACCOUNT   1. An arrangement between a buyer and seller in which the buyer receives no written confirmation of a purchase. Rather, the seller debits the buyer's account. **2.** A credit order that has not yet been paid.

OPEN-ENDED QUESTION   A survey question asking the respondent to answer the query in his or her own words. It is different from **closed-ended question,** in which the respondent chooses from a list of answers provided by the researcher. There is a drawback to using open-ended questions: It creates less uniformity of respondent answers, thus making the data tabulation process difficult. See also **questionnaire.**

OPINION LEADERS   People who wield influence over others in the same social group. That is, the opinion leaders' ideas and behavior serve as a model to others. People turn to opinion leaders for advice and information, which is why marketers will often attempt to reach opinion leaders through marketing communications. For example, in marketing a new type of aspirin companies may target doctors. As opinion leaders, doctors recommend certain medications to patients, who generally heed the doctor's advice. Marketers seeking to reach opinion leaders must develop *demographic* and *psychographic* profiles of them, as well as determine what media or communications channels would best be used to contact them. See also **reference group.**

OPINION RESEARCH   Market research designed to determine people's thoughts and beliefs toward a given object or situation. Opinion research is intended to elicit feedback on what people *think* is true about something in their environment. For example, opinion research would be used to gauge people's beliefs about political, economic, or social issues. Opinion research firms use questionnaires and personal interviews to solicit market data.

ORANGE GOODS Consumer products that have a relatively long life span but are replaced after a certain period of time. An example of orange goods is clothing. People wear clothes for months or years. Eventually, however, the garments are discarded when they become tattered or when fashion trends make them no longer desirable. See also **red goods.**

ORDER ENTRY The procedures involved in entering customer orders into some kind of **order processing** system. Orders are entered a variety of ways. For example, a salesperson can write up a customer's purchase request manually or buyers can place product requests via a computer terminal linked to the seller's computer. Speed and accuracy are the most important aspects of the order entry process to ensure that customers receive the goods they ordered in timely fashion. See also **data entry.**

ORDER FORM The document on which customers indicate their product requests. Information provided on the order form includes the product, the quantity ordered, the date of delivery, and shipping (address) instructions. Order forms are used to request merchandise from wholesalers or manufacturers. They are frequently included in such direct-marketing materials as catalogs.

ORDER PROCESSING The system whereby an organization places and tracks customer orders. Order processing involves managing an **order entry** system as well as determining how to use purchase information to support the business and customer service initiatives.

ORDINAL SCALE A level of measurement that describes a variable in terms of a rank order (e.g., more than, less than). Assume the level of college education of a group of people is being measured. Here, college education is the shared attribute. The people could then be ranked on an ordinal scale as having more, less, or the same level of college training. Examples of other measurements that can be ranked via an ordinal scale are social class, religiosity, and political orientation (e.g., liberalism, conservatism). See also **nominal scale; ratio scale.**

ORGANIZATIONAL BEHAVIOR The study of how and why people act as they do in organizations. Organizational behavior studies typically relate to such areas as communication (the flow of communication between people and groups in the hierarchy), power and authority, policy formulation and decision making, and organizational roles. The goal of organizational behavior studies is understanding and improving individual and group performance in the corporate hierarchy.

ORGANIZATIONAL MARKET   The market segment comprised of individuals and companies that purchase goods and services for purposes other than personal consumption (e.g., goods used in the production of other products).

Compared to the *consumer market*, the organizational market is significantly smaller. Yet its buyers engage in large-volume, highly professional, and detail-oriented purchasing activities. Corporate purchasing departments have become profit centers unto themselves. Today, a company's large-scale investment in the goods and services it procures is managed to enhance the profits and competitive position of the business.

Components of the Organizational Market

The organizational market consists of three areas: the industrial market, the reseller market, and the government market. Organizational buyer behavior varies within each area.

• *Industrial market*—comprised of companies involved in obtaining goods and services to produce goods that are sold, rented, or supplied to other companies. Examples of industries in the industrial market are agriculture, construction, transportation, telecommunications, and public utilities. The increased complexity of industrial purchasing departments and the corporate purchasing function has led marketers to identify **buy classes, buying centers,** and **buy phases** to understand organizational buyer behavior.

• *Reseller market*—comprised of the organizations that acquire goods to resell or rent to others at a profit. In short, the reseller market is made up of companies that distribute products to the final buyer through selling intermediaries. Wholesalers and retailers are examples of reseller organizations. Resellers must decide which assortment of products to carry, from what vendors to purchase them, and at what prices. In general, buying procedures and decisions in the reseller market are similar to those in the industrial market. Yet they vary by the size of the organization. For example, the owner of a small retail outlet would make all purchasing and assortment decisions. Conversely, a large department store would employ specialist buyers responsible for making these decisions.

• *Government market*—comprised of federal, state, and local governmental agencies. These organizations purchase goods and services to meet the public's needs in the areas of defense, health and education, and public welfare. Governmental spending decisions are subject to public review and scrutiny by "watchdog" groups. Therefore, organizations selling to the government market must expect to prepare significant amounts of paperwork before purchase decisions are approved.

ORGANIZATION CHART   The hierarchy of a corporation as visually depicted in a diagram. An organization chart shows each unit of the organization in relation to another unit. That is, it graphically illustrates executives' positions and lines of reporting (the people to whom they report and those who report to them). Organization charts show company positions and/or departments as squares or rectangles. Names of persons or groups are indicated within the boxes. Solid lines are drawn to and from these boxes to cite reporting relationships. Dotted lines are sometimes used to illustrate advisory relationships between people or groups (e.g., where there is no formal reporting relationship). See page 246.

OUT-BOUND TELEMARKETING   The direct-marketing technique of contacting customers and prospects via the telephone. Out-bound telemarketing programs involve sales representatives calling people to both generate and qualify leads. Some out-bound telemarketing programs use *automatic dialing and recorded message players (ADRMPs)*. These machines dial a prospect's telephone number and initiate a prerecorded message when someone picks up the phone. The system enables the customer to place a product order (leaving a message on the answering machine); or it instructs the customer to punch in select digits to speak with a sales representative. Out-bound telemarketing programs must be carefully scheduled. That is, it is important not to have out-bound calls made at inopportune times (such as early-morning hours or dinner time) since this can cause customer resentment to the solicitation. See also **in-bound telemarketing.**

OUTDOOR ADVERTISING   The various forms of print communications that appear in outdoor locations. The most common form of

Organization Chart

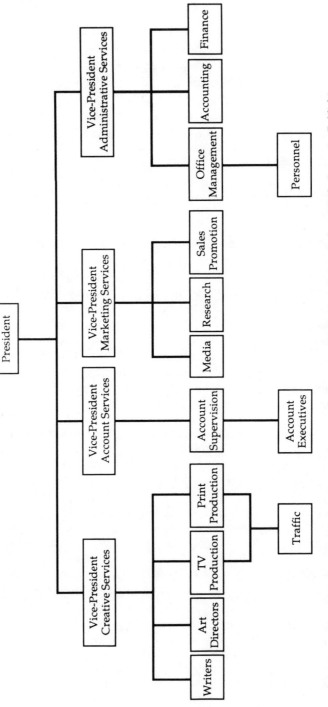

From *Advertising: Theory and Practice*, by C. H. Sandage, Vernon Fryburger, and Kim Rotzoll. Copyright © 1989 by Longman Publishing Group. Reprinted by permission of Longman Publishing Group.

outdoor advertising are billboards, which are large posters anchored in the ground or attached to building exteriors or rooftops. Outdoor advertising is strategically situated in high-volume traffic locations (e.g., on highways, near the entrances to tunnels). The benefit of this advertising approach is that it provides high repeat exposure at a very low cost (outdoor advertising has the lowest **cost per thousand** of any advertising medium). The limitation of outdoor advertising is that there is very little audience selectivity. Media buyers who specialize in outdoor advertising purchases are called *outdoor buyers.*

OUTER-DIRECTED   Term describing a consumer purchase that is based on how the consumer perceives others view him and his actions. Outer-directed purchase behavior is influenced by a person's desire to conform to peer group pressures. For example, a consumer buys an expensive car to impress the neighbors. See also **VALS.**

OUTER ENVELOPE   In direct mail, the envelope that houses the package's promotional materials. The design of the outer envelope is critically important because it is the first thing the consumers see and it must make them sufficiently interested in opening it. For this reason, outer envelopes often feature **corner card** copy and graphics to encourage the recipients to open them (for example, "Free Gift Inside!"). However, some outer envelopes use no such copy or graphics so as not to appear like a promotional piece.

OUT-OF-HOME MEDIA   Advertising seen or heard by people outside their dwellings. Out-of-home media include billboards, transit advertising, outdoor displays, and skywriting. Out-of-home media are different from *in-home media,* which include radio, television, newspapers, and magazines. See also **alternative media.**

OVERFULL DEMAND STATE   The market situation in which a company has more business than it can or wants to handle. Consider a popular tourist attraction. If the facility attracts more visitors than it can physically accommodate, it is faced with an overfull demand state. Companies contending with such a market situation will often engage in **demarketing,** which is marketing to lessen demand on a temporary or permanent basis. Companies do so either by raising prices or by decreasing service or promotional activities. See also **demand states.**

OVERLAY A transparent sheet of paper that is placed over a piece of **mechanical art.** The overlay serves to protect the artwork. It is also the page on which written changes to copy, illustrations, or photographs on the mechanical are indicated (changes are never indicated directly on the mechanical). An overlay may either be a piece of acetate or tissue typewriter paper.

OVERNIGHTS A preliminary report of household *ratings* and *audience share* of network program time slots in the top 25 markets in the United States. Overnights are estimated audience figures that are compiled the day after the programs in those time slots air. Official figures of viewership are distributed approximately one week later. Overnights are furnished by the A. C. Nielsen Company.

OVERRUN The quantity of publications printed beyond the number that is actually needed. Companies typically print overruns of magazines, brochures, and catalogs to meet unexpected contingencies such as copies getting lost. Magazine overruns are produced to allow distribution of copies to prospective advertisers or buyers, as well as to readers who request back issues.

P

PACKAGED GOODS   Consumer products sold in small packages and generally made available in grocery and drugstores. Examples are food, health and beauty aids, toiletries, and household products. Packaged goods are low-cost items that are consumed frequently. Companies typically promote packaged goods heavily via mass media advertising.

PACKAGE INSERT   A promotional piece inserted into a product package to sell the same or other products made by the manufacturer. A merchandise catalog, for instance, can be used as a package insert. Thus, when a consumer is sent a product ordered from the catalog, another copy of the catalog is included in the product shipment. This provides a replacement catalog that includes a new order form for future purchases. Also known as *package stuffer*.

PACKAGE TEST   A test conducted on a small scale by direct mailers to measure response rates and, thus, determine which package elements should be included in the full mailing. For example, the company may alter the envelope in which the promotional materials are contained (perhaps by featuring different copy or graphics on the envelope). The altered envelope would be sent to a sample of names. Sent to another sample would be a *control package* that is identical to the test package except for the envelope design. The company would then compare the responses of the two samples to see which drew the higher response. The full mailing would use the package design/ elements that effected the higher response. Direct mailers must alter only one variable in a test package because if more than one element is changed it is difficult to determine which change effected the higher response. See also **offer test.**

PACKAGING   The decisions and procedures involved in developing the containers that hold products. Packaging involves decisions on a package's size and shape, color and artwork, labeling, and closure (for consumers' convenience and for protecting the product itself). Packaging concepts are extensively tested before being introduced in the marketplace. Testing is done to see if the package will stand up to normal usage; if its colors and design are appealing to consumers; if its shape enables easy handling and shelving by retailers; and if its physical attributes (e.g., its ability to be resealed) are desirable to consumers. Today, many packaging decisions are based on environmental considerations—that is, if the package is recyclable or will decompose easily in landfills.

PACT (POSITIONING ADVERTISING COPY TESTING)   A report prepared by a number of leading American advertising firms in 1982 to form a consensus on advertising testing. The report recognized that advertising messages have a number of different objectives (e.g., to reinforce or change consumer perceptions, to encourage product trial, to announce new product features). Moreover, the report suggested that ad testing must either gauge advertising's ability to be received by the consumer, comprehended, or responded to. Thus, advertisers must first determine upon which of these levels advertising is to act. Then, testing measures must be selected to accurately gauge the advertising's ability to do so.

PAGE PROOF   Printout of typeset copy that shows a client how the pages of a booklet or brochure will look in sequential order. The proofs show the typeset material and illustrations on each page. They are then numbered to show the client how the piece will look upon completion. Page proofs are generally produced for the client's final review before the start of production. Any changes made at the page proof stage of production are more expensive than those made on **galleys.**

PAID CIRCULATION   The total number of copies of a periodical sold either through subscriptions or by single-copy (newsstand) sales. It is tabulated on an issue-by-issue basis or as an average over a period of six months. **ABC statements** and **BPA statements** are audits of periodicals' paid circulation figures.

PALLET   A wooden platform on which products are stacked for shipping and storage purposes. Pallets measure 40'' by 48'' and can hold 2,000 pounds of merchandise. They are constructed so as to allow truck unloading and warehouse storage by means of a forklift. Pallets are sometimes used to transport mailing packages. The benefit is that there is less damage to packages than if they were transported by mail sack. Additionally, pallets allow faster movement of the materials to and from delivery trucks. Also known as *skid*.

PANEL RESEARCH   Consumer research technique in which a group of people are queried about their attitudes and opinions toward a product(s) over time. That is, the group members are not interviewed once. Rather, they are interviewed on several different occasions. There are two types of panel research. *Omnibus* panel research refers to the same group of respondents being interviewed about different issues in different sessions. *True* panel research involves the respondents being asked about the same product or service in a series of sessions (so as to gauge attitude changes toward the item over time).

PAN-EUROPEAN   The practice of standardizing products and/or marketing communications for dissemination to countries in Europe. Pan-European marketing suggests the need to modify products and promotional strategies to contend with the varying languages and cultural norms in different European countries. However, with the unification of the European market in 1992, some marketers have adopted standardized **marketing mix** combinations as a means of effecting cost savings and enhancing communication effectiveness. See also **Euro-ad; Eurobrand.**

PASS-ALONG CIRCULATION   A magazine's readers who receive the publication by means other than purchase or request. For example, pass-along circulation may involve people getting the magazine from a friend, a public library, or in a doctor's office waiting room. Calculating a magazine's total circulation includes paid and nonpaid circulation, as well as pass-along circulation. Readers included in pass-along circulation figures are called *secondary readers*, in contrast to the people who purchased or requested the publication, who are called **primary readers.**

PASTE-UP   A graphic artist's preparation of finished **mechanical art.** Paste-up involves adhering to the mechanical the copy and other elements that will comprise the printed design, such as type, photos, and illustrations. Paste-up involves cutting, trimming, and pasting these elements into place. With the advent of **desktop publishing,** however, computers can now do the paste-up work previously performed by graphic artists. See also **layout.**

PAY-PER-VIEW   Individualized programming provided by a cable television service. A cable subscriber arranges to receive a movie, sporting event, or concert and is billed separately for the show (not as part of the subscriber's basic service cost). Pay-per-view requires a special converter box to receive the transmission. As of the late 1980s, only 20% of American homes were equipped to order and receive pay-per-view programming. That figure has continued to increase rapidly.

PENETRATION   In general, the extent to which a given product has ever been purchased in a particular market. Penetration, however, also refers to the level of sales of a specific company's product in a particular market. Penetration, from the generic standpoint, can be illustrated by this example: Oriental soup mixes have high penetration levels in geographic areas of the United States where there are high concentrations of citizens of Oriental descent. Such products would have low penetration in other areas where there are not a significant number of Oriental residents or where people's tastes in food are more traditional. The term *market penetration* describes the degree to which a specific company is selling its product within an existing market (e.g., how much the maker of a consumer product is selling in the Dallas market). Companies attempt to increase their market penetration by adopting more aggressive marketing tactics, such as increasing their advertising, organizing special promotions, or raising incentives for their sales force or channel intermediaries.

PENETRATION STRATEGIES   Pricing and promotional strategies employed when a product is first being introduced in a market. There are two basic kinds of penetration strategies. A *rapid penetration strategy* involves establishing a low product price and allocating a large amount of money to promotion, thus effecting the fastest market penetration and the largest market share. A rapid penetration strategy is used when a market is large and there is a low level of product awareness. A *slow penetration strategy* calls for establishing a low product price and spending little on promotion, thus encouraging speedy market acceptance of the product (due to its low price) and keeping down costs (due to the low levels of promotional expenditures). A slow penetration strategy is utilized when the market is large and when product awareness in the market is relatively high.

PEOPLE METER   A mechanical audience measurement device that is situated in people's homes to monitor their TV viewing patterns. People meters are similar to remote controls. Attached to television sets, they feature buttons that are pressed by household members or visitors when viewing programs (with each member being assigned a specific button). Thus, the meters generate information on how long a particular family member watches a given program. Consequently, this information provides data that can be used by advertisers in targeting various market groups for media planning purposes.

PER CAPITA INCOME   The average level of income of an individual in a given population. Per capita income is calculated by dividing the total income of the population by the number of people comprising it.

PERCEIVED RISK   People's tendency to modify, postpone, or avoid making a purchase when they are unsure of the outcome or expect negative consequences. For example, the purchase of a high-priced item will be perceived as risky in that consumers fear losing a lot of money if they are unhappy with the purchased item. Perceived risk may also be socially based. For instance, consumers may feel their purchase of a particular garment will not be deemed fashionable or socially acceptable. Marketers attempt to understand the factors that create perceived risk. Thus, they must provide product information and support to minimize it or to help consumers justify their purchase decisions. See also **dissonance-reduction.**

PERCEIVED VALUE PRICING   The strategy of pricing a product based on how consumers discern its value, as opposed to on the seller's costs. For example, if the market perceives a brand of wristwatch as being technologically superior, the manufacturer may set a higher than normal price. The key to this pricing strategy is correctly gauging consumers' perceptions of the product. The danger of perceived value pricing is overestimating consumers' perceptions (and charging too much) or underestimating perceptions (and charging too little). Companies influence the market's perception of a product by altering non-price **marketing mix** variables such as promotion (e.g., advertising in **upscale** publications) and distribution outlets (e.g., making the product available only in fancy boutiques).

PERCEPTION   The cognitive process by which a person selects, organizes, and interprets stimuli from the external environment (e.g., an advertisement) or from internal sources (e.g., a physical need such as hunger or thirst). How people perceive stimuli is determined by their prior attitudes, beliefs, and/or needs in a given situation. Thus, perception becomes the basis for how a person behaves and acts in given situations or toward specific objects. Perception is one of the key variables studied in analyzing **consumer behavior.** See also **selective perception.**

PERCEPTUAL MAPPING   A representation of information on consumers' perceptions of existing products, generated via the process of **multidimensional scaling.**

PERFORMANCE-BASED COMPENSATION   In advertising, payment by companies to their agencies based on the latters' performance rather than on a retainer or project basis. Performance-based compensation is measured generally in terms of sales of the products for which the agencies create advertising. Performance may also be based on subjective criteria such as the advertisers' satisfaction with the agency's creative output or its level of client service.

PERGAMON AGB   A British research firm that generates TV audience data for sale to advertisers. Similar to the A. C. Nielsen Company, Pergamon utilizes such audience measurement tools as **people meters** to compile viewership data. More than 8,500 such devices are used by Pergamon in households in the United Kingdom, Ireland, the Netherlands, Belgium, Spain, Italy, Greece, Portugal, Turkey, Hong Kong, Thailand, the Philippines, New Zealand, and France.

PERSONAL INFLUENCE   An individual's ability to impel others to think or behave in a certain way. Personal influence generally connotes social interaction. That is, one person's influencing of others' beliefs usually occurs in a one-to-one or group encounter. Identifying the people who exert influence over others is an important element of marketing strategy, which is why marketers attempt to reach **opinion leaders** through communications. *Note:* Personal influence can also be psychologically driven. For example, it can take the form of thought processes a consumer undertakes in deciding to buy a certain product to conform to peer pressure.

PERSONAL INTERVIEW   A method of gathering survey data via a face-to-face meeting between a researcher and respondent. Personal interviews are conducted in people's homes, in the researcher's office, or in pedestrian locations (e.g., a **mall intercept interview**). Personal interviewing is the most expensive method of gathering survey research, yet it is the most valuable because the interviewer can generally ask more questions, clarify ambiguous answers by respondents, and record additional information about the respondent (e.g., his or her clothes, facial expressions, body language).

PERSONALITY   The combination of an individual's psychological traits that leads to consistent responses to environmental stimuli. Personality describes the characteristics that account for differences between people and lead to relatively predictable responses to certain recurring situations. Such consistency of response allows classification of people into *personality types* (e.g., dominant, self-confident, autonomous, sociable, defensive). Marketers attempt to influence **consumer behavior** by identifying the link between personality types and certain products. For example, the autonomous personality type is the likely consumer for do-it-yourself products found in home-improvement and building-supply stores.

PERSONALIZED AD   A specially bound magazine insert that features the individual subscriber's name. Personalizing ads was devised to create insertions that have the impact of a direct-mail letter. Similarly, they are used to communicate a special offer or invitation. For example, a car manufacturer ran personalized ads concurrently in several national magazines. The ads invited readers to test drive the company's new model, using the coupon as authorization to do so and to receive a free gift. The personalized information also included the dealer located closest to the subscriber. *Note:* The drawback of personalized ads is their cost. The **selective binding** insertion process can add up to 50% to the price of a full-page, four-color ad.

PERSONAL SELLING   The tool of promotion whose main benefit is being able to tailor the sales message to the particular prospect and situation. Personal selling can be conducted in face-to-face encounters, over the telephone, or through personalized correspondence. It is a very costly technique primarily because of the sales personnel that need to be trained, managed, and deployed. Yet there are three key advantages to personal selling: (1) The seller is able to observe reactions by the prospect and modify the sales approach as needed; (2) the seller can establish a long-term relationship with a prospect (which can lead to multiple sales over a period of time); and (3) the buyer generally feels obligated to listen and respond (either negatively or positively) to the sales pitch. *Note:* Personal selling is a *direct-promotion* technique designed to capitalize on the functions of the *indirect-promotion* techniques of *advertising, sales promotion,* and *publicity.*

PERT (PROGRAM EVALUATION AND REVIEW TECHNIQUE) A planning tool that graphically depicts the events and activities required to complete a large-scale project. The goal of developing a PERT chart is not only to outline specific activities but also to estimate the time needed to complete them. A PERT chart appears as a *network diagram* that uses arrows to indicate the tasks that require time and resources (and the interrelationship of people and groups responsible for them) and circles to show the completion of one or more activities that signal the start of subsequent steps. Indicated on the lines connecting the arrows and circles are numbers noting completion dates. Since completion dates may only be estimated (as opposed to being indicated precisely), PERT chart numbers show three possible duration periods: most optimistic, most likely, and most pessimistic. *Note:* In marketing, PERT charts are utilized for major, long-term

PERT Network Diagram

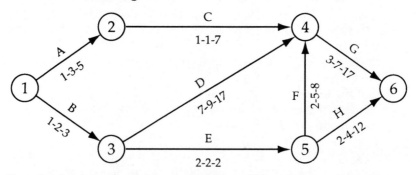

From *Encyclopedic Dictionary of Accounting & Finance* by Jae K. Shim and Joel G. Siegel. Copyright © 1989. Reprinted by permission of the publisher, Prentice Hall/Business & Professional Division/A Division of Simon & Schuster, Englewood Cliffs, N.J. 07632.

initiatives such as new product introductions. See also **critical path method.**

PHYSICAL DISTRIBUTION MANAGER   The corporate manager responsible for the flow of materials used in manufacturing and in distributing finished goods to the market. The physical distribution manager, who typically reports to corporate or division management, coordinates the work of the corporate departments responsible for procuring raw materials used in manufacturing, and, ultimately, delivering finished products to channel intermediaries or end-users. Also known as the *logistics manager.*

PIE CHART   A graphic used to pictorially present data. It is a circle divided into slices that indicate different percentages. For example, a pie chart can be used to show the levels of market share held by different companies. Thus, a company holding 25% of the market would have a slice representing one-quarter of the circle; a company with 50% of the market would have a slice representing one-half of the circle. The different pieces of the pie chart have separate mark-

Pie Chart

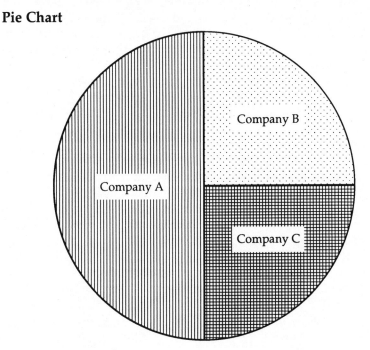

ings. For example, Company A's share would be shown as solid lines, Company B's share as dotted lines, and Company C's share as crossed lines. See also **bar graph.**

PIGGYBACK   Broadcast media term for two commercials by the same advertiser that appear one after the other. The spots may be for the same or different (albeit complementary) products. Piggyback commercials are typically purchased by the advertiser as one unit of commercial time. That is, two 15-second spots that will be piggy-backed are purchased as one 30-second unit. Piggyback spots are also referred to as *back-to-back* commercials. See also **bookends.**

PIMS (PROFIT IMPACT OF MARKETING STRATEGIES)   A study conducted by the Strategic Planning Institute to generate information on the profit performance of businesses under different competitive conditions. The study resulted in a model of the major variables that influence a company's **return on investment** and account for differences in profitability and cash flow. Data from the study were generated from analyzing some 2,800 businesses in different industries. Three basic variables were identified as having the most impact on ROI: (1) *competitive position,* as indicated by market share and product quality; (2) *production,* as measured by a company's intensity of investments and manufacturing productivity; and (3) *market attractiveness,* based on the market's growth rate and the characteristics of its consumers. Companies use PIMS data to compare their performance with those of their peers—that is, the profitability of companies with similar strategic positions (but they may be in different industries).

PITCH   A personal or telephone solicitation to obtain new business. A salesperson's pitch is an attempt to get an order from a new or existing customer. Advertising professionals make a pitch to obtain new accounts. For example, an advertising agency will make a *speculative pitch* to secure new business, which entails developing a proposed advertising campaign complete with print ads and/or television **storyboards,** and media strategies. *Note:* PR professionals seeking publicity for clients may make a telephone pitch of a news story idea to editors, or the publicists detail the suggested story in a **pitch letter.**

PITCH LETTER   One of the main tools used by public-relations professionals to generate publicity. Pitch letters detail a news or feature story idea being proposed by the PR representative to a journalist. They provide information on the story idea, while explaining the connection between it and the publicist's client. The letter is persuasively written to highlight the story's news value insofar as it relates to the editorial needs of the target medium. Pitch letters are usually directed to one media outlet at a time, wherein the editor is offered exclusivity on story usage. However, they are sometimes mass mailed to media with no exclusivity suggested.

PLACE   One of the *4 P's of marketing,* referring to the tactics and distribution channels used to make a product physically available to consumers. Place considerations relate to the physical handling and distribution of the product, such as warehousing, packaging for transportation, modes of transportation, and the number of wholesale and/or retail outlets through which the product will be made available.

PLACEMENT   See **media placement.**

PLANNED OBSOLESCENCE   The practice of designing products that become obsolete or must be replaced after a certain period of time. Manufacturers have been criticized for this product strategy. For example, consumer advocates have condemned goods that are intentionally designed to have short life spans. They argue that such goods, if manufactured differently or with different materials, would last longer and would not require repurchases or frequent repairs.

PLANNING   In general, the process of attempting to capitalize on market opportunities in the external environment as determined by the competences of the organization. Planning is a systematic process that involves defining specific actions to be undertaken, assessing environmental factors, setting objectives and developing strategies to achieve them, and gauging performance. *Marketing planning* is the process that results in a strategy to sell a specific product or service. See also **marketing plan.**

PLANOGRAM   A computerized diagram used in merchandising to design the optimal display of products on retail store shelves. Computerized "planogramming" enables a store owner to determine the best layout of products and product categories vis-à-vis the store's customers. That is, it aids in making decisions on where to situate products to maximize their visibility to the customers most likely to buy them. Planogramming is a simulation that allows the retailer to conduct "what if" analyses. Thus, different planograms can be developed to compare shelf layouts and their varying impact on purchase behavior.

PLATES Metallic sheets created for use in the printing process. Through a photographic procedure, plates are made to feature the image to be reproduced. Then, placed on a printing press, they imprint the image on paper, labels, or other materials. *Color plates* are used in the reproduction of two-, three-, and four-color artwork.

PMS COLORS (PANTONE MATCHING SYSTEM) The industry standard for shades of ink used in printing. Graphic designers select PMS colors when creating designs for print advertising and collateral materials. The designers indicate which colors should be used by noting the PMS number on the **mechanical art.** Often, designers will also attach a color swatch to the mechanical's **overlay.**

POINT-OF-PURCHASE ADVERTISING (P-O-P) One of the main tools of sales promotion, which involves creating in-store merchandise displays that are designed to catch the consumer's eye and effect **impulse buying.** P-O-P materials include on-shelf displays, window arrangements, banners, and freestanding units that conveniently stack the merchandise being promoted. P-O-P materials are developed by manufacturers and distributed to retailers who sell their merchandise. Many retailers, however, are reluctant to accept P-O-P displays. Consequently, manufacturers offer retailers discounts on merchandise or other incentives to encourage their use of the displays. P-O-P materials often are designed to be visually consistent with the manufacturer's other marketing communications such as print and TV advertising, coupons, and **freestanding inserts.**

POINT-OF-SALE **1.** Term frequently used synonymously with **point-of-purchase advertising** (referring to promotional displays erected in retail outlets). **2.** Also used to describe displays that are situated directly near cash registers and checkout counters so as to effect **impulse buying.**

POLITICAL ENVIRONMENT See **macroenvironment.**

POLITICAL MARKETING   The marketing of ideas and opinions that relate to public or political issues or to specific candidates. In general, political marketing is designed to influence people's votes in elections. It is different than conventional marketing in that *concepts* are being sold as opposed to products or services. Political marketing, however, employs many of the same techniques used in product marketing, such as paid advertising, direct mail, and publicity.

POLYBAG   A bag used by direct marketers to ship multiple pieces of merchandise or sheets of promotional literature. For example, poly-bags are used to mail **card decks.** Polybags are made of polyethylene. The bag is either heat-sealed (with a tear-away strip to allow opening) or left open at one end. Polybags sometimes feature copy and illustrations on them.

PONY SPREAD   A print advertising format comprised of two **junior page** ads that appear on facing pages in a periodical. That is, the spread consists of two ads that occupy equal portions of the adjoining pages but they are combined to visually form one ad. Also known as *junior spread*.

POP-UP   Print advertisements and magazine inserts designed to rise when the reader opens it. A pop-up is created by using a special **die-cut** fold that causes part of the design to rise from the piece's center and create a third dimension. It is a very costly graphic design

Pony Spread

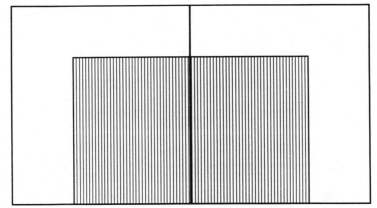

approach. Pop-ups are used when the advertiser seeks to create an attention-getting special effect.

PORTFOLIO ANALYSIS   An evaluation of the products and **strategic business units** comprising a diversified company's portfolio. Companies periodically conduct portfolio analyses to measure the units' market performance. The portfolio analysis is done to assess the financial resource needs of individual SBUs. It is also done to review the different contributions being made by the SBUs toward achieving the company's corporate objectives. The main goal of a portfolio analysis is to determine the company's investment strategy—that is, to determine whether to continue investing funds in an SBU, to curtail its investment, or to withdraw the SBU from the market. Portfolio analyses generally use a two-tiered matrix to assess SBU performance. One level of the matrix measures the market's *growth rate* or its overall attractiveness. The other level indicates the SBU's competitive position in the market. Two common tools used in conducting portfolio analyses are the **growth-share matrix** and the **market attractiveness-competitive position matrix.**

POSITION   The location of an advertisement or commercial in a given **vehicle.** In print media, position refers to the ad's situation within sections of the publication or on a given page. In broadcast media, it describes the particular time slot at which a commercial airs. Advertisers must sometimes pay a premium for a *preferred position.* For instance, the back cover of a magazine is a preferred position because it is very likely to be seen and read by a large number of people. Similarly, certain preferred positions on broadcast stations command higher rates than other time slots. See also **island position.**

POSITIONING   Marketers' strategic attempt to influence how consumers perceive their product in relation to others in the same product category. Positioning involves designing the company or product's image so that consumers can understand and appreciate it on its own merits, as well as in comparison to competitors' offerings. For example, the maker of an office photocopy machine may position it as being the most reliable (and the least in need of frequent repairs); or the manufacturer of running shoes might position its product as being the best to avoid leg injuries. Developing a positioning strategy is done after identifying the product's **competitive advantage** and determining the ways to best communicate it to the market. The next phase involves developing **marketing mix** strategies to effectively position the product in consumers' minds. See also **multidimensional scaling.**

POSITIVE APPEAL   A thematic approach to developing advertising copy in which the benefits of the product and product usage are highlighted. The copy generally explains how a consumer's anxiety about a certain situation or issue can be alleviated by using the advertised product. In **negative appeal** the copy emphasizes the adverse consequences of *not* using the product.

POSITIVE OPTION   The direct-mail selling technique in which a consumer is required to indicate whether or not he or she wants to receive a regularly scheduled product shipment. For example, a positive option in a book club membership (where the consumer is offered a new book each month) requires the person to notify the publisher of the former's acceptance or refusal of the next installment. With a **negative option,** the consumer automatically receives the next order without initially being given the opportunity to refuse it. Using a positive option will result in less revenue per customer than a negative option. Yet offering a positive option generally attracts more buyers.

POSTING   The placement of outdoor advertising such as billboards, transit ads, or any of a variety of painted displays. An ad's *posting date* refers to the date on which it is first displayed. Its *posting period* is the amount of time it will remain on display. For instance, a billboard's posting period might be anywhere from three months to a year. Painted displays, such as those found on building exteriors, have posting periods of up to three years.

POSTMARK ADVERTISING   A slogan, **logo,** or message that appears in a company's postal meter stamp. Postmark advertising must meet specifications set by the U.S. Postal Service. For instance, the message must not relate to a controversial or political topic, and the design itself can in no way resemble official postal markings. Postmark advertising is frequently used by business and trade associations, hotels, and charitable organizations.

POSTTEST   The process of measuring the effectiveness of advertising after it has appeared in the marketplace. Advertisers conduct posttesting to gain insight into consumer responses to certain advertising approaches and to avoid making costly mistakes in the future. Posttesting should only be done after specific, measurable objectives have been set. *Note:* Posttesting is employed to measure both the impact of an advertising message as well its ultimate effect on product sales. See also **pretest.**

PREDICTIVE RESEARCH   Survey information that enables cause-and-effect meanings to be applied to the data. Predictive research is the third level in the hierarchy of research projects—a structure based on the extent to which research elicits predictive findings. The first level is *descriptive research,* which merely states that something exists or happened in the past. The second level is *evaluative research,* which adds value judgments to data to create comparisons.

PREDICTOR VARIABLE   See **independent variable.**

PREFERRED POSITION   An advertiser's specification of where in a print medium (or when in a broadcast medium) its advertisement will appear. These choice locations sometimes require advertisers to pay a surcharge to secure them. For example, a magazine's back cover is a preferred position. The fact that many people are likely to see and read it often makes the back cover a magazine's most expensive page. A preferred position also refers to an ad's placement in the section of the medium appropriate to the advertised product. For instance, a wine retailer would secure a preferred position in a newspaper's food or lifestyle section. In publishing, a preferred position is the opposite of a *run-of-paper* placement, in which the ad's location in the medium is determined by the publisher.

PREMIUM   **1.** A gift or bonus given free to consumers as a means of providing an inducement to purchase a product. Distributing premiums is a popular sales promotion technique. It is used to effect higher sales, both by generating product trials among nonusers as well as encouraging more purchases by current users. Two examples of premium offers are a manufacturer gives away free silverware in exchange for a dozen **proof-of-purchase** seals; or a magazine publisher offers free pocket calculators to first-time and renewal subscribers. The premiums themselves are usually imprinted with the name of the company that distributed them, providing a reminder to consumers of where they received the items and, thus, stimulating future purchases. **2.** The highest-priced product in a given category (e.g., Godiva chocolates). Premium products have been shown to attract an identifiable market segment: those people who insist on buying only top-of-the-line goods. See also **coupons.**

PRE-PRINT ADVERTISEMENT   **1.** An advertisement distributed to retailers prior to its appearance in advertising media. Pre-print ads are sent to show the type of advertising support a given product will be given by its manufacturer. Pre-print ads are generally larger than they will appear in publications and are mounted on poster board for in-store display purposes. **2.** Materials that are printed ahead of the publication's regular printing schedule. These include **freestanding inserts,** multipage brochures, and ads printed on special paper stock.

PRESORTING   The act of segregating pieces of mail by destination or by type of handling class (e.g., first-class, second-class, bulk mail) before mailing. Presorting is done in large-scale direct mailings to lessen postal costs. That is, the advertiser often receives a discount from the U.S. Postal Service for presorting mail because it saves the post office the time and expense of doing it.

PRESS   The print news media, or term used by public-relations professionals to assess publicity about their clients appearing in those media. That is, press may be favorable ("good press") or unfavorable ("bad press").

PRESS AGENT   See **public relations manager.**

PRESS KIT   A compilation of news releases and other publicity materials that provide the news media with information about a company's product(s), services, or corporate activities. Press kits are usually developed to announce a particular public-relations initiative. The information contained in the kit is timed to a specific **release date.** However, many companies develop generic press kits that provide standard company information (content that is not time-sensitive). In addition to editorial materials, press kits often include biographies and photographs of company executives, product photographs, and reproduceable art (e.g., charts and graphs). The actual kit is usually a specially designed folder whose editorial enclosures are printed on graphically similar letterhead.

PRESS PARTY   A news media event of a social nature. A press party is where members of the media are convened to receive information about the host company for the purpose of generating publicity or to, in general, engender favorable attitudes toward the company. Information on the company or product being highlighted is distributed to the attending media in **press kits.** The events typically feature food, drink, and entertainment of some kind. Press parties are frequently used by publishers to introduce new books to publishing trade magazines and to critics.

PRESSURE-SENSITIVE LABEL   Labels with an adhesive back that enables them to be easily removed from their original sheets and affixed to mailing envelopes. The ease with which they are handled is why pressure-sensitive labels are more expensive than **Cheshire labels,** which must be cut by machine and affixed to envelopes with glue. Mailing lists are available on pressure-sensitive labels. They are particularly valuable in direct-mail packages where the label shows through a **window envelope** and the recipient is able to remove the label from the mailing address spot and affix it to an enclosed order form. This convenience to the recipient can result in an increased response to the mailing.

PRETEST   The process of gauging the effectiveness of advertising and other marketing communications prior to their appearance in the marketplace. Pretesting is used to measure the impact of advertising copy, design, or any other element of an ad or promotional campaign. Pretesting is done to spot ineffective promotional approaches that can be corrected prior to a costly, full-scale launch in a media schedule. See also **posttest.**

PRICE   The amount of money asked for in the transfer of products and services from their providers to consumers. Price is one of the 4 *P's of marketing.* That is, it is one of the controllable variables that a company regulates to maximize sales and to enhance a brand's image among consumers. Price is the only element of the **marketing mix** that generates revenues; the others (place, product, and promotion) generate only costs. Establishing a product's price involves addressing numerous issues that relate to a product's current market standing and the financial objectives of its manufacturer. See also **pricing.**

PRICE COMPETITION   Competition among companies that seek to differentiate their products based on price. Products are marketed as being preferred based on how much less they cost. In **nonprice competition,** marketers differentiate their products on variables such as quality, customer service, product attributes, or availability.

PRICE CUTTING   A company's decision to lower its product price (temporarily or permanently) from the standard rate. Companies cut prices when they have excess capacity and want to generate additional business without increasing selling efforts or improving the product. Companies also cut prices when they are losing market share to competitors, or when they are attempting to dominate the market by attracting purchasers of competing products. There are dangers to price cutting, however. For example, price cuts may cause consumers to perceive that the product is of inferior quality compared to other products, or that the manufacturer is encountering financial problems. *Note:* Companies cut prices either by lowering a product's retail price, offering coupons or **rebates,** or by providing a larger package (e.g., bonus size) at the same price.

PRICE DISCRIMINATION   The practice of charging different customers different prices for the same product. Price discrimination is illegal, except where the seller can prove its costs are different when selling the same product to different customers (e.g., when a retailer buys large volumes of product and earns a discount from the manufacturer).

PRICE ELASTICITY OF DEMAND   In general, how much market demand changes as a result of a change in a product's price. Demand is either elastic or inelastic. *Elastic demand* is where a price decrease causes the percentage increase in the quantity of product sold to exceed the percentage drop in price. With *inelastic demand,* a price increase causes the percentage decrease in the quantity of product sold to be less than the percentage increase in price. Price elasticity varies with the nature of individual products and services.

PRICE FIXING   An illegal act in which two or more companies, in collusion, agree to set a standard price for similar goods and services. Price fixing limits market competition. The Federal Trade Commission—whose function is to protect the free-enterprise system and ensure competition—is empowered to take legal action against companies found to engage in price fixing.

PRICE LEADER 1. The company in a given product category that initiates price changes. Other firms in the category tend to follow suit, either lowering or raising prices in response to the price leader's move. For example, if the price leader in the transportation industry raises fares, other companies will do the same. **2.** A piece of merchandise whose price has been abnormally lowered to build store traffic. See also **loss leader pricing.**

PRICE LINING Retailing practice in which products are grouped into different categories based on set price parameters. For example, a men's store may price line its suits. The garments may be grouped into ranges, for example, $200 suits, $300 suits, and those priced $500 and above. Merchandise that has been price lined is typically situated in different areas of the retail outlet to make the merchandise easily accessible to buyers seeking goods in specific price ranges.

PRICE-OFFS Products whose cost has been lowered. The percentage reduction is usually indicated on the product package. For example, a price-off item may carry **flagging** that states "30% off the manufacturer's suggested retail price."

PRICE PACK A sales promotion tool in which the consumer receives savings off a product's regular price. A message announcing the savings is generally indicated on the package. There are two types of price packs. *Reduced-price packs* are two single packages sold together at a reduced rate (e.g., a two-for-the-price-of-one offer). *Banded price packs* feature two related items (e.g., a hair brush and comb set) bound together and sold at a price lower than what it would be if they were purchased separately.

PRICE SENSITIVE The situation in which a change in a product's cost (either raising or lowering it) significantly affects market demand for it. Price sensitivity varies by the nature of given products. Companies that produce price-sensitive products must test the effect of price changes on demand prior to instituting changes. See also **price elasticity of demand.**

PRICING The systematic process of establishing and/or modifying the cost to the consumer of a product or service. Following are the basic steps involved in determining a product's price:

- *Set the marketing objective.* Determine whether the goal is to maximize sales, maximize profits, or merely survive in the marketplace.
- *Determine demand levels.* Project the varying levels of product that will be sold at different prices (since different prices will result in various levels of market demand).
- *Estimate costs.* Identify the **fixed** and **variable costs** at different levels of production. That is, ascertain how much it will take to produce and market the product at different output quantities.
- *Identify competitors' prices.* Note at what level competitors price their product. Compare their products' quality and features insofar as they determine the price.
- *Determine the pricing method.* Decide which pricing method, i.e., **mark-up pricing; target-return pricing; perceived-value pricing; going-rate pricing; sealed-bid pricing,** is appropriate, depending on the product market situation.
- *Select the final price.* Decide price based on consideration of the above factors, but also in concert with other **marketing mix** elements to ensure it is acceptable to customers, sales force members, channel intermediaries, and suppliers.

The reaction to pricing decisions of various publics must be predicted. For example, too much of a price increase (or one that is deemed unjustified by the market) may cause consumer resentment or reluctance on the part of retailers to carry the product.

Second, price changes by competitors must be anticipated. Plans must always be in place to respond to competitors' price increases or decreases.

PRIMARY ADVERTISING   Advertising in which the marketer attempts to build demand for a general product category. Primary advertising is often undertaken by trade associations. For example, a dairy trade association conducted a primary advertising campaign to promote milk. A subsequent program by the group promoted cheddar cheese. Also known as *generic advertising*.

PRIMARY METROPOLITAN STATISTICAL AREA (PMSA)   A geographic area that is populated by at least one million people and where residents of a large urbanized county (or a group of counties) have certain socioeconomic ties. For example, people living in a PMSA work, attend school, and generally travel to and from the contiguous counties frequently. When two PMSAs overlap, they're known as a *consolidated metropolitan statistical area (CMSA)*.

PRIMARY RESEARCH Market data collected in the field by a company to study a particular marketing situation or problem. Generating primary research is a costly process. Its key value is that the investigation may be tailored to meet specific research objectives, and the findings are often more relevant than those gathered from other sources (e.g., *secondary research*—data gathered from published sources or from **syndicated service research firms**).

PRIME TIME The time period when TV or radio stations attract their largest audience. Consequently, advertising rates during prime time are higher than any other time slot sold by the broadcaster. Prime time on television is 8 P.M. to 11 P.M., Monday through Saturday, and 7 P.M. to 11 P.M. on Sunday. Radio's prime times are its **morning-drive** (6 A.M. to 10 A.M., Monday through Friday) and **afternoon-drive** (3 P.M. to 7 P.M., Monday through Friday) periods. See also **dayparts.**

PRINT MEDIA The various forms of printed communications that provide informational content and sell advertising. Examples are newspapers, magazines, newsletters, directories, and books. Print media may be local or regional in scope, or may be distributed nationally. Print media offer distinct benefits to advertisers. For example, advertising in newspapers and magazines allows advertisers to provide a high level of detail in product descriptions. Moreover, readers are able to clip out an ad—or a coupon from it—to make an inquiry or purchase. See also **broadcast media.**

PRINT-RUN The quantity of pieces (e.g., brochures) that will be printed. For example, the print-run for a brochure might be 10,000 copies (8,000 for actual distribution and a 2,000 **overrun** for contingency purposes). The per-unit cost of printing decreases as the print-run increases. Thus, the per-unit price of printing a brochure might be $5.00 when producing 10,000 copies. The price might drop to $3.50 per brochure when the print-run is increased to 20,000 copies.

PRIVATE BRAND Products that are owned by resellers as opposed to by their manufacturer. Thus, private brands are sold by manufacturers to **middlemen,** who in turn package and sell them under the latter's label. Private brands are sold at a lower cost than nationally advertised brands because middlemen do not have the high promotion expenses that national manufacturers do. Another defining characteristic of private brands is that they are generally available locally or regionally, as opposed to nationally. Their low cost makes them alluring to bargain-conscious consumers. An example of private brands are the Ann Page products sold at A&P supermarkets. Also known as *private labels*.

PRIZM   Research data used in segmenting a market based on both geographic and demographic variables. PRIZM data define areas by zip code, census tract, and block group. Residents of these areas are grouped into lifestyle clusters on the basis of hundreds of variables keyed to people's level of education, ethnicity, **family life cycle** stage, mobility, and housing. Marketers use PRIZM data after they have defined the desired target market. That is, the data are used in devising **marketing mix** variations and **media planning** to effectively reach the people most likely to buy the sellers' products. PRIZM data are compiled by the Claritas Corporation of Alexandria, Va. See also **ACORN.**

PROBABILITY SAMPLING   The sampling technique in which all members of a population under study have an equal and known chance of being selected. Used to test hypotheses in the final stages of the marketing research process, probability sampling has several advantages over **nonprobability sampling** methods: (1) It rules out human bias in the selection of people to be interviewed; (2) it enhances the likelihood that the sample is representative of the total population; and (3) it allows an estimate of the degree of **sampling error** that can be expected. Also known as *random sampling*.

PROBABILITY THEORY   Concept referring to the number of times that research results will occur if the objects or situations under study are subject to chance. Probability theory can be illustrated by the act of flipping a coin. The theory holds that there is a 50–50 chance that the coin will come up either heads or tails. That is, if you flip the coin 200 times, probability theory holds that heads will come up approximately 100 times and tails will come up approximately 100 times. However, the theory acknowledges that rare events will happen occasionally (for example, it is possible—yet highly unlikely—that heads will come up 200 times in a row). Thus, probability theory states how often (e.g., what the probabilities are) things should happen when the objects under review are based on chance alone.

PROCUREMENT See **purchasing.**

PRODUCER PRICE INDEX (PPI) A monthly index produced by the U.S. Bureau of Labor Statistics of the prices of some 2,800 commodities. The PPI measures the prices of raw materials and semifinished goods. Increases in the PPI mark changes that will subsequently occur in the *consumer price index.* See also **economic indicators.**

PRODUCT A manufactured good that possesses objective and subjective characteristics that are manipulated to maximize the item's appeal to consumers who purchase it to satisfy a given need. Product is one of the *4 P's of marketing.* That is, it is one of the four controllable variables a company regulates in its efforts to generate sales.

PRODUCT AND BUSINESS PORTFOLIO MODEL A type of **model** that assists management decision making in regard to resource allocations to products and **strategic business units** in the organization's portfolio. The model might be used, for example, in determining which products should receive additional funding or which ones should be withdrawn from the marketplace. In general, the model is used in determining the optimal product portfolio mix that will help the company achieve its corporate objectives.

PRODUCT DELETION See **abandonment.**

PRODUCT DESIGN MODEL A **model** used in the **new product development** process to determine the most desirable attributes for the new item. The goal of using a product design model is to create the ideal combination of product features and attributes to enhance its marketability. Input data used in the model are typically based on consumer research, such as buyers' profiles and data on their perceptions and preferences toward existing brands. See also **conjoint analysis; multidimensional scaling.**

PRODUCT DIFFERENTIATION **1.** The distinguishing characteristics of various products. That is, the attributes that make products different from one another. **2.** A marketing strategy in which a company attempts to modify a product to appeal to different market segments. The company employs a different **marketing mix** for each differentiated product. See also **differentiated marketing.**

PRODUCT IMPROVEMENT   A company's efforts to increase sales by enhancing a product's attributes to attract new users or to encourage current users to purchase the item more frequently. Product improvement is effected one of three ways: (1) *Quality improvement* refers to increasing the functionality of the item (e.g., making it more durable); (2) *feature improvement* entails adding new features to expand the product's versatility or convenience to consumers (e.g., adding new accessories); and (3) *style improvement* refers to changing the product to enhance its aesthetic appeal (e.g., altering the product's look, such as in introducing a new car model that is sportier than a previous model). Also known as *product modification.*

PRODUCT INTRODUCTION STAGE OF THE PRODUCT LIFE CYCLE   See **product life cycle.**

PRODUCTION   1. In manufacturing, the procedures involved in physically assembling a product designed for a given target market. 2. The creation of print and broadcast advertising materials. In print media, production refers to the preparation of **mechanical art,** including selecting a type style, paper stock, photos, and illustrations. Production in the development of broadcast advertising (and other forms of video communications) involves scripting, filming, editing, casting, and management of audiovisual studio facilities.

PRODUCTION COSTS   The total monies expended in manufacturing a product for market consumption. Production costs are categorized as either fixed or variable. *Fixed costs* do not vary with the size of the production output, for example, overhead costs for rent, salaries, and interest paid on debt. *Variable costs* increase or decrease in direct proportion to the volume of production, for example, raw materials and packaging. A company's *total production costs* are the sum of its fixed and variable expenditures. Product pricing is based, in part, on covering total production costs (after which some percentage markup is determined to generate a profit).

PRODUCTION HOUSE   A company that produces audiovisual materials for corporate clients. Production houses are equipped with facilities to produce a wide range of visual communications such as

slides, computer graphics, videotapes, and **video news releases.**
Production houses are staffed by producers, editors, and script writers. Such companies may handle all aspects of production for a
client; or they may provide select functions as needed by the client
(e.g., the client furnishes the script, while the production house
assumes responsibility for all other aspects of the project).

PRODUCT LIABILITY   A manufacturer's legal obligation to ensure
the safety of a product. Manufacturers are required by law to provide
adequate instructions on labels and/or packaging to warn consumers
about a product's inherent dangers (e.g., an electrical product can
cause electric shock if improperly connected) and its correct usage. In
general, product liability relates to injuries that can result from
defective products—that is, defectiveness in terms of their manufacture, processing, or distribution. See also **warranty.**

PRODUCT LIFE CYCLE (PLC)   The four sequential stages (a life
cycle) that products entered into a commercial market go through.
The four stages pose unique opportunities and threats to maintaining
profitability. The competitive climate in each phase is different. Thus,
changes to marketing strategy are required. The stages are characterized as shown on the next page.

The Product Life Cycle

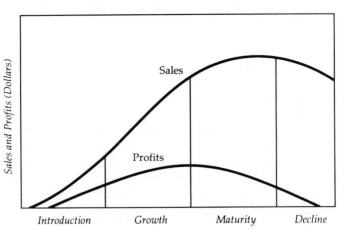

Source: *Sales Management: Concepts, Practices, and Cases* by Eugene M. Johnson, David
L. Kurtz, and Eberhard E. Scheuing. Copyright © 1986 by McGraw-Hill, Inc. Reproduced with permission of McGraw-Hill, Inc.

• *Introduction.* The product is first introduced. Marketing activity is designed to create consumer awareness and to encourage product trials (often through the sales promotion techniques of distributing coupons and free samples). Limited competition exists, yet profit margins are low for two reasons: (1) The size of the market is not as large as it should eventually become; and (2) production and marketing costs reflect the substantial start-up expenditures.

• *Growth.* Product sales increase and management attempts to expand distribution and the range of product alternatives (e.g., new models or variations of the original product). Competition increases as other companies vie for the burgeoning number of consumers.

• *Maturity.* Sales stabilize as the market reaches saturation and competition continues to increase. Promotional strategies must emphasize the product's **differential advantage.** New product models, service options, and lower prices are introduced to generate sales. The market typically expands as the average-income mass market now begins to purchase the product, which is offered in more distribution outlets and at a wide range of prices.

• *Decline.* Market size and consumer demand dwindle as competing products become more attractive to consumers. Industry sales decline, forcing marketers to decrease promotional programs and reduce the number of distribution outlets through which the product is sold.

Marketers whose products are in the decline stage have three basic options. They can:

1. *Reduce marketing programs,* cutting back on distribution outlets and promotional activity.
2. *Revive the product* by repositioning it. For example, a company that manufactured baking soda suffered a severe drop in sales when premixed cake batters obviated the need for the product as a baking ingredient. The brand was repositioned as a way to absorb refrigerator odors. It was also promoted as a tooth brightener. Both were highly successful **repositioning** strategies.
3. *Delete it,* either by phasing out the product or discontinuing it immediately. See also **abandonment.**

PLC models are valuable planning tools. However, marketing managers must realize that each PLC stage is influenced by many environmental factors that often are difficult to predict or identify (i.e., inflation, changing consumer lifestyles, competitor activity).

PRODUCT LINE   The group of products developed by a company that feature similar characteristics, applications, or markets (e.g., a consumer products company that produces health and beauty aids). Four basic product line decisions are made. They relate to *product line length,* where products are added when they contribute to profits and do not erode the sales of existing products (brand extension); *product line stretching,* where products are added to attract less profitable or more profitable markets; *product line filling,* involving the addition of products to fill gaps in the line to gain additional profits or to counter competitors' moves; and *product line featuring,* where products are highlighted in promotional campaigns to generate sales for other products in the line. See also **product mix.**

PRODUCT MANAGEMENT ORGANIZATION   A large consumer goods company that produces numerous products and/or brands, and where the marketing for individual brands is coordinated by an assigned **brand manager.** Kraft General Foods, for example, is a product management organization. This company assigns different brand managers for each of its breakfast cereal, beverage, and pet food brands.

PRODUCT MANAGER   See **brand manager.**

PRODUCT-MARKET GRID   A chart used by companies to identify which market segments to target. The grid is comprised of nine cells, the axes for which indicate *product characteristics* (based on customer needs) and *market characteristics* (relating to different customer groups). Identifying desirable market segments is done by crossing the two or more variables. The grid is used to develop **market coverage** strategies.

PRODUCT MIX   The totality of **product lines** offered by a company. Product mix decisions involve varying their width, depth, and consistency. *Mix width* refers to the number of different product lines offered by the company. *Mix depth* measures the total number of products in each line. *Mix consistency* involves assessing the relationship between product lines in terms of their end uses, distribution channels, or target consumers.

PRODUCT PLACEMENT Arranging to have a product seen in a TV show or motion picture or used by the actors. An advertiser pays to have its product or an identifier (e.g., a sign or billboard carrying the brand name or **logo**) appear on-screen typically for just a few seconds. For example, in the movie *E.T.* a youngster leaves a trail of Reese's Pieces candy for the extraterrestrial to follow. The visibility gained for the product in this highly popular film resulted in a sharp increase in sales. See also **cinema advertising.**

PRODUCT PLANNING MANAGER The manager employed in a company that does not have **product managers.** Product planning managers are responsible for all aspects of planning and developing products, as well as monitoring their market performance. Product planning managers serve as liaisons with functional units involved in planning and developing the company's product line.

PRODUCT PORTFOLIO The collection of products sold by a company. Large, diversified companies periodically assess their product portfolios to evaluate the individual units' market performance. This formal **portfolio analysis** is designed to help the company determine its investment strategy for each unit. That is, assessing product performance helps companies spot where weaknesses exist, and it aids in decision making on whether to invest more money in the product or to withdraw it from the market. See also **growth-share matrix.**

PRODUCT PUBLICITY Publicity designed specifically to promote a new or existing product. It involves arranging for news coverage of the product in print and/or broadcast media that reach the target market. It is generally easiest to achieve product publicity when the item creates a new product category (e.g., an invention) or when it is significantly different from related products already on the market (e.g., a product that employs a new technology). In general, however, as a product matures it becomes more difficult to secure publicity about it, which is why many public relations programs for such products are often built around special events or social causes to which the product's use favorably relates.

PRODUCT QUALITY An objective measure of a product's conformance to requirements. That is, the ability of the product to perform as intended. **2.** An item's performance as subjectively measured by

consumers, referring to whether the product delivers more performance attributes of value to consumers than other brands in the same
category. A product's quality is communicated to consumers by its
price, packaging, promotion, and channels of distribution. Each of
these **marketing mix** elements must collectively and consistently
communicate quality.

PRODUCT RESEARCH   Market research designed to generate data
about a product either before or after it has been introduced in the
marketplace. That is, product research studies may test the potential
market acceptance of an item prior to its commercial introduction; or
it can evaluate consumers' feelings toward the product after it has
been on the market for a period of time. Other forms of product
research include studies of competitors' products, or tests of an item's
package design or physical characteristics (e.g., how well a resealable
package holds up after prolonged use).

PRODUCT-STRUCTURED SALES FORCE   The sales force structure
in which sellers are assigned specific products or product lines. A
product-structured sales force is appropriate in companies that market technically complex products that are numerous and/or unrelated.
The benefit of this structure is that salespeople become expert in
understanding their assigned product's attributes and target customers' needs. The drawback is that there may be duplication of effort
when different salespeople contact the same target customer in
attempting to sell their assigned products. See also **market-structured
sales force; territory-structured sales force.**

PROFESSIONAL SERVICES MARKETING   Marketing activities undertaken by professional groups or practitioners such as accountants,
lawyers, architects, engineers, doctors, and management consultants. Professional services marketing requires tactics different from
those employed in consumer product marketing. Several factors
illustrate why:

• *Provider's inability to differentiate itself from competitors.* Clients
often view professional services providers as offering identical, undifferentiated service capabilities (e.g., an accounting firm's audit or
tax planning services). Thus, it is difficult for professional services
firms to communicate how their technical services are better than
those of competitors.

- *Clients' inability to evaluate services.* The complex, technical services provided by professionals (e.g., legal advice, structural engineering design) are often difficult for clients to understand and even more difficult to evaluate after the service has been rendered.

- *Clients' negative view of marketing.* Many clients negatively perceive aggressive marketing by professional services firms because some clients feel that a firm's need to market itself reflects negatively on its professionalism. Thus, firms must devise **soft-sell approaches** that communicate their sales messages in a way that is acceptable to their corporate clients.

- *Providers functioning as marketers.* Buyers of professional services generally require that the people who sell those services are the same ones who will provide them, which presents a challenge to professional services firms: finding professionals with the right mix of technical skills and sales and marketing ability.

Note: Two key factors have effected the upsurge in professional services marketing in the United States. First, legal restrictions on marketing by professional groups (prevalent until the late 1970s) have largely been eliminated. This has spawned an increase in competitive marketing activities. Second, the proliferation of services firms— consistent with the country's move away from a manufacturing- to a service-oriented economy—has necessitated that companies aggressively market their services to protect and expand their client bases. See also **consultative selling.**

PROFITABILITY CONTROLS   A company's measurement of the profitability levels of its various products, sales territories, customer groups, or distribution channels. Companies maintain profitability control measures to periodically evaluate the success of their marketing activities. The objective is to determine which of these activities should be expanded, reduced, or eliminated. Thus, if a profitability control study shows that sales in a given territory have fallen significantly (perhaps due to an increasingly strong competitor), the company may decide to redirect its sales activities away from this area and into another.

PROFIT MAXIMIZATION   The corporate strategy to achieve maximum long-term profits from a marketing undertaking. Although this would seem to be the obvious goal of any company, some companies adopt a **satisficing** philosophy rather than a profit maximization strategy; satisficing refers to the goal to achieve the stated profit objective while not striving to surpass that figure (even though the company conceivably can). Profit maximization suggests the fact that companies differ in the importance they place on short- versus long-term profits. That is, some companies may be more concerned with increasing sales growth or market share than with generating maximum profits. Also known as *profit optimization.*

PROGRAMMING   The decisions by a television or radio station on which types of programs to air and in what time periods. Programming decisions are primarily determined by the station's **format.** Thus, if a television station's format is all news (such as Cable News Network) its programming will include news reports, interviews with news makers, panel discussions, and so on. A station's programming is important from a **media planning** standpoint because different programming formats appeal to different audiences. Thus, media planners may base advertising buys on the criterion of programming (e.g., buying airtime on MTV and other music video stations to promote a new album).

PROMOTION   The activities designed to communicate a product's features, benefits, and availability to the target market. Promotion is one of the *4 P's of marketing.* Promotion is a central element of effective marketing because no matter how good a product is, consumers have to have heard about it and be convinced of its benefits for them to want to purchase it. The basic objectives of promotion are to either inform, persuade, or remind consumers about a product's attributes and availability. See also **promotion mix.**

PROMOTIONAL ALLOWANCE   An incentive given by a manufacturer to a wholesaler or retailer for the latters' participation in a promotional program. For example, a retailer who agrees to feature a point-of-purchase display furnished by the manufacturer might receive a promotional allowance to cover the expenses involved in doing so. Allowances take the form of gifts, discounts on merchandise, or free merchandise. See also **trade promotion.**

PROMOTIONAL PRICING   The strategy of lowering a product's price, below its list price, for a brief period of time to provide an incentive to consumers to purchase it. Examples of promotional pricing are *cash refund offers* (which are intended to get consumers to buy a product within a specified time period) and *low-interest financing* (as in the sale of an automobile).

PROMOTION MIX   The combination of promotional techniques used to communicate information about a product or service to a target market. The promotion mix is divided into two categories: (1) *Direct promotion* involves personal selling to consumers (either face-to-face or via telemarketing); and (2) *indirect promotion* involves the use of advertising, publicity, and sales promotion—the tactics of communicating product information via nonpersonal channels. Devising a promotion mix strategy is based on identifying the target market and establishing communications objectives (e.g., deciding what information needs to be communicated, as determined by consumers' varying levels of product awareness or attitudes).

PROOF   A printed piece reviewed to gauge the correctness and quality of a printing or production job. Consider the printing of a brochure cover. A proof might be the first cover off the press, which is checked for errors and for the color quality of the design. See also **page proof.**

PROOF-OF-PURCHASE   Evidence of a product purchase, taking the form of either a box top, label, or removable seal from the product container. Proofs-of-purchase are a popular sales promotion device. Many sales promotion programs involve offering gifts, merchandise, or discounts to consumers in return for a stated number of proof-of-purchase seals. Programs that require collecting multiple proofs-of-purchase over a period of time (usually in return for gifts from a special catalog) are known as *continuity programs.*

PROOFREAD   The practice of checking typeset copy to catch errors and to make editorial changes prior to further production. For example, a printer's **proof** or word-processed text would be proofread before the materials go to press. *Proofreaders* are the people who perform this function. They are either agency staff members or freelancers.

PROSPECT   A potential buyer of a product or service based on the criteria that he or she has the financial capacity and/or desire to acquire it. The defining characteristic of a prospect is that the person has never purchased the item before. Salespeople develop *prospect* *lists,* which are compilations of qualified buyers maintained in the expectation that they might become customers. The practice of identifying qualified buyers is called **prospecting.**

PROSPECTING The systematic process by which a salesperson attempts to identify new customers. Two popular prospecting techniques are using the **endless chain** method and contacting **centers of influence.** The endless chain technique involves asking current customers for the names of friends or business associates who might also be interested in the seller's product or service. Prospecting through centers of influence entails querying influential persons (i.e., bankers, lawyers, politicians) for the names of potential customers. Prospecting is the first phase of the selling process. The second phase is **qualifying,** in which identified prospects are assessed using criteria that determine if they are valid potential customers.

PROTECTIONISM Legal measures enacted by a government to limit the importation of foreign-made goods (e.g., establishing quotes or high import tariffs on such items). Protectionism denotes a country's discrimination against imports in an attempt to protect industries and job employment in that country. Protectionist practices hinder marketing activities by companies seeking entry into foreign markets. Thus, a foreign government's protectionist policies must be factored into the marketing planning of companies attempting to sell products in that country.

PSYCHIC INCOME The intangible benefits or satisfaction a person gets from purchasing a product or service. Psychic income is the benefit gained beyond the functional value of the item or activity. Consider the person who buys an expensive home. The buyer benefits not only from the shelter the home provides but also from the improved self-image of living in an affluent neighborhood.

PSYCHOGENIC NEEDS A person's psychological or emotional needs that influence his or her **consumer behavior** patterns. For example, psychogenic needs include a person's need for love, self-esteem, and social status. Consequently, many products are designed to appeal to consumers' psychogenic needs for status or social belonging (e.g., luxury cars, yachts). Psychogenic needs contrast *biogenic needs,* which are those basic requirements human beings have for food, drink, air, and so forth.

PSYCHOGRAPHICS The analysis of consumer groups based on their members' *activities, interests, and opinions*—that is, their overall lifestyles. Psychographic analyses entail studying how people live, as well as determining their interests and likes and dislikes. Market segments are often described by consumers' psychographic characteristics. See also **psychographic segmentation.**

PSYCHOGRAPHIC SEGMENTATION The **market segmentation** strategy that involves analyzing market composition and buyer behavior based on consumers' lifestyles, personality characteristics, and product consumption patterns. Lifestyle groups are generally defined by their members' *activities, interests,* and *opinions.* Personality categories may describe people in terms of their being, for example, aggressive, self-confident, dominant. Consumption patterns relate to when, why, and how often people buy particular goods and services. A market's psychographic characteristics influence **marketing mix** strategies such as product design, promotional approaches, and distribution channel decisions.

PUBLIC AFFAIRS The corporate function devoted to maintaining a favorable relationship between a company and the society in which it operates. Public affairs generally involves communications directed at government, special-interest groups, and community organizations. It is similar to public relations (and the function is often resident in a company's PR department), but it differs in the sense that it is usually not related to the company's marketing initiatives.

PUBLICITY The practice of creating and disseminating information about a company, its products, services, or corporate activities to secure favorable news coverage in media reaching identified target audiences. (Publicity is often used synonymously with public relations. Publicity, however, is just one of many tactics that comprise the PR function.)

Different means are used to generate publicity, such as personal contacts with the media and the distribution of news releases, press kits, video news releases, and so on. Central to effective publicity is content that is topical and appeals to the editorial needs of the media to which the publicity is targeted. As a promotional tactic, publicity provides the greatest credibility of any marketing communications approach because of the implied or overt endorsement of the marketing message by impartial news media. A product message contained in a news or magazine article is not perceived by the reader as a form of promotional communication. Thus, news coverage is more believable than an advertisement. In addition to its high credibility, publicity can often deliver more information about a company or product than paid advertising. That is, the high cost of media limits the amount of detail advertisers can provide in broadcast and print ads.

There is one key drawback to publicity. Since there is no contractual arrangement between publicist and the medium, the former exercises *no control* over how the marketing message is presented or whether it is presented at all.

Note: The marketing value of publicity sparked the creation of **advertorials,** which are articles that appear in print media as regular editorial content but whose space is sold as advertising. See also **media tour.**

PUBLIC RELATIONS (PR)   One of the key elements of the **marketing communications mix** whose function is creating a positive image about a company, its products, services, or people via the use of *nonpaid* forms of communication. Public relations differs from advertising and other marketing communications (e.g., sales promotion), which disseminate marketing information primarily through paid media.

The main goal of PR is influencing the perceptions, opinions, and beliefs about an organization among its relevant publics, for example, customers, shareholders, government agencies, and the general public. In general, PR employs the following tools and tactics:

- *Publicity*—involving the creation and dissemination of news materials (e.g., news releases, press kits, informational documents) about the company to secure favorable coverage in news media reaching the company's target markets.
- *Special events*—creating and publicizing company-sponsored seminars, conferences, competitions, anniversary celebrations, and so on, the goal being to create forums to disseminate company information *directly* to members of its target publics and to generate publicity.
- *Speeches*—involving the arrangement and scheduling of speaking engagements by company executives in forums that reach a specific target audience (e.g., arranging speeches before key industry or trade associations).
- *Public-service activities*—creating opportunities to establish or support community-oriented initiatives that benefit the well-

being of society and can be promoted via publicity and other forms of communication. An example is a consumer products company that sponsored free computer seminars for local public schools and donated hardware and software to them in the process.

- *Promotional materials*—developing annual reports, brochures, newsletters, audiovisual presentations, and so forth to highlight the company and its corporate activities. (These materials may be designed to generate publicity or to provide company information to target publics.)

Public relations is a marketing function that can support other promotional initiatives. Ideally, PR strategies should be developed based on the company's strategic or marketing objectives. PR is used in the following marketing situations:

- *Product publicity*—obtaining news coverage about new or modified products in media that reach consumer, trade, or business audiences.
- *New product launches*—creating market awareness of a new item prior to disseminating advertising or other promotional communications (e.g., sales promotion, direct mail).
- *Promotion of generic product categories*—activities designed to rebuild interest and/or increase consumption of products whose market demand is low or has fallen (e.g., a publicity campaign promoting the unique new uses of a product). This activity sets the stage for promoting the company product that would benefit from the increased public awareness of the category.
- *Defending of problem products/situations*—generating publicity to counter negative coverage resulting from such occurrences as product recalls, product tamperings, and other *crisis communications* situations.
- *Enhancement of corporate image*—creating a favorable impression of the company in order to project a positive image on its products or services.

Note: Public relations is a corporate function handled by a company's own PR or corporate communications professionals and/or by retained public relations agencies that provide a wide range of communications and media consulting services. See also **issues management; media training.**

PUBLIC RELATIONS AGENCY A company that provides the full realm of PR services to clients, such as publicity; media relations; writing of annual reports, newsletters, brochures, and speeches; **media training; crisis management;** public affairs counseling; and special events management. PR agencies are retained by companies that do not have in-house PR capabilities, or they are hired to supplement the work of the organization's corporate communications staff. PR agencies are engaged on a retainer basis or are hired for a specific short-term project.

PUBLIC RELATIONS MANAGER The corporate executive responsible for coordinating public relations activities on behalf of the company. The PR manager is responsible for getting publicity and developing other communications programs to present a favorable image of the company to its relevant publics. Included in the PR manager's responsibilities is overseeing the work of retained public relations agencies. The manager generally reports to the director of PR or corporate communications. In some cases, he or she reports directly to senior management. In large consumer product companies, PR managers responsible for **product publicity** report to a marketing or brand manager. *Note:* A *press agent* is a type of PR manager whose sole function is generating publicity.

PUBLIC RELATIONS SOCIETY OF AMERICA (PRSA) National professional society of public relations practitioners from business and industry, as well as from PR firms, government agencies, trade associations, schools, and nonprofit organizations. The PRSA sponsors seminars, maintains a speakers' bureau and job referral service, and provides research services. The group also offers an accreditation program. Its headquarters is in New York City. See Appendix A for address and phone number.

PUBLICS The groups to which a company markets its products and services or that impact the company's ability to reach its organizational goals. Publics can be customers, shareholders, distribution channel intermediaries, or government groups.

PUBLIC SERVICE ADVERTISING Social-oriented advertising designed to benefit society and the general public's welfare. An example of public service advertising is that which promotes worthy causes such as education, crime and drug abuse prevention, and the Red

Cross. Public service advertising is normally developed by nonprofit organizations, with the print media space or commercial air time donated by the media in which the advertising appears. Broadcast advertisements of this nature are called *public service announcements* (PSAs). See also **Advertising Council; special marketing.**

PUFFERY   1. Advertising messages of a shallow nature that make unsubstantiated or exaggerated claims. An example of puffery is an ad that claims the product is "the best," the "most unique," "the one and only." **2.** In publicity, a story idea or news release that lacks news value or is overly self-serving to a single product or company.

PULLING POWER   The ability of an advertisement to effectively elicit the desired response by the target audience. Pulling power also relates to the effectiveness of other promotional initiatives such as sales promotion campaigns.

PULL STRATEGY   The marketing strategy designed to get consumers to request a specific product or brand from retailers. That is, promotional communications are intended to persuade consumers to ask retailers to carry the product or brand, thus "pulling" the product through distribution channels. With a *push strategy*, promotional initiatives are concentrated at the retailer and wholesaler level, with the goal of getting retailers to stock the advertised product or brand and to promote (push) it to consumers.

PURCHASING   The corporate function that coordinates the acquisition of materials and services required in producing and distributing goods and services. Purchasing is a multifaceted process. It involves selecting vendors from which materials are obtained, assuring the quality of those materials, and negotiating prices and delivery schedules. Purchasing also involves decisions about procuring sufficient amounts of supplies and materials needed to meet production schedules. Most large companies have purchasing departments. Sellers of industrial products analyze the purchasing departments of their different customers to effectively tailor their selling strategies. See also **buying center.**

PURCHASING AGENT   A purchasing department manager who is responsible for acquiring one or more products required by the company in its production and distribution of goods and services.

Not all purchasing agents, however, are employed as company staffers. Some are independent **middlemen** who work for a company (a retailer or wholesaler) on a contractual basis and are paid by commission. These purchasing agents typically have long-term relationships with the companies they represent. Moreover, their responsibilities transcend purchasing to include activities such as receiving, inspecting, warehousing, and shipping merchandise.

PURE COMPETITION   The market situation in which many different sellers of a product offer similar products to many buyers. Understanding pure competition is important in devising marketing strategy because it is one type of economic situation that defines the marketer's *competitive environment.* Three characteristics define pure competition. First, there is a large degree of homogeneity between products (that is, nominal differentiation between them exists in the minds of consumers). Second, the number of sellers is so large that the **marketing mix** variations by one seller will not affect market prices, which relates to the third characteristic: In a pure competition milieu, sellers have virtually no need for a price policy since the market itself determines the price. That is, the product quantities that sellers are willing to sell mirror the quantities consumers are willing to buy.

PURE MONOPOLY   The economic situation in which one company is the sole provider of a product or service. A pure monopoly denotes the total absence of competition. Thus, the company holding the monopoly enjoys complete control over market supply of the product, price setting, and the ability to prevent competitors from entering the market. Many marketing theorists believe a pure monopoly can never exist in the real world. Their contention is that there is always a substitute product or service. For example, assume one airline company enjoyed a monopoly over air travel. People would still have at their disposal other means of travel, such as trains.

PURPOSIVE SAMPLE   See **judgment sample.**

PUSH MONEY   Money given to retail salespeople by a manufacturer for encouraging the sale of the manufacturer's product to consumers. For example, a manufacturer might offer $1 for each unit of product the salesperson is able to sell. Push money, in general, refers to incentives to sellers to promote a product over competing brands.

These incentives also take the form of gifts, vacations, and other nonmonetary inducements. Also known as *spiffs*. See also **trade promotion.**

PUSH STRATEGY Marketing strategy in which products are promoted directly to retailers and wholesalers instead of to consumers. That is, it is designed to get channel intermediaries to stock and promote specific products to customers. A push strategy is different from a *pull strategy*, which is when marketing communications are targeted at consumers, who are encouraged to ask retailers and wholesalers to carry the product (thereby "pulling" the product through distribution channels).

PYRAMIDING A direct-mail technique in which promotional materials are sent to small samples of a mailing list one at a time. In pyramiding, the marketer mails to one sample of names. For example, the company might mail materials to the first 1,000 names of a 10,000-name list. If the return of the first mailing is deemed sufficient, the marketer then mails to another portion of the list. The process continues (assuming the return rates are favorable) until materials have been mailed to the entire list. Pyramiding is a form of testing a mailing list. It is done to avoid wasting money on a one-time mailing to a list that may not draw the desired response.

Q

Q-RATING   Audience research term relating to the level of awareness people have about a broadcast program or personality. Q-ratings
measure how many TV viewers or radio listeners are familiar with a
given program and how many regard it as their favorite. Q-ratings
also gauge a given person's popularity based on how well viewers or
listeners can recognize him or her. Also known as *Q-score*.

QUALIFICATIONS, STATEMENT OF   A list of credentials and relevant company information prepared by an organization seeking business from a potential client. Statements of qualifications are usually
requested of professional services firms in proposal situations. The
document illustrates the company's ability to provide the requested
service. It includes information about the company and its key
executives, its experience in serving other clients in the same industry, and other relevant aspects of the organization. Companies reviewing services firms generally request a statement of qualifications
from each firm making a proposal.

QUALIFIED CIRCULATION   See **controlled circulation.**

QUALIFIED LEAD   A prospect who has shown an interest in buying
a product or who has the financial means or authority to purchase it.
For example, a person who inquires about a product (and has, thus,
shown interest in the item) is a qualified lead. In short, a qualified
lead is a prospect who is deemed a valid potential customer after
having been evaluated by a salesperson against certain criteria. See
also **qualifying.**

QUALIFYING   The process of evaluating whether or not a sales
prospect is a valid potential customer and, thus, worth pursuing. The

goal of qualifying is to avoid wasting time trying to get business from people or businesses that do not have the desire or financial means to purchase the seller's product. There are three criteria used in qualifying prospects: (1) The seller determines whether the prospect has money to buy the product; (2) whether he or she has the authority to make the purchase decision (this is usually the case in industrial selling, where a given corporate officer has the final say in making the decision); and (3) whether the prospect has the *need* to obtain the product or service (if a prospect does not, he or she will either refuse the offering or ultimately be dissatisfied with it if agreeing to the sale). See also **prospecting.**

QUALITATIVE RESEARCH   Market research of a nonstatistical nature. Qualitative research describes the nature, type, or components of a consumer group or market situation. Qualitative research is undertaken to gain insight that is useful in defining the group or situation—that is, in narrowing down the subject area from broad categories into more defined terms. For example, in developing a new product, the researcher might conduct **focus groups** or one-on-one interviews to generate anecdotal data about consumers' general interest in or likes and dislikes about the new product. The resultant qualitative data would be used to develop hypotheses, which would then be probed further through **quantitative research.** *Note:* Results of qualitative research generated cannot be extrapolated to larger populations.

QUALITY CONTROL   The procedures involved in ensuring that manufactured goods are free from defects and meet design specifications. For instance, in a manufacturing operation, units coming off an assembly line might be randomly selected to represent the entire production output for quality assessment. Quality controls are established not only for manufactured items but also for sales and distribution activities. The goal of quality control is to ensure that quality levels of goods and services are being maintained.

QUALITY OF LIFE   A person's subjective appraisal of his or her lifestyle as indicated by various socioeconomic variables such as income, social status, level of education, and health. This concept is important in marketing because consumers generally strive to maintain or increase their quality of life, thus impacting their **consumer behavior** patterns and product preferences. Quality of life varies on a person-by-person basis, as well as by social-cultural factors. Thus, a person living in an economically deprived country would have different quality of life criteria than a person living in an affluent nation.

QUANTITATIVE RESEARCH   Market research of a statistical nature that involves the measurement of quantifiable amounts. Quantitative research entails collecting data, the result being statistics that are assigned particular attributes or values as variables. For example, in developing a new product, quantitative research would be undertaken to measure the size of the population that would be interested in the new item. In measuring the audience of a given TV or radio program, statistics would be generated about the number and types of people watching the program (information used in the **media planning** process). Quantitative research involves representative samples of respondents. Selecting those respondents and analyzing the feedback obtained from them would both be undertaken using scientific methods designed to provide definitive, quantified results. Quantitative research differs from qualitative research in that **sampling error** can be measured and the results can, therefore, be used to predict the behavior of large populations. See also **error; marketing research; sampling.**

QUESTION-AND-ANSWER   Advertising format in which a spokesperson or acknowledged expert answers questions relating to the sponsored product. The questions ostensibly are those that would be asked by interested consumers. In print media, the questions are typically printed in boldface or italicized type. The answers are set in a regular type style. The question-and-answer format is generally used in print media, but is sometimes employed in broadcast advertising.

QUESTION MARK   See **growth-share matrix.**

QUESTIONNAIRE   The main survey tool used to generate market research data. Questionnaires contain a series of questions that are designed to solicit information on respondents' demographic characteristics, attitudes, perceptions, and beliefs about a product or issue. Questionnaires are self-administered by a respondent; or they are used by an interviewer to record data when conducting a face-to-face or telephone interview.

Designing a questionnaire first involves setting research objectives (answering the question, "What information do I want to generate?"). Identifying the information needed to achieve research objectives determines the way questions should be structured and phrased. There are three common approaches to structuring questionnaire items: closed-ended questions, open-ended questions, and scale items:

1. *Closed-ended questions* require the respondent to choose from a list of answers provided by the researcher. In crafting closed-ended questions, the researcher must ensure that the respondent is presented with all possible answers—that is, the choices must be *exhaustive*. Moreover, choices must be mutually exclusive—that is, respondents should feel that only one answer applies. For example:

What is your annual income?

☐ $10,000–$19,000
☐ $20,000–$29,000
☐ $30,000–$39,000
☐ $40,000–$49,000
☐ $50,000 and above

Note: Sometimes a closed-ended question calls for only a yes or a no answer. This is called a *dichotomous question*. For example:

Did you vote in the last presidential election?

☐ Yes
☐ No

The main benefit of closed-ended questions is the ease with which they are tabulated. The finite number of responses allows quick, accurate coding of responses.

2. *Open-ended questions* require the respondent to answer in his or her own words. For example:

What personality traits do you look for in a presidential candidate:

_____
_____
_____

The drawback of open-ended questions is researchers' difficulty in tabulating answers. Since the respondent is not given choices, there is a wide range of possible answers, which makes the data inputting complicated and time-consuming.

3. *Scale items* gauge the *degree* to which a respondent holds a given attitude toward an object or concept. These items involve a

series of statements. Respondents are asked to indicate whether they "strongly agree," "agree," are "uncertain," "disagree," or "strongly disagree." For example, **Likert scale** questionnaire items:

I think it is important to vote in every election.

Strongly Agree	*Agree*	*Uncertain*	*Disagree*	*Strongly Disagree*
☐	☐	☐	☐	☐

Note: The wording of all questionnaire items is critical to eliciting reliable feedback. Questions and statements should be phrased in simple, direct, and unbiased terms. Researchers must avoid questions that evoke irrelevant responses, may be misunderstood by the respondent, or are worded in such a way as to influence the respondent's answers (**leading questions**). See also **ranking; Thurstone scale.**

QUOTA A prescribed level of performance of a salesperson as measured by specific objective criteria. For example, a salesperson might be required to meet a quota of selling at least 100 units of a product per month. Quotas might also be measured in terms of the amount of dollar sales, the number of sales calls made, visits to prospects, or product demonstrations given to customers. Quota figures might be a prescribed number, or they are stated as a percentage of output in comparison to prior results.

QUOTA SAMPLE A form of **nonprobability sampling** in which a select number of respondents in a given category must be interviewed as part of the research initiative. Assume the study calls for interviewing at least 1,000 women aged 25 to 40. The researcher must find and interview this prescribed number of respondents in this category.

R

RACK JOBBER   A type of **limited-service wholesaler** that coordinates the installation and stocking of display racks in retail food and drug outlets. Rack jobbers typically deal in such nonfood items as paperback books, toys, and certain health and beauty aids. Rack jobbers deliver the goods by truck and set up the displays themselves. Periodically, they visit the retail outlets to replenish the inventory of display items.

RADIO   A major broadcast advertising medium that is included in virtually all major campaigns, often as a supplement to TV and magazine/newspaper ads. Radio offers distinct benefits as a media category. First, advertisers can control precisely when an ad will appear, specifying the day, hour, and minute to reach highly segmented audience groups. Second, radio offers great flexibility in creating messages that can be adapted to sound (e.g., via the use of *special effects*). Third, production costs are generally low. Radio advertising has several drawbacks, however. There is a tremendous degree of competition in radio broadcasting, with scores of other stations competing for listeners' attention. Next, it is difficult to provide detailed product information in radio commercial time spots (generally sold as 30- and 60-second segments). Last, there is much less audience research data on radio listenerships in comparison to TV audience information.

RADIO PROMOTION   A sales promotion technique in which a company ties in with a radio station to promote a product, special event, or ongoing campaign. Assume a corporate advertiser is sponsoring a rock concert. A radio promotion might involve arranging with a station that reaches the target audience (geographically and/or demographically) to publicize the event over a period of time by making announcements of the time and place (and sponsor) of the event, offering gifts or T-shirts to listeners who call in to answer contest questions, and so on. In exchange, the company would feature the station's logo or **call letters** in promotional materials such as advertising, event signage, fliers, and news releases.

RAGGED LEFT/RIGHT   Typesetting term referring to copy that has uneven margins on the right (ragged right) and/or left (ragged left) sides of the page. Ragged type is different from *flush right/left* or *justified* type, which is copy that extends to the end of the margin on one or both sides of the page. Also known as *unjustified* type.

RANDOM-DIGIT DIALING   A technique for selecting household telephone numbers to be called as part of a research study. Random digit dialing is a sampling method in which numbers are generated randomly. The first three digits (the exchange digits) are kept standard to ensure that the calls are made to the geographic area under study. The final four digits, however, are selected at random. The key benefit of this sampling technique is the ability to gain access to households with unlisted telephone numbers.

RANDOM SAMPLING   See **probability sampling.**

RANKING   A survey question format in which respondents are asked to indicate their responses in order of importance. For example, a questionnaire item might ask, "Please rank the attributes of this new product (i.e., price, quality, durability, convenience) in order of importance, with 1 being the most important and 4 being the least important." The benefit of ranking questions is that they are easy to tabulate when seeking information on a group of items (e.g., product characteristics). The drawback of ranking questions is that they do not reflect the degree of difference between answers. For example, the respondent might feel there is minimal difference between items 1 and 2 but that there is a great deal of difference between items 3 and 4.

RATE BASE   The figure on which a publication's advertising rates are based, as determined by its **average net paid circulation.** A rate base is a guarantee established by the publisher, reflecting the number of copies of the publication that are expected to be circulated on a regular basis. Since it is a guarantee, if the issue in which a company's ad appears does not meet the rate base, the advertiser receives a **make-good**—compensation in the form of a refund or a discount on a subsequent insertion.

RATE CARD   A document listing the rates of a given advertising medium. Rate cards might be single sheets or booklets that detail the medium's standard ad rates, as well as discounts (e.g., for volume purchases) and surcharges (e.g., for **preferred positions**). Magazine rate cards indicate both costs and publishers' specifications for preparing **mechanical art**. Rate cards are usually included in **media kits** furnished to advertisers.

RATE DIFFERENTIAL   The numerical difference between the advertising rates charged to local advertisers and those charged to national advertisers. Local advertisers are charged less for advertising than national advertisers. For this reason, many national advertisers engage in **cooperative advertising** with local companies when promoting goods in specific markets. That is, national advertisers tie in with a local retailer, with the latter buying ad space at the discounted local rates.

RATINGS   A measurement of the size of a viewing/listening audience of a given TV or radio program. Ratings are stated as a percentage of the number of households in the audience (those watching or listening to the program) as compared to the total potential audience (those households that have a TV or radio). A rating point represents 1% of the total potential audience. In the United States, one rating point equals 931,000 households. Media planners often base broadcast advertising buys on a program's rating, since the higher the rating the larger the audience. See also **A. C. Nielsen Company; audience measurement; cost per gross rating point**.

RATIO SCALE   A level of measurement that allows for comparisons of the magnitude of the numbers on the scale. Ratio scales have a natural or absolute zero; thus there are measurable intervals between scale points. Consider, for example, a ruler. This ratio scale shows that 12″ is twice as long as 6″ and four times as long as 3″. Also known as *interval scale*. See also **nominal scale; ordinal scale**.

REACH   See **cumulative audience**.

READERSHIP   The total number of people who read a given periodical. Readership includes those people who pay for the publication **(paid circulation)** as well as those who see it by means other than purchase **(pass-along circulation).** Publishers periodically conduct *readership studies* to determine the demographic and socioeconomic characteristics of their readers—information that is ultimately submitted to advertisers for **media planning** purposes. *Note:* In audience research, readership is a measure of the people who actually report having read a particular advertisement. See also **Starch ratings.**

REASON-WHY ADVERTISING   An approach to writing advertising in which a fact about the product is stated and then proved or explained. Reason-why copy is intended to give the consumer a reason to purchase the advertised product or service. For example, an ad's headline may state, "Why This Rare Coin Is the Best Investment You Can Make." The copy would go on to explain why this is true. Reason-why copy usually requires ample space to prove the point, which is why this approach is generally used only in print advertising, where the advertiser can go into greater detail than in a broadcast spot.

REBATE   A sales promotion technique in which the consumer is refunded a portion of the purchase price as an incentive to buy the item. For example, a consumer purchases an automobile and subsequently receives a $500 rebate. Rebates are similar to cents-off coupons, which also offer a discount off a product's cost. Rebates differ, however, in that the price reduction occurs after the purchase as opposed to at the point of sale, as with coupons.

RECALL   A test to determine advertising effectiveness. Recall measures the degree to which a person can remember the elements of an ad to which he or she has been exposed. In recall tests, the respondent is asked to describe the advertisement: its sales message, points made in the copy, campaign theme, and so forth. There are two types of recall tests. *Aided recall* refers to the researcher showing the ad to the respondents (providing a reminder), after which questions are asked. *Unaided recall* involves simply querying the respondents about an ad they have seen without first showing them the ad. See also **recognition.**

RECOGNITION   An advertising effectiveness test that involves showing a respondent an ad to determine if he or she has seen it.

Respondents are shown the advertisement and asked if they remember seeing it and whether or not they read it. Recognition tests measure consumer awareness of an individual advertisement. If an ad is deemed to have high recognition, it is assumed that the communication is effective. See also **Starch ratings.**

RED BOOKS   See **Standard Advertising Register.**

REDEMPTION   The practice of submitting coupons or **proofs-of-purchase** to receive a discount or **premium.** For example, a consumer who furnishes coupons to a retailer to receive product discounts is engaging in redemption. Companies track *redemption rates* to measure the success of a given promotion. That is, the redemption rate is a percentage of the number of coupons redeemed by consumers in comparison to the total number of coupons that were originally distributed to the market.

RED GOODS   Low-profit-margin consumer products that people purchase frequently. Examples of red goods are milk, bread, cigarettes, and soap. See also **orange goods.**

REFERENCE GROUP   Sociological concept referring to the fact that human behavior is influenced by a person's interaction with members of groups to which he or she belongs. Identifying reference groups and their impact on individuals is important to studying **consumer behavior.** Social scientists distinguish between three types of reference groups: (1) *Membership groups* are those to which the individual actually belongs (e.g., family, work, clubs, political parties); (2) *aspirational groups* are those to which the individual hopes to belong (e.g., fraternities); and (3) *dissociative groups* are those whose values the individual rejects and does not aspire to join (e.g., religious cults, radical political groups). Reference groups directly or indirectly influence individuals' attitudes and serve to expose people to new products and practices. Identifying reference groups to which consumers belong is an important step in defining target markets and in devising **marketing mix** combinations.

REFERRAL   Sales technique of using a person's name (usually a current customer) in introducing oneself to a prospective customer. For example, a salesperson will say, "Mr. Jones, your attorney, suggested I contact you." Some marketing programs are designed to solicit referral names from current customers in exchange for some kind of incentive. The resultant list of referrals then constitutes a group of prospects whom the salesperson can contact. See also **friend-of-a-friend promotion.**

REFUND OFFER   The ability of a customer to receive his or her money back if dissatisfied with a purchased product. See also **rebate.**

REGIONAL EDITIONS   Advertising sections of a national magazine that allow companies to market their products and services to select geographic regions. Assume a company markets its products solely in the northeastern and southeastern United States. The company would buy advertising space in the magazine's regional editions for those two areas. Regional editions were created to allow advertisers to geographically target their products, without having to buy the magazine's entire national circulation. *Note:* The editorial content is standard in all regional editions; what varies is the regionalized advertising sections.

REGRESSION ANALYSIS   Statistical technique used to estimate the contribution of an **independent variable** to changes in the **dependent variable,** for example, determining the effect of increasing advertising expenditures (independent variable) on product sales (dependent variable). Using regression analysis, an equation would be developed to show how much sales would increase if advertising were increased. When one independent variable is studied, the technique is called *simple regression analysis.* With *multiple regression analysis,* two or more independent variables are studied. The goal of this statistical technique is to identify the most significant *predictor variables* in a marketing situation. Thus, in the above example, advertising might *not* be the best variable to alter to effect higher sales; increasing the size of the sales force might prove to be more important.

RELAUNCH   The reintroduction of a product or promotional campaign after a period of inactivity. That is, relaunch suggests that the product or initiative was introduced into the marketplace then discontinued for one reason or another. For example, a soft drink manufacturer had to stop a promotion that involved having prizes pop out of its soda cans when the container mechanism proved faulty. Subsequently, the company considered relaunching the promotion after the mechanical problem was corrected. A relaunch generally involves some change to the product or promotional strategy before it commences.

RELEASE DATE   Publicity term referring to the day and time at which a news announcement will officially be made to the media. News releases indicate the date in a line that states: "For Release: __(date)__ , __(time)__." Release dates are set so that every target news medium receives the story at the same time. PR professionals establish release dates in an attempt to maximize news coverage because if one news medium reports a story before others, the latter may be discouraged from doing so because one publication has already run the story. See also **embargo.**

RELIABILITY   Research term denoting the extent to which data will be similar in comparable measurements of the same units of study. Reliability relates to the *consistency* of test results. That is, in two independent measurements of the same objects or situation, the research methodology will be deemed reliable if the same results can be expected. See also **validity.**

REMAINDER   Merchandise that has not been sold because of a lack of market demand. Remainder merchandise is ultimately lowered in price to sell the goods. For example, Valentine's Day candy boxes that have not been sold are remainder merchandise whose price is reduced after the February 14 occasion.

REMINDER ADVERTISING   Advertising designed to remind consumers about a particular product's attributes or availability. Reminder advertising often takes the form of brief mentions of the product because it is assumed that consumers are already aware of its existence from having seen other advertising for it. Examples of reminder ads are those which appear on matchbooks or on a **premium.** *Note:* Reminding consumers about a product is one goal of advertising strategy. It is different from the other strategies of *alerting* consumers to a product's existence or *persuading* them to prefer the advertised brand over competing brands. See also **message development.**

RENEWAL PROMOTION   A mailing to subscribers of a periodical to encourage renewal of their subscriptions. Renewal promotions typically commence six months before the subscription expiration date.

Such promotions involve mailing reminder notices of the imminent expiration. Telemarketing, however, is also sometimes employed. Renewal promotions often offer subscribers a discount on the subscription price (e.g., the ability to renew at the original subscription rate). Promotional materials might state, "Renew now before the subscription price goes up."

REPEAT RATE   The rate at which a consumer purchases the same product, usually within a given period of time. Identifying a product or brand's repeat rate is an indicator of the item's success. That is, a high repeat rate suggests a high degree of customer satisfaction. Data on repeat rates are also used in making general marketing decisions. For example, measuring repeat rates can be used to assess levels of advertising expenditures (a low repeat rate suggests advertising might have to be increased); to assess levels of advertising effectiveness (a low rate might mean the advertising is not working); or to determine whether or not a product should be kept on the market (such as when repeat rates are particularly and consistently low).

REPETITION   The act of frequently communicating an advertising message, slogan, or theme to reinforce it in consumers' minds. For example, a company will advertise in an **across-the-board** TV time period (that occurs on the same channel and at the same time each day) to effect message repetition to the target audience.

REPLY ENVELOPE   A piece of **business reply mail** sent to the addressee (the company that issued it) at no cost to the mailer. For example, reply envelopes are included in direct-mail packages, enabling the recipient to mail back the order form with payment or to request additional information. Most reply envelopes are postage-paid so as to provide an incentive to the consumer—that is, the envelopes provide a measure of convenience and cost savings. In fact, higher response rates typically occur when postage-paid reply envelopes are included in direct-mail solicitations. See also **return postcard.**

REPOSITIONING   The strategy of changing how a product is perceived by the market. Positioning refers to influencing people's perceptions of the product so that they come to believe that it is preferable to competitors' goods. Repositioning denotes altering the original positioning strategy, which might be required when a competing product begins to dominate and a new strategy is needed to contend with it; or if the product is in the decline stage of the **product life cycle** and its uses, benefits, or new attributes must be repositioned to save it from extinction. See also **positioning.**

REPRINT   The reproduction of an advertisement that has already appeared in the marketplace. A reprint is often mounted on cardboard and distributed to retailers for in-store display purposes (similar to a **preprint advertisement**). Reprints are also made of newspaper or magazine articles in which a company or its products are favorably portrayed. These editorial reprints can then be used as sales literature or as direct-mail pieces.

RESEARCH AND DEVELOPMENT (R&D)   The phase of the **new product development** process in which a prototype of the item is created. R&D begins after a product concept has been approved by company management. The research phase involves using new technologies and scientific procedures to engineer the product. Development involves devising procedures to produce and test it. In general, however, R&D is the corporate function that entails discovering new ways to design and manufacture new, modified, or improved products. Most large companies have formal R&D departments that coordinate these activities.

RESEARCH DIRECTOR   The corporate or advertising agency executive who heads the organization's market research function. The research director either conducts research studies or oversees the work of market research firms retained to do so. Such firms either provide **secondary research** data or conduct customized market research studies. In both cases, the research director assists management in devising marketing goals based on the data accumulated. *Note:* In an advertising agency, the research director typically reports to the vice-president of marketing services.

RESEARCH INSTRUMENTS   The various tools and techniques used to collect **primary research** data. There are two basic categories of research instruments. The first is *questionnaires,* which are printed documents featuring a series of questions and/or statements to which people are asked to respond. Questionnaires are either self-administered by respondents or are used by interviewers to record data in face-to-face or telephone interviews. The second category, *mechanical* *instruments,* include laboratory testing devices such as **galvanometers** (which measure sweating in the palm that accompanies emotional arousal in the respondent) and **eye cameras** (which record respondents' eye movements when reading an ad or viewing a picture—information that is ultimately used in designing print advertisements). See also **cathode ray tube.**

RESEARCH REPORT Document summarizing the findings of a research study. A standard research report has three sections: (1) The *digest,* which is a description of the study stating why it was undertaken and what the major findings were (the digest is intended for review by senior management); (2) the *detailed findings,* which discuss the results in a broader level of detail (with wording that is designed for review by product or marketing managers—that is, it is not overloaded with too much research and/or statistical jargon); and (3) the *tabulations,* which contain tables of statistics (where the level of detail is designed primarily for the market researchers). Research reports are designed to provide the information that is needed to make decisions about the marketing situation or problem the study was designed to address. See also **top-line report.**

RESEARCH STUDY A project contracted by a company to elicit market research on a given marketing problem or situation. Formal research studies are conducted by **custom marketing research firms** that participate in designing the study and in coordinating its implementation. The firm generates the research data and analyzes the results, which become the property of the client.

RESELLER MARKET The collective of businesses and individuals who purchase goods in order to resell or rent them at a profit. Retailers and wholesalers are two types of companies that comprise the reseller market. The vast majority of products sold to consumers are sold through such selling intermediaries. See also **organizational market.**

RESIDUALS Payments to an actor who appears in a commercial that airs more than once. Residuals are paid to actors either by the advertising agency that cast them or by the TV or radio stations on which the commercial appeared. Large advertising agencies have *talent payment departments* that coordinate payments of residuals to actors who have appeared in commercials developed by those agencies.

RESPONDENT   A person who takes part in a research study and provides information being collected for that initiative. Respondents complete questionnaires or agree to be queried by a researcher in a face-to-face or telephone interview. Respondents are selected for the research study either by **probability** or **nonprobability sampling.** See also **sampling.**

RESPONSE   1. A person's reaction to an external stimulus. **2.** In marketing, response can refer to a consumer's action after having seen an advertisement (e.g., the consumer does or does not purchase the item) or whether or not the consumer acted upon a direct-mail solicitation. Response is an important concept in direct marketing, where measurements are taken of the number of people who buy the advertised merchandise (orders) or request information (inquiries). A direct-mail campaign's *response rate,* for instance, refers to the number of people who responded to the promotion in comparison to the total number of people who received the promotional packages. Direct-mail companies regularly conduct *response analyses* to evaluate the success of a given initiative. These statistical assessments review different aspects of the campaign as individual determinants of its success, for example, the mailing list, the product offer, the mailing package design or contents. **3.** In market research, a person's answer to a question.

RESPONSE-HIERARCHY MODEL   A paradigm used in establishing communications objectives and strategies. A response-hierarchy model is used by marketing communicators to help determine what response they seek from the target audience: (1) *cognitive* (e.g., alerting consumers to a product's availability); (2) *affective* (e.g., getting buyers to perceive the product in a certain way); and (3) *behavioral* (e.g., moving consumers to purchase the item or to request additional information). See also **awareness, interest, desire, action; hierarchy of effects.**

RETAILER   A **middleman** company that purchases goods from a manufacturer or wholesaler for resale to the goods' ultimate consumers at a profit. Retailers usually sell merchandise for personal and household consumption, with the merchandise both stored and displayed on the store's premises. *Store retailers* are the operators of department stores, supermarkets, clothing boutiques, and so on. *Nonstore retailers* include companies that sell through mail-order catalogs, engage in direct selling (e.g., house-to-house), or operate vending machines. See also **organizational market.**

RETAILING The practice of making goods available to consumers for their personal use in a location or situation that provides a forum for exchanging those goods. There are four basic functions of retailing: (1) buying and storing goods; (2) transferring title of those goods; (3) providing information on the nature and uses of those items; and (4) (in some cases) extending credit to consumers.

RETAINER A method by which a services firm (e.g., an advertising agency, management consulting firm) is compensated. A retainer arrangement involves establishing a standard monthly fee to be paid to the firm by the client. The fee is based on the scope of the work— a predetermined level of service the client expects to need. However, the firm provides unlimited service and the client can call upon the agency anytime to handle specific assignments. In a retainer arrangement, out-of-pocket expenses—such as travel costs, payments to vendors—are billed to the client separate from the retainer fee. A retainer is different from a *project fee* arrangement, which is where the money paid to the firm is based on the scope of a specific assignment and payment stops once the work is complete. See also **performance-based compensation.**

RETURN 1. Another term for *response* in a direct mail campaign, referring to the number of people who either purchased merchandise or requested additional information. Return is a percentage of the number of people who acted upon the solicitation in comparison to the total number of people who received the promotional materials. 2. In market research, the number of people who mailed back a questionnaire that was issued to a sample of respondents.

RETURN ON INVESTMENT (ROI) A measure of profitability calculated by taking **net profit** and dividing it by *total assets*. Assume net profits are $50,000 and total assets are $200,000. The ROI is

$$\$50,000 \div \$200,000 = .25 = 25\%$$

Companies measure ROI to make comparisons between units in their **product portfolios,** as well as between their own and competitors' products. The resultant comparative data are used to make decisions about pricing, inventory levels, and corporate spending (e.g., how much capital to allocate to given products or marketing activities). See also **break-even analysis.**

RETURN POSTCARD   A postage-paid reply card sent by a consumer to the selling company to order merchandise or receive product information. The seller's address is preprinted on the card, which usually features an **indicia** signifying that postage costs will be borne by the company. The convenience and no-cost mailing of the card provide an inducement to consumers to return it. See also **reply envelope.**

RETURNS AND ALLOWANCES   In retailing, the total dollar amount of products that were returned to the seller by dissatisfied customers (returns) and the total price reductions/discounts that were granted to consumers by the seller (allowances). The monetary amount of returns and allowances is deducted from the store's *gross sales* to arrive at total *net sales.*

REUSABLE CONTAINER   A sales promotion technique in which a product container serves a purpose after it has been emptied. For example, an empty jelly jar can be designed to serve as a drinking glass. In short, a reusable container refers to a product package that eventually becomes a **premium.**

RIFLE APPROACH   1. Term denoting selectivity in targeting new business prospects. Rifle approach is used in the context of sales planning, where it refers to focusing the selling effort on buyers who have the greatest purchase interest and/or ability. 2. The distribution of publicity materials (e.g., a news release) to select news media instead of mass mailing them to many different media. See also **shotgun approach.**

RISK   Concept referring to the fact that purchase decisions by a consumer involve varying levels of chance taking on the buyer's part. For example, buying an expensive product (such as a car or home) involves a significant degree of risk because the consumer fears losing a large amount of money if the wrong purchase decision is made. Risk creates anxiety in the consumer. Thus, people strive to minimize risk by seeking product information from friends, or by purchasing only well-known brands or goods that offer warranties. Marketers attempt to understand the factors that create risk in consumers' minds and take measures to reduce it (e.g., by offering customer service support or instructional literature). See also **dissonance-reduction; perceived risk.**

RISK ANALYSIS Strategic planning function in which the external threats of the marketplace are identified and assessed in terms of their potential impact on the organization and their likelihood of occurrence.

ROLE AND STATUS 1. Sociological terms referring to the position a person occupies in a given social group and the expected modes of behavior of the individual in that setting. A person's *role* is determined by the needs, goals, beliefs, and values the group expects of him or her. A person's *status* is the level of esteem accorded the role by the social group. People have different roles and statuses in different social groups: family, work, professional associations, clubs, and fraternities. 2. Also used to describe the expected behavior of a company or individual serving as a marketing channel member. See also **channel behavior.**

ROLE SET Term denoting the fact that a sales manager must assume different roles when interacting with salespeople, as a means of maximizing the efficiency of the organization's sales efforts. For example, the sales manager must be an *effective performer*, able to provide counsel on sales and marketing issues; an *inspirational leader*, getting salespeople motivated and, thus, to be successful sellers; an *innovator*, able to devise solutions to salespeople's problems; a *parent image*, setting the rules and establishing criteria for salespeople's performance; and an *information provider*, offering input to the sales force on the company's procedures and policies.

ROLLOUT 1. Merchandising term referring to the formal introduction of a product into the marketplace. Rollout is generally used to denote the full-scale launch of a product—that is, after the item has been *test marketed* in one or more geographic areas. 2. In direct mail, the largest mailing in a campaign. For example, a rollout would be sending promotional materials to the remainder of a mailing list after successful test mailings to small samples of the list. See also **pyramiding.**

ROUTING   Sales term referring to the pattern of travel by a sales representative through a given geographic territory. Routing denotes strategically scheduling visits to customers to maximize efficient servicing of accounts while minimizing travel and expenses. For example, a salesperson covering the southwestern United States would plan to call on customers in New Mexico and Arizona on the way to visit accounts in California (as opposed to starting in California, moving east to New Mexico, and then moving back west to Arizona). Salespeople engage in routing to ensure that a territory is sufficiently covered at the lowest possible cost to the selling organization. See also **territory management.**

RUN-OF-PAPER (ROP)   Publishing term referring to the placement of an advertisement at the publisher's discretion. That is, an advertiser submits an ad and the publisher decides where it will appear in the publication. Advertisers, however, can request a **preferred position,** in which case the advertiser negotiates the cost to have the ad placed in a specific section of the newspaper or magazine. Also known as *run-of-press.*

RUN-OF-SCHEDULE (ROS)   The broadcast equivalent of **run-of-paper.** Run-of-schedule is the situation in which an advertiser furnishes a TV commercial and its air time is determined by station management. (On radio, ROS refers to *run-of-station.*) Advertisers, however, can negotiate to receive a **preferred position** for the commercial at an agreed-upon rate.

S

SADDLE STITCH The technique of binding a booklet in which a thread or wire is stitched through the center fold of the publication's pages. Saddle stitching is used only for very thin booklets. Larger publications (such as mail-order catalogs or research reports) require alternate forms of binding, such as stapling or a comb-bound spine (a plastic spine with spiral "teeth" that fit through perforations in the text pages).

SALES AGENT An individual or company serving as a seller of a manufacturer's products or services. Sales agents operate independently and typically do not take title to the goods they sell. Depending on their contract with the manufacturer, sales agents may or may not exercise control over setting prices and other terms of the exchange between buyer and seller.

SALES ANALYSIS The periodic examination of a company's sales figures to assess company performance and to improve the accuracy of **sales forecasts.** Sales analyses are done for specific territories, products, or salespeople. Such analyses may be conducted monthly, quarterly, or annually. The process involves gathering, classifying, and analyzing sales data to interpret the pattern of sales orders obtained in the marketplace. See also **cost analysis.**

SALES AND MARKETING RESEARCH Market research designed to generate data on a specific sales and marketing situation or problem. For example, such research is undertaken to gauge the market potential of a product; the percentage of market share held by a company; specific characteristics of a market or market segment; or the efficiency of **channels of distribution.**

SALES AUDIT An in-depth analysis of a company's overall sales operation. (A sales audit is different from a **sales analysis** in that the latter is merely a review of sales results.) The sales audit is designed to review the company's total sales strategy as measured against its overall sales objectives. The audit involves determining whether or not the objectives are realistic, appropriate, and attainable. It also assesses the company's sales plans and policies that are being employed to achieve its objectives. Moreover, the audit reviews organizational details, determining whether or not sales force staffing is adequate and if the organizational structure needs to be changed. The audit ultimately results in an assessment and a series of recommendations for future actions. To elicit objective data, the sales audit should be conducted by an outside consulting firm.

SALES BUDGET The monies allocated to finance sales force activities such as salesperson training, compensation, and travel and expenses. The sales budget is a component of a company's marketing budget and represents the money to be dedicated to sales department activities over a specified period of time.

SALES COMPENSATION The various methods by which a salesperson is paid. There are three basic forms of sales compensation: (1) *Straight salary* involves paying the salesperson a fixed annual stipend; (2) *commission basis* refers to compensation based on the salesperson's level of performance (e.g., as a percentage of sales he or she generates); and (3) *combination compensation* plan mixes a straight salary arrangement with commission. In general, sales compensation should be based on providing incentives to reward outstanding performance by the salesperson. Moreover, it should be designed to motivate the sales force to do the things management wants (e.g., maintaining accurate customer records and/or furnishing periodic progress reports).

SALES CONTEST An intracompany competition in which salespeople vie for gifts, money, or vacations, with the winner being the seller who accomplishes or exceeds the company's stated sales objective. A sales contest, however, may also be arranged by a manufacturer that establishes the competition among its independent sales agents.

SALES FORCE ORGANIZATION How the members of a company's sales force are organized and deployed to engage in personal selling to customers. Sales forces may be organized by geographic territory, product, market, or a combination of these variables. In general, an effective sales force organization minimizes duplication of effort (e.g., avoiding having more than one seller handle the same area of responsibility); specializes labor (e.g., having people handle the jobs for which they are best suited); and coordinates the activities of different salespeople and departments in the seller company. Determining the appropriate sales force organization first involves establishing specific sales goals and objectives. See also **complex sales force organization; market-structured sales force; product-structured sales force; territory-structured sales force.**

SALES FORECAST   A projection of the amount of sales a company expects to achieve over a future period of time, as determined by a specific marketing program. Sales force projections are stated in terms of dollars or unit sales. Companies normally conduct market research before developing sales forecasts. For example, estimating future market demand generates data on which sales forecasts can be based. A company can collect such data through *buyer intention surveys,* interviews with sales force members and channel intermediaries or by reviewing various **economic indicators.** See also **forecasting model.**

SALES LETTER   A correspondence developed by a selling organization and issued to customers or prospects. In sales, the letter may simply be a communication sent by a sales representative to a target customer. In direct mail, a sales letter is the first element seen in the promotional package. The letter details the product or service being offered and explains why the recipient should act upon the offer. The main goal of a sales letter is to get the reader's attention and to highlight the advertised product's attributes and benefits. Sales letters are often personalized with the name and address of the recipient. However, some sales letters carry a generic salutation (e.g., "Dear Business Executive")

SALES MANAGEMENT   The overall process of coordinating an organization's personal selling efforts to customers and prospects. In general, sales management entails:

- *Devising a sales program*—which involves such things as account management policies, sales forecasts, sales force organization decisions, and territory assignments

- *Implementing the sales program*—coordinating all activities involved in hiring, training, compensating, and providing motivation/incentives to the sales force
- *Evaluating sales force performance*—establishing methods for monitoring and assessing salespeople's work

See also **sales analysis; sales audit.**

SALES MANAGEMENT INFORMATION SYSTEM (SMIS) The system by which sales data are collected, analyzed, interpreted, and distributed to a company's sales managers. A company establishes an SMIS to continually monitor the market to spot important trends, changing customer needs, and opportunities for market growth. Information comprising the SMIS is collected from salespersons' field reports, internal sales records, and historical data on the company's individual products, accounts, and territories. SMIS data are used primarily to spot problems and opportunities and to develop projections of future occurrences for sales program planning. See also **marketing information system.**

SALES MANAGER The executive in a company who is responsible for overseeing the organization's personal selling function. The sales manager coordinates either all or part of the company's sales efforts. That is, the manager may be responsible for national sales activities or those for a particular region or territory. In general, the manager plans the company's sales objectives and devises tactics to achieve them. In addition, he or she organizes and directs the activities of the sales force; monitors external developments and market trends to develop sales programs; and enacts controls to gauge the company's overall sales performance in relation to its stated sales objectives. See also **role set; sales force organization; sales management.**

SALES PROMOTION One of the main elements of the **marketing communications mix.** Sales promotion involves using specially designed materials, devices, and programs that communicate product information, provide an incentive to consumers to purchase the product, and spur them to engage in the transaction immediately. Sales promotions may be targeted to these audiences:

- *Consumer users*, where the initiative is intended to encourage more product usage
- *Consumer nonusers*, to encourage product trial

- *Retailers,* to urge them to carry more inventory of a product and to offset competitors' promotions
- *Sales force,* to assist them in introducing new products to **middlemen** and to complement other promotional activities such as advertising, publicity, and personal selling

The tools employed in sales promotion include:

coupons	contests
rebates	sweepstakes
continuity programs	incentives
price packs	point-of-purchase
premiums	advertising
samples	events marketing

See also **trade promotion.**

SALES PROMOTION MANAGER   The corporate executive responsible for developing and implementing sales promotion programs. He or she also oversees the work of retained sales promotion agencies. The sales promotion manager typically reports to a marketing manager or advertising manager.

SALES QUOTA   A performance standard that states, in terms of dollars or units, the sales that must be achieved over a specific period of time. Quotas are sales objectives established by the company's sales management for individual sales representatives, territories, or specific customers (e.g., a wholesaler or retailer). Evaluating of a salesperson's performance is often based on the actual sales generated compared with the sales quota. See also **activity quota.**

SALES REPORT   A salesperson's summary of his or her activities in an assigned area of responsibility such as territory, product, or market. Sales reports include data on sales generated, number of phone calls and visits made to customers, or the number of product demonstrations given. Sales reports may also detail customers' feedback to products or company procedures, as well as competitors' activities.

SALES REPRESENTATIVE   An employee of the selling organization or an independent operator **(sales agent)** that conducts personal selling on behalf of the company. Sales representatives typically report to a sales manager. Also known as *salesperson.*

SALES TERRITORY   See **territory**.

SALTING   The practice of inserting fictional names/addresses into a mailing list to discover unauthorized usage of the list. Salt names (also called *decoys* or *dummy names*) are included by list owners, since the list rental is usually for one-time usage. Thus, if a company attempts to reuse the list, it will unknowingly mail to the salt names. The materials will then be received by the list owner. Salt names are also used to determine the speed with which postal delivery of a mailing is made or to review/verify the work of the **lettershop** that conducted the mailing.

SAMPLE   **1.** In sales promotion, a small amount of product distributed free or at a reduced cost to consumers to encourage product trial and future purchases. For example, in introducing a new brand of cereal a company mailed one-portion samples (*trial-size* packages) to consumers. **2.** In marketing research, a subset of a population which, when surveyed, yields information deemed to be representative of the total population. See also **sampling**.

SAMPLING   The phase of marketing research in which members of a population are scientifically selected to yield findings that reflect the characteristics of the total population.

Sampling is necessary to help assure accurate, valid results in marketing research. It is also needed to effect logistical and cost savings. For instance, it would be very costly and difficult to survey every member of a market consisting of one million people. Sampling allows a select number of people to be surveyed—the theory holding that the sample would tend to have the same characteristics and yield data in the same proportions as the total population. Samples in marketing research studies are either probability or nonprobability samples.

Probability samples are those in which every member of the total universe of respondents has an equal and known chance of being selected. Assume a survey is being conducted of people's feelings on the food/beverage service in a new football stadium. If that arena is filled to its capacity with 50,000 people, each person would have one chance in five of being selected if the probability sample being sought is 10,000. There are three types of probability samples:

1. *Simple random sample.* This process typically involves assigning numbers to units of the population. A set of random numbers

is then generated and the units having those numbers are selected for the sample. Thus, numbers would be assigned to the 50,000 ticket stubs; then 10,000 of those would be selected based on the preassigned numbers.

2. *Stratified random sample.* The population is divided into mutually exclusive groups (such as gender groups), and samples are drawn from each. Thus, football fans could be divided into males and females; samples would then be drawn accordingly.

3. *Cluster (area) sample.* The population is divided into arbitrary groups based on their location (e.g., those fans in different sections of the stadium), and the researcher draws a sample of the designated groups.

Nonprobability samples are based on criteria that ensure that some members of the population have a higher probability of being sampled than others. There are three kinds of nonprobability samples:

1. *Judgment samples.* The researcher subjectively selects survey respondents whom the researcher feels will yield accurate information. For example, the researcher chooses those stadium fans waiting in line at concession stands.

2. *Convenience samples.* The researcher interviews those people who are accessible to the researcher (e.g., those fans sitting in the same section of the stadium as the researcher).

3. *Quota samples.* The researcher interviews a set number of people from several categories (e.g., men, women, and those children between the ages of 10 and 15).

There are three main advantages to probability sampling. First, such samples rule out human biases that might be involved in subjectively selecting people to be interviewed (as in judgment sampling). Second, probability samples increase the likelihood that the sample drawn is representative of the broader population. Third, probability sampling is the only sampling method that offers measurable estimates of accuracy. That is, **sampling error** can be determined by computational methods that estimate the degree of error to be expected in a given sample.

SAMPLING ERROR   Term referring to the inherent imperfections in **probability sampling.** Sampling error denotes the fact that no probability sample can ever represent the exact characteristics of the total population. Researchers determine sampling error to indicate the difference among figures generated in repeated measurements of the population. This **confidence range** means that researchers can conclude after a sample is drawn that the actual data fall within that specified range (stated as a percentage). For example, if researchers have a test sample average of 80, they will also say within a high degree of confidence that the actual population average is 80 ± (say) 3%, or between 77 and 83. *Note:* Sampling error decreases as the size of the sample increases.

SAMPLING FRAME   The group of sampling units from which a sample is to be drawn. A sampling frame can be a list of people (e.g., from a telephone directory), geographic areas (as used in **area sampling**), or companies or institutions. Researchers must ensure that the sampling frame is accurate, up-to-date and, most importantly, relevant to the research initiative. For example, to draw a sample from a list of Houston city residents, a telephone book listing households in Houston suburbs would not be used. See also **universe.**

SATISFICING   The corporate strategy of aiming to achieve a specific corporate or financial objective, and not attempting to exceed that level even if it is possible to do so through other strategies or increased activities. For example, if a company meets its year-end sales objective for a product after only 10 months, it may stop promoting the product. Satisficing is different from a **profit maximization** strategy, in which a company strives to realize as great a profit as possible.

SATURATION   See **burst advertising.**

SCALES   Survey research questions designed to gauge the nature and strength of respondents' attitudes or beliefs toward an object or concept. Scaling questions are **closed-ended questions.** That is, the respondent chooses from a list of answers provided by the researcher. Examples are **Likert** and **Thurstone** scales. See also **questionnaire.**

SCANNER   An electronic device that reads **bar codes** and other graphic symbols that appear on product packages, coupons, and mailing envelopes. For example, electronic cash registers are scanners that read the bar codes on product packages, recording the product's price and entering data used for inventory management and accounting purposes. Similarly, scanners are used to record information from coupons, tabulating the number of coupons redeemed and identifying from which sources (e.g., magazines, newspapers, **freestanding inserts**) they emanated. Scanners are also used by the U.S. Postal Service to read bar codes on envelopes for the purpose of sorting mail. See also **electronic marketing; universal product code.**

SCATTER PLAN   Media planning term referring to the purchase of advertising at different times and on a variety of broadcast programs. A scatter plan gives the advertiser a wider and more diverse audience than when it concentrates its advertising on one given show.

SCIENTIFIC EVIDENCE APPROACH TO ADVERTISING   A thematic approach to writing advertising in which the copy presents scientific or survey data in support of the product sales message. This approach is designed to illustrate through empirical facts that a brand is superior to its competitors. An example is advertising copy that discusses how one toothpaste has been scientifically proven to fight cavities better than other brands.

SCRATCH-AND-SNIFF   The technique of implanting a fragrance into an area of a postcard that releases the scent when scratched. Many perfume ads use this technique. See also **action device.**

SCRATCH OFF   A device used in sales promotion materials in which the consumer scratches off (usually with a coin) the area of a card that reveals a special message. For instance, a fast-food restaurant chain ran a promotion in which consumers received a scratch-off card with each purchase. The cards indicated whether the consumer was an instant winner of a contest and noted the prize. See also **action device.**

SCREENER   A person retained by an advertiser to view **prime-time** network programming (prior to its airing) to spot objectionable material that might harm the advertiser's image. Screeners are hired to identify shows that contain acts of violence, sex, profanity, drugs, alcohol, and so forth. The screener then reports to clients, which then determine if advertising on a particular show will reflect badly on the clients' products.

SCREENING   1. In direct mail, the deletion from a mailing list of names based on a particular criterion. For example, a list may be screened to discard names of people outside the geographic area being targeted; or screening may be based on criteria such as gender or income level. **2.** In broadcast advertising, the showing of a commercial prior to its appearance in the marketplace. A commercial is usually screened for final client approval before its distribution to the intended advertising media.

SEALED-BID PRICING   Pricing mechanism in a **competitive bid** situation, where the company bases its price on what it expects its competitors to charge. That is, the company's price is determined by expectations of what competitors will bid as opposed to the company's own costs or demands. Sealed-bid pricing poses a challenge to companies: The company must not set its price so low that it will lose money if it gets the contract; conversely, the company must not set its price so high that it lessens its chance of getting the contract. The *process* of sealed-bid pricing involves the submission of confidential bids, all due at a specified time, with the contract awarded to the lowest bidder.

SEASONAL DEMAND   Market situation in which the amount of product taken by the market varies significantly by season or time of year. For example, the market for swimwear in the northern United States is active in the summer but dormant in the winter. Similarly, demand for Halloween costumes and accessories is high in the weeks preceding the occasion and virtually nonexistent at other times of the year. Also known as *seasonality*. See also **demand states.**

SECONDARY RESEARCH   Research information that is available from published sources (e.g., census data, studies conducted for another person or group). Secondary research also includes data available to clients for a fee or on a subscription basis (e.g., the marketing and media research available from the A. C. Nielsen Company). Secondary research is different from *primary research,* which are data of a proprietary nature that have been generated for a specific company.

SECOND-CLASS MAIL   Mail service that is used primarily for sending magazines and newspapers that are published on a continuous basis or have been requested and/or paid for by the addressee. Second-class mail is less expensive than first-class mail, but is more costly than third-class and fourth-class postage. Thus, second-class mail is almost never used for direct mailings, which typically involve the distribution of thousands of envelopes.

SEGMENT   A subgroup of people within a market. The members of a market segment show a commonality of one or more demographic or psychographic characteristics, or they share some special need or attribute. See also **market segmentation.**

SELECTIVE BINDING   The process of binding different printed elements into a publication in different combinations in one binding run. Selective binding is used, for example, in the insertion of **personalized ads** in a national magazine. These are ads that feature individual magazine subscribers' names and provide localized information on product availability (e.g., dealer locations). Here, selective binding is used to group the personalized insert cards by geography. Selective binding was created by the R. R. Donnelley & Sons Company. The trademark name is *selectronic gathering.*

SELECTIVE DISTRIBUTION   The distribution strategy in which a manufacturer makes its product available in one or just a few outlets in a given geographic area. A manufacturer decides on a selective distribution strategy when it wants to concentrate its sales efforts on only a few dealers, choosing the best dealers and ignoring marginal dealers. Consequently, the manufacturer can expect a strong commitment by the dealer since the dealer enjoys limited competition from other sellers. Selective distribution is usually employed for high-margin consumer goods such as furniture and large household appliances (e.g., refrigerators). See also **exclusive distribution; intensive distribution.**

SELECTIVE PERCEPTION   People's cognitive ability to shield themselves from the barrage of external stimuli to which they are exposed in an attempt to create order and avoid psychological chaos. In marketing, selective perception is important to understanding how consumers react to stimuli such as advertising and other sources of information. There are three aspects to selective perception: (1) *Selective exposure* suggests that people select only certain messages from the mass of external stimuli to which they are exposed; (2) *selective distortion* relates to the fact that when confronted with general, limited, or dissonant information, people will unconsciously supplement the information with their own perceptions, the goal and result of which is a message that is understandable and consistent with their feelings and beliefs; and (3) *selective retention* refers to people's tendency to remember external stimuli that are similar to their preconceived notions and beliefs, and to forget stimuli that are not. See also **consumer behavior; perception.**

SELECTIVITY INDEX A measurement technique used in **media planning** to compare print advertising vehicles in a given geographic area. The index is determined by dividing a medium's audience size by the percentage of the population in the target market. For example, if newspaper A's readers in the target market make up 20% of the market and population in the target market is 40%, then

$$20\% \div 40\% = 50 \text{ (selectivity index)}.$$

Or if newspaper B's readers in the target market make up 30% of the market and the population in the target market is 40%, then

$$30\% \div 40\% = 75 \text{ (selectivity index)}.$$

Here, newspaper B is more efficient for reaching the target market, since it has a higher selectivity index than newspaper A. See also **cost per gross rating point; cost per thousand.**

SELF-CONCEPT The mental picture people have of themselves. Self-concept, as a component of an individual's personality, is an important influencer of **consumer behavior.** For example, if people have a very strong self-concept (e.g., as being proud or very accomplished), they may believe that they deserve the very best items and will buy the most expensive brands in a given product category. Marketers attempt to create a **brand personality** that is consistent with the self-concept of the target buyer (e.g., creating an aura of affluence around a product targeted to upscale buyers).

SELF-LIQUIDATING OFFER In sales promotion, a **premium** gift sold at a cost lower than its retail price to generate sales for a given product. A self-liquidating offer is designed to get consumers to purchase large amounts of a product because they want to acquire the premium at a desirable price. For example, a manufacturer advertises on its product packages the offer of a cooking skillet for $9 (the unit cost the manufacturer pays for the item) that would retail for a higher price. By getting consumers to want the premium, the manufacturer effects increased unit sales. Thus, the self-liquidating offer lets the manufacturer have the premium "pay for itself" while using it as a promotional tool to sell more product.

SELF-REGULATION   In general, the procedures enacted by an industry to monitor its activities and ensure that standards of professional behavior and business practices are maintained by its members. For example, the **National Advertising Review Board** is the advertising industry's self-regulatory body. The organization reviews complaints of false or deceptive advertising.

SELF-SERVICE   A type of retail outlet where consumers search for and select products with no (or minimal) assistance from the store's personnel. Examples of self-service outlets are discount stores and supermarkets. In self-service stores, checkout counters are situated in different sections of the outlet or in a central location.

SELLER'S MARKET   The economic situation that favors sellers as opposed to buyers. In a seller's market, demand for a product outweighs its supply. Thus, sellers have the upper hand in setting prices and purchase terms. For example, a seller's market in real estate exists when the supply of homes on the market is significantly lower than the number of people seeking to purchase them. In a seller's market consumers buy what they can get if they cannot get what they want. See also **buyer's market.**

SELLING AGENT   An independent person or company that sells all or part of a manufacturer's line of merchandise. Selling agents typically work on an extended contractual basis with the manufacturer and usually have full authority for setting prices. A key defining characteristic of selling agents is that they may provide financial assistance (e.g., working capital for promotional expenditures) to the manufacturer. Selling agents may work for more than one manufacturer. *Note:* Selling agents differ from **sales agents** in that the latter do not have authority over prices and terms of sale and never get involved in advertising and promotion (as selling agents sometimes do).

SEMANTIC DIFFERENTIAL SCALE   A questionnaire item used to gauge consumers' feelings toward a brand, company, or object. This attitude measurement method involves constructing a list of opposite adjectives (good–bad, strong–weak, high–low, etc.) with cells to let the respondent indicate how strongly he or she feels the adjective applies (e.g., extremely good, very good, somewhat good).

SEQUENTIAL SAMPLES A series of samples drawn from the same **universe,** in which a small sample is first taken and then subsequent samples are drawn if the preceding ones do not provide conclusive evidence.

SEQUENTIAL TESTING A form of consumer **product research.** Sequential testing involves having a respondent test one product and then assess another in the same category. The consumer is ultimately asked to evaluate and compare the products he or she has tried.

SERVICE BUREAU A company that provides administrative and other support services to individuals or other companies. Marketing-related service bureaus offer such capabilities as mailing list maintenance (e.g., compiling and/or updating lists) and computer operation (such as for database management). Companies retain service bureaus when they do not have the capability resident in their organization or when they need to supplement their own resources on a temporary basis.

SERVICE LINE The group of capabilities offered by a services organization that are related in nature and which may be marketed to the same clients. For example, an accounting firm may offer such services as management consulting; tax return preparation; and actuarial, benefits, and compensation planning. See also **product line.**

SERVICES **1.** Activities provided by a person or company to another person or company that are intangible and do not relate to a physical product. Marketed services include accounting, legal services, medical services, management consulting, architecture, and engineering. As a commodity, services have several defining characteristics that distinguish them from products: *intangibility,* the buyer cannot see the service before it is rendered; *inseparability,* that is, the service requires involvement by the provider; *variability,* that is, services by different providers may vary in terms of quality and level of service; and *perishability,* that is, service value exists at the time the buyer receives it (services cannot be stored for use at a later time). **2.** Services also denote the activities performed by a company for a consumer who has purchased a product. For example, customer services include information support, product usage instructions/ guidance, and product repairs. See also **professional services marketing.**

SHARE OF AUDIENCE   See **audience share.**

SHARE OF MARKET   See **market share.**

SHARE OF MIND   Concept referring to how much the general public associates a particular brand with a specific product category. For example, a product with the largest share of mind is the one that most consumers will mention when asked to cite a brand in the category. Share of mind is directly related to **share of voice** because the more a company advertises its product (thus gaining a large share of voice), the more people will have heard of it. Consequently, the product earns a greater share of consumers' minds in comparison to other products (that may not advertise as frequently).

SHARE OF VOICE (SOV)   The level of advertising by a brand in a given product category in comparison to others in the same category. The higher a brand's SOV, the greater the number of advertising messages being disseminated to consumers. There is a high correlation between a product's SOV and its market share. That is, companies that advertise more frequently gain a greater level of market share in the product category.

SHELF LIFE   The amount of time a product can stay in storage before it can no longer be sold or consumed. Products have varying shelf lives. For example, bread and milk have very short shelf lives in comparison to, say, boxes of cereal or household products. Many products carry expiration dates to indicate the date after which the items are no longer fit for consumption. In general, shelf life denotes the maximum amount of time a product can be stored between the time it is produced and consumed. See also **stock rotation.**

SHELF TALKER   An in-store sales promotion device designed to draw attention to a product or to announce a sale or promotion relating to the item. Specifically, a shelf talker is a sign or printed card that is attached to the shelf or railing of a display on which the featured merchandise is stacked. Shelf talkers are found in supermarkets, discount stores, and variety stores.

SHERMAN ANTITRUST ACT   Federal legislation enacted in 1890 that prohibits efforts by companies to restrain interstate and foreign trade or to try to monopolize a market. The Sherman Antitrust Act makes illegal any effort by a company to create a monopoly or to limit free trade. See also **Clayton Antitrust Act.**

SHOPPING CENTER   A group of retail stores that are similar in size and architectural design and are located on one site. There are two basic types of shopping centers. *Regional shopping centers* are large facilities (e.g., suburban malls) that contain approximately 50 to 100 stores and attract consumers from a 5- to 10-mile radius. These shopping centers typically feature one or two **anchor stores** (well-known retailers) and numerous smaller retailers. The benefits of regional shopping centers are that they offer shoppers ample parking and restaurants (in addition to just retail outlets), and they allow one-stop shopping. *Community shopping centers* are much smaller than regional centers. They may have only one anchor tenant (or none at all) and feature fewer stores. Community shopping centers draw consumers from a smaller geographic radius than regional shopping centers. *Note:* Both types of shopping centers are usually planned, developed, and owned by one company. See also **superstores.**

SHORT LIST   The list of finalist service providers in contention for a contract to provide services to a prospective client. For example, a company seeking to hire an engineering firm first interviews 10 firms. After reviewing their qualifications, the company eliminates several contenders and develops a short list of three or four candidates. These candidates will then be invited to formally make proposals for the work. Thus, when a company *has made the short list,* it is one of the last few firms being considered for the contract.

SHOTGUN APPROACH   **1.** A broad-based approach to disseminating sales and marketing information. Using a shotgun approach, a company will distribute materials to as wide an audience as possible to generate maximum returns. **2.** In publicity, mailings of news releases or **pitch letters** to many different media outlets as opposed to select outlets. See also **rifle approach.**

SHOWINGS   **1.** Term used in outdoor advertising to describe the number of displays to be erected and the size of the population expected to be exposed to them. For example, a "100 showing" of billboards means that the entire population of a market will pass by the billboard at least once on any given day; a "50 showing" means half the population will do so. **2.** Also used in planning the display of transit advertising. In this context, it refers to the proportion of cars in a transportation system fleet (e.g., subway cars, buses) that will carry the ads. Thus, a "full showing" means that all cars in the system will feature the ads; a "half showing" means half the cars will; and so on.

SHRINK WRAP   A technique for packaging one or more printed materials for a direct mailing. A shrink wrap is a clear plastic bag that is shrunk by heating it, thus making the package fit snugly around the materials. Shrink wrapping is used in mailing multicomponent promotional packages (such as a catalog and an accompanying flier). See also **polybag.**

SIC CODE   (**STANDARD INDUSTRIAL CLASSIFICATION CODE**) The U.S. government's system of defining individual industries and specific trades within them. SIC categories are broken down into code numbers that identify industries in terms of products manufactured or functions performed. Other information includes the number of companies in a given category, the number of total employees, and the average number of employees per organization. Marketing planners use SIC information to assess the nature and scope of **organizational markets**—information used in identifying, defining, and segmenting those markets. Direct-mail advertisers can obtain mailing lists that are based on SIC codes.

SIMMONS MARKET RESEARCH BUREAU (SMRB)   A market research firm that provides data on the audience composition of various print and broadcast advertising vehicles. SMRB data are based on demographic and product-use categories, with the data providing information on product purchases by different market segments. SMRB information is frequently used by media planners in determining which media would be the most effective for reaching consumers of a particular product category. Thus, if furniture polish is being sold, SMRB data would indicate which advertising vehicles are heard/read/viewed by the audiences that purchase the largest quantities of that product.

SIMPLE RANDOM SAMPLE   A **probability sample** in which units in the population are given numbers, after which random numbers are selected and the sample is drawn based on the population units that have those numbers. For example, a sample of 100 is to be drawn from a population of 1,000 people. In simple random sampling, each person is assigned a number from 1 to 1,000. Then, a random sample is drawn to select 100 numbers. The people interviewed are those whose assigned numbers were drawn. See also **sampling.**

SIMPLE REGRESSION ANALYSIS   See **regression analysis.**

SIMULATED TEST MARKET   A form of **market testing** in which consumers are exposed to a simulated purchase situation to gauge their reactions to a product, advertising, or **marketing mix** combinations. For example, a company may create in a research facility a storelike environment to see how consumers maneuver through the store and view the products on display. This simulated test market would generate information on consumer responses to the marketing stimuli, with the resultant data used in marketing planning, estimating market demand, and sales forecasting.

SIMULATION   Computer-based statistical modeling used to predict how certain variables affect other variables. For example, simulation by economic forecasters would involve using mathematical **models** to estimate changes in the economy by manipulating variables such as changes in government fiscal policies or **economic indicators.** Such information might ultimately be used in sales forecasting.

SIMULCAST   A television program that airs simultaneously on radio. For example, a televised concert would be simulcast on a radio station to enable viewers to receive the audio portion in stereo.

SITUATIONAL ANALYSIS   A main element of a marketing plan. The situational analysis summarizes the internal and external forces affecting the company and its product(s) and makes quantitative and qualitative projections for the marketing actions being proposed. Among the variables addressed are industry developments affecting the marketing environment: new competitors, technological innovations, and social and political developments that may impact the marketing strategy. An assessment of the company's strengths and weaknesses is made of the company and its product (as well as those of competitors and their products). The situational analysis may also include information on market characteristics, buyer needs, purchase patterns, and other variables that may influence the outcome of the marketing initiative.

:60   Designation for a 60-second television or radio commercial, as indicated on a script.

SKIMMING   A new product pricing and promotion strategy in which the item carries a high cost in an attempt to attract consumers willing to pay more for a premium product (thus "skimming" the top level of a market's buyers). There are two skimming strategies. With a *rapid skimming* policy the new product is launched at a high price with a high level of promotion. The goal is recovering as much gross profit per unit while communicating the item's premium value to consumers. With a *slow skimming* policy the product carries a high price with a low level of promotion, the goal being to recover the maximum gross profit per unit while keeping marketing expenditures low. See also **penetration strategies.**

SLICE-OF-LIFE ADVERTISING   A form of advertising message execution where the product is shown in a real-life situation. Many slice-of-life ads are mini-dramas in which a common problem is depicted, the product is introduced, and the problem is solved by using the advertised item. For example, a family on vacation is shown having its luggage stolen but is able to recoup monetary loss by having traveler's checks (the advertised product) promptly replaced.

SLIPPAGE   The percentage of people who buy a product to receive an advertised rebate or **premium** but who fail to submit the **proofs of purchase** required to do so. This figure is called the *slippage rate*.

SLOGAN   A phrase that summarizes the theme or central idea communicated in an advertisement or ad campaign and that is used repeatedly in the ads. A slogan that is highly memorable will ultimately define the characteristics of the product or service being advertised. For example, the Prudential insurance company's OWN A PIECE OF THE ROCK slogan attempts to connote the stability of the company and the solid level of service it strives to provide to policy holders. Slogans serve to lend continuity to an ad campaign. That is, the ads in the campaign are different but they are linked in the consumer's mind by the slogan.

SOCIAL CLASS   The grouping of people in a society into classifications based on income, level of education, profession, or any other criterion of prestige or esteem. Social class is an important determinant of **consumer behavior** because people of the same social class tend to exhibit similarities in product and brand preferences and recreational activities. Social class is frequently used as a criterion for **market segmentation**. See also **socioeconomic classifications**.

SOCIAL-CULTURAL ENVIRONMENT   See **macroenvironment**.

SOCIAL GROUP   An aggregate of individuals who interact with each other while maintaining specific roles within the group. Examples of social groups are families, friends, co-workers, clubs, and fraternities. Social groups are significant in marketing because people's beliefs and actions are influenced by the social groups to which they belong. That is, social groups exert pressure on individuals to conform to accepted modes of behavior as established by the groups. These social pressures may influence people's actions as buyers of goods and services. See also **consumer behavior.**

SOCIAL MARKETING   The area of marketing concerned with applying marketing methods to disseminate societally beneficial ideas (e.g., cancer research, energy conservation). The scope of social marketing has broadened in recent years to also cover services rendered by public and nonprofit institutions whose focus is controversial in nature (e.g., abortion rights, gun control). Also known as *societal marketing*. See also **advocacy advertising; public service advertising.**

SOCIOECONOMIC CLASSIFICATIONS   The grouping of a market's members into categories based on social and economic characteristics. Socioeconomic classifications suggest similarities in their members' behavior, values, and lifestyles. There are considered to be seven basic socioeconomic classifications in the United States: *upper-uppers,* the country's social elite who live on inherited wealth; *lower-uppers,* people who earn high incomes due to great success in business; *upper-middles,* people who are highly concerned with their careers and who have done well as professionals such as entrepreneurs and corporate managers; *middle class,* average-income white- and blue-collar workers who strive to live better-than-average lifestyles; *working class,* people with average or slightly below average incomes, mainly blue-collar workers; *upper-lowers,* people whose standard of living is just about at the poverty level, who perform unskilled work and receive low salaries; *lower-lowers,* people on welfare who are poverty stricken.

SOFT GOODS 1. Consumer products that are soft to the touch (e.g., clothing, linen, and textiles). **2.** Consumer products with a short life span (less than six months). Also known as *nondurable goods.* See also **hard goods.**

SOFT OFFER A direct-marketing term denoting the advertiser's offer to consumers to review merchandise prior to paying for it. That is, a consumer can order merchandise and use it for a stated period of time before deciding whether or not to buy it. A soft offer is different from a *hard offer,* in which payment must be received with the product order. Soft offers typically yield higher responses than hard offers. Soft offers, however, leave open the possibility that the manufacturer will incur *bad debt* (when people who try the product keep it without ever paying for it).

SOFT-SELL APPROACH Selling technique marked by subtlety in delivering the sales message and in asking for the order. A soft-sell approach is different from a *hard sell* or high-pressure sales approach where the seller attempts to control the sales situation and force the prospect to agree to the sale. See also **consultative selling.**

SOUND EFFECTS Audio techniques used in TV and radio commercial production to lend atmosphere to the advertisements. Sound effects include ambulance sirens, crowds, footsteps, and explosions. Sound effects may be created by an individual (e.g., a person making bird sounds) or are available as recordings on albums or audiotapes. Sound effects are indicated by the symbol SFX on **storyboards** and theatrical scripts.

SOURCE The person who communicates an advertising message. Choosing the source in an advertisement is an important consideration in developing the promotional strategy because highly credible sources are more persuasive. The credibility of the source is usually based on three factors: *expertise,* when the communicator appears to possess specialized knowledge (.e.g., a doctor endorsing a new medication); *trustworthiness,* when the person is perceived to be honest and objective; and *likability,* when the person is attractive to consumers in terms of his or her naturalness or humor. See also **message development.**

SPECIAL EFFECTS   Visual techniques used in TV commercial production to create images that cannot be produced firsthand. For example, a commercial may call for rain or fog that would be created using special effects for an indoor filming. Other special effects used in commercial production are lightning, fire, snow, and smoke. Special effects are indicated by the symbol FX on **storyboards** prepared for the commercial.

SPECIAL EVENTS   See **events marketing.**

SPECIALTY-LINE MARKET RESEARCH FIRM   A research company that provides data collection or analysis services to other research firms or corporate marketing research departments. Specialty-line firms, for example, might conduct field interviewing on behalf of a **custom marketing research firm** or a company conducting its own market research study. See also **syndicated service research firm.**

SPECIALTY PRODUCTS   Consumer products with unique characteristics that people will make a special effort to obtain. Buyers are willing to travel long distances and otherwise make an extra effort to purchase specialty goods. Indeed, a significant number of consumers will insist on obtaining such products and will accept no substitutes. Examples of specialty products are certain luxury cars, consumer electronics equipment, and designer fashions.

SPECIALTY STORE   A retail outlet that has a narrow product line and caters to a highly defined market segment. Specialty stores carry only one type of product, but they offer many different brands of that item. An example is Athlete's Foot, a chain of stores that only sells athletic shoes. Other types of specialty stores carry such product lines as apparel, sporting goods, and furniture. See also **assortment.**

SPECULATIVE PITCH   A new business presentation by an advertising agency in which the firm develops an entire ad campaign to try to win the account. Making a pitch *on-spec* means the agency will only get paid for the work if it is hired by the client. Speculative pitches involve considerable time and out-of-pocket expenses to the agency. Thus, they are usually made only by firms seeking a very large account or those wanting to build their reputation.

SPIFFS   See **push money.**

SPLIT-RUN RESEARCH   A method of advertising testing. In split-run research two variations of an ad are run in the same publication but are distributed to different readership segments. (The segments might be based on geography or subscriber/newsstand sales.) For example, researchers determine which advertising approach is more effective in a couponed ad carrying two different headlines based on the number of coupons received from the different ads. In addition to copy, split-run research may involve variations to an ad's layout, type of illustration, product price, or whether or not a **premium** is offered.

SPOKESPERSON   The individual hired to promote a product or service. A spokesperson could be a celebrity or an expert in a given subject area. In advertising, the spokesperson appears in print or broadcast commercials to discuss the product and its benefits. In publicity, the spokesperson gives news media interviews to discuss the product or company being promoted. For example, in introducing the first foods to use the artificial sweetener aspartame, General Foods used staff nutritionists as spokespeople to discuss how the sweetener was made and to espouse its safety to consumers. Spokes-people used in publicity campaigns are usually extensively trained for interviews and presentations to the media. See also **celebrity endorsement; media training.**

SPONSOR   An advertiser that underwrites all or part of the cost of a TV program. Sponsoring a program usually requires the advertiser to purchase the majority of commercial announcements made on the program. However, the actual amount of commercial time the spon-sor is required to purchase is related to either the time at which the program airs and/or various station regulations depending on whether it is a local or network broadcast. The sponsor is usually mentioned in the **billboard** announcements made at the beginning and end of the show.

SPORTS MARKETING   The sponsorship of or corporate involve-ment in sporting events to promote a specific product or company. A company sponsoring a golf or tennis tournament (and financing the costs of the event logistics and prize money) is one example of sports marketing. Another is a company's contributions to support an Olympic team by providing for its uniforms or travel expenses. Sports marketing programs nearly always are promoted by advertising, sales promotion, and public relations activities. Often, the sponsoring companies display signage bearing their **logos** at the event sites. Companies sponsoring cars in an auto race, for example, usually have their logos emblazoned on the vehicles themselves. See also **events marketing.**

SPOT The designation for a specific time period on broadcast media for the airing of commercials, station announcements, and *public service advertisements* (PSAs). Also known as *time slots*. See also **spot tv/radio.**

SPOT TV/RADIO Broadcast commercial time purchased on individual stations on a market-by-market basis. A spot buy is different from a *network buy*, in which the advertiser makes one ad purchase to air commercials on all stations affiliated with the network. Spot tv and spot radio refer to the commercial time that broadcast media collectively set aside for spot purchases. See also **AAAA spot contract.**

STANDARD ADVERTISING REGISTER A two-volume set of directories listing major advertising firms *(Standard Directory of Advertising Agencies)* and national advertisers *(Standard Directory of Advertisers)* in the United States. The National Register Publishing Company of Wilmette, Illinois, produces these directories. Also known as the *red books*.

STANDARD ADVERTISING UNITS (SAU) Standardized sizes of advertising space established by newspapers for national advertisers. SAUs are unit sizes of varying columns (width) and inches (depth). SAUs were established to simplify the purchase of ad space in newspapers by national advertisers. Prior to their introduction, the different space sizes of newspapers required advertisers to incur extra expenses in preparing different-size ads for virtually every separate newspaper buy.

STANDARD DEVIATION A statistical measurement that indicates the degree to which individual values are clustered around the average value. Thus, standard deviation measures the aggregate difference between the **mean** of a sample or population and the values distributed around it. For example, if in a sample of personal computer prices the standard deviation is ± $200, then most of the brands will fall within ± $200 of the average. If the standard deviation is ± $1,000, there is much more variation around the mean (thus indicating a large price differential between the various brands).

STANDARDIZATION   The practice of grading products by their respective levels of quality, for example the designation of Grade A by the U.S. Department of Agriculture (as in poultry). Standardization was initiated to facilitate the comparing of different products by consumers. Standardized products carry either letters or numbers as set by the government or trade group assessing the products. Also known as *grade labeling.*

STANDARD RATE AND DATA SERVICE (SRDS)   Company that publishes a series of directories listing information about print and broadcast advertising vehicles. SRDS directories group media by newspaper (U.S. daily and Sunday papers); consumer and farm magazines; radio and TV stations and networks; and business publications. SRDS publications include information on the vehicles' ad rates, their circulation or audience figures, advertising **closing dates,** contract and copy regulations, and requirements for preparing **mechanical art** (for print insertions). One SRDS publication, *Direct Mail List Rates and Data,* includes information on some 75,000 mailing lists available to direct marketers.

STAPLE GOODS   Products that are bought and consumed frequently, the purchases of which are characterized by minimum effort by consumers in terms of comparison shopping. There is little differentiation between staple goods. Thus, they are marketed primarily on the basis of price. Examples of staple goods are milk, bread, and sugar. Also known as *commodity products.*

STAR   See **growth-share matrix.**

STARCH RATINGS   A measurement of consumers' **recognition** of an advertisement. Starch ratings, produced by the firm Daniel Starch and Associates, gauge the extent to which consumers have seen or heard an advertising message as a test of its communication effectiveness. Starch ratings are determined using this process: (1) The researcher determines if the respondent is a reader of a given magazine issue; (2) the researcher goes through the magazine with the respondent, asking the latter if he or she saw the particular ad; (3) if the respondent says yes, the researcher asks the respondent what he or she saw or read in the ad. Starch ratings result in three levels of readership: (1) *noted,* the percent of issue readers who said they saw the ad in the specific issue; (2) *associated,* the percent of issue readers who said they saw and read any part of the ad that contained the name of the product/advertiser; and (3) *read most,* the percent of issue readers who said they read 50% or more of the ad. See also **adnorm.**

STATISTICAL ABSTRACT OF THE UNITED STATES   An annual publication produced by the U.S. Department of Commerce, Bureau of the Census. This guide contains statistical data on social and economic characteristics of the country and includes sections on recent national trends. For example, the consumer market data features statistics on income, employment, housing, and population characteristics broken down by state, large cities, and major metropolitan areas. An appendix, *Guide to Sources of Statistics,* alphabetically lists major private and public sources of statistical information.

STATISTICAL DEMAND ANALYSIS   Forecasting technique used to identify the variables that have the greatest direct impact on sales. In statistical demand analysis, sales are always the **dependent variable.** The **independent variables** altered to assess their relationship to the dependent variable are prices, consumers' incomes, population figures, and the level of promotional expenditures. This forecasting technique typically applies **multiple regression analysis.**

STIMULUS-RESPONSE THEORY   Theory of learning holding that every stimulus evokes a response in the person experiencing it. In marketing, stimulus response is used to understand how linking two ideas can create in the consumer's mind a positive or negative relationship between them. That is, the marketer's goal is determining which stimulus will elicit the desired response in the target consumer. For instance, a marketer will attempt to link a brand's name (stimulus) with the perception of value or quality (the consumer's response). The objective of devising marketing strategy based on stimulus-response learning is engendering routinized buying behavior, thus limiting the influence of people's perception and insights in purchase decision making. See also **classical conditioning.**

STOCK 1. Inventory. When a product is in stock, it means it is in storage on the retail store's premises. 2. In printing, paper of different weights, textures, or finishes (e.g., coated stock).

STOCK ROTATION The inventory management practice of moving stock to ensure freshness and to sell products before their **shelf life** expiration. For example, a grocer moves milk containers that have not been sold to the front of the display when stocking newly arrived containers because the new containers have more distant expiration dates than those that have not yet been sold. The unsold containers are moved up front to encourage consumers to buy those first.

STOCK SHOT Previously used photograph or video footage available for use in publications or films. For example, a manufacturing magazine would maintain stock shots of an assembly line; or a manufacturing company might use its stock footage of workers on an assembly line when producing a corporate training video. Companies maintain stock shots in their photo or film libraries. Stock shots are also available from vendor companies that specialize in furnishing such visuals. These vendors sell the rights to stock shots on a one-time-use basis.

STORECAST A simulated radio broadcast aired in a retail outlet that contains announcements of sales or special items available in the store, for example, the announcements followed by the introduction, "Attention, K-Mart shoppers." Retailers that use storecasts situate loudspeakers around the store. Storecasts may air music as well as product-related announcements.

STORYBOARD A series of drawings that depict the sequence of visual elements in a TV commercial, accompanied by the copy that will be heard as each visual is shown. Storyboards are the broadcast equivalent of rough layouts produced for print ads. That is, storyboards are developed to show the client how a commercial will look upon its completion. Storyboards are produced in the initial stages of designing and producing the commercial. See also **animatic.**

STRAIGHT COMMISSION/SALARY Terms referring to one of two ways a salesperson is compensated. Straight salary means the seller receives a fixed stipend, as determined by the amount of time worked. Straight commission refers to seller compensation based on level of performance, which is a stated percentage of either dollar or unit sales of a product. *Note:* Some salespeople are paid both salary and commission in an arrangement known as a *combination compensation plan.*

STRATEGIC ALLIANCE   A joint initiative by two companies seeking to exploit the same marketing opportunity. Consider a company seeking entry into a foreign market. The company might establish a strategic alliance with a company based in that country by arranging a licensing agreement, which would enable the company seeking entry to have its products sold by the company already based there, thus quickly introducing its products without having to first develop manufacturing and distribution capabilities. Conversely, the foreign-based company enjoys the ability to market an established product without having to invest in research and development and start-up costs. Also known as *joint venture.*

STRATEGIC BUSINESS UNIT (SBU)   A component of a company that contributes to but is independent of other elements of the organization. SBUs may be individual products, product portfolios, divisions, or separate businesses. SBUs have several defining characteristics: They have a specific *corporate mission* (different from, albeit complementary to, the organization's mission) and the ability to determine strategies and objectives independent of other areas of the company; *operational capabilities* and control over the resources required to implement corporate activities; distinct *competitors;* and a *manager* responsible for the unit's operations and ultimate profitability. SBUs are smaller and more centralized than the parent organization, with lines of authority and responsibility less clearly defined. Herein lies the benefit of SBUs: their ability to respond more quickly to marketplace threats and opportunities, which is a direct result of their looser organizational structure.

STRATEGIC PLANNING   Management function concerned with ensuring that the company's businesses and products are coordinated to generate the desired level of profits and growth. Strategic planning involves the continual adaptation to changing marketplace conditions to capitalize on market opportunities vis-á-vis the organization's objectives and resources. Strategic planning is conducted at the corporate level of an organization. A strategic plan drives the development of marketing plans for the company's individual services or products, product portfolios, and divisions. Four basic activities comprise the strategic planning process:

1. Developing a clear statement of the company's guiding mission and objectives (thus giving employees a shared sense of direction).
2. Identifying, developing, and evaluating SBUs, or **strategic business units.**
3. Allocating financial and human resources to those SBUs, thus determining how much capital to invest in SBUs. The determination is based on their varying levels of market potential and competitive positions in the market.
4. Expanding existing businesses and creating new ones through **integration** or **diversification** growth strategies.
   See also **growth-share matrix.**

STRATEGIC WINDOW A narrow time period during which a company can capitalize on a given marketing opportunity. The term connotes a period when the window is "open" (when the company can act) and when it will "close" (when the company can no longer make the move). Consider a company that installs single master antennae for cable TV reception in areas that have not yet been wired for cable. If legislation has been enacted that will grant a cable franchise license in three years, the company has a strategic window to provide its service before the market area is wired. If it waits too long to act, the strategic window will close and the company will have lost its marketing opportunity.

STRATEGY A plan for achieving a specific goal or objective. Strategy denotes the direction a company will take in attempting to capitalize on opportunities in its chosen market. Developing a strategy guides the allocation of resources. Moreover, it enables the company's departments and operating units to head in the same direction.

STRATIFIED SAMPLE A type of **probability sample** in which units of a population are grouped into homogeneous subsets (strata) prior to drawing a sample from each of them. For example, the population is divided into mutually exclusive groups (e.g., males, females). Then a **random sample** of elements from each group is chosen such that the proportion of males and females in the sample is the same as that for the entire population. See also **sampling.**

STRIP PROGRAMMING   See **across-the-board.**

SUBCULTURE   A separate segment of a culture whose members share common traits based on race, nationality, religion, or geography. Identifying the subculture to which people belong is a key factor in analyzing **consumer behavior** because members of a subculture tend to exhibit similar preferences for art, music, food, recreation, politics, and so forth. Subcultures, therefore, represent distinct market segments. Marketers must be cautious, however, not to assume that all members of a subculture will exhibit identical behavior. For example, in the Hispanic subculture in the United States all people of Spanish descent are classified as Hispanic. But this group can be further categorized into subgroups of Mexicans, Puerto Ricans, Cubans, Dominicans, and so on. Although all these groups tend to share certain common characteristics (e.g., a strong family orientation), they vary significantly in terms of preferred foods and music, as well as in socioeconomic respects. Thus, marketing planners must factor into the marketing planning process a subculture's similar and dissimilar characteristics. See also **market segmentation; target marketing.**

SUBHEAD   A line of copy in a print advertisement that is used to visually break up the text for the reader's benefit. Subheads are used in ads containing lengthy wording in which a reader might be discouraged from reading the ad because of the large amount of copy. Subheads are typically set in type larger than the text (but smaller than the headline type) or in boldface so as to visually stand out. In addition to breaking up the copy, subheads are used to provide more information. For example, a subhead appearing under the headline can be used to amplify or explain the headline's message.

SUBLIMINAL ADVERTISING   The practice of presenting ad messages that are received below a person's level of consciousness. That is, the messages are unconsciously (rather than consciously) perceived by consumers, for example, when a movie theater's management flashed the image of a box of popcorn during a film for only one or two seconds. The brief message was not consciously registered by the viewers, who nonetheless received the message subconsciously. See also *Hidden Persuaders.*

SUBWAY-SHELTER ADVERTISING   A form of outdoor advertising featuring displays on canopies that have been erected for waiting mass-transit travelers. These structures include bus-stop shelters and those on elevated train stations. Subway-shelter structures are maintained by outdoor advertising companies. This medium is a useful form of **reminder advertising**—that is, as a supplement to ads appearing in print and broadcast media.

SUPER   Short for *superimpose,* which is the process of displaying an image on a video screen that already features an image. Words, graphics, or prices shown at the bottom of the TV screen during a commercial are examples of superimposed images. Supers are used to provide additional information about the visual being shown.

SUPERMARKET   A large retail establishment that contains a wide variety of products and brands. Supermarkets are designed to meet consumers' every need for food and household goods. These stores generally offer low-cost, low-margin products that customers select on a self-serve basis. Generally, supermarkets feature a departmentalized layout (e.g., with household products in one section, canned goods in another, and meats and poultry in another). Supermarkets occupy approximately 25,000 square feet. See also **superstores.**

SUPERSTATION   A television station that broadcasts its programming signal via satellite for reception by cable television systems across the country. The systems, in turn, disseminate the signal to household subscribers via coaxial cable. Examples of superstations are WGN-TV in Chicago and WTBS-TV in Atlanta.

SUPERSTORES   Retail establishments that are larger than supermarkets and offer consumers an even wider selection of goods and services. In addition to foods and household products, superstores offer facilities such as dry-cleaning, shoe repair, and bargain lunch counters. They were created to meet consumers' needs for every food and nonfood product routinely purchased. Superstores range in size from 50,000 square feet to 200,000 square feet.

SUPPLEMENT   A printed section in magazine-style format that is added to a newspaper for distribution to the newspaper's circulation. An example of a supplement is the *Parade* magazine that appears in many Sunday newspapers. Supplements feature both editorial content and advertising. Some supplements are produced by the host publication itself. Others, such as *Parade* magazine, are produced by independent **syndicates.**

SUPPLIER   A company that provides goods used in the manufacturing process but that are not included in the product itself. For example, a supplier will sell a manufacturer the materials used in packaging products for distribution. See also **maintenance, repair, operating (MRO) items.**

SUPPLY AND DEMAND   Economic theory relating to the amount of product to be entered into a market over a period of time (supply) and the number of units of product to be sold in that period (demand). Understanding supply and demand relationships is important to marketers because it is essential to appraise the economic climate of a market to devise **marketing mix** strategies. For example, supply and demand patterns influence product pricing. That is, when supply of a product is low and demand is high, prices may be set at high levels. On the other hand, when supply is high and demand is low, prices must be set at lower levels. See also **demand states.**

SURVEY RESEARCH   Research designed to yield descriptive data about a marketing problem or situation. Survey research is employed to gain insight into consumers' knowledge, beliefs, and preferences toward a product or issue, as well as to measure magnitudes of these variables among a population. As a methodology, survey research is midway between the investigative nature of **exploratory research** and the statistical precision of **experimental research.**

SWEEPS   The month-long period during which the audience size of network television time slots is calculated for the purpose of setting advertising rates at local stations. During the sweeps, networks typically air highly popular shows and movies to generate maximum viewership because the larger the audiences, the higher the rates the networks' local stations can establish.

SWEEPSTAKES   Sales promotion technique in which prizes are awarded to participants who are selected in a random drawing. The key defining characteristic of a sweepstakes is that no product purchase is required of entrants. Sweepstakes involve submitting an entry form with one's name and address and returning it to the sweepstakes organizer (either by mail or by dropping it off at a retail location). Similar to other sales promotion programs, the goal of a sweepstakes is creating consumer involvement with a brand to foster consumption. See also **contests.**

SYNDICATE   1. An organization that furnishes editorial or broadcast subject matter to print and electronic media for a fee. For example, a newspaper syndicate supplies columns, offers supplements, cartoons, and crossword puzzles to its subscribers. There are also syndicated art services that sell photos and illustrations to ad agencies and other companies needing artwork for various forms of print communications. **2.** A group of newspapers owned by the same company, such as those published by S. I. Newhouse. See also **syndication.**

SYNDICATED SERVICE RESEARCH FIRM   A company that periodically gathers market research data for sale to clients on a fee or subscription basis. An example is the A. C. Nielsen Company, which collects marketing and media research data for sale to advertisers and manufacturers.

SYNDICATION   The sale or distribution of radio and TV programming to local stations by the owner of that programming. There are two types of broadcast syndication: (1) *First-run* syndication involves the distribution of original shows that were produced specifically for the syndication market (e.g., TV movies and specials); (2) *off-network* syndication is the distribution to local stations of shows that previously aired in **prime time** on network television (e.g., situation comedy reruns).

SYNECTICS   An idea generation technique used in **new product development** and in devising strategies for promotional campaigns. Synectics is a group problem-solving exercise that involves two steps: distorting or transposing a familiar way of looking at an object or situation in order to develop new ways of perceiving it; and taking an unfamiliar concept or situation and redefining and restating it until it becomes familiar in terms of the group members' knowledge and experiences. The central defining characteristic of synectics is the use and building of *analogies:* direct analogies, personal role-playing analogies, fantasy analogies, or symbolic analogies. See also **brainstorming.**

SYSTEMATIC SAMPLING   See **nth name selection.**

SYSTEMS BUYING/SELLING   The purchasing or selling of a multi-faceted product or service. Companies that engage in systems buying do not want to make many different purchase decisions in *buying* a complex product (e.g., a telecommunications network). That is, instead of dealing with multiple vendors, the company deals with one contractor who is responsible for bidding and assembling subcontractors to provide the total package. Conversely, companies that provide systems *selling* market the capability to assemble all the products and services needed by the buyer. An example is a company that markets the ability to assemble a complex manufacturing production system complete with equipment, inventory controls systems, and other services required to effect a fully functional operation.

T

TABLOID A newspaper format that has the appearance of a magazine but is not bound. Tabloids measure approximately 14″ deep by 10″ to 12″ wide. They typically include many pictures and illustrations, and most of the articles are brief. Tabloids are smaller than **broadsheet** newspapers. In fact, tabloids were originally developed to be easier to handle than broadsheets by commuters in crowded buses and subways. Tabloids generally contain the same amount of content as broadsheets, but given their smaller size, they appear to contain more information.

TABULATIONS The process of grouping research statistics into categories for the purpose of data reduction and analysis—that is, reducing a large amount of data into a manageable format (tables) for review and study by the researcher. The "tabs" are usually a separate part of the final **research report** because they contain a level of statistical detail of interest only to the researcher, as opposed to senior management or marketing managers who generally need only a summary analysis of the findings. See also **cross-tabulation.**

TACHISTOSCOPE (T-SCOPE) A laboratory testing device used in measuring advertising effectiveness. A t-scope flashes an ad to a respondent at different exposure intervals, ranging from less than a hundredth of a second to several seconds. After each exposure, the respondent is asked to describe what he or she recalls from the ad. See also **galvanometer.**

TACTICS The activities designed to execute the strategies outlined in a marketing plan. Tactics may also involve the steps taken to manipulate the context in which a product is sold—activities designed to alter the market's political, legal, social, or cultural landscape.

TAG LINE   The final line of copy at the end of a print ad or TV commercial that summarizes the communication's message. Tag line is often used synonymously with *slogan,* which is used repeatedly in an advertisement or an ad campaign and is usually stated at the end of the communication.

TAKE-ONE   A print advertisement that features coupons, refund blanks, or contest entry forms in a pocket or pad that is attached to the ad. **Car cards** in transit advertising often use this format. For example, a vocational school ad featured a take-one pad of postage-paid reply cards that enabled interested people to receive information about the school. Take-one advertisements generally carry an extra charge to advertisers, which covers maintenance services rendered by the transit system operator.

TALENT   **1.** The actors in a TV commercial or a broadcast program. Large advertising agencies have *talent payment departments* that coordinate payment of residuals to actors who appear in commercials that are shown repeatedly. **2.** TV news shows use the term to describe anchor persons and news readers.

TARGET AUDIENCE   The segment of a population to which advertising and other marketing communications are directed. Target audiences are usually defined in terms of geographic, demographic, and/or psychographic attributes. Marketers study target audiences and their characteristics in order to devise impactive promotional strategies. Also known as *target market.* See also **market segmentation; target marketing.**

TARGET MARKETING   The strategy of identifying the different groups that comprise a market and developing corresponding products for each group. Target marketing is the opposite of **mass marketing,** which is when a company develops and mass markets one product that is designed to appeal to all buyers. Target marketing involves three basic steps:

1. **Market segmentation.** The company defines its market segments based on the variables of geography, demographics,

psychographics, and/or behavioral characteristics (e.g., product usage patterns).

2. **Market targeting.** The company decides which of those market segments to pursue by evaluating the profit potential of each segment, then determining a market coverage strategy. **Undifferentiated, differentiated,** and **concentrated marketing** relate to the kinds of market offerings (different products or variations of an existing product) that are suitable to each segment.

3. **Positioning.** The company makes decisions on how to portray the product offerings to make them more appealing to consumers than competitors' offerings.

TARGET-RETURN PRICING   The strategy of establishing a product's price to yield a specific **return on investment.** Target-return pricing is calculated using the formula

$$\text{target return price} = \text{unit cost} + \frac{\text{desired return} \times \text{invested capital}}{\text{unit sales}}$$

For example, suppose a company has invested $2 million in developing a new type of can opener and wants to earn a 15% return. Each unit costs $10 to produce and estimated unit sales are 50,000. The target-return price is calculated as

$$\$10 + \frac{.15 \times \$2,000,000}{50,000} = \$16$$

Thus, the company must charge $16 per unit to realize a 15% return on investment.

The drawback of the target-return pricing method is that it ignores such factors as competitors' pricing and *price elasticity.* See also **break-even analysis.**

TEAM SELLING   The selling approach used by organizations that market highly complex products because one salesperson cannot be expert in all aspects of the product offering. Team selling involves assembling a group of salespeople who are technically conversant in different features of the product. However, the sellers are all familiar with the general capabilities of the product, and the viewpoints and concerns of the key decision makers in the customer company. Team selling is used, for example, in the sale of multifaceted industrial or electronics products (e.g., an advanced weapons system). See also **systems buying/selling.**

TEAR SHEET An ad or news article torn from the magazine that is sent by the publication to an advertising or PR firm. Tear sheets of ads are sent to advertisers as verification of the insertion. They are usually sent with the invoice for the ad. News article tear sheets are sent to the PR professional who arranged for placement of the article or who assisted in its preparation. Whereas an ad tear sheet is sent as a matter of course, editorial tear sheets are usually sent only upon request by the PR representative. See also **Advertising Checking Bureau.**

TEASER AD An advertisement that intentionally contains limited information about the product so as to pique people's interest and generate curiosity. For example, in promoting the movie *Batman,* teaser ads showing only the Batman **logo** appeared in many print and outdoor advertising vehicles. Subsequent ads provided progressively more information about the movie and its premiere date. Teaser ads are usually used in the beginning of an ad campaign or to introduce a new product.

TEASER COPY See **corner card.**

TECHNICAL EXPERTISE APPROACH A thematic approach to advertising copy in which a company's proficiency in manufacturing a product is highlighted. Examples are a car maker that promotes its pioneering use of air bags and other technologically advanced safety features, or a vintner that painstakingly ages its wines to achieve the highest quality.

TECHNOLOGICAL ENVIRONMENT See **macroenvironment.**

TELECONFERENCE The technique of holding a multilocation conference by means of telecommunications technology. The facilities that serve as conference sites are equipped with rooftop satellite dishes to receive the signal from the broadcast location. Teleconferencing has become a popular means of holding news conferences where media in many different cities can be reached simultaneously. It is also a popular technique for internal communications in multioffice corporations where a CEO delivers an address to his or her company's offices around the country or world.

TELEMARKETING   The direct-marketing technique of communicating with customers and prospects via telephone. Telemarketing is either in-bound or out-bound. With *in-bound* telemarketing consumers dial toll-free **800-numbers** or minimum-toll **900-numbers** to order products, make inquiries, or voice complaints. *Out-bound* telemarketing is the proactive tactic of contacting buyers to sell products or qualify leads. Some outbound telemarketing systems are automated. Through the use of **ADRMPs (automatic dialing and recorded message players),** buyers' telephone numbers are dialed automatically and a prerecorded announcement is activated when someone picks up the receiver. The consumer is able to order products by leaving purchase information on an answering machine, or the system routes the call to a salesperson. Telemarketing is used both in consumer and business-to-business marketing.

TELEVISION   The electronic communications medium with the ability to produce impactive advertising messages by using a combination of sight and sound. With TV advertising vivid and memorable images relating to products can be created, including the ability to actually show products in use. From a **media planning** standpoint, TV advertising allows sellers to achieve great selectivity in targeting viewers both geographically and demographically since there are an abundance of audience measurement and composition data available. TV advertising has its drawbacks, the first of which is cost. TV commercial time and production costs are extremely expensive. Thus, advertisers lack the ability to provide detailed product information given the relatively brief length of TV commercials (most often 30- and 15-second spots). Moreover, TV commercials are fleeting messages that contend with the **clutter** of many competing commercial messages and station announcements. See also **cable television.**

TELEVISION HOUSEHOLD   A household with at least one television set. A TV household is the basic unit of measurement used in calculating the size of a program's audience. For example, the A. C. Nielsen Company's term **households using television (HUT)** refers to the percentage of TV households in a given geographic area that have their sets turned on at a specific point in time, in comparison to the total number of TV households in the area under study.

TELEVISION RATINGS   See **ratings.**

TERRITORY   A salesperson's assigned area of responsibility in serving customers and contacting prospects. A territory may be a given geographic area, but it may also be defined as a particular customer group, product line, or any other defined segment of a company's market. See also **territory-structured sales force.**

TERRITORY MANAGEMENT   The tactics and strategies a salesperson employs in conducting selling activities within his or her assigned territory. The primary goal of territory management is maintaining regular contact with customers and prospects. Territory management involves effectively planning and scheduling visits and phone calls to customers, as well as maintaining favorable relationships with them. See also **routing.**

TERRITORY-STRUCTURED SALES FORCE   The sales force structure where each salesperson is assigned an exclusive geographic territory. There are three advantages to this organizational structure: First, it gives salespeople a clear definition of their area of responsibilities; second, it increases the salesperson's ability to cultivate relationships with local businesspeople and other influencers; third, it minimizes travel expenses. See also **market-structured sales force; product-structured sales force.**

TEST GROUP   The group in a research study that is exposed to the experimental **variable.** The resultant effect of the variable in the test group is measured against the results of that in the **control group** to determine the variable's true effect. Consider research being conducted for a new medication. The test group would receive the medication while the control group would receive a placebo. The results of the two groups would then be compared to determine the actual effect of the medication. Also known as *experimental group.*

TESTIMONIAL ADVERTISING   See **celebrity endorsement.**

TEST MARKET   A geographic location selected as the site to test a new product, promotion, or advertising campaign prior to its full-scale market introduction. The test market is generally an area that has as its center a major city or commercial center. Introducing a product in a test market is the final stage of the **new product development** process. See also **test marketing.**

TEST MARKETING   The practice of testing a new product, promotion, or advertising campaign to assess the impact of the chosen **marketing mix** combination. In **new product development,** test marketing is the final phase of the process, where the item is tested under real-life conditions. The goal of test marketing is to generate feedback for predicting the success of the product or promotion and to make any necessary strategic/tactical modifications prior to a costly, full-scale launch. Three negative factors, however, can complicate test marketing. First, costs are high to maintain a test long enough to generate reliable data on consumer purchase patterns and product satisfaction. Second, manipulating price and promotion tactics in different test markets may lessen the reliability of the findings. Third, competitors may steal a new product concept or distort the opponent's test results by manipulating marketing tactics (e.g., pricing) for their existing products (which are similar to the product being tested). The competitive risk inherent in test marketing has moved companies to explore other ways of eliciting consumer feedback, such as conducting **focus group** interviews. See also **in-home use test; simulated test market.**

THIRD-CLASS MAIL   The class of mail utilized for most direct-mail campaigns. In general, third-class mail is used to send bulk mail and other materials weighing less than one pound. Sending materials via third-class mail requires the mailer to obtain a permit from the U.S. Postal Service. It appears as an **indicia** on the envelope's postage meter stamp. Third-class mail is less expensive than first- and second-class mail. Yet it has a lower priority of service than these more costly postal rates and is, therefore, not delivered as quickly.

:30   Designation for a 30-second television or radio commercial, as indicated on a script.

THROUGH-THE-BOOK METHOD   Research technique conducted by the Simmons Market Research Bureau, Inc., to measure the actual number of *readers* of a given issue of a publication. The process involves one-on-one interviews in which the researcher asks respondents about articles contained in the issue. This is done after the researcher reviews the articles with the respondent by going "through the book." Only people who said they actually read the magazine are counted as readers. The Simmons organization conducts this research for all issues of some 50 major publications.

THURSTONE SCALE   Research technique used to gauge a respondent's attitude, preference, or opinion toward an object or subject. Thurstone scales consist of 7 to 10 statements that relate to the issue under study—statements ranging from very favorable to very unfavorable expressions of sentiment toward the issue. The respondent is asked to choose the statement that most closely reflects his or her attitude. Each statement is assigned a score. These scores are ultimately tabulated (typically along with the scores from other sets of statements) to characterize the respondent's overall feeling toward the object or subject. See also **Likert scale.**

TICKLER LIST   A list of action items distributed to a company's sellers to remind them of specific areas of their sales responsibilities. For instance, a tickler list might provide information on which clients/ customers need to be called, which need to be visited, which need to be entertained, or which referral sources need to be interviewed. Tickler lists are issued periodically by the company's management. They are often used in professional services organizations to make the selling function more convenient for sellers (who must also act as service providers).

TIE-IN ADVERTISING/PROMOTION   **1.** In advertising, an ad purchased by a retailer featuring a manufacturer's product available in the retailer's store. Tie-in ads may contain several different products by various manufacturers. **2.** In sales promotion, promotional tactics that thematically relate to other marketing communications for the same product such as advertising and **point-of-purchase** displays. These tactics are designed to complement and enhance the other marketing communications materials. **3.** Also a joint marketing initiative by two or more companies, for example, when companies team up to offer coupons or refunds, or when they sponsor contests to promote their respective (usually complementary) products. For example, an airline may tie in with a luggage manufacturer to promote travel to specific vacation spots. Also known as *cross-promotion.*

TIME-SERIES ANALYSIS   A **sales forecasting** method in which a projection of future sales is based on the level of past sales.

TIME SLOT   See **spot.**

TOMBSTONE AD   An advertisement that features no illustration and is strictly informational (as opposed to promotional) in nature. The ad is called a "tombstone" because its copy is laid out as several horizontal lines. An example is an ad that announces a lease arranged by a commercial realtor, or a securities offering announced by the investment banker underwriting the issue.

TOP-DOWN PLANNING   A corporate planning approach in which senior management develops action plans for implementation by lower levels of management. It is different from *bottom-up planning,* in which lower levels of management develop their own plans and submit them for review by senior management. In a top-down organization, for example, senior management would create the marketing plans to be carried out by its various divisions.

TOP-LINE REPORT   A report summarizing the preliminary findings of several questions being asked in a research study. That is, it reports data on several key questions that have been answered by the total sample of respondents. The information included in a top-line report generally relates to the question areas of greatest importance to the company's management or to areas of the study on which management needs immediate feedback.

TOP-OF-MIND   The brand that respondents mention first when asked to name one in a particular product category. Top-of-mind is the highest level of **share of mind,** which is determined by a company's level of advertising, resulting in respondents knowing more about one brand than others in the same category. Thus, if a brand has the highest share of mind it enjoys top-of-mind response in a consumer research study. See also **share of voice.**

TOTAL MARKET POTENTIAL   An estimate of the maximum number of sales of a product that might be available to all companies in an industry during a given period of time. Total market potential is calculated using the formula:

$$Q = n \times q \times p$$

where Q is the total market potential, n is the number of buyers in the market, q is the quantity bought by an average buyer, and p is the price of the unit. For example, if there are one million buyers of shampoo in a market, and the average buyer purchases three bottles a year at a price of $2, the total market potential for shampoo in that area is $6 million (1,000,000 × 3 × $2). Total market potential is stated in terms of units or dollars. See also **chain ratio method.**

TOTAL PAID CIRCULATION The total number of people who actually pay for a periodical, as opposed to those who receive it by means other than purchase. Total paid circulation includes subscriptions, newsstand, and single-copy sales. A magazine's total paid circulation is calculated to determine its **base rate** for advertising. Also known as *total net paid.* See also **controlled circulation.**

TOUCH-SCREEN VIDEO A type of video system that enables a viewer to select information by touching a portion of the screen that activates a visual image. For example, the viewer of an **electronic catalog** would like to receive information about a particular product. With touch-screen technology, the viewer is instructed to touch the section of the screen that calls up the desired information. Touch-screen videos, similar to other video systems, are usually found in retail stores and in high-pedestrian-traffic locations such as shopping malls.

TRACKING In direct marketing, the process of monitoring the elements of a campaign to ensure its success. Tracking generally is done at three stages in the program: (1) *early response,* to estimate the projected number of gross responses; (2) *halfway response,* to project gross and net paid responses for the total program; and (3) *final response,* to calculate the total number of orders (not including cancellations or returns of merchandise) and to evaluate the program's overall profitability. Tracking involves assessing the entire promotion, as well as its individual components such as the mailing list, direct-mail package elements, and the product offer.

TRADE ADVERTISING Advertising directed at the retailers and wholesalers of consumer products. Trade advertising is designed to promote the stocking of merchandise by these channel intermediaries. That is, it is designed to broaden distribution of a product by increasing the number of outlets that carry it, or by increasing the amount of product taken by existing distribution outlets. See also **business-to-business advertising.**

TRADE ALLOWANCES   Special incentives given by a manufacturer to retailers and other channel intermediaries to stock, display, or promote the manufacturer's product. Examples of trade allowances are discounts on merchandise (usually on a per-case basis), advertising allowances (compensation for advertising the manufacturer's product), and display allowances (compensation for using the manufacturer's **point-of-purchase advertising** materials). See also **trade promotion.**

TRADE MAGAZINE   A publication whose editorial and advertising content are geared to the members of a given industry or profession. Trade magazines are very narrow in scope (such as *Business Insurance* magazine, read by insurance executives); or they are broad in content to appeal to executives in different business categories (such as *Industry Week,* read by manufacturing and industrial professionals in many business categories). Trade magazines offer advertisers the ability to reach highly defined business audiences both through print advertising and via the acquisition of mailing lists for direct marketing. See also **horizontal publication; vertical publication.**

TRADEMARK   The legal term for *brand.* A trademark is a name, symbol, title, slogan, or designation that identifies one seller's product from another seller's product. Trademark protection ensures that a company's product identifier cannot be infringed upon by a competitor. Advertisers, manufacturers, and merchants may obtain trademarks, the registration for which is made through the U.S. Patent Office.

TRADE PREMIUM   An incentive given by a manufacturer to a retailer or wholesaler who achieves a specific level of sales of the manufacturer's product. Examples of trade premiums are vacations, prizes, and free merchandise.

TRADE PROMOTION   Sales promotion activities directed at retailers and wholesalers. Trade promotions provide incentives to **middlemen** to carry the manufacturer's product or to stock additional inventory. Examples of trade promotion tools are **price-offs,** in which the retailer is granted a discount on merchandise for a specified period of time; allowances such as *advertising allowances* (price discounts in exchange for inclusion of the manufacturer's product in the retailer's advertising) and *display allowances* (incentives granted in exchange for the retailer's agreement to feature **point-of-purchase advertising** materials); and *specialty advertising items* such as calendars, pens and pencils, memo pads, and yardsticks that are imprinted with the retailer's name for distribution to customers.

TRADE SHOW   A forum for companies in a given industry to display products and to distribute information to persons working in that industry. Trade shows are often annual events sponsored by an industry association. They are attended by manufacturers, suppliers, and distributors. Companies that exhibit at trade shows do so to generate new sales leads and to maintain customer contacts. In general, company sales representatives seek to educate attendees about their companies by distributing sales literature and **premiums.**

TRADE SHOW BOOTH   The area of an exhibition hall that is rented by a company participating in the trade show there. Trade show booths are manned by company representatives, whose role is to meet customers and prospects and distribute company-related information. Many companies erect special displays in trade show booths. These feature graphics and other visuals that identify the company, its products, or its services. Many displays are portable; they can be dismantled and packaged for shipment to other trade shows and exhibitions.

TRADING STAMPS   A sales promotion technique in which consumers receive stamps with product purchases and ultimately redeem them for gifts and merchandise, for example, S&H Green Stamps. These are pasted into special booklets by consumers. When the booklets are filled, the consumer redeems them to receive gifts from a special catalog. The amount of trading stamps received by the consumer per purchase is generally based on the dollar amount of the purchase—that is, the more expensive the bill, the more stamps received. See also **continuity program.**

TRAFFIC AUDIT BUREAU   Nonprofit organization comprised of outdoor advertisers and plant operators whose function is conducting research on the number of people who will see outdoor advertisements (e.g., billboards). In short, the Bureau gauges the size of the population that will pass by outdoor advertisements, generating audience size information for use by advertisers in media planning. See Appendix A for address and phone number.

TRAFFIC DEPARTMENT   The group within an advertising agency that is responsible for the overall production of advertisements and their distribution to the media in which they will appear. The traffic department sees to it that production schedules are met to ensure that ads are shipped in time to meet the target media's deadlines. The traffic department maintains information on the status of advertisements in production.

TRANSACTION   The exchange of items of value between two parties to meet their respective wants and needs. For example, a monetary transaction is the transfer of money for merchandise. A *barter* transaction involves giving an item of value in exchange for an item of comparable value. For a transaction to take place, there must be at least two parties offering items of value, agreed-upon conditions of the transaction, and a time and place of agreement.

TRANSIT ADVERTISING   Advertising that appears in transportation vehicles or in the stations where people board those vehicles. Transit advertising is found in subway trains, buses, ferries, and taxis. The value of transit advertising is the ability to reach large numbers of people in a specific geographic area at a high rate of repetition. That is, the people who use transit systems do so frequently and, thus, see transit ads over and over again. See also **car cards.**

TRANSPORTATION   The process of physically moving goods from one location to another, such as in moving a product from its manufacturer to the **middleman.** There are several modes of transportation (i.e., railroads, airlines, trucks, and barges). Product manufacturers must decide on the most appropriate means of transportation from the standpoint of cost, speed, and safety to the merchandise being shipped. The selected mode of transportation affects the pricing of products. That is, an expensive means of transportation may necessitate factoring this cost into a product's price.

TREND ANALYSIS   The use of analytical techniques to determine patterns of growth or decline of a variable in a specific period of time. For example, trend analysis might be used to study population growth in a given geographic area. The resultant information would be used to project sales and, thus, determine production and manpower requirements. Trend analyses are developed using data from various sources of public information as well as from company records.

TRIAL OFFER 1. The offer to a consumer to try a product for a stated period of time before deciding whether or not to purchase it. A trial offer is an important aspect of direct marketing because consumers do not have the opportunity to examine a product as they could when shopping in a store. See also **soft offer. 2.** The situation in which a product's cost is reduced for a first-time buyer.

TRIAL SIZE A product package that is smaller in size than the product's usual container quantity. Trial-size packages are distributed free or at a reduced cost to prospective customers to encourage them to try the product. This consumer promotion technique is an effective way to introduce a new product. Trial-size packages are delivered by mail or are made available in retail outlets.

TRUCK JOBBER A type of **limited-service wholesaler** that sells and delivers food and snack items directly to store owners. A truck jobber makes periodic visits to customers (supermarkets, grocery stores, hotels, restaurants), selling goods from the truck to the facilities' owners for cash. Also known as *truck wholesaler.* See also **cash and carry wholesaler.**

TRUTH-IN-ADVERTISING The issue relating to the requirement of companies to truthfully explain the attributes and benefits of products in their advertising. Companies that do not engage in truthful advertising (that is, those engaging in deceptive practices) are subject to disciplinary action by the Federal Trade Commission. See also **consumer protection legislation.**

TRUTH-IN-LENDING The Truth-in-Lending Act of 1968 requires lenders to state the true costs of credit transactions, as well as to fully disclose terms and conditions of financing arrangements. Such is the case, for example, when a car maker offers financing to buyers. The Truth-in-Lending Act prohibits companies from using or threatening to use violence to collect loans, and it restricts the amount of garnishment of a buyer's wages.

TURNOVER The number of times a store sells its average amount of inventory over a designated period of time. For example, if a store normally stocks $20,000 worth of merchandise and it achieves $200,000 worth of sales in one year, it has turned over its inventory 10 times. Stores track turnover of their different products to determine sales rates—information used in deciding which products to carry (or not to carry) in the future.

TWO-COLOR   The printing production technique in which two colors of ink are used. Different design effects can be achieved while using only two colors by creating various hues of the colors or by using colored paper stock (as opposed to white stock). Two-color printing is less expensive than four-color printing, which reproduces artwork in the same colors as the original image.

TWO-STEP FLOW OF COMMUNICATION   Theory of communication stating that people generally do not receive information directly from the message **source,** but rather from an **opinion leader.** Information emanates from a source (e.g., the mass media), it is received by an opinion leader, and it is then passed on to an individual. For this reason, some marketing strategies are based on identifying and communicating with opinion leaders within the target market.

TYPEFACE   Another term for *font,* which is the design of the letters of a given type style. A typeface includes all letters of the alphabet as well as commonly used symbols such as the percent sign (%) and the ampersand (&). Selecting the typeface to be used in a printed communication is one aspect of **typography.**

TYPOGRAPHY   The process of selecting and arranging **typefaces** to be featured in a print communication (e.g., advertisement, brochure, catalog). Typographical decisions relate not only to the typeface but also to its size, the length of the lines of copy (column width), and the vertical spacing between lines. The goal of typography is to make the printed piece legible and visually appealing, vis-à-vis the amount of page space in which the copy must fit.

U

UNAIDED RECALL   A test of advertising effectiveness. Respondents are queried about an ad they have seen *without* having it in front of them. (Unaided recall is different from *aided recall,* where respondents answer questions about an ad that is shown to them while being asked about it.) In unaided recall, respondents are asked to describe what they remember about the ad's content—the product, slogan, sales message, and so forth. Unaided recall is generally used in **posttesting.** That is, it is a test of advertising effectiveness after the ad has appeared in the marketplace.

UNDIFFERENTIATED MARKETING   The strategy of selling one product to all people within a market, without modifying it to meet the different needs of the market's segments. In undifferentiated marketing, the company ignores segment differences. It seeks to satisfy the market with one product offering. Consider a company that sells coffee. The company has adopted an undifferentiated approach if it offers just one type of coffee. If it adopted a **differentiated marketing** strategy, it would develop different types to appeal to the market's various segments—people seeking decaffeinated coffee, instant coffee, drip, and so on.

UNDUPLICATED AUDIENCE   See **cumulative audience.**

UNFAIR COMPETITION   Any unethical business practice that proves injurious to competitors or that is deemed *not* to be in the public interest. An example of unfair competition is the **dumping** of goods in foreign countries. Another is advertising that is designed to mislead or confuse consumers. Practices are considered unfair when they violate regulations established by judicial, legal, or administrative agencies. See also **Federal Trade Commission.**

UNIQUE SELLING PROPOSITION (USP) Concept relating to the differentiating quality of a product on which advertising strategy is based. There are three characteristics of an effective USP: (1) It must make a proposition to the consumer, implying that buying the item will offer a specific benefit; (2) the proposition must be one that the competition cannot make—that is, the brand or the advertising claim made must truly be unique; (3) the proposition must be strong enough to attract a significant number of new customers. The USP concept was developed by Rosser Reeves, a founder of the Ted Bates advertising agency. See also **message development.**

UNIT PRICING The system of pricing in which a product's cost is indicated as a per-unit charge in addition to a charge based on quantity. Consider a package of chopped meat that sells for $2 per pound. Unit pricing would indicate on the package label that a package containing 2 pounds of it costs $4 (2 lb × $2). The goal of unit pricing is to facilitate comparing of products by consumers.

UNITS OF ANALYSIS The people, objects, or areas being observed in a research project study. For example, the units of analysis of a population could be women aged 18 to 34; units that are *objects* could be types of automobiles (compacts, convertibles, four-wheel drive cars); units that are *areas* could be zip codes within a city (as in **area sampling**). See also **sampling.**

UNIVERSAL PRODUCT CODE (UPC) A system developed to identify products by type and by manufacturer. UPCs are comprised of 11 digits. The first 6 indicate the manufacturer (these digits are standard for all products made by company). The last 5 digits describe the product itself. UPCs appear on product packages as **bar codes.** These are the graphic symbols that are read by optical **scanner** devices to record prices and to generate sales data for inventory and product ordering purposes. UPCs are assigned by the Uniform Code Council of Dayton, Ohio.

UNIVERSE In research, the collection of all possible entities that fit the designated characteristics of interest—characteristics that define the target market or the group under study. For example, if a neighborhood with 50,000 people is being studied, the universe is 50,000. The units of study to be analyzed in a research initiative are drawn from the universe via **sampling.** Thus, a sample is a subset of the universe. See also **sampling frame.**

UNJUSTIFIED TYPE   See **ragged left/right.**

UNWHOLESOME DEMAND STATE   Demand situation in which a deleterious product spawns marketing efforts to discourage consumers from purchasing it. Unwholesome demand states exist for products such as cigarettes, alcohol, and pornography. The marketing objective in contending with an unwholesome demand state is getting people to give up something they like (e.g., health groups using **fear appeals** to discourage cigarette smoking). See also **demand states.**

UPFRONT SELLING SEASON   The period (typically in May and June) when TV networks negotiate with advertisers on the cost of commercial time on shows in the upcoming fall TV season. Networks grant guarantees of program ratings as the rationale for setting prices for commercial time. (If these guarantees are not met, advertisers receive **makegoods.**) The upfront season is a time of extensive deal making and competition among advertisers to secure **preferred positions** for desirable network program time slots.

UPPER/LOWER CASE   Typesetting term referring to letters set in both capitals and small letters. Upper case means letters are set as capitals; lower case means they appear as small letters. Upper/lower case is abbreviated as U&L. This specifies to a typesetter or printer that capitals and small letters should be used in normal fashion. A lower-case letter, word, or phrase that should be set in upper case is indicated with the proofreading symbol of two or three lines underneath it. An upper-case letter, word, or phrase that should be set in lower case is shown with the proofreading symbol of a diagonal line going through it.

UPSCALE   Affluent buyers. Upscale people are consumers with high incomes and ample buying power, or they are people with high levels of professional status or education. Certain products are geared specifically to upscale buyers such as sports cars, jewelry, and yachts.

Similarly, many media are targeted to upscale buyers, such as *Town & Country* magazine. See also **downscale.**

UPWARDLY MOBILE   Members of a market who are striving for and achieving higher socioeconomic status. They include successful entrepreneurs, professionals climbing the corporate ladder, and others making significant gains in income, lifestyle, and material goods. Many products are geared to this market segment (such as educational materials that help people learn or help enhance skills to advance professionally).

U.S. BUREAU OF THE CENSUS   The division of the Department of Commerce that collects demographic information on the U.S. population. The bureau conducts a census every 10 years to measure the size and geographic distribution of the population. Census data report information organized by people's geographic area of residence on such variables as age, gender, race, marital status, education, and employment. Most of the information collected by the bureau is available free of charge (and generally obtainable in libraries). The bureau publishes a quarterly catalog listing all data files and tabulations available, as well as other unpublished and published materials. Examples of Census Bureau publications are the *Census of Business: Retail-Area Statistics—U.S. Summary,* which provides statistical totals for each region, state, city, and "standard metropolitan area" by type of retail establishment; and *County Business Patterns,* which presents employment and payroll statistics by county and by industry for all 50 states, as well as for the District of Columbia and Puerto Rico.

V

VALIDATION The process of following up with respondents who have been interviewed for a research study to ensure the interviews were conducted correctly. Validation involves querying a select number of respondents to see if they were, in fact, interviewed and if the research questions were asked properly. Validation is undertaken to assure the quality of the research data. It is also done to evaluate the performance of the researchers who conducted the interviews.

VALIDITY Relates to whether or not a research methodology accurately measures or predicts the variable it is designed to gauge. Assume a person's intelligence is being studied. Measuring the respondent's IQ would be more valid than gauging, say, the number of hours he or she spends studying in the library. Validity is also used to assess the viability of measurement techniques. That is, it relates to the degree to which a given measurement process is free of systematic errors. See also **reliability.**

VALS Market data based on people's *values and lifestyles.* VALS data are used to understand consumers' purchase decision making as determined by their activities, attitudes, opinions, and lifestyle characteristics. VALS data group consumers into segments comprising three main categories: (1) *need-directed,* consumers who make purchases based solely on needs; (2) *outer-directed,* consumers whose purchases are influenced by how they think other people perceive them; and (3) *inner-directed,* consumers whose purchases are based primarily on satisfying some inner (psychological) need. Each of these categories is broken down into three subcategories that collectively comprise nine value lifestyle groups (see following diagram). Marketers use VALS information in defining target markets as well as

The Nine VALS Segments

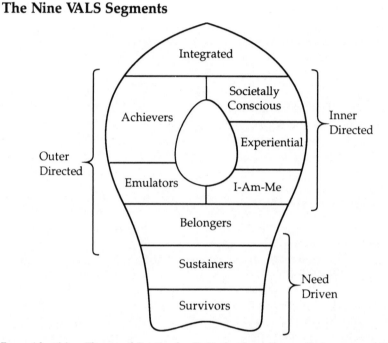

From *Advertising: Theory and Practice*, by C. H. Sandage, Vernon Fryburger, and Kim Rotzoll. Copyright © 1989 by Longman Publishing Group. Reprinted by permission of Longman Publishing Group.

in devising effective promotional strategies. VALS research is developed by the California consulting firm of SRI International, which furnishes the data to clients on a subscription basis.

VALUE-ADDED   Concept referring to what a manufacturer adds to raw materials to ready them for consumption by the market as products. For example, a company purchases a steel plate to make a metal ruler. Thus, it takes a basic raw material and transforms it into an item for market consumption. Value-added relates directly to product pricing. That is, the time and expense the company incurs in manufacturing the ruler out of a metal plate is reflected in what the finished product will cost.

VALUE ANALYSIS   A cost-reduction technique in which the costs of a manufacturing operation are studied to determine ways to reduce expenditures and/or eliminate unnecessary steps. Product engineers perform value analyses to identify new and less expensive ways to design and manufacture products. For example, the engineer will try to determine whether the cost of a mechanical part or subassembly can be reduced (or its production standardized) to effect greater savings to the organization. Also known as *value engineering*.

VALUES The ideas and beliefs people hold to be important, as determined by the social-cultural groups to which they belong. Values are the things people believe are good (e.g., honesty, loyalty) and those they feel are bad (dishonesty, theft, etc.). Values are passed on from generation to generation and are reinforced through such institutions as education and religion. Values influence people's behavior in social interactions and in purchase situations.

VARIABLE The element of a research study that changes or is altered to make observations about the marketing situation being studied. For example, if investigating product sales in a given market, sales would be the dependent variable—that is, the variable being studied. The independent variables—those altered to estimate their effect on the dependent variable—might be the product's price, the level of promotional expenditures, or sales force size.

VARIABLE COSTS The expenditures that vary in direct proportion to decreases or increases in the level of an organization's activity (e.g., manufacturing, sales). For instance, the variable cost of raw materials increases as more units of product are manufactured. Variable costs are different from *fixed costs*. These are the expenditures that do not change with changes in the level of activity (e.g., rent, personnel salaries, insurance costs).

VARIABLE PRICING Pricing policy in which the seller offers different prices to different people at different times. That is, prices are adapted to customers based on their individual purchasing power or ability to bargain. Products sold by street vendors are generally offered at variable pricing levels. Another example is when a seller offers a discount for high-volume purchases. For instance, the seller may decrease the per-unit price of an item if the buyer purchases a large number of units. Variable pricing is the opposite of products sold at a *flat rate*, which is when the price of a product never varies under any circumstances.

VARIANCE   In statistics, the square of the **standard deviation.** Variance represents the degree of clustering of a sample of values around the average of the sample.

VARIETY STORE   A retail establishment that sells a wide range of low-cost merchandise. Variety stores offer items such as stationery, confectionery products, light hardware items, and toys. An example is a five-and-dime store.

VCR (VIDEO CASSETTE RECORDER)   A machine that attaches to a television set to enable viewers to record programs or to play prerecorded videotapes. The proliferation of VCRs first posed a competitive threat to TV advertising because broadcast and cable television viewing decreased. However, the ubiquitousness of VCRs prompted the creation of new promotional techniques using this device such as **video commercials** and direct mailing of videotapes to consumers and businesses. VCRs also spawned a variety of new products. These include instructional videotapes (e.g., home-improvement and household repairs) and accessories for the machines themselves (video head cleaners, cassette holders).

VEHICLE   A particular advertising medium within a media category. For example, *Better Homes & Gardens* is one vehicle in the media category of magazines. Advertisers devise a **media mix** strategy for advertising campaigns that details general media categories and the target vehicles within them.

VENDOR   In general, any person or company that sells products or services. Vendors that provide goods and services to advertisers furnish art supplies, stationery and office materials, **premiums,** graphic arts supplies, stock photos, and so forth.

VERTICAL HALF-PAGE   A print advertisement that occupies the complete right or left half of a periodical's page. That is, the ad appears as half the width of the page, extending from the top to bottom of the page. A vertical half-page is typically sold at half the cost of a full-page ad. This layout is different from a *horizontal half-page*, where the ad divides the page horizontally.

VERTICAL INTEGRATION   The corporate growth strategy in which a company expands by acquiring or developing businesses that

Vertical Half-Page

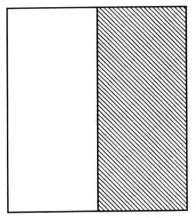

support the production or distribution of its products. Two types of vertical integration exist. *Forward vertical integration* is when a manufacturer acquires/develops wholesalers or retailers; *backward vertical integration* is when a retailer acquires/develops a manufacturing or wholesaling capability.

VERTICAL MARKET   A situation in which the market for an industrial product is narrow, but most companies operating in the market need the product. Consider the electrical part needed to make a VCR work. A narrow market exists for the company that holds the patent for the part. But the market is deep in that every VCR manufacturer needs the component part.

VERTICAL MARKETING SYSTEM (VMS)   A system in which the wholesaler, retailer, and manufacturer are unified in the production/ distribution of products. (In a conventional marketing system the wholesalers, retailers, and manufacturer are all independent and none exercises control over the others.) Examples of vertical marketing systems are a manufacturer owning retail outlets or controlling them via franchising; or a hotel chain owning a carpet mill and furniture manufacturer that furnish these hotel accessories. Vertical marketing systems were established to enable companies to control **channel behavior.** For example, vertical systems eliminate conflicts between channel intermediaries pursuing their own financial objectives. See also **horizontal marketing system.**

VERTICAL PUBLICATION   A trade magazine whose advertising and editorial content are geared to a specific industry or profession. An example is *Metalworking News,* which is produced for metalworking and metallurgy professionals. **Horizontal publications** are trade magazines whose content appeals to professionals in many different industries (e.g., *Industry Week*).

VIDEO COMMERCIAL   A commercial that appears at the beginning of a rented videotape movie. Video commercials are often used as a supplement to other promotional activities developed in conjunction with a film. For example, Coca-Cola created TV advertising and sweepstakes in promoting the movie *Indiana Jones and the Last Crusade.* A video commercial was included in the videotapes that ultimately became available to consumers for sale or rental.

VIDEO NEWS RELEASE (VNR)   The electronic equivalent of a printed news release. VNRs are broadcast news stories used to generate television publicity. VNRs generally run the length of an average news report, which is two to three minutes. VNRs are usually accompanied by a transcript, as well as by supplemental information identifying the people appearing in the segment. VNRs are distributed to TV stations either by hard copy (videocassette) or via satellite feed. They are offered both with and without voiceover and graphics—the raw footage version enabling film editors to add their own audiovisual treatments. *Note:* VNRs are generally created by companies that specialize in their production and distribution. Some large public relations agencies, however, have the in-house facilities to produce and disseminate VNRs on their own.

VIDEO SYSTEMS   Electronic sales and marketing tools that provide product information via video technology. There are two basic kinds of video systems. **Electronic catalogs** are displays that communicate information about a company's product line. Some electronic catalogs are interactive. That is, they enable consumers to choose the product information they want and to order goods directly from the video source. Electronic catalogs that are not interactive do not allow consumers to order products from the video display. *Video networks* are comprised of series of video monitors located in areas with high levels of pedestrian traffic (such as in a mass transit station). The monitors are connected via closed circuit and run multiple promotional messages from the same or different advertisers. Video networks are often established in supermarkets and department stores.

VIDEOTEX   An interactive video system that transmits information to consumers via computer and can serve as an advertising medium. Videotex systems enable consumers to bank at home, receive news and stock market quotes, make travel arrangements, and send electronic correspondence. Access to videotex systems is sold on a subscription basis. Users pay a standard rate plus a separate charge for the length of time they spend on the system.

VIGNETTE   1. A photograph or illustration that does not have a distinct border. That is, the illustration has an indefinite border because it blends into the surrounding blank area of the page. 2. A television commercial format in which several situations relating to the advertised product are shown in rapid succession. For example, a commercial for premoistened towelettes might show a person using the product in a car, people using it on a picnic, and a secretary using it at her desk.

VISUAL   1. A rough sketch of a print advertisement or communication (e.g., brochure cover). A visual shows the layout of the design, indicating the elements and their respective positions in the design. 2. In film production, that which is shown (as opposed to what is heard) in a given scene.

VOICE MAIL   A telephone system that automatically routes calls to the appropriate person or corporate department, and that functions as an answering machine. For example, direct marketers employ voice mail systems to enable consumers to place product orders without having to speak to salespeople. The system also allows the caller to leave a voice mail message to make inquiries or to voice complaints—calls that are ultimately returned by sales representatives. See also **ADRMP.**

VOICEOVER   The words spoken in a TV commercial by an unseen announcer. Voiceover supports the visual being shown. That is, the viewer concentrates on the on-screen image while the voiceover explains the visual or offers additional information. Voiceover is indicated as V.O. on a **storyboard** or broadcast script. Also known as *announcer voiceover.*

W

WANTS One of the most fundamental concepts in marketing. Wants refer to people's desire for specific products and services that satisfy their needs. For example, a hungry person needs food. Wants are the type of food he or she desires to eat. People's wants are influenced by socioeconomic and cultural forces. Thus, a poor person who is hungry may simply want (can afford) a sandwich, whereas an affluent person would want a gourmet meal. Wants are influenced by such institutions as family, religion, and schools.

WAREHOUSE The facility used for storing merchandise before it is distributed to retailers and other channel intermediaries or sold to consumers. Having warehouse storage space is necessary because rarely do consumption and production cycles match exactly. Companies store merchandise in private warehouses that they own, or they rent space in public warehouses along with other companies.

WAREHOUSE STORE A large retail establishment designed to sell discounted merchandise at high volume. Warehouse stores are no-frills facilities with vast inventories. Store managers offer virtually no customer assistance and simply display products for consumers' perusal. Customers decide what merchandise they want and pick it up themselves at a loading dock. Examples of goods sold at warehouse stores are furniture and building-supply products.

WARRANTY A written guarantee by a seller that the product sold is of high quality and free of defects. Warranties state that the seller will provide a refund on faulty merchandise, will replace it, or will repair it at no cost to the buyer. Warranties apply for a limited period of time. The time period commences when the buyer receives a warranty application (not when the purchase is made). See also **expressed warranty; implied warranty.**

WEBER'S LAW   A psychological theory that, in marketing, is generally applied to understanding consumers' perceptions of brands. Weber's law suggests that people assess a product based not on its individual attributes but rather on their perceived differences between it and alternative brands. See also **just noticeable difference.**

WEB PRESS   Printing press that employs curved plates to imprint images on a continuous paper roll as opposed to individual sheets. Web presses operate at high speeds for high-volume printing jobs. Web presses are used, for example, in printing newspapers and catalogs. They are also employed in printing labels and other materials on foil paper and plastic.

WEEKLY   A periodical published on a weekly basis. Many magazines and newsletters are published as weeklies, as well as many community newspapers and "penny-savers." See also **dailies.**

WEIGHT   Term referring to the thickness of paper stock. For example, paper used for a brochure cover, known as *cover stock,* is of a heavier weight than paper used for the brochure's pages, *text stock.* Weight is stated in terms of pounds. That is, it's determined by the actual weight of a ream of paper—approximately 500 sheets.

WEIGHTING   In research, the statistical procedure used when units drawn with unequal probabilities to form a sample are assigned weights to make them comparable for analytical purposes. For example, two samples of equal size have been drawn—one from a city and one from a suburb. Since there is a vast difference in population size between the areas, people have different probability levels of being selected for the sample. Thus, weights would be assigned to the units from each area to make the entire combined sample representative of the city/suburb population from which it was drawn.

WHITE GOODS   **1.** Large household appliances (such as refrigerators, dishwashers, washing machines). The name comes from the white enamel finish found on many of these products. **2.** Sheets, pillowcases, and linen.

WHITE MAIL Consumer correspondence sent to a business in the sender's own envelope, as opposed to **business reply envelopes** provided by the company. White mail usually contains customer inquiries, complaints, or address changes. Large volumes of white mail are very time-consuming to open because the mail comes in a variety of envelope sizes generally not suited to the envelope-opening machines companies operate.

WHOLESALER A company serving as the **middleman** between a manufacturer and a retailer. A wholesaler buys goods from the manufacturer for resale (at a profit) to retailers and, occasionally, directly to consumers. There are two basic types of wholesalers: (1) *Full-service wholesalers* provide services such as carrying stock, maintaining sales forces, and offering management and credit assistance to buyers; and (2) *limited-service wholesalers* offer some, but not all, of the services rendered by full-service wholesalers. See also **cash and carry wholesaler; rack jobber; truck jobber.**

WHOLESALING The process of buying merchandise in large quantities from a manufacturer for resale to retailers or business users. Unlike retailing, wholesaling generally does not involve actively promoting products, nor does it involve establishing the wholesale outlet in a location convenient to or appealing to buyers. This is because wholesaling entails selling products primarily to businesses that come from a wide geographic area and that are generally indifferent to promotional trappings.

WIDOW Typesetting term for a single word or portion of a word (such as one that has been hyphenated) that appears on one line of text at the end of a paragraph or at the top of a page. Widows are generally avoided in typesetting. Consequently, efforts are made to eliminate them by editing the text or by changing the spacing of the copy.

WINDOW ENVELOPE An envelope with a transparent plastic or paper opening through which the addressee's information is seen. Window envelopes generally reveal only the address. However, the window sometimes shows other contents of the envelope (such as copy or graphics). Window envelopes are expensive but they save the mailer money by eliminating the cost of addressing envelopes (e.g., typing the addresses or affixing mailing labels).

WITHDRAWAL   See **abandonment.**

WORD-OF-MOUTH ADVERTISING   The personal communication channels through which people receive product or service information, as opposed to from an advertising medium. Word-of-mouth advertising is not advertising per se, since no money is expended by the seller. Word-of-mouth involves getting satisfied customers to recommend the product or service to family, friends, and co-workers. For example, a doctor can generate word-of-mouth advertising by giving patients a brochure to distribute to people they know.

WRAPAROUND   A decorative banner that circles or is draped around an in-store merchandise display. A wraparound may simply be an ornamental design or it may carry a promotional message relating to the featured product. Wraparounds are one form of **point-of-purchase advertising.**

X

XEROGRAPHY   The printing method used in photocopy machines. Copies are made via a process that applies an electrical charge to the image to be reproduced. Pigment becomes bonded to the image area and, with the application of heat, is made permanent. That is, the image is baked onto the page.

Y

YELLOW GOODS   Household products that are not consumed, are high-priced, and are replaced after several years. Examples of yellow goods are ovens, dishwashers, and refrigerators (although these are sometimes referred to as **white goods** for the white enamel surfaces they frequently feature). See also **brown goods; orange goods; red goods; white goods.**

YELLOW PAGES ADVERTISING   Advertisements for business and consumer services that appear in the nonresidence sections of telephone books. Yellow pages advertising is the most common form of **directory advertising.** Yellow pages ads are display ads that consist primarily of copy indicating the advertiser's address and telephone number, product/service offerings, brands carried, and store hours. There are some illustrations in yellow pages advertising.

Z

ZAPPING   The practice of using a TV remote control to change channels during a program's commercial breaks to avoid seeing ads. (Viewers watching recorded programs on a VCR engage in zapping when they fast-forward through the commercials.) Zapping is a concern of TV advertisers in that it lessens the number of potential viewers of a commercial. See also **flipping**.

ZERO DEFECTS   The ideal situation in which no unit coming off a manufacturer's assembly line is defective. Companies strive to limit defects in the hope that they will ultimately achieve a zero-defect level. Companies have adopted various kinds of advanced manufacturing technologies and planning techniques to achieve zero defects (e.g., robotics, Total Quality Management).

ZIP CODE   The U.S. Postal Service's system of designating geographic areas for mail sorting and delivery. The first zip codes introduced were five digits. The USPS, however, is moving toward standard use of nine-digit zip codes (referred to as *zip* + 4). Zip is an abbreviation for *zoning improvement plan*.

ZIP CODE ANALYSIS   The technique of evaluating the success of a direct-marketing program in different geographic areas based on zip codes. In a zip code analysis, a company will review the number of orders received from different zip codes to determine the varying levels of sales from those areas. This information is used for future direct-mail programs. That is, the company may subsequently concentrate on areas that showed the highest sales response rates and avoid areas that showed the lowest. Zip code analysis is based on the assumption that people living in the same geographic area (e.g., an affluent neighborhood) tend to exhibit similar consumption patterns.

ZONE PRICING   The practice of determining the price of a product based on the geographic area (zone) receiving it. The price of merchandise is based not only on a unit's cost but also on the shipping and handling costs the company incurs in mailing to a specific area. In general, the further away a product has to be mailed, the higher the shipping and handling costs and, thus, the higher the product's cost.

ZOOM IN/OUT   A film production term referring to a camera movement that creates a closeup of the image (zoom-in) or shows a broad area or scene (zoom-out). The technique is achieved by using a special *zoom lens*, which does not have to be focused each time the camera is moved. That is, the camera can zoom-in or zoom-out without being refocused to shoot at varying distances.

Appendix A

Marketing and Media Trade, Commercial, and Business Organizations

Advertising Club of New York (ACNY)
155 E. 55th St., Ste. 202
New York, NY 10022
(212) 935-8080

Advertising Council, Inc. (AC)
261 Madison Ave.
New York, NY 10016
(212) 922-1500

Advertising Research Foundation (ARF)
3 E. 54th St.
New York, NY 10022
(212) 751-5656

Advertising Women of New York (AWNY)
153 E. 57th St.
New York, NY 10022
(212) 593-1950

Affiliated Advertising Agencies International (AAAI)
2280 S. Xanadu Way, Ste. 300
Aurora, CO 80014
(303) 671-8551

American Advertising Federation (AAF)
1400 K St. NW, Ste. 1000
Washington, DC 20005
(202) 898-0089

American Association of Advertising Agencies (AAAA)
666 Third Ave., 13th Fl.
New York, NY 10017
(212) 682-2500

American Business Press (ABP)
675 Third Ave., Ste. 400
New York, NY 10017
(212) 661-6360

American Marketing Association
(AMA)
250 S. Wacker Dr., Ste. 200
Chicago, IL 60606
(312) 648-0536

American Newspaper Publishers
Association
Box 17407 Dulles Airport
Washington, DC 20041
(703) 648-1000

American Telemarketing
Association (ATA)
5000 Van Nuys Blvd., Ste. 400
Sherman Oaks, CA 91403
(818) 995-7338

Art Directors Club (ADC)
250 Park Ave. S.
New York, NY 10003
(212) 674-0500

Association of National
Advertisers (ANA)
155 E. 44th St.
New York, NY 10017
(212) 697-5950

Audit Bureau of Circulations
(ABC)
900 N. Meacham Rd.
Schaumburg, IL 60173
(708) 605-0909

Business/Professional
Advertising Association
(B/PAA)
Metroplex Corporate Center
100 Metroplex Dr.
Edison, NJ 08817
(201) 985-4441

Corporation for Public
Broadcasting (CPB)
901 E St. NW
Washington, DC 20004
(202) 879-9600

Council of Sales Promotion
Agencies (CSPA)
750 Summer St.
Stamford, CT 06901
(203) 325-3911

Direct Marketing Association
(DMA)
11 W. 42nd St.
New York, NY 10036
(212) 689-4977

Institute of Outdoor Advertising
(IOA)
342 Madison Ave., Rm. 702
New York, NY 10173
(212) 986-5920

International Advertising
Association (IAA)
342 Madison Ave., Ste. 2000
New York, NY 10017
(212) 557-1133

International Association of
Business Communicators
(IABC)
One Hallidie Plaza, Ste. 600
San Francisco, CA 94102
(415) 433-3400

International Federation of
Advertising Agencies (IFAA)
1450 E. American Lane, Ste. 1400
Schaumburg, IL 60173
(708) 330-6344

Magazine Publishers of America
(MPA)
575 Lexington Ave., Ste. 540
New York, NY 10022
(212) 752-0055

National Association of
Broadcasters (NAB)
1771 N St. NW
Washington, DC 20036
(202) 429-5300

National Cable Television
Association (NCTA)
1724 Massachusetts Ave. NW
Washington, DC 20036
(202) 775-3550

National Mail Order Association
(NMOA)
5818 Venice Blvd.
Los Angeles, CA 90019
(213) 934-7986

National Newspaper Association
(NNA)
1627 K St. NW, Ste. 400
Washington, DC 20006
(202) 466-7200

National Newspaper Publishers
Association (NNPA)
948 National Press Building
Washington, DC 20045
(202) 662-7323

Newspaper Advertising Bureau
(NAB)
1180 Ave. of the Americas
New York, NY 10036
(212) 921-5080

Newspaper Advertising Sales
Association (NASA)
c/o Don Waddington
Branham Newspaper Sales
733 Third Ave.
New York, NY 10017
(212) 490-1200

Outdoor Advertising Association
of America (OAAA)
1212 New York Ave. NW,
Ste. 1210
Washington, DC 20005
(202) 371-5566

Point-of-Purchase Advertising
Institute (POPAI)
66 N. Van Brunt St.
Englewood, NJ 07631
(201) 894-8899

Promotion Marketing
Association of America
(PMAA)
322 Eighth Ave., Ste. 1201
New York, NY 10001
(212) 206-1100

Public Relations Society of
America (PRSA)
33 Irving Pl.
New York, NY 10003
(212) 995-2230

Publishers Information Bureau
(PIB)
575 Lexington Ave., 5th Fl.
New York, NY 10022
(212) 752-0055

Radio Advertising Bureau (RAB)
304 Park Ave. S., 7th Fl.
New York, NY 10010
(212) 254-4800

Technical Marketing Society of
  America (TMSA)
P.O. Box 7275
Long Beach, CA 90807
(714) 821-8672

Television Bureau of Advertising
  (TvB)
477 Madison Ave., 10th Fl.
New York, NY 10022
(212) 486-1111

Traffic Audit Bureau (TAB)
114 E. 32nd St., Rm. 802
New York, NY 10016
(212) 213-9640

Appendix B

Marketing and Advertising Trade Publications

Ad Business Report
919 Third Ave.
New York, NY 10022
(212) 421-3713

Advertising Age
220 E. 42 St.
New York, NY 10017
(212) 210-0100

Advertising Communications
  Times
121 Chestnut St.
Philadelphia, PA 19106
(215) 629-1666

Adweek/East
49 E. 21st St.
New York, NY 10010
(212) 529-5500

Adweek/Midwest
435 N. Michigan Ave., Ste. 819
Chicago, IL 60611
(312) 467-6500

Adweek/New England
100 Bolyston St.
Boston, MA 02116
(617) 482-0876

Adweek/Southeast
6 Piedmont Center, Ste. 300
Atlanta, GA 30305
(404) 841-3333

Adweek/Southwest
2909 Cole Ave., Ste. 220
Dallas, TX 75204
(214) 871-9550

Adweek/West
5757 Wilshire Blvd., Ste. M-110
Los Angeles, CA 90036
(213) 937-4330

Adweek's Marketing Week
49 E. 21st St.
New York, NY 10010
(212) 529-5500

American Demographics
P.O. Box 68
Ithaca, NY 14851
(607) 273-6343

Art Direction
10 E. 39th St.
New York, NY 10016
(212) 889-6500

B/PAA Communicator
100 Metroplex Dr.
Edison, NJ 08817
(201) 985-4441

Bulldog Reporter
2115 4th St., Ste. A
Berkeley, CA 94710
(415) 549-4300

Business Marketing
740 Rush St.
Chicago, IL 60611
(312) 649-5260

Cable TV Advertising
126 Clock Tower Pl.
Carmel, CA 93923
(408) 624-1536

Catalog Marketer
228 N. Cascade Ave., Ste. 307
Colorado Springs, CO 80903
(719) 633-5556

Communication Briefings
700 Black Horse Pike, Ste. 110
Blackwood, NJ 08012
(609) 589-3503

Communication World
One Hallidie Plaza, Ste. 600
San Francisco, CA 94102
(415) 433-3400

Corporate Communications
  Report
112 E. 31st St.
New York, NY 10016
(212) 889-2450

Creative, The Magazine of
  Promotion & Marketing
37 W. 39th St.
New York, NY 10018
(212) 840-0160

Dartnell Sales and Marketing
  Newsletter
4660 N. Ravenswood St.
Chicago, IL 60640
(312) 561-4000

Dartnell Sales and Marketing
  Executive Report
4660 N. Ravenswood St.
Chicago, IL 60640
(312) 561-4000

Direct Marketing Journal
605 Third Ave.
New York, NY 10158
(212) 850-6000

Direct Marketing Magazine
224 Seventh St.
Garden City, NY 11530
(516) 746-6700

DM News
19 W. 21st St.
New York, NY 10010
(212) 741-2095

Educational Marketer
P.O. Box 7430
Wilton, CT 06897
(203) 834-0033

Franchising World
1350 New York Ave. NW, Ste. 900
Washington, DC 20005
(202) 628-8000

Healthcare Marketing Quarterly
Haworth Press
10 Alice St.
Binghamton, NY 13904
(800) 342-9678

Hi-Tech Alert for the
  Professional Communicator
Communication Research
  Associates
10606 Mantz Rd.
Silver Spring, MD 21093
(301) 747-8241

International Advertiser
342 Madison Ave., Ste. 2000
New York, NY 10017
(212) 557-1133

International Product Alert
33 Academy St.
Naples, NY 14512
(716) 374-6326

Jack O'Dwyer's Newsletter
  (Public Relations)
271 Madison Ave., Ste. 600
New York, NY 10016
(212) 679-2471

Journal of Business and
  Industrial Marketing
108 Loma Media Rd.
Santa Barbara, CA 93103
(805) 564-1313

Journal of Business-to-Business
  Marketing
Haworth Press
10 Alice St.
Binghamton, NY 13904
(800) 342-9678

Journal of Consumer Marketing
108 Loma Media Rd.
Santa Barbara, CA 93103
(805) 564-1313

Journal of Euromarketing
Haworth Press
10 Alice St.
Binghamton, NY 13904
(800) 342-9678

Journal of Food Products
  Marketing
Haworth Press
10 Alice St.
Binghamton, NY 13904
(800) 342-9678

Journal of Global Marketing
Haworth Press
10 Alice St.
Binghamton, NY 13904
(800) 342-9678

Journal of International
  Consumer Marketing
Haworth Press
10 Alice St.
Binghamton, NY 13904
(800) 342-9678

Journal of International Food &
  Agribusiness Marketing
Haworth Press
10 Alice St.
Binghamton, NY 13904
(800) 342-9678

Journal of Health Care
  Marketing
American Marketing Association
250 S. Wacker Dr., Ste. 200
Chicago, IL 60606
(312) 648-0536

Journal of Hospitality & Leisure
  Marketing
Haworth Press
10 Alice St.
Binghamton, NY 13904
(800) 342-9678

Journal of Hospital Marketing
Haworth Press
10 Alice St.
Binghamton, NY 13904
(800) 342-9678

Journal of Marketing
American Marketing Association
250 S. Wacker Dr., Ste. 200
Chicago, IL 60606
(312) 648-0536

Journal of Marketing Channels
Haworth Press
10 Alice St.
Binghamton, NY 13904
(800) 342-9678

Journal of Marketing for Higher
  Education
Haworth Press
10 Alice St.
Binghamton, NY 13904
(800) 342-9678

Journal of Marketing Research
American Marketing Association
250 S. Wacker Dr., Ste. 200
Chicago, IL 60606
(312) 648-0536

Journal of Nonprofit & Public
  Sector Marketing
Haworth Press
10 Alice St.
Binghamton, NY 13904
(800) 342-9678

Journal of Pharmaceutical
  Marketing & Management
Haworth Press
10 Alice St.
Binghamton, NY 13904
(800) 342-9678

Journal of Professional Services
  Marketing
Haworth Press
10 Alice St.
Binghamton, NY 13904
(800) 342-9678

Journal of Promotion
  Management
Haworth Press
10 Alice St.
Binghamton, NY 13904
(800) 342-9678

Journal of Restaurant &
  Foodservice Marketing
Haworth Press
10 Alice St.
Binghamton, NY 13904
(800) 342-9678

Journal of Services Marketing
108 Loma Media Rd.
Santa Barbara, CA 93103
(805) 564-1313

Licensing Journal
P.O. Box 1169
Stamford, CT 06904
(203) 358-0848

Mail Order Digest
3875 Wilshire Blvd., Ste. 604
Los Angeles, CA 90010
(213) 380-3686

Marketing & Media Decisions
401 Park Ave. S., 7th Fl.
New York, NY 10016
(212) 545-5100

Marketing News
American Marketing Association
250 S. Wacker Dr., Ste. 200
Chicago, IL 60606
(312) 391-2155

Marketing Review
310 Madison Ave., Ste. 1211
New York, NY 10017
(212) 687-3280

Marketing Strategist
51 E. 42nd St., Ste. 417
New York, NY 10017
(800) 962-7538

Media Industry Newsletter
145 E. 49th St., Ste. 7B
New York, NY 10017
(212) 751-2670

Medical Marketing & Media
7200 West Camino Real, Ste. 215
Boca Raton, FL 33433
(407) 368-9301

Non-Store Marketing Report
228 N. Cascade Ave., Ste. 307
Colorado Springs, CO 80903
(719) 633-5556

P-O-P Times
2000 N. Racine Ave., Ste. 3600
Chicago, IL 60614
(312) 281-3400

Potentials in Marketing
50 S. 9th St.
Minneapolis, MN 55402
(800) 328-4329

Premium/Incentive Business
1515 Broadway
New York, NY 10036
(212) 869-1300

Product Alert
33 Academy St.
Naples, NY 14512
(716) 374-6326

Promo
47 Old Ridgefield Rd.
Wilton, CT 06897
(203) 761-1510

P.R. Reporter
P.O. Box 600
Exeter, NH 03833
(603) 778-0514

Public Relations Journal
Public Relations Society of
  America
33 Irving Pl.
New York, NY 10003
(212) 995-2230

Public Relations News
127 E. 80th St.
New York, NY 10021
(212) 879-7090

Public Relations Quarterly
44 W. Market St.
P.O. Box 311
Rhinebeck, NY 12572
(914) 876-2081

Public Relations Review
10606 Mantz Rd.
Silver Spring, MD 21093
(301) 747-8241

Public Service Advertising
  Bulletin
Advertising Council, Inc.
261 Madison Ave.
New York, NY 10016
(212) 922-1500

Quirk's Marketing Research
  Review
6607 18th Ave. S.
Minneapolis, MN 55423
(612) 861-8051

Ragan Report
407 S. Dearborn St., Ste. 1360
Chicago, IL 60605
(312) 922-8245

Rep World
P.O. Box 2087
Sinking Spring, PA 19608
(215) 678-3361

Research Alert
37-06 30th Ave.
Long Island City, NY 11103
(718) 626-3356

Sales & Marketing Digest
Marsili Publishing
P.O. Box 4365
Rockford, IL 61110
(815) 547-4311

Sales & Marketing Management
633 Third Ave.
New York, NY 10017
(212) 986-4800

Sales Executive
13 E. 37th St., 8th Fl.
New York, NY 10016
(212) 683-9755

Signs of the Times
407 Gilbert Ave.
Cincinnati, OH 45202
(513) 421-2050

Social Science Monitor
Communication Research
  Associates
10606 Mantz Rd.
Silver Spring, MD 21093
(301) 747-8241

Special Events Report
213 W. Institute Pl., Ste. 303
Chicago, IL 60610
(312) 944-1727

Specialty Advertising Business
1404 Walnut Hill Lane
Irving, TX 75038
(214) 580-0404

Target Marketing
401 N. Broad St.
Philadelphia, PA 19108
(215) 238-5300

Target Market News
4849 S. Greenwood Ave.
Chicago, IL 60615
(312) 268-4444

Tradeshow & Exhibit Manager
1150 Yale St., Ste. 12
Santa Monica, CA 90403
(213) 828-1309

Tradeshow Week
12233 W. Olympic Blvd., Ste. 236
Los Angeles, CA 90064
(213) 826-5696

Youth Markets Alert
37-05 Thirtieth Ave.
Long Island, NY 11103
(718) 626-3356

Appendix C

Selected Bibliography "How-To" Books in Marketing

General Marketing

- *AMA Handbook of Marketing for the Service Industries*, Carole A. Congram and Margeret L. Friedman, AMACOM, 1991.
- *Bottom-up Marketing*, Al Ries and Jack Trout, McGraw-Hill, 1988.
- *Catalog Marketing*, Katie Muldoon, AMACOM, 1988.
- *Competitive Advantage: Creating & Sustaining Superior Performance*, Michael E. Porter, Free Press, 1985.
- *Competitive Strategy: Techniques for Analyzing Industries & Competitors*, Michael E. Porter, Free Press, 1980.
- *Concept Testing*, David Schwartz, AMACOM, 1987.
- *Faster New Product Development: Getting the Right Product to Market Quickly*, Milton Rosenau, AMACOM, 1990.
- *How to Prepare a Results-Driven Marketing Plan*, Martin L. Bell, AMACOM, 1987.
- *Manager's Guide to Competitive Marketing Strategies*, Norton Paley, AMACOM, 1990.
- *Managing New Products: Competing Through Excellence*, Thomas Kuczmarski, Prentice-Hall, 1987.
- *Marketing Edge: Making Strategies Work*, Thomas V. Bonoma, Free Press, 1985.

- *Marketing Imagination,* Theodore Levitt, Free Press, 1986.
- *Marketing Management: Analysis, Planning, Implementation & Control,* Philip Kotler, Prentice-Hall, 1988.
- *Marketing Problem Solver,* Cochrane Chase, Chilton, 1988.
- *Marketing Professional Services,* Philip Kotler & Paul N. Bloom, Prentice-Hall, 1984.
- *Marketing to Win: How You Can Build Your Client Base in the New Highly Competitive Service Economy,* Frank Sonnenberg, HarperCollins, 1990.
- *Marketing Warfare,* Al Ries and Jack Trout, McGraw-Hill, 1985.
- *Maximarketing: The New Direction in Advertising, Promotion & Marketing Strategy,* Stan Rapp and Tom Collins, McGraw-Hill, 1989.
- *McGraw-Hill 36-Hour Marketing Course,* Jeffrey L. Seglin, McGraw-Hill, 1990.
- *Moments of Truth,* Jan Carlzon, Harper & Row, 1989.
- *Romancing the Brand, The Power of Advertising and How to Use It,* David N. Martin, AMACOM, 1989.
- *Social Marketing: Promoting the Causes of Public & Nonprofit Agencies,* Seymour H. Fine, Allyn, 1990.
- *Social Marketing: Strategies for Changing Public Behavior,* Philip Kotler and Eduardo L. Roberto, Free Press, 1989.
- *Successful Product Development: Strategies for High Growth from a Market-Based Approach,* Axel Johne and Patricia Snelson, Basil Blackwell, 1990.

Advertising

- *Advertising Pure & Simple: The New Edition,* Hank Seiden, AMACOM, 1990.
- *Confessions of an Advertising Man,* David Ogilvy, NTC Business Books, 1987.
- *Herschell Gordon Lewis on the Art of Writing Copy,* Herschell G. Lewis, Prentice-Hall, 1988.
- *Ogilvy on Advertising,* David Ogilvy, Random House, 1985.
- *Tested Advertising Methods,* John Caples, Prentice-Hall, 1986.

Direct Marketing

- *Business-to-Business Telemarketing,* Jeffrey L. Pope, AMACOM, 1983.

- *Database Marketing Strategy & Implementation*, Robert Shaw & Merlin Stone, Wiley, 1990.
- *Direct Marketer's Idea Book*, Martin Gross, AMACOM, 1989.
- *Direct Marketing Handbook*, Edward L. Nash, McGraw-Hill, 1984.
- *Successful Direct Marketing Methods*, Robert Stone, NTC Business Books, 1988.
- *Successful Telephone Selling in the '90s*, Martin D. Shafiroff and Robert L. Shook, HarperCollins, 1990.

Sales Promotion

- *Best Sales Promotions*, Bill Robinson, NTC Business Books, 1989.
- *Handbook of Sales Promotion*, S. Ulanoff, McGraw-Hill, 1985.

Sales/Customer Service

- *At America's Service: How Corporations Can Revolutionize the Way They Treat Their Customers*, Karl Albrecht, Dow Jones-Irwin, 1988.
- *Consultative Selling*, Mack Hanan, AMACOM, 1990.
- *Customer Connection: Quality for the Rest of Us*, John Guaspari, AMACOM, 1988.
- *How to Master the Art of Selling*, Tom Hopkins, Warner Books, 1988.
- *How to Win Customers & Keep Them for Life*, Michael Le Boeuf, Berkley Publishing, 1989.
- *Keeping Customers For Life*, Joan K. Cannie With Donald Caplin, AMACOM, 1990.
- *Major Accounts Sales Strategy*, Neil Rackham, McGraw-Hill, 1989.
- *Service America!*, Karl Albrecht and Ron Zemke, Warner Books, 1990.
- *Service Within: Solving the Middle Management Leadership Crisis*, Karl Albrecht, Dow Jones-Irwin, 1990.
- *S.P.I.N. Selling*, Neil Rackham, McGraw-Hill, 1988.
- *Strategic Selling*, Robert B. Miller, Warner Books, 1988.
- *Value-Added Selling Techniques: How to Sell More Profitably, Confidently & Professionally*, Tom Reilly, Congdon & Weed, 1989.

Public Relations

- *Complete Book of Product Publicity,* James D. Barhydt, AMACOM, 1987.
- *Lesly's Handbook of Public Relations & Communications,* Philip Lesly, AMACOM, 1990.
- *Power & Influence: Mastering the Art of Persuasion,* Robert L. Dilenschneider, Prentice-Hall, 1990.
- *Public Relations Handbook,* Robert L. Dilenschneider and Dan J. Forrestal, Dartnell, 1987.

Marketing Research

- *Do-It-Yourself Marketing Research,* George Breen and A. B. Blankenship, McGraw-Hill, 1989.
- *Practical Marketing Research,* Jeffrey L. Pope, AMACOM, 1981.